AMERICAN CASTE AND THE
NEGRO COLLEGE

AMERICAN CASTE
AND THE
NEGRO COLLEGE

BY

BUELL G. GALLAGHER

WITH A FOREWORD BY

WILLIAM H. KILPATRICK

GORDIAN PRESS, INC.
NEW YORK
1966

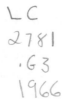

To J. S. G.
IN GRATEFUL AND
ASTONISHED LOVE

FOREWORD

THE adjustment of the Negro justly and satisfactorily into American life remains as yet a most serious problem. But meanwhile certain of the conditions that originally determined the problem are now changing. Many individual Negroes have made most impressive use of the highest available culture, while the group as a whole has, considering the circumstances, advanced notably. The crux of the problem has perhaps shifted, as the title and discussion of the book before us seem to indicate. We may now fairly ask not so much how to solve the problem in terms of the original elements as why the problem is not now more surely in process of solution. What is it that is holding up the process?

It seems quite possible that a principal factor hindering a solution of the problem lies in the historic separation of understanding between the two parties to the problem. For the solution to any problem, if it is to be sought and found, must start from the common ground of understanding held by the opposing sides. The less of common understanding between any two parties the more difficulty in general will they have in finding a common basis of agreement.

To this suggested explanation of difficulty some will immediately object. Many who live close to the problem, and see it from the vantage side, will assert that it is the outsiders who create trouble and prevent a just and friendly solution, and further that those on the grounds, from both sides, are the only ones who really see things as they are. And they will go on to add that the two groups as they live in historic continuity utterly deny the intimation of lack of common understanding; on the contrary, they meet daily in friendly intercourse as they have done for generations and understand each other as could no others with less knowledge of actual conditions.

The writer of these lines is not a stranger to the conditions referred to in the preceding paragraph. He was reared under those very conditions. He has himself possibly as long a line of slaveholding ancestry as any who will read his words, and during his whole life he has known the former slaves of his father (until the last one died a few years ago). He understands what is meant by the trouble which ignorant outsiders can create. But for all these things, partly in spite of them, partly because of them, he reasserts the lack of a common understanding. To be sure, many from the two groups do meet every day, usually in or about the home or the office of the dominant group, and these meetings are often, perhaps generally, on very friendly terms, more friendly possibly than is common with master and servant the world over. However, these meetings are not now in general, and never were in the past, on such terms as furnish a meeting of minds on the matter at issue in the problem under consideration. It is astonishing how closely two distinct groups may be associated and how much they may have in common and yet fail to have the necessary basis of common understanding as regards the crucial elements of a problem that divides them. And it is the dominant group that will fail to understand how the other feels rather than the other way about.

It appears practically certain that this matter just here under discussion is one of the most serious constituent difficulties in the greater problem faced by President Gallagher. When the two peoples first met as masters and slaves respectively and on that basis of relationship for 200 years wrought bases of communication, the communication so effected was designed from the point of view of the master class to carry forward its concerns, not for the purpose of a free exchange, back and forth, of ideas and feelings as to how it felt to be master and still less as to how it felt to be slave. Means of communication designed primarily to enable the master to make his commands effectively known to a slave are not the means suitable for communicating with respect to a difficult problem of readjusted social relationships. Nor, as we shall in a moment see, has the abolition of slavery yet resulted in the needed kind of communication.

We have thus far spoken of the lack of common bases of communication and understanding. It is possible to dig yet deeper. The master-slave relationship of the two centuries prior to 1860 entered characteristically into the very constitution of the personal selves of the constituent members of the two groups. No one is ever born a self. Selfhood has to be achieved, and it is achieved in the give-and-take of social relationships and—be it noted—in terms of the cultural pattern. In the case at hand the self of the young master and the self of the young slave were formed respectively on two correlative patterns to fit the situation created by the demands of the dominating master class. For at that time this class could and did control the educative conditions of life in a manner and degree now almost incomprehensible. The one pattern of self or personality was built to rule as master and to demand and receive the docile obedience of the other, while the other pattern of self or personality was built, in intent and surprisingly so in fact, to accept subordination as right and proper. The most astonishing characteristic of man is his wide-range malleability. Let the conditions, by custom or otherwise, seem inevitable, and the growing self will accept them as part and parcel of its own being. So in the early days of our country, under the domination of master-class purposes, master and slave each, in order to be as best it could under the available conditions, built its type of self or personality, each the correlative of the other as the master class wished it done.

Let no one begin to say that something in the innate nature of the two groups determined the respective patterns. The more we know of man, the less reason we find for believing in the existence of any such innate racial natures. Indeed the history of such matters belies and denies the theory. It would be false to suppose that these opposed master-slave mentalities or personalities were peculiar to American slavery. Wherever there has been hereditary slavery or any form of serfdom more or less of the same thing has been found. Classical Greece is an excellent instance in point. The peculiar pattern of our own Southern slavery was largely British in origin, more or less of a transplanted pattern from their hereditary master class controlling a hereditary servant class in Great Britain— Nordic ruling Nordic, if one is interested in a discussion of race. So deeply was this British prototype imbedded in British life that traces of it may easily be seen to this day. But the British cultural mind which came to America went also to India and later to China and Africa. In every case where conditions permitted the British have built the same master pattern in themselves even if, as was true of most cases, they did not have so free a hand to mold their servants. One reason their descendants in America succeeded more definitely was that the Negroes were torn from their own cultural connections and transplanted largely as individuals in a strange land, knowing little or nothing of each other. Under such conditions the old culture did not remain to supply a personality pattern after its kind. They could therefore make no effectual resistance against the pattern supplied them. It was in this manner that the master culture had its effectual way in the old South.

The abolition of slavery in 1865 did not at once destroy the old personality patterns nor did it completely abolish the conditions that had originally made the patterns. What had been a master-slave relationship was continued in intent and largely in fact as a master-servant relationship, using much of the former patterns of respective personality attitudes and again at the wish of the continuing master class. It is this fact still supported by differences of wealth, control, and opportunity that constitutes largely the present "race problem" in the United States. The present culture of the country, more definitely in the South, somewhat less definitely so elsewhere, still upholds to a greater or less degree the historic relationship.

And here comes the new phase of the problem. The old personality patterns could be built only on condition that the Negro was kept ignorantly thinking that his slave status was both inevitable and proper. Difference of skin proved useful in maintaining this belief and acceptance. Under existing conditions no such belief can hold. Means of communication are too free and open. The best patterns that the world has to offer are available to the Negro, and he is increasingly building himself and even more his children on the world outlook. In this, by the use of schools and literature as well as by the more popular radio and talking pictures, he finds the means of communication that allow him to rise out of his former relative ignorance of his situation and of the dominant master mentality into an understanding of it all and of how and why it came into being.

The members of the continuing master class, curiously enough, have no such easy access to an understanding of how the other group feels. Particularly they can hardly learn how the others feel about their denial of opportunity. Ordinary intercourse never even starts out in the direction of an understanding on this point. Not only is the topic taboo when members of the two groups meet, but the ordinary member of the dominant group feels committed in advance to a kind of universal negative regarding the whole matter. There is literature available that could help, but it is not of the best-seller type and so is easily disregarded; while no radio or talking picture even begins to help open up the subject, rather the contrary. So the dominant group that lives in closest contact is most in danger of not understanding what has come to constitute the modern phase of the problem.

And this leads us to President Gallagher's book. In its larger setting, it is an appeal to all concerned to see and understand present actual conditions. He has here in masterly fashion seized upon the conception of caste as the key element in his treatment of the problem, key element to bring the needed common understanding, key element to the treatment of his specific problem of a proper educational program for a segregated cultural college. To seize upon the conception of caste as the key marks a firm grasp of the realities of the situation.

A further significance to the book lies in Dr. Gallagher's modern understanding of the educative process and the consequent promising program mapped out not only for his college, but for any college that accepts a social mission, particularly for any Negro college in America. It is a pleasure to see how surely he has cut through accumulated tradition to the heart of college education and has proposed a workable scheme for bringing into effective coöperation all the constituent factors in the college situation—trustees, administration, staff, and students. And he has not only proposed it, he has actually put it to work. And it works.

As one who has from his youth up lived more or less intimately with this most serious problem and has all the while been concerned to help improve relations between the groups, the writer takes this opportunity to testify that President Gallagher's discussion has brought to him a clearer view than ever he had before of what the problem now means, particularly what it means to those who live among us a life of perpetual denial of full life and opportunity. If this book is sufficiently studied, it will do much good, good to those who from the vantage side fear to lose what they ought not to wish, good to those who on the other side yearn for the fuller life and have not known what road to take. Not that the book offers any panacea, far from it; but it does offer a program that all men of good will can study to advantage.

The South and the nation must face this problem and face it more resolutely and more understandingly than has hitherto been true. We must face it determined to give justice to every color, irrespective of previous lack of opportunity. Anything else or less is wrong, and being wrong must result in multiplied evil. The path of education is the path we must follow, education whether in school or out, an education to see more intelligently and to will more justly.

WILLIAM H. KILPATRICK

New York City
August, 1938

PREFACE TO THE
SECOND PRINTING

THIRTY years ago, having read (so far as I know) every book in the English language dealing with the problems of race in the United States, I sat down to write this book. I structured my analysis around the concept of caste as the conviction then controlling American life. I believe that the intervening years have validated both the tools and the conclusions of the book, which was to be out of print within eighteen months.

To be asked by a publisher to permit a re-issue after all these years is both pleasing and disquieting—pleasing, because all authors are vain; disquieting, because much has happened since this book took shape, and its data are dated.

Perhaps the most revolutionary change in human history is now underway, illuminated by one startling fact. In 1936, as I finished my research, I had found not one responsible writer who asserted, on the record, his belief that legalized segregation of the races could be eliminated in the United States. Many inveighed against it; but none passed from hope to conviction in stating that legally supported segregation could be eliminated. Today, the situation is completely reversed. All the weight of the constitution, of legislation, of the courts and of the executive branch of government (even in a few hold-out States) admits — no, asserts — that legalized segregation is on the way out.

Just as the first half of the twentieth century in this nation was preoccupied with the struggle for the rights of Labor, so the second half will be preoccupied with the struggle for integration. Now that legalized segregation

PREFACE

is in its final death struggle, and desegregation has become a purposeful objective, the possibility of equality of opportunity becomes real. In time, and with much effort, the opportunity to be equal will emerge.

And, for the record, I assert my belief that the end of the century will see an America which is greatly strengthened and enriched because, on the whole, it will be an integrated America, safe for diversity. If the writing, and the reprinting, of this book play a constructive part in this total effort, I shall be content.

BUELL G. GALLAGHER

The City College
     of the
City University of New York
August 15, 1966

PREFACE

NINETY-NINE years ago, intended slaves on the *Amistad* mutinied. They killed the captain, threw the crew in chains, and ordered the captive helmsman to steer for Africa. Through his ingenious navigation, the vessel anchored in Long Island Sound. The Africans were promptly clapped in prison, charged with mutiny and murder on the high seas. A fund was raised by popular subscription; the case was successfully defended; the Africans were repatriated. The defense of the *Amistad* mutineers led to the founding of the American Missionary Association with its avowed purpose of attack on "the sins of slave-holding, polygamy, and caste." Today, slavery is gone. Since our marriage and divorce laws permit only one legal spouse at a time, polygamy is prohibited except in serial form. But caste is as firmly entrenched and as powerful as it was a century ago.

Our caste-controlled America, in the main, presents to the Negro today the same alternatives it held out to the illicit cargo of the *Amistad*—servitude or mutiny. Not yet has the Negro been granted the option of normal, constructive citizenship. No individual or group within either race can be charged with the responsibility for this denial; it rests with the continuance of the caste system. The critical problem then becomes, how to modify caste or to make it irrelevant.

Caste will not be modified or made irrelevant unless the transformation is preceded or accompanied by a profound shift in individual and group attitudes. But these attitudes are largely a reflex of the social pattern in which persons live. To learn new attitudes, people must have new experiences. How can these experiences be obtained in a caste-controlled society? One method is that of carving out some areas of experience in which the code of caste does not control.

The college campus, Negro or white, can be such a center

of emancipation. In the widest and most inclusive sense of the term, education is the best answer to the challenge of caste. If well-meaning persons can be induced to stop prattling about "the race problem" and to set to work seriously to find what makes it impossible for Negroes and whites to live constructively as fellow-citizens, the time may come when the Negro will find that the old alternative of mutiny or subservience is replaced by the possibility of citizenship.

It may be too much to expect this transition to be completed within the lifetime of anyone now living. History will give its answer. In the meantime, the least which could be expected of an allegedly Christian and democratic nation is a rigorous, determined, good-humored, and persistent effort to understand the nature of the social forces which control it, and how these forces may be channeled in new directions. This book is offered as a tool for use in this effort. The first eight chapters carry through an analysis of caste and the social forces which work through the caste system. Chapters IX and X analyze the educational structure in the light of its social task. The remaining chapters work out details of principle and practice for the college which seeks to discharge its social function.

There is a sense in which a man's book is not his own. Only its deficiencies and errors are his. Whatever of excellence there may be in this book I owe indirectly to the six or eight hundred men and women whose writings I have read in preparation for my own; and I acknowledge more direct specific indebtedness to a number of counselors and aids.

Dr. William H. Kilpatrick has watched the study from its inception, spending many hours in conference with me, and as the work began to take shape, criticizing it both in the large and in detail, never intruding his point of view, and jealously guarding his counsel with the intention of helping me to discover better what I saw in the situation. He has patiently worked with me through revisions of the manuscript. Dr. Donald P. Cottrell has not only read the entire manuscript

PREFACE

(portions of it twice) and offered valuable criticisms and suggestions, but he has also assisted in the effort to work out the application of some of the principles emerging from the study in practical form on the campus of Talladega College. To both of these men I am indebted quite beyond the possibility of adequate acknowledgment.

Dr. John L. Childs has been helpfully critical at several points of educational philosophy. Dr. Edmund de S. Brunner contributed to the initial stages of the research, but leave of absence prevented his continuing participation. Dr. Otto Klineberg clarified my thinking at certain critical junctures. Dr. Helen M. Walker has been of invaluable help in the statistical aspects of the study and has reviewed that portion of the work. Professor Mabel Carney has contributed her stimulating counsel. Dr. R. Bruce Raup has been particularly helpful in the problems of methodology. Mr. Walter White furnished information not otherwise available, adding reliable counsel and comment. Dr. Charles S. Johnson and Dean Horace Mann Bond have read the manuscript and made suggestions.

Several co-workers in the Advanced School of Education of Teachers College have been of service; and in particular, Mr. Bernard Carp helped with his criticisms of the diagrams in Chapter IV, and Mr. Kenneth Benne stimulated sections of the discussion in Chapters X and XI.

I am indebted to the American Missionary Association and to the Trustees of Talladega College for the leave of absence which enabled me to complete the work. In one sense my greatest debt is to my colleagues who have carried on in my absence—especially Dean James T. Cater on whom fell much of my administrative load. Miss Eleanor Thompson has spent long weeks at the typewriter in preparation of the manuscript.

It would be gratuitous to thank my lady for participation in what is so intimately her own shared achievement.

BUELL G. GALLAGHER

Talladega, Alabama
August, 1938

CONTENTS

TABLES

FIGURES

I

NO ARMOR FOR HIS BACK

But now in this Valley of Humiliation poor Christian was hard put to it. . . . Then did Christian begin to be afraid, and to cast in his mind whether to go back, or to stand his ground. But he considered again that he had no armor for his back . . . ; wherefore he resolved to venture, and to stand his ground.

—JOHN BUNYAN, *The Pilgrim's Progress*

THE American college, like Bunyan's Christian, faces a decision—whether, in the Valley of Humiliation, to stand its ground, or to retreat? And, like Christian, the college may discover that it has no armor for its back, and (contrary to the adage) that valor is the better part of discretion.

Especially is this the circumstance of the segregated college for Negroes which feels all the stresses and strains of the society of which it is a part and from which it sometimes vainly tries to keep apart. The problem of the races—often wrongly called "the Negro problem"—is as inescapable as the future, as tenacious as the past. Twelve millions of Negroes and ten times that number of non-Negroes must live in the same land, making their livelihoods, rearing their children, finding their satisfactions in life. How they are to make a living, where they shall bring up their children, and what satisfactions they are to find, will depend in part upon whether the segregated college decides to retreat or to stand its ground. If the Negro college can discover its social opportunity, and if it can find or fashion means to meet that opportunity, the races in America may be aided in going forward out of their Valley of Humiliation.

Numerically not a large group, the slightly over one hundred institutions of higher learning for Negroes in the United States are strategically important. Training the intellectual representatives of twelve million people, they are highly important centers for attack upon the internal problems of the Negro group—both the problems which are primarily engendered within the group and those which result principally from external social pressures. It is also thought by many that the segregated college may contribute, to a significant degree, to the disentanglement of the larger complex of problems which confront the two races as together they face the future. In facing American society, not in retreat from it, will the Negro college probably find its fulfillment.

American history chronicles few more vividly interesting chapters than the story of the founding and growth of the colleges for Negroes.[1] The way along which they have come from the dubious days of the Reconstruction period to the promising days of the present, has not been an easy road. Marked with difficulty and disappointment, yet studded with hope and inspiration, the story of the rise of higher education for Negroes in America approaches heroic proportions when set over against its historical background. This climactic development emphasizes the necessity for clear thinking and fearless acting in the present decade, if the gains of the past are to be conserved and the hopes of the present are to be justified.

THE ADMINISTRATOR'S PREDICAMENT

If the administrator in the Negro college is to be intelligent about his job, he must make practical decisions *now*. He must make up his mind as best he can—for he must act now and therefore he must decide now. This does not mean a dogmatic attitude or a closed mind. Rather the contrary. It does mean that he must take into account all available information and value judgments, and, in the light of such fragmentary knowledge as he can command, attempt to construct a more useful frame of reference.

It is possible for the researcher arbitrarily to select one single aspect of the problem of the Negro college in its social setting, and to isolate it from its context for special study. This is already being done, and it needs to be done with increasing effectiveness and intensity until the area is systematically and adequately covered.[2] But in the nature of the case, our knowledge of a dynamic phenomenon will always

[1] D. O. W. Holmes, *The Evolution of the Negro College,* "Teachers College Contributions to Education," No. 609 (1934).

[2] For summaries of current research in the field of Negro education, see the *Journal of Negro Education,* April, 1933; April, 1934; April, 1935; and October, 1936.

be less complete than a picture of a static whole. And in the meantime, the college goes on. Like it or not, as far as his college and its social setting are concerned, the administrator is forced to try to

. . . grasp this sorry scheme of things entire,

to examine the relationships, the wholeness, the composite complexity, the total configuration of which the college is a part. This present book is written not so much with the hope of making a descriptive inventory of collegiate opportunities for Negro Americans, as with the desire of finding key meanings which may be useful in making the Negro colleges effective servants of the group they are set apart to serve.

The study starts, therefore, in the midst of a complex entanglement[3] of historical, sociological, economic, psychological, educational, anthropological, biological, aesthetic, ethical, religious, and philosophical problems, any one of which, taken by itself, would readily be considered as sufficient for scores of atomistic researches. But the interest here is not so much in any of these problems in and of themselves, as it is in the interrelation of a multitude of factors as they functionally and organically combine in the society which confronts the Negro college. The problem of finding insights for the administration of such a college in American society is complex, varied, highly charged with emotional overtones. The approach must be as varied and as comprehensive as the problem itself; and the study must attempt to be as objective as the limitations of human frailty permit.

TREATING CONTROVERSIAL MATERIALS

The controversial nature of the materials sets a special problem for the author. There appear to be six options, between which one must choose in his treatment of the highly volatile questions which cluster around the Negro college.

---

[3] "We must begin with things in their complex entanglements rather than with simplifications made for the purposes of effective judgment and action; whether the purpose is economy or dialectical, esthetic or moral." John Dewey, *Experience and Nature*, p. 32.

First, one might refuse to touch directly or indirectly upon the more dynamic aspects of the problem, choosing instead to concentrate on some more or less neutral (because arbitrarily insulated from its context) problem. This would mean that the discussion would be limited to matters of secondary and tertiary importance, and that even these could not be treated with candor.

Secondly, one might select for emphasis certain of the less highly charged aspects of the problem, hoping in the discussion to touch obliquely upon critical and controversial issues, and trusting to indirection for ultimate outcomes. Both of these possibilities seem uninviting, if not cowardly; and both of them would lead to something less than the inclusive pattern of thinking which we desire. Embracing less than the whole, they would give results which were partial in both senses of the word—biased and fragmentary.

A third possibility which would lead around the controversial aspects of the problem might be that of frankly assuming a stated attitude, and then proceeding with the discussion of less controversial matters. There are some pragmatic arguments which would appear to support this alternative.[4] It would enable one quickly to come to grips with the so-called practical issues of college administration rather than delaying him with the seemingly more theoretical discussion of issues which are hidden in the subsoil of the field. It might lift the whole study out of the area of mundane and banal controversy and pitch it on a higher plain of intellectual objectivity. But one would pay a price for his serenity, a price in academic irrelevancy when the situation demands realism and functional relevancy; and even more in the threat of hidden danger in the subtle undermining of the entire structure of the study because the currents of subterranean controversy would con-

[4] See, for example, R. B. Vance, *Human Geography of the South*, p. 463: "In a field where doubts abound, let us make one sweeping statement. If biological inferiority of the whole Negro group were a proved fact, it would, nevertheless, be to the benefit of both white and black to behave as though it did not exist. Only in this way can the Section be sure of securing, in the economic sphere, the best of which both races are capable."

tinue to eat at the sands of uncertainty into which assumptions were driven like bearing piles for false foundations. No matter how pure one's motives might be, he would be accused by friend and foe alike of side-stepping the main issues.

If one does not dodge the underlying controversial issues, if he does not give them oblique treatment, and if he does not gloss them over with irenic assumptions, three possible courses remain. He may (fourthly) include all the important relevant issues, making the test one of relevance and importance rather than of possible emotional overtones. He may hew to the line and let the chips fall where they will. If this course is followed, controversial materials will need to be treated in a noncontroversial spirit.

Fifthly, one might make a study which included all matters germane to the problem, whether controversial in context or not, but without publishing the results. A long-time program of development could then be projected without exciting aggressive opposition. A college which wishes to serve the needs of a minority group in a hostile society may well avoid stirring up unnecessary opposition. But this procedure would still imply that there was something which must be hidden from public gaze, something which could not stand the light of day, something which was not quite open and aboveboard, not quite "safe"; and it is probable that the vague uneasiness which might grow out of a whispered report that "something funny was going on" would in the long run be more serious than possible opposition to an announced policy. Moreover, the whole idea of "putting over" some preconceived plan of action, of imposing some blue-printed Utopia upon a recalcitrant society, is completely foreign to the spirit and attitudes of the writer. For strategic, logical, and psychological reasons, this fifth course is rejected.

The sixth possibility can be rejected merely by naming it. There are some who feel that, far from avoiding the controversial issues, these issues ought to be the primary subject of research, for the purpose of settling them once and for all—in the "right" way. Starting with preconceived notions (prejudices) about matters of race, the research (if it could be called research) proceeds to buttress the preconceptions. This is the method of the propagandists of the Left and of the Right. Both the social reformer and the Bourbon use it. With the sixth alternative, all matters of method, procedure, and results are dictated in advance by the preconceptions with which the researcher sets out. Not a little of the alleged research in the fields of Negro education and race relations has gone down this blind alley of prejudice.

The fourth possibility therefore remains as the only serious bidder for preference. The writer feels that he must hew to the line and let the chips fall where they may. He feels that he must try to include all significant and relevant data, without regard to whether or not controversial overtones can be associated with these data; but he is also aware that he must constantly be on guard against inevitable tendencies of some personal bias of the researcher to intrude itself into the investigation. The approach must be noncontroversial in tone and in fact.

At the same time, the research worker must make every effort to be conscious of his own bias or "slant," and to make explicit provision for it. The reader has a right to know the point of view of the writer, the procedure for setting facts in order. "Objectivity," as the term is sometimes used in the humane sciences, is synonymous with omniscience; and as such it is beyond the reach of men. There are some who dare to think that even the Omniscient is biased in favor of truth, goodness, and beauty, that broadmindedness is compatible with a belief in justice, equity, and brotherhood.

POINT OF VIEW

The point of view of this book is indicated in two groups of facts, one having to do with the life experience of the writer, and the other having to do with more general considerations.

The autobiographical facts which influence the writer, and for which both author and readers need constantly to make implicit and explicit correction in findings of fact and in inference from fact, grow out of the life of the writer: a son of the Middle West, of Caucasian ancestry, educated in the Middle West, the East, and in England; and during the period of study and writing of this book the president of a liberal arts college for Negroes in the heart of the Deep South. Throughout the four and one-half years of study and writing which have gone into the making of this book, the author has rigorously attempted to make allowance for the particular autobiographical circumstances which might color his findings or bias his conclusions. Every value judgment which has consciously entered into the discussion has been given empirical reference, in the conviction that it is better to state the value judgment openly, and to subject it to critical examination, than to permit an uncriticized preference to prejudge the issue. But no absolute claim to alleged "objectivity" is made by the writer, any more than he can expect it in his readers. Each of us approaches the issues of life with the total equipment of experiences which life has given him up to the moment; and it is for us rather to admit that we are what we are, and to make explicit provision for our personalities, than to fall back on the dangerous assumption that we can be completely objective. We can strive toward objectivity; and one of the best means of reducing the error of our findings is to acknowledge our own limitations so that we may correct them or introduce counterbalancing factors in our research.

The second group of influencing factors, which describe the general point of view of the writer, are stated in the following assumptions:

1. That all human beings are human beings, which means from the actual figures that the majority of human beings in this world are "colored" people;

2. That a college which is set apart by law or custom or both, often largely against the will of the segregated group, has a primary obligation to see that the welfare of that group is not neglected in its efforts;

3. That the fullest ethical consideration urges that the welfare of the segregated group is best served when the college works to integrate the narrower group purposes with the wider and larger service of human welfare;

4. That the college must concern itself intelligently with the processes of social change, since if it does not thus exercise an intelligent concern, its activity (or inactivity) is likely to have an unintelligent and therefore undesirable effect upon the social process;

5. That, in social evolution, it is possible for intelligent and conscious purpose to play a normative part, the contrary assumptions of both theistic and nontheistic determinists being rejected.[5]

This last assumption does not postulate the independence of human purpose from the experiences which have been built into individual and group life. Rather the contrary. What is assumed is that it is possible for intelligent action to be projected on the basis of purposes and desires which in turn have grown out of a study of the situation, and that this action may conceivably have some influence upon the speed and the direction of social movement.

THE AREA TO BE COVERED

Geographically, the study is limited mainly to the Southern United States. A glance at the map shows that most of the segregated colleges are located in these Southern States. Historically, the particular set of attitudes which cluster about Negro-white relationships are a product principally of Southern culture. For this reason, the study deals mainly with the

---

[5] An example of theistic determinism: "Many governments have been founded upon the principle of enslavement of classes, but the classes thus enslaved were of the same race in violation of the laws of nature. . . . The negro by nature or by the curse of Canaan is fitted for that condition which he occupies in our system. . . . The substratum of our society is made up of the material fitted by nature for it, and by experience we know that it is best not only for the superior race but for the inferior race that it should be so. It is indeed in conformity with the ordinance of the Creator." From the speech on the Constitution of the Confederate States of America, delivered by the Honorable Alexander Stephens.

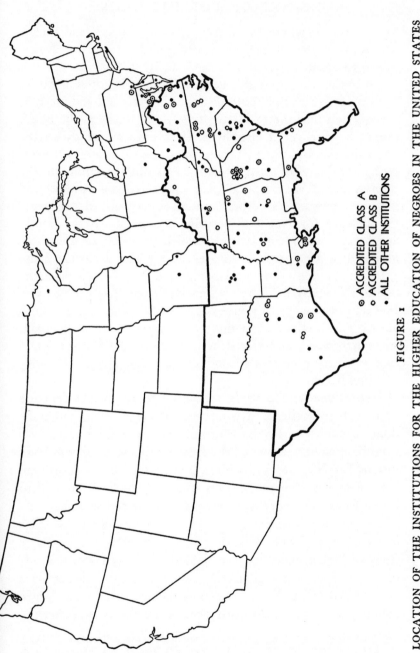

ACCREDITED CLASS A
ACCREDITED CLASS B
ALL OTHER INSTITUTIONS

FIGURE 1

LOCATION OF THE INSTITUTIONS FOR THE HIGHER EDUCATION OF NEGROES IN THE UNITED STATES

South—that is where the segregated colleges are, and that is where race relationships originally got their peculiar American formulation.

To concentrate upon this geographic area is not to point an accusing finger at the South. Neither directly nor indirectly is it suggested that the racial attitudes to be found in the South cannot be discovered elsewhere. If this were a study of the entire national pattern of race relationships, quite an interesting catalogue of culture conflicts in other sections of the country could be compiled—not only involving whites and Negroes, but several other minorities as well. But because the colleges for Negro Americans are mainly in the South, and because the racial attitudes which characterize the whole nation to a greater or lesser degree are found clearly delineated in the immediate environs of the Negro college in the South, this study is limited primarily to one geographic area. It is not an attempt to revive old sectional controversies or to pillory any section. It is merely an attempt at a clear-cut, straightforward, and sympathetic study of the historical and contemporary processes which have dug this particular Valley of Humiliation.

Institutionally, the study is limited to the social function of the Negro college. A companion study of what might be done through and by the white colleges would be useful,[6] as would companion studies of the elementary and secondary institutions for Negroes and whites, and of the adult educational movement for both races. This study is arbitrarily limited to the colleges for Negroes, merely to make it compassable.

Functionally, the line is drawn even more narrowly. This is not a general study of higher education, nor even a general study of higher education for Negroes. This is a special study of those aspects of higher education for Negroes which bear upon the central problems raised by the presence of the Negro college as a segregated institution in the midst of American

---

[6] Materials on what is actually being done in the white colleges of the South are available from the Southern Interracial Commission, 706 Standard Building, Atlanta, Georgia.

society. The reader who looks in these pages for a full and rounded discussion of the Negro college is forewarned: this is not a general discussion, but primarily a discussion of the particular problems of higher education for Negroes which grow out of the relationship of the college to the social process.

THE PROCEDURE

There are three major stages to the study. Logically they follow one another in the order in which they are given; but actually the process of exploration has been one of constant alternation and movement from one aspect to another as the study has progressed.

Following the introductory chapter, Chapters II to VIII analyze the social setting of the segregated college, uncovering the basic sociological factors which are principally relevant to the college. A statement of the psychological processes in which the individual acquires race attitudes dominant in his society is given empirical reference both historically and sociologically. How these race attitudes function as stereotypes, and how a social system is built up which expresses and nurtures these stereotypes and attitudes, is given as the social background in which the segregated college faces its dilemmas and must find its answers.

Chapter IX analyzes and rejects several notions of Negro education which appear not to be adequate to the demands of a socially functional college, and in the light of this negative analysis Chapter X attempts a positive statement of the notion of a college which would be more effective socially.

After the idea of the functional college has thus been constructed in the light of the sociological analysis, Chapters XI to XIII discuss in general outline three concrete areas of particular interest in the actual operation of such a college.

Certain materials which seem essential to the main argument of the book, but which could not be incorporated in the text without unduly slowing the discussion, are included in three Appendices.

II

THE NATURE OF PREJUDICE

The outside world does not know, neither can it appreciate, the struggle that is constantly going on in the hearts of both the Southern white people and their former slaves to free themselves from racial prejudice; and while both races are thus struggling they should have the sympathy, the support, and the forbearance of the rest of the world.

—BOOKER T. WASHINGTON

THE dominant difficulty confronting the Negro college graduate as he faces the world is symbolized in the phrase "race
prejudice." Many of his problems within the racial group,
and most of the extra burdens which society imposes upon
him are expressions of race attitudes. To be intelligent about
the college for Negro students, we must begin with the question: What is this thing called race prejudice? Any attempt
to orient the Negro college in its social environment must
begin with this question.

Is race prejudice inborn? Is it innate and unchanging, immutable and unavoidable? Or does it arise out of circumstances, and is it therefore subject to change? And if it is
subject to modification, how, and under what circumstances,
do these modifications appear? What determines race attitudes?

A prolific literature has grown up around this question of
the nature of attitudes in general and of race prejudices in
particular. Much of what is contained in this chapter, and in
the three which follow it, has been said by scores of writers
far abler than the present one (as the footnotes testify); and
several of these writers have been particularly concerned with
the bearing of the study upon educational problems and procedures. The reader who is well versed in the literature of
racial attitudes and of the caste structure of American society
may find the present discussion elementary. But it is precisely
because it is elementary and therefore basic that it is included
here. Without any claim to originality either in materials or in
the treatment of data, the present writer feels compelled to
begin his study of the social task of the Negro college by
depicting in brief the present state of knowledge about race
attitudes in the American caste system. The educational importance of this excursion into psychology and sociology becomes

more fully apparent as the study proceeds. We begin, then, with a naïve inquiry into the nature of race prejudice.

THE GROWTH OF PSYCHOLOGICAL PATTERNS

It is "human nature" for a child to be hungry; but his society largely determines the methods he uses to satisfy that hunger. The random movement, the kicking and crying of the infant, is gradually replaced, under parental guidance, with the "Say please" pattern. A little later in life he may learn to find the cookie jar for himself. As he comes into maturity, he may learn to respond to the urge of hunger not by kicking and crying, not by stealing cookies, but by laying aside a part of his monthly salary to be put at the disposal of the cook. This is still human nature at work. Looking ahead, he may decide that if he wishes to eat in his old age, he must save. Then, widening his perspective, he may advocate an old-age insurance plan in the board of directors of his company; and later he may lend his support to the national security legislation, or become interested in the proposal for an ever normal granary for supplying the needs of the nation. This is still human nature.

Like any other adult pattern of conduct, it involves the whole complex set of experiences and relationships which have been built into the life process of the individual. The outcomes are the joint product of the evolving personality and the social fabric in terms of which that personality finds expression.

Let the societal pattern be different, and the developing infant will learn a quite different set of responses and habits. He may begin with the same random crying and kicking to satisfy his hunger urge. If, however, he grows up among a tribe of head-hunters and cannibals, his methods of satisfying that hunger urge as an adult will differ strikingly from the procedures of the corporation director. A different social matrix provides different patterns for individual development into matured attitudes.

In this process of individual growth, there is no point up

to which human nature is at work, and beyond which something else takes over the controls. Nor can it be maintained that there is a gradual diminution of the working of "natural" forces and a gradual increase of some other kind of force or factor. On the contrary, there is an increasing use of intelligence, itself one of the native potentialities of humanity. The stuff of experience from the cradle to the grave is a single continuum. The nature of experience does change; but it cannot be said that it is human nature to seek more immediate and limited rather than more remote and more inclusive goals. True, the complexity of the action pattern may vary from the simplest to the most elaborate. The ratio of effectiveness of the higher mental processes may increase; but if we say that "human nature" was at work in the first instance, it is still human nature at work in the last of a series of experiences in a long development.

Three observations may be made. First, whatever human nature may mean, it does not mean something fixed and immutable. What individuals and groups do when confronted by recurring situations is profoundly modified from time to time.[1] Secondly, these modifications are carried through in terms of realized capacities, and they are largely determined by the matrix of contemporary social life in which they find themselves carried out.[2] Thirdly, the creative element, the thing which makes possible the fashioning of new goals and of implements for realizing these goals, is action in accordance with intelligently conceived plans. "Human society is not controlled chiefly by ready-made reactions, but is largely a product of human experience, that is, of what man has learned through

[1] See E. Faris, "The Concept of Social Attitudes" in *Social Attitudes*, pp. 3-16. The basic stuff of human-nature-in-performance is not an irreducible set of instincts of "drives," but rather, "acts and experiences are the determining antecedents beyond which it is not profitable or even possible to seek any stable elements or absolutes." Attitudes, therefore, are not inherited absolutes, but cultivated predispositions. An attitude, however real, is inferential. There is no one-to-one correspondence of specific responses to specific stimuli.

[2] See Max C. Otto, "Philosopher of a New Age," *The Social Frontier*, III (June, 1937), 266. "Man cannot be anything without incorporating his environment; and he cannot be human without vital interplay of his activities and ideals in super-personal endeavors."

the centuries by means of his intelligence.[3] This does not mean that everything now included in society is intelligently conceived. It does, however, suggest that the contemporary social matrix is a part of a process of continuous interplay of individuals and groups, in which there may be basic motives at work, but in which the reaction pattern varies widely.

In his study of the growth of social norms, Sherif[4] shows that the basis of accepted reaction patterns which are social norms—such stereotypes and conduct-controls as fashions, conventions, customs, values, and attitudes toward these—is the formation of a common frame of reference through the contact of individuals. Social attitudes, once formed in the individual, serve as frames of reference in the situations into which he enters, determining to an important degree the preferences, likes, and dislikes of the individual. The properties of any part are determined by its relationship to the whole, its membership in the total functional experience. The setting up of a reaction pattern which is universally adopted within a group, and which thereafter enters into the experience of all members of that group as one of the important determining factors in the experience of its members, is the process of building an attitude.

One of these patterns of reaction is the social attitude called race prejudice. As such, it is a fairly sophisticated development including a complex of many interrelated factors. It is not always present where there are noticeable physical differences between groups of people; and, conversely, it sometimes appears in spite of the fact that the alleged "races" cannot be sharply distinguished. The definite pattern of social attitudes which we, today, call race prejudice is of comparatively recent origin. Lord Bryce is responsible for the statement[5] that "down to the days of the French Revolution there had been very little in any country at any time, of self-conscious racial feeling."

[3] Charles A. Ellwood, *Psychology of Human Society*, p. 310.
[4] M. Sherif, *The Psychology of Social Norms*.
[5] See W. D. Weatherford and Charles S. Johnson, *Race Relations*, Ch. III.

It does not appear from scientific study that racial antipathies are "instinctive," something to be charged to a mysterious, immutable "human nature."[6] Bruno Lasker's study of race attitudes in children finds no support for the notion that there is an instinctive reaction of aversion or antipathy between members of differing groups. Each child has an experience of race feeling which is peculiar to him, built upon experience or lack of experience with members of other groups, but "the nature of these contacts is largely determined by a much larger and more inclusive influence: the adult-made environment."[7] And while reserving final decision until experimental evidence can be amassed, Lasker concludes tentatively that "the evidence makes it probable that the attitudes unconsciously transmitted are much more effective than those deliberately taught."[8] This conclusion was much more strongly indicated than had been anticipated in advance of the study.

For, although we were prepared for much evidence concerning the pressure of adult attitudes upon those of children, the actual evidence of the staggering weight of prejudices with which it burdens the rising generation is beyond all expectation. One might almost say that it makes no difference whether the child is born with natural aversions or not; he is certain to have his mind canalized, even before he starts going to school, into habitual acceptance of the prevailing attitudes of the group within which he lives. Personal experience, when hedged around with prohibitions and protective care, is no gateway to realism. The average child is

[6] "Race prejudice has often been asserted by popular writers to be instinctive or hereditary. While this is apparently a complete misstatement it is a very excusable one. The error arises from the normal tendency of unsophisticated people to confuse the customary with the natural. When children grow up in a community, they take on the customs and attitudes prevailing . . . and when the attitudes have become second nature they are often thought of as inherent or natural." E. Faris, *"Natural History of Race Prejudice"* in *Ebony and Topaz*, ed. Charles S. Johnson, pp. 107-10.
[7] Bruno Lasker, *Race Attitudes in Children*, p. 371.
[8] *Ibid.*, p. 371. So also R. E. Park, in his "Human Nature, Attitudes, and the Mores" contributed to *Social Attitudes*. An attitude is a tendency to act with reference to a given value; it represents a tension within the individual while it is latent; it may differ in intensity with different individuals or at different times in the same individual. "Attitudes are rooted in experience, but it is this experience in all concreteness that finally determines the character of an attitude, both as to its direction and its intensity." (P. 32.) Attitudes are communicable, even contagious, and the slight subtleties of behavior are much more important than overt instruction in this process of contagion.

made to accept outer differences, and to accept them as inner differences of value. His very contacts are regulated for him, if not by precept, then by example. So it comes that the child—since his experience is not the same in classroom and Sunday School, on the street and on the playground, at home and in the social center—acquires a mixture of contradictory attitudes towards those of other races which he is quite unable to explain to himself or to others.[9]

Nor does it appear to make much difference what the temperament of the particular child is, or his special physico-psychic characteristics. "Generally speaking, even in those reactions which seem most closely bound up with the physiological equipment, the part played by the individual character in the formation of racial attitudes is small, apparently, compared with that played by the weight of surrounding adult opinion and its conscious and unconscious influence."[10]

Some writers on this question have made a good deal of the fact that children tend to fear the intrusion of strange and unaccustomed factors in experience. A strange face, a strange noise, may call out a violent reaction of fear or aversion in the child. In the youth this may be changed to disgust or to amusement. Such reactions, it is said by some, indicate an instinctive base for race attitudes. The point does not need argument. The close and intimate relationship between the white infant and the Negro nurse, common practice in thousands of the best homes throughout the South, and the cementing of genuine lasting attitudes which are at least cordial on both sides, indicates that the alleged instinctive attitude of aversion is not operative in these cases at least. Moreover, it is clear that while the new or the strange may call out fear it may also evoke curiosity. Which of the two attitudes will be called into play depends upon a complex of factors, not least important of which is the attitude of adults and older children present. Initial contacts, plus habituation, fix the attitude; and these contacts depend upon the adult-managed social framework. If the first reaction toward a stranger— of whatever race—is reënforced by fear reactions on the

[9] Lasker, op. cit., p. 370.
[10] Ibid., p. 262.

part of the mother, the feeling is exaggerated and the fixation of prejudice has begun. If the mother is hesitant about
contacts only with certain kinds of strangers, such as the
physician or street children, the child is imperceptibly but
effectively pushed in the same direction. Much depends upon
the first few contacts with members of another group; and
the adult attitude determines whether the child will build up
habits of friendliness or of withdrawal. Both attitudes are
possible as far as human nature is concerned. This appears
to apply to all races and to all situations.[11]

Through childhood and adolescence, then, the individual
might develop attitudes of race friendliness or of antagonism.
The degree to which he develops either (or both) depends
upon the manner in which his experience combines the inter-
acting factors of his contradictory environment. "Pugnacity
and fear are no more native than pity and sympathy. The
important thing morally is the way these native tendencies
interact, for their interaction may give a chemical transformation not a mechanical combination."[12] As a child, the individual will probably not take a consciously aggressive part
in deciding his course. As he comes into adulthood, it is
likely that he will still be relatively passive, his attitudes having been formed in terms of experience in the group of which
he is a member. He follows the path of negative race adjustment rather than the building of positive attitudes because, although either development was a potentiality of his
nature, that one won out which was most heavily weighted
for preference, most consistently and effectively learned
through experience in his society.

But it may be asked: If race prejudice is not instinctive,
then why is it prevalent? The first answer is that attitudes
of antagonism or of discrimination between racial groups are
not universally prevalent. The French, for example, during
the World War seemed to show little or no race prejudice
toward the Negro American.

---

[11] *Ibid.*, pp. 34 f.
[12] John Dewey, *Human Nature and Conduct,* p. 111.

A reasonable hypothesis for as much prevalence as we see in particular societies is that there are conflicts in society which, by their continuance, support attitudes of antipathy rather than of friendliness; and that these basic conflicts fasten themselves upon the individual members of the several groups, calling out the responses of antagonism and prejudice rather than of understanding and friendliness. "Race" then becomes important not as a biological description or ethnic classification, but primarily as a symbol of conflict between groups in the culture. After examining the inadequacies of attempts by biologists, anthropologists, psychologists, and others to agree on a satisfactory classification of races, Krout concludes that the term "race" has relatively little actual biological significance due to the acknowledged hybridization of races, and that racial differences turn out to be cultural differences, which leads him to the conclusion that "the real significance of the term 'race' lies in its employment as a culture symbol of group conflict and group organization."[13] Race is not itself the cause of conflict; but men organize themselves for conflict according to observable lines of demarcation such as skin color and hair texture. Having so organized, they rationalize the division, call it "racial," and use the symbol thus created as a device for furthering covert ends.

Racial antagonisms are therefore not unlike other group antagonisms between classes or nations.

The fundamental causes of racial dislike and hostility, where these exist, are similar to those which give rise to hostility within communities of the same race. They are moral rather than racial. There is no necessity to postulate the existence of a specific and universal instinct of racial antipathy; while on the other hand there is strong, positive evidence that such an instinct does not exist. An adequate explanation of racial antagonism can be found in impulses and motives that are independent of race. These impulses and motives, however, though not racial in their origins, may become racial through being connected in the mind with the thought of another race. When

[13] Maurice H. Krout, "Race and Culture: A Study in Mobility, Segregation, and Selection," *American Journal of Sociology*, XXXVII (1931-32), 175-89.

this association takes place the feelings may be aroused by contact with any member of that race, and operate with all the force of an instinctive antipathy.[14]

When cultures which have marked surface differences come into contact, conflict is likely to result, because the habit patterns of the individual are formed in terms of his own particular group culture, and any effort at adaptation, implying loss of status on his part, is unwelcome. Or, within a given culture, groups with noticeable physical differences may come into sharp competition in the economic sphere, with resulting conflict and the organization of sentiments and emotions around the central fact of struggle for a livelihood and for comparative status on the economic ladder. "Race prejudice may be regarded as a phenomenon of status. Race prejudice is like class and caste prejudices—merely one variety of a species."[15]

The focal point of race antagonisms is likely to be some threat to existing status.

Every change in status, whether of an individual or of a group, involves a change in social organization. Prejudice—that is, caste, class and race prejudice—in its more naïve and innocent manifestations, is merely resistance of the social order to change. Every effort of the Negro, for example, to move, to rise and improve his social status, rather than his condition, has invariably met with opposition, aroused prejudice and stimulated racial animosities. Race prejudice, so conceived, is merely an expression of conservatism.[16]

"Where there are social classes, there will inevitably be corresponding attitudes and sentiments. Racial distinctions, where they exist, will always be supported by racial prejudices."[17] The prejudice expresses itself in the acceptance by the individual of the stereotype or social norm which appears to fit the needs of his group in the conflict. If the basic pattern is that of the economic structure, then the lines of economic conflict determine the racial conflict, and the racial attitudes

---

[14] J. H. Oldham, *Christianity and the Race Problem,* p. 43.

[15] R. E. Park, "Bases of Race Prejudice," *Annals* of the American Academy, CXL (November, 1928), 11-20.

[16] *Ibid.,* p. 13.

[17] *Ibid.,* p. 14.

conform to the economic processes. "Racial animosities supplement group symbols, or fictions, and make possible connected group activities. Group prejudices are rationalizations by which the individual maintains his self-esteem and advances his economic and other interests."[18] It is this line of thought which leads Herbert A. Miller to conclude, "I am convinced that practically all race concepts are not race at all, but concepts derived from economic situations. There are certain economic advantages to be derived from having one group subordinated to another."[19] Following the same line of thought, Reuter states the same conclusion a little more moderately. "Race is made the symbol of cultural status, and thus serves to justify the exploitation of the weaker group with the inevitable political and cultural consequences. Being a symbol of cultural status, it serves to classify individuals, and so to retard their advance by limiting their freedom and determining the cultural values to which they have access."[20]

The notion to which the discussion has brought us, then, is that when two groups of people are engaged in a chronic conflict of interest, largely economic, centering around the problems of security and status, each group having a high degree of visibility in skin color or other group characteristics; there is a conscious drawing of racial lines of demarcation and the use of the concept of race as a tool in the struggle. Feeling, strong emotion, is called into play, and race prejudice results. In this sense, race prejudice is a convenient device for the exploitation of one group by another.

But it is not enough that this general notion of the nature of race prejudice should appear plausible. It must square with sociological facts as far as these facts are obtainable. And if the evidence in sociological data is at all clear, it ought to be possible for persons with quite diverse attitudes on race matters to peruse the data and see substantially the

[18] Daniel Katz and Kenneth Brady, "Racial Prejudice and Racial Stereotypes," *Journal of Abnormal and Social Psychology,* XXX (July-September, 1935), 182.

[19] Quoted in Weatherford and Johnson, *op. cit.,* p. 57.

[20] E. B. Reuter, *American Race Problem,* p. 34.

same conclusions, even though other considerations, such as judgments of value, may lead each to draw his own inferences from these conclusions. In the remaining section of this chapter, two sets of data will be examined in an effort to give empirical reference to the idea that race attitudes are bound up with social processes, and particularly related to economic processes. First, the historic development of race attitudes and economic processes in the South is to be studied to reveal possible connections or lack of connections between *economic processes* and race attitudes; and, secondly, a study of fluctuations in *economic conditions* as related to fluctuations in race attitude should reveal the degree of sensitivity of response existing between the two factors.

HISTORICAL RELATIONSHIP BETWEEN ECONOMIC PROCESSES AND RACE ATTITUDES

1. *The problem defined.*—When we make the hypothesis that there may be an interrelationship of economic processes and race attitudes, we do not imply either the presence, or the lack, of a causal nexus. A student of population areas (to take an illustrative example from another field) may be interested in tracing the high correlation between overcrowding and high mortality rates. That does not mean that he concludes that congestion of population is the cause of disease. It does make it possible for him to say that, by and large, where there is overcrowding, there is also a high death rate. The fact that the two things go together is of great importance; for although poor housing may not *cause* disease, the chances for infection and communication, with fatal results, appear to be much higher in certain congested areas. The basic operational relationship between housing and disease therefore becomes highly important.

In a somewhat analogous fashion, if it can be shown that a basic relationship of interconnection exists between the nature of the economic process and the shaping of race attitudes, it is not necessary to argue the point as to whether there is a causal connection or not. Concomitance is significant not necessarily of cause and effect but of interconnection in some form. Of course, if it should appear that it is purely accidental that such a concomitance occurs, and that the apparent relationship is specious, the concomitance would be declared as of no significance. But a functional interrelationship discernible beneath the phenomenon of concomitance is highly significant for the analysis of social processes. The high correlation between the presence of a "C" on a faucet and the fact that cold water comes out of that faucet does not imply that the "C" is the cause of the water being cold. But it does imply that, usually, when everything is working normally, one may expect the water to come out cold when one turns a faucet marked "C." High correlation in this case is significant not of a causal nexus but of an operational or functional nexus.

So, when we ask whether there is a basic relationship between economic processes and race attitudes we are not asking whether the economic interpretation of history is valid, nor are we asking whether the economic factor is the *only* one which enters the picture. A common-sense, naïve view of the matter immediately suggests that a large number of factors —physical, geographical, climatic, religious, educational, etc.— do affect race attitudes. It is shown, for example, that there is a high degree of correspondence between the predominance of evangelical fundamentalism and the number of lynchings[21] in America. We readily admit that a great many sociological and psychological forces are brought to bear in determining race attitudes. All that is implied in the question as to whether economic processes and race attitudes are basically related is the inquiry as to whether there is not a strong tendency for "racial" attitudes to be drawn and to be intensified in rather general correspondence with the patterns of economic conflict or coöperation as these economic patterns develop. If the dominant psychological attitude developed under the aegis of the economic processes is an attitude of competition, and if there are easily recognized surface differ-

[21] Walter White, *Rope and Faggot*, Ch. III and pp. 245-50.

ences between large groups of persons engaged in this competitive struggle, the question is whether the process of drawing the lines of conflict on economic matters may not actually be the pragmatic process through which "races" are defined and race attitudes built up. In a world of conflict, men tend to take sides according to superficial and easily recognized differences if such differences exist; and when they cannot find such surface differences, they invent others, as in Nazi Germany today. As Todd points out, "It makes not the slightest difference whether there is any such reality as race or not. It is enough that people believe that there is."[22] When the struggle in the economic arena is the conflict which looms largest in men's minds (as it does during most of the peace-time years of modern life), the lines of "racial" grouping tend to correspond to the lines of economic conflict, whether the former actually correspond to biological realities or not. Two groups which are thrown together as economic competitors develop feelings of difference which are reënforced by skin color, hair texture, and other surface differences which make the distinctions between the two groups highly visible, and the correspondence between the economic matrix and racial categories is emphasized. Antagonisms and rivalries develop. Slogans and stereotypes are invented to facilitate the process of conflict. If the struggle is long enough and bitter enough, very strong "racial" antagonisms develop, and the prejudice is established as a continuing part of the accepted mores. Then it is that we say that there is a basic relationship between the nature of the economic process and the nature of race attitudes. Then it is that we conclude that race prejudice has a basic relationship to economics. The question, then, is: Does this basic relationship actually exist in American life?[23] First, is there a historical correlation in

---

[22] A. J. Todd, *Theories of Social Progress*, p. 224.

[23] Faris is of the opinion that "undoubtedly economic competition does occasion such sentiments, but it appears not to be everywhere the case." ("Natural History of Race Prejudice" in *Ebony and Topaz*, p. 90.) But the example he cites, of antagonism of Chinese students to foreign powers, is basically an economic conflict in which the students become involved through inclusion in the group attitude, allegiance to the stereotype, which in turn is closely related to the economic conflict.

development of the economic and "racial" lines of cleavage and conflict? Secondly, is there any sensitive index of concomitance of fluctuation in the two factors?

2. *The data examined.*—"Racial prejudice," says Reuter, "against the Negro in America is a heritage of slavery but it is very largely a development and characteristic of freedom."[24] The seeds were sown in the relatively peaceful and stable times before the Civil War; the harrowing of war and Reconstruction plowed under any sentiments of conciliation or moderation; and having sown the wind, America reaped the whirlwind. To understand the contemporary situation, two earlier phases of historical development of race attitudes must be considered; namely, the ante-bellum and the Reconstruction periods.

Despite the persistence of the tradition of idyllic plantation days,[25] there was a noticeable growth of race prejudice during slave times, particularly as between the white worker and the slave. During the period of slavery, the poorer white occupied the marginal acreage and hated the Negro who lived on the good land owned by the master of the plantation. He envied the slave who, while bound to the land, was not allowed to starve. "The poor white envied the slave's security and hated him for his material advantages, while the slave envied the white man's freedom and hated him for the advantages of his whiteness. Each group, in an effort to exalt itself, looked down on the other with all the contempt which the planter aristocracy showed for both."[26] The dominant pattern of economic processes was the plantation economy; and the lines of cleavage were sharply drawn between the white and black farm workers. The poorer white saw himself occupying a position in the agricultural economy which was, in many instances, worse than that of the slave. Crowded off the fertile

[24] Reuter, *op. cit.,* p. 147.
[25] Cf. Ulrich B. Phillips, *Life and Labor in the Old South;* Francis P. Gaines, *The Southern Plantation: A Study in the Development and Accuracy of a Tradition;* and B. Schrieke, *Alien Americans: A Study of Race Relations.*
[26] S. C. Spero and Abram Harris, *The Black Worker,* p. 4. I am indebted to this book for much of the data on the status of Negro labor before emancipation.

lands, left to fend for himself while the slave was "looked out for," the poorer white grew to hate the black slave, his competitor for a position of security on the bottom rung of the economic ladder.

This hatred was further aggravated by competition between black and white craftsmen in the towns. . . . The ablest and most promising slaves who were not assigned to service in the great house were trained in the skilled crafts. . . . The masters found it easier and cheaper to have their slaves trained in carpentry, masonry, blacksmithing and the other mechanical trades than to depend upon outside free white labor.[27]

Exceptionally fine slave craftsmen were not infrequently sent to the cities where they were hired out to master craftsmen or sometimes contracted their labor directly to the public. There were some masters who permitted their skilled slaves to hire themselves out in their free time in return for a fixed sum to the master or a certain percentage of the slaves' earnings.[28] The quality of the work turned out by the two groups of artisans was, generally speaking, about equal in excellence, the work of one group excelling on some occasions, and that of the other group being superior at other times. Yet, quite aside from the question of the quality of the work, the slave group had a decided advantage over the free whites in competing for contracts.

The poor white artisan was not competing with the black slave artisan any more than the independent store keeper of the present is competing with the manager of the chain store in his territory. The white mechanic was competing with the slave owner whose cheap slave labor, financial resources, and political power gave him every advantage . . . "I am aware," said a citizen of Athens, Georgia, in an open letter to the local contractors, "that most of you have too strong antipathy to encourage masonry and carpentry trades of your poor white brothers, that your predilections for giving employment in your lines of business to ebony workers have either so cheapened the white man's labor, or expatriated hence with but a few exceptions all the white masons and carpenters of this town. . . . As masters of the polls

[27] *Ibid.,* p. 5. See also, W. W. Alexander, "Negroes and the Economic Structure," *Southern Workman,* LX (June, 1931), 269-77.
[28] Harris and Spero, *op. cit.,* p. 6.

in a majority, carrying all before them, I am surprised the poor do not elect faithful members to the Legislature who will make it penal to prefer Negro mechanic labor to white men's."[29]

In 1845, the Georgia legislature passed a law prohibiting slaves from bargaining their services for hire as artisans and craftsmen and fining their owners for permitting slaves to enter the field of competition with white free workers in this fashion. But twelve years later the white artisans petitioned the city council to correct the difficulty which the law seemed ineffective in meeting, asking that Negro mechanics belonging to plantation owners from outside Atlanta be prevented from competing in the Atlanta labor market.[30] White mechanics in Virginia petitioned the state legislature to prevent Negroes from being apprenticed in any craft or trade. In North Carolina, they protested against the use of slave artisans to underbid them in contracts and take away "business that belongs to white laborers."[31]

As an instance of the kind of race attitudes nurtured by this conflict, consider the case of one Andrew Rock, shipwright, who petitioned the South Carolina commons in 1774 on behalf of himself and other shipwrights. He complained that Negro slaves worked in Charleston and surrounding towns at the shipwright's trade, and "were chiefly employed in mending, repairing, and caulking of ships, other vessels, and boats"; that as a result white shipwrights had almost no opportunity to work, were therefore reduced to poverty and ultimately driven from the colony. A bill to prohibit slaves from being used in shipwright's work and another bill to prevent apprenticeship of slaves in "Mechanic's Trades both in Town and in Country" failed to pass the South Carolina Commons because of opposition of slave owners, despite urgent appeals from nonslave-owning white craftsmen.[32] A

---

[29] *Ibid.,* p. 7. The letter was printed in 1838.
[30] *Ibid.,* p. 8.
[31] *Ibid.,* p. 9.
[32] Marcus Jernegan, "Slavery and the Beginnings of Individualism in the American Colonies," *The American Historical Review,* XXV (January, 1920), 237.

by-law of the Trustees of Georgia, in 1750, forbade any artificers, except coopers, to take Negroes as apprentices, or planters to lend or to let out their slaves "to be employed otherwise than in manuring and cultivating their Plantations in the Country." Later, in 1782, Virginia forbade masters to hire out their slaves and to receive the pay.[33] From colonial times right down to emancipation, the white and black workers had ample opportunity to develop attitudes of mutual hostility. Summing up his investigation of slave artisans in colonial and post-colonial times, Jernegan says:

The weight of evidence shows that there was a great increase in numbers [of slave artisans]; that they were of much greater [market] value than untrained slaves; that they were much sought after; that they did compete with free white labor, especially in the towns; and finally, that they were the most important agency in the rise of plantation manufactures.[34]

In addition to this sharp and widespread competition between the artisans of the two races in the towns, and the antipathies of the farm laborers of the two races in the country, there appears to have been an even more effective and drastic competition between the unskilled labor groups of the two races whenever construction work or industrial employment called for hands. The slave owner used his slave principally during the two relatively short periods of planting and chopping in the spring and early summer and picking in the fall. For the rest of the time, anything the owner could get for the slaves' services was clear profit to him. It was not uncommon for contractors to time their enterprises to take advantage of this reservoir of ready, cheap labor rather than to use white workers. The rate for white workers was thus cut below the subsistence level. Once again, the white unskilled worker found himself competing not with the individual Negro but with the great plantation system which backed the black worker and put him on the labor market at a ridiculously low wage.

[33] *Ibid.*, p. 238.
[34] *Ibid.*, p. 239.

Negro slaves were employed in foundries as foremen, blacksmiths and founders. They were used to mine both coal and ore. They worked along the water front as longshoremen. With the exception of conductors, they worked on the railroads in every capacity including that of locomotive engineer, and they piloted the steamboats that plied on southern waters. They were even used to some extent as hands in the textile mills and formed a large portion of the workers in the tobacco factories. In all these employments they came into competition with white workers. . . . A factory near Columbia, S. C., reported the average cost per annum of its slave operatives at a minimum of $106. Whether the slave was rented or owned, slave labor was cheap and operated to depress the wages of white labor.[35]

It is understandable that this should have been the case. The master class had large investments in slaves, and the seasonal nature of cotton growing meant that they must use the slave labor in the off-season to get a steady return on their investment. It also meant that the plantation economy paid the bill of supporting the slave labor, while the industrial use of the slave was merely a marginal device for increasing income and was therefore perfectly calculated to undermine the wage levels of the free white industrial workers.

The master class insisted on employing its slaves in whatever manner it found profitable. If they were not needed on the plantations they were rented out to dig ditches. If they were too weak to stand the strain of working in the fields, they were sent to the cotton mills to "attend to the looms and spindles." The slave owner demanded a steady income on his investment. Furthermore, what there was of southern industry and enterprise was owned by the slaveholding class.[36]

During slave times, it would appear, the lines of economic cleavage between white and black workers were clearly drawn and intensified by decades of irritation. In agriculture, in the crafts and building trades, in industry, in transportation, and in the unskilled labor market, the slave was thrust by his owner into sharp and devastating competition with the free white. The latter, instead of marshaling his political power to strike back against the planter class, exhibited an increasing hatred for the black man with whom he was in immediate

[35] Spero and Harris, *op. cit.,* p. 10.
[36] *Ibid.,* pp. 10 f.

competition. (Two cats, their tails tied together, will scratch and fight each other in mutual recrimination.) Racial prejudice in America between working-class whites and blacks roots back in the competition of slavery with free labor.

So, too, racial attitudes between the white aristocracy and the Negro have their beginnings in the master-slave pattern. Despite atrocity stories like *Uncle Tom's Cabin* which played their part in inflaming public opinion on both sides of the conflict which developed between the North and the South, the planters as a class do not appear to have been cast in the mold of Simon Legree. A good deal of sentimental building of dream pictures of ante-bellum days can be charged to wishful thinking; but it still remains that common sense would prompt an owner to treat his slaves at least as well as the money investment would demand. In addition, the house slaves occupied a peculiarly high position in the master's estimation. The house slave generally was thought of very much as another child. He was treated as a child, perhaps a step-child, but nevertheless, part of the whole family. The master expected the slave to respond as a child (but one who would never achieve majority), and there developed a paternalistic attitude with its correlative dependency complex which was as firmly fixed between master and slave as was the bitter hatred between white and black worker. There grew up an elaborate system of etiquette which was at once the vehicle of expressing this master-slave relationship and of perpetuating it psychologically.[37] The slave was addressed by his first name, as a child always is. Indeed, he had only a first name. He, in turn, treated all members of the master's family as worthy of the respect due adults, calling the children of the master "Young Master" and "Young Missy." In a case of disagreement, the master was always right, and the slave escaped punishment by assuming the rôle of the childlike, smiling, simple-minded person who was not expected to know any better. He pulled at his forelock, dropped

---

[37] Bertram W. Doyle, "The Etiquette of Race Relations—Past, Present, and Future," *Journal of Negro Education*, V (April, 1936), 191-208.

his eyes and grinned. He might be cuffed; he might even be chastised severely on occasion. But the attitude developed was one of paternalistic dominance by the master and of childish submission by the slave. The racial attitudes were developed in accordance with the economic pattern of owner-slave.

There was a third set of circumstances which was partly geographic and partly economic in nature, and which was responsible for a special kind of race antipathy, the antagonism of the white highlander who was at once anti-slavery and anti-Negro. Thrusting itself down from the North in a long, sprawling series of ridges and valleys, the wedge of the mountains divides the broad coastal plains from the rich lands of the Mississippi and its tributaries. Down through its valleys, pushing southwestward from Pennsylvania and Maryland, the Scotch-Irish and German pioneers of the eighteenth century injected into the South through the Appalachian wedge a culture which was more Pennsylvanian in character and contacts than Carolinian or Georgian. Economically, politically, and socially, these pioneers in their mountain fastnesses were cut off from the seaboard life. Not only the falls of the rivers, which marked the head of navigation, but also a parallel strip of pine barrens, cut the mountains off from the plain. It was an area which Turner called:

The first distinctively western region, non-slaveholding, grain and cattle raising, a land of dissenting sects, of primitive democratic conditions, remote from the coast, and finding the connection with Baltimore, Philadelphia, and the Pennsylvania valley, both in spiritual and economic life, more intimate than with the tide-waters of Maryland, Virginia, North Carolina, and South Carolina, within whose boundary lines it chiefly lay.[38]

What contacts there were between the mountaineers and the coastal-plain dwellers were principally irritating and contentious contacts. Politically, the tidewater minority area

[38] "Is Sectionalism in America Dying Away?" *American Journal of Sociology*, XIII, 665, quoted in H. P. Douglass, *Christian Reconstruction in the South*, p. 67. I am indebted to Douglass for the accompanying insight into the attitudes of nineteenth-century mountaineers toward Negroes.

ruled the more populous upland interior counties "by apportionment of the legislatures so as to secure the effective
majority of representatives. Unjustly taxed, deprived of due
participation in government, their rights neglected, they protested, vainly for the most part."[39]

Economically, the clash of mountain and plain was even
more irritating. Previous to 1830, the mountain people had
begun to push on down into the Piedmont and out into the
plains where (as in central North Carolina, and northern
Alabama, for example) they were the spear-thrust of a non-
slaveholding agricultural economy. But with the invention of
the cotton gin, plantation farming became a very lucrative
business, and the plantation system rapidly pushed the intruders back into their mountains and gulleys and unwittingly
caused a wave of migration which swept right over the ridges
and into the broad valleys of the interior. Especially between
1830 and 1840, the census figures show marked declines in
the rate of increase of the white population of states like
North Carolina.[40] Up in the hills and mountain retreats, the
disgruntled farmers nursed their grudges, oiled their guns,
and bided their time. The wealthy plantation owners, resting
their power on the use of Negro slaves, had beaten them back
—temporarily; but with the war, these highlanders in large
numbers swelled the ranks of the Union Army. The mountains of Virginia tore themselves loose from the mother
state and became West Virginia. All down the range of the
Appalachians almost to the very heart of Alabama where the
last red hills drop off to the black plains, there came many
recruits to join the Northern army, singing as they joined:

> To the flag we are pledged, all its foes we abhor,
> And we ain't for the nigger, but we are for the war.[41]

Here were a great group of whites, living in the South but
not of it, strongly opposing and often despising the landed
aristocracy, and with equal heartiness disliking the Negro and

[39] Turner, *op. cit.,* p. 666.
[40] Douglass, *op. cit.,* p. 68.
[41] W. E. B. DuBois, *Black Reconstruction,* p. 56.

the institution of slavery by which the aristocracy used the Negro to defeat the single-handed white farmer. They were both anti-slavery and anti-Negro. When the war came, they were for the Union and against the Negro.

And when the war came, it let loose another storm which had been brewing for decades. With each year the increasing tension between North and South, between slaveholder and nonslaveholder, and between free and white worker and slave, had tightened the lines of class and caste cleavage, deepening the racial antipathies and grooving the habituation. The altruistic thrust of Beecher, Garrison, Frederick Douglass, and the Abolitionists was backed by the desire of Northern industrialists to cripple the plantation South. All the forces of pent-up emotion were marshaled on both sides. All the rapiers of keen intellect were summoned to thrust invective and vilification. Blundering, stumbling, the nation plunged into four years of weary, dirty warfare. In its earlier stages, it was not intended as a war to free the Negro. As Frederick Douglass put it in Boston in 1865, the Civil War was begun "in the interests of slavery on both sides. The South was fighting to take slavery out of the Union, and the North fighting to keep it in the Union; the South fighting to get it beyond the limits of the United States constitution, and the North fighting for the old guarantees;—both despising the Negro, both insulting the Negro."[42]

As the war progressed, it gradually became clear that the North could not win unless the slaves were freed. When the planters went off to fight, they left their plantations and their families in charge of their slaves. It was on the continuing loyalty and submission of the slaves that the South relied in its struggle against the powerful North. As long as the plantations were worked and the crops were harvested, the South had strength. But let the slave once go free, and the backbone of Southern resistance would be broken. At the same time, the North was having difficulty in whipping up an army strong enough to defeat the stubbornly battling South. It became

[42] *Ibid.,* p. 61.

clear that unless some great moral push could be put behind the effort to subjugate the South, the result of the war was in doubt. Emancipation, accordingly, had a triple objective: to afford this moral issue for prosecuting the conflict, to increase the ranks of the Northern armies with black recruits, and to break the backbone of Southern resistance by taking the slaves off the plantations. Long before emancipation, however, the black man had begun to decide for himself that the issue lay in his hands. Slowly at first, and then in increasing numbers, the slaves entered into a general strike, laying down their hoes and joining the nearest Union forces. This withdrawal of black labor from the side of the South and the presence of black fighters in the depleted ranks of the Northern forces are two of the underlying facts helping to explain the collapse of the South. Also of great significance was the increasing disaffection of the lower-class whites in the Confederate armies. It was called "a rich man's war and a poor man's fight," and the poorer white recruits wearied of the dreary business. In accelerating tempo, desertion sapped the strength of the Confederate forces, just as Negro revolt followed by emancipation stopped the pulse of the plantation economy. Principally over two bridges, the North marched victorious—disaffection in the Confederate ranks, and lack of labor on the plantations. And at the same time, the Union forces felt the stimulus of fresh black recruits, troops which the South had preferred not to use. The South preferred to surrender to the North rather than to the Negroes.[43]

Thus it came about, through historical accident, that the black man, for generations the unwitting and unwilling instrument of exploitation of both himself and the white workers of the South, found himself thrust into the vortex of the conflict which was to result unexpectedly in his freedom. The inevitable effect was the intensifying of racial lines of antagonism beyond anything previously known. In the new society the old controls were no longer operative. Before the war the master had known what to do and what to expect; the

[43] *Ibid.*, p. 121.

slave had known "his place." With the new freedom came tremendous social upheaval. No one knew what the next day might not bring. No one felt secure. The wealth of the planter class had been swept away by the crushing blow of the war and emancipation. The lot of the white worker was no better than before the war. But into this shifting scene of instability, where the white aristocrat was struggling without solid footing and the white worker was left stranded without employment and without means of support, stepped the black freedman, bewildered by the sudden change in affairs, un-equipped for the new and uneven struggle that was to be his —but free, and therefore a potential equal of other free men.

How, then, was this freedman to be controlled? asked the white. The white aristocrat, the former owner, resented the assumption of adulthood and independence by his erstwhile "children." The white worker still smarted under the sting of devastating competition. Some means of preserving status must be found. The poorer white particularly needed some-thing to bolster his weakened sense of self-importance, for now there was nothing to distinguish him from the colored poor man. Both shared the bed of poverty, while the shackles of slavery no longer confined the black man. The caste preju-dice, which this changed situation intensified, was directed not so much against the Negro as a person, but primarily it be-came an expression of "dislike for him in a certain relation. The prejudice expressed itself as an intolerant insistence upon the customary caste relationship."[44] Poorer and richer white alike insisted that the etiquette of slavery should hold in spite of the nominal freedom of the Negro. Some means of preserving status must be assured.

The history of the Reconstruction period is the story of the fashioning of new controls to replace those destroyed by war; but the aftermath of war is not a time when moderation and common sense ride easily in the saddle. Good will and native decency did not have a free opportunity to fashion race attitudes in the United States as Negroes emerged from

[44] Reuter, *op. cit.*, p. 149.

bondage. It is futile to discuss what might have been if some other method of ending slavery had been discovered, even though the example of other situations, like that of Jamaica, points to a possibly different outcome if events had followed a different course in the United States. The tragedy of the "Tragic Era" lies in the fact that through its years the emerging Negro was shackled with new chains, chains which were fashioned out of the attitudes carried over from ante-bellum days, attitudes which had been heated to white heat in the fires of fratricidal warfare, and from which new social chains were beaten out on the anvils of sectional pride by the twin hammers of fear and fury. The hope of benefit from the years of struggle was indefinitely deferred. For a brief moment, the Negro enjoyed a measure of freedom; but as the army of occupation, and the Freedmen's Bureau, withdrew their coercive presence, the ante-bellum South reasserted itself. What else could have been expected?

The Reconstruction chaos was immeasurably aggravated by the wave of graft and corruption, unbelievably far-reaching and vicious, which swamped every department of American public life in the middle third of the nineteenth century and did not miss the South.

The basic fact is that the entire South was poor, desperately poor. The emancipated slave was poor; he had been freed, but given no means of livelihood or support. He was free to starve. He was without clothes, without a home, without employment, without land, without cash. He might beg or steal and fend for himself and his family as best he could, much after the fashion of refugees from a war zone. The white workers were equally poor, except for two minor factors: with emancipation some found it possible to appropriate pieces of former plantations, as squatters; and, secondly, emancipation had removed the direct threat of competition of the owner-backed slave artisan. The planter class, the merchants and professional men, the entire aristocracy of pre-war times, came out of the conflict with their resources decimated and their incomes cut off.

In this setting of poverty, as nearly universal as one could have under modern conditions, must come the effort to set up a new state, and it is clear to the unprejudiced observer that no matter who had conducted that state, if there had been no Negro or other alien elements in the land, if there had been no universal suffrage, there would have been bitter dissatisfaction, widespread injustice, and vast transfer of wealth involving stealing and corruption.[45]

In such an atmosphere of bitterness, hatred, contempt, and distrust were the new social controls to be fashioned. Here were formed the race attitudes with which the South entered the new century. What chance did tolerance have?

Political disfranchisement, legal and extra-legal segregation and Jim Crowism, inequality in educational facilities— the whole pattern of social life which was hammered out of the chaos of post-war confusion—can be understood in terms of the desperate effort of white men of all classes to maintain some degree of security and status by achieving a sense of permanent differentiation from the emancipated black man. The old patterns of aristocratic paternalism and of envious mistrust and contempt were merged into a new potpourri of racial attitudes centering around the problem of "keeping the Negro in his place."

The changes in economic processes had their influence upon the emerging racial attitudes. The freedman, no longer backed by a master who wanted profit from his labors, and thoroughly schooled in the attitude of dependence, turned to philanthropically inclined persons for employment and apprenticement. Gradually, with the backing of social pressure, the white artisan replaced the colored artisan. For a time, the white employers continued to hire workers of both races to labor side by side; but this only rubbed salt in the wound. Steadily the pressure to eliminate the Negro from apprenticeship opportunities and ultimately from the crafts made itself felt. The freedman who had previously depended upon his master to protect him and support him in competition with the white worker, "now looked to his new master, the em-

[45] DuBois, *op. cit.*, p. 599.

ployer, when the pressure of white labor's competition pushed him back."[46]

Not infrequently Negroes were used as strikebreakers, which served to increase the bitterness with which Caucasian labor attacked them. For decades, the labor unions debated the issue of whether Negroes should be included or excluded. "Include them that they may not break our strikes!" demanded one wing of the labor movement. "Take them in and swamp ourselves with the great wave of black labor?" shouted their opponents. Some maintained that if the Negro were not included in the labor movement he would become a threat to the very existence of white labor; but the long-standing antipathies, developed in slave days and irritated by the war and Reconstruction, prevailed over the nascent class interest which might have united white and black workers. The Negro was excluded. The trade unions which did not admit Negroes were adamant in their stand, and by their action forced the more liberal unions and the National Labor Union to conform, lest the whole movement be split on the rock of "racial equality."[47] In the long run, this meant that the Negro was pushed out of the skilled crafts into the un-skilled class of unorganized labor. The union refused to permit Negro apprentices. Such employment as the Negro did get was made possible by the hangover from slave times which permitted white labor and white employers, for a time, to sanction the hiring of Negroes on a definitely lower wage scale. The defense for the wage differential was given in the sophistry that the Negro was, by nature, best fitted for the rough and menial tasks, heavy or agricultural work—he was not "amenable to the 'laws of political economy.' "[48]

Thus the majority of Negro workers was shunted away from industry and the crafts, away from the labor movement, and into agriculture and domestic service. And the sense of distance between the white and black workers was empha-

[46] Spero and Harris, op. cit., p. 15.

[47] Ibid., pp. 31-47.

[48] A. A. Taylor, The Negro in Reconstruction Virginia, Ch. V, p. 85, cited by Spero and Harris, op. cit., p. 33.

sized and deepened by the psychological patterns built up as this process of economic differentiation proceeded, first in the white heat of Reconstruction and then through the weary years of the post-bellum doldrums.

Whether the contemporary (1930s) development in apparent coöperation between white and colored workers in the coal mines and the cotton belt will mean a new departure it is too soon to say. In previous times of depression and difficulty, white workers have been known to open their ranks to black men; but "only when the very life of the union is in danger is there a likelihood that Negro membership will be solicited. Thus in times of strike the Negro is often welcomed, and then he may be thrown out as soon as the strike is over."[49] If the white unions persist in excluding the Negro, the latter cannot be blamed too much for using the only weapon left to him in the struggle for admission to the unions.

The Negro reserve has proved the reënforcement that has weakened the morale of the strikers and made it difficult or impossible for them to win their objectives. Of several conspicuous instances of this result which have attracted nation-wide attention, the use of Negroes in the steel strike of 1919 is perhaps best known. If the Negro has to depend upon a strike to gain employment, he cannot be blamed for feeling somewhat like the undertaker who is suddenly saddened at the decline of deaths.[50]

Place alongside this continuing hostility of black and white labor the continuing racial feeling of the dominant whites. The former masters could not readily accustom themselves to the freedom of their former slaves. A man who had previously been forced to respond without question to his master's bidding might now walk about and ignore the wishes of his former master. If he failed to respond, he was "insolent." If he worked unwillingly, he was "lazy." If he resolved to face his lot with a song on his lips, he was "happy-go-lucky." It was too much to expect that the master class could quickly accustom themselves to the complete shift of affairs—and

[49] Herman Feldman, *Racial Factors in American Industry*, p. 29.
[50] *Ibid.*, p. 32.

they were afraid. They were afraid of the rising tide of black political power. They were afraid that the black and white workers together might overwhelm the aristocracy and the middle classes.[51] In desperation, the aristocracy and the middle classes made common cause with the white workers and raised a new oligarchy on the tottering foundations of the old aristocracy. Out of this experience emerged the "Solid South"—a solid phalanx of whites, drawn together in common opposition to the upsurging blacks. Thus, by one stroke, the dominant upper- and middle-class whites defeated both the "radical" aspirations of the agrarian movement and the democratic hopes of the freedmen. A single feat served

[51] The testimony given before the special Congressional Committee appointed to investigate the alleged political activities of the Ku Klux Klan (1872) is replete with illuminating comment which is the more convincing because it is apparently quite naïve in its identification of economic influences in the shaping of racial attitudes. Thus, for example, one William H. Forney of Jacksonville, Alabama, testified: "I will state you another reason why I think it [the Klan] originated. Immediately after the surrender, and when the Freedmen's Bureau was established through our country, it was right difficult for some men to realize the fact that their slaves did not belong to them. A colored man would work for them, but when the Negro would say something they did not like, probably the white man would slap him as usual. The Negro would report that to the officer of the Bureau, and he would immediately have the man seized, carry him up there, and the matter would undergo an investigation; probably they would send for him some fifteen or twenty miles. Now the class of Negroes that did that were generally very bad, lazy, indolent ones. I am inclined to think that a good many persons thought they would band together and be a kind of patrol for that class. I think that was about the original cause of the patrol, where the Bureau-men would invariably, or nearly invariably, believe the colored man, when you probably never could tell the real truth or how the thing originated. . . . I think this thing was started pretty much to frighten that class of Negroes" in "The Ku Klux Conspiracy," *Report* of the Joint Select Committee on the Condition of Affairs in the Late Insurrectionary States, VIII (Ala., Vol. I), 477.
General Samuel W. Crawford, Colonel 2d regiment infantry and Brevet Major General U. S. Army, stationed in Alabama, testified: "I do not think that the planter has any antagonism to the Negro at all; I think he wants his labor. I think it is a class of white men, not possessed of wealth or real estate, that exists in Alabama, many of them in the mountains, that is hostile to the Negro. Those people see him on the rich lands and possessed of political privileges, which increases the old jealousy, and they know that if they can get rid of the Negro, have him colonized for instance, it will be better for both of them on the point of association and the division of political rights. I believe that the planter has no antagonism whatever to the Negro; he wants his labor." *Ibid.*, IX (Ala., Vol. II), 1175.

both ends: it kept the Negro in "his place" and prevented (for the time) the white worker and small farmer from wresting political control from the conservatives.

One of the most interesting phases of the story, which is yet to be traced in historical detail, is the part played by the newly emergent middle classes of both white and black groups. For those who know the recent history of the South, or who are conversant with incidents of tension and stress in Northern urban centers where the Negro population greatly increased during the migration of the 1920s, no extended documentation will be necessary to suggest the outlines of the development. There is a field for study here, however, which may well engage the efforts of competent investigators. When this story is pieced together, it will probably show how the emerging middle class of Negroes find themselves at the vortex of the difficulty, struggling for new status in a society which, by inertia and by deliberate effort of some of its component parts, jealously attempts to prevent shifts in status. The terrific outbursts of community opposition when a moderately well-to-do Negro professional man erects a decent home on a good home site—a story which can be documented with scores of instances of mob violence and near lynching as a result of such steps; the white opposition to the successful Negro merchant; the insistence that salaries for Negro teachers shall be lower than salaries for whites performing the same services; these examples suggest the wealth of material which is available to make this story. It is not yet clear whether the resentment against this emerging Negro middle class is greater among the poorer whites or among the newly emerging white middle classes.

For purposes of conciseness and clarity, let the argument be summarized and restated at this point:

1. Economic competition causes sharp rivalry between the poorer whites and Negroes—a rivalry beginning in slave times and continuing to the present.

2. The general poverty of the South following the Civil

War keeps great sections of the population, both whites and Negroes, below the subsistence level, serving to aggravate racial antipathies, emphasizing the disadvantages of both groups by their mutual jealousy of any slight advancement of the other group.

3. The old adjustment between master and slave is perpetuated in the post-bellum paternalism of the white upper- and middle-class members, with the etiquette of slave times being used as an outward expression of the acceptance of differentiated status.

4. The high visibility of Negroes prevents an easy solution of racial antagonism by the disappearance of the exploited group (as various European groups have escaped from the cellar of economic opportunity by being assimilated in the general body of the population).

5. This same high visibility serves to increase the ready acceptance of the prejudices which are born of the conflict.

6. These considerations point to the conclusion that, given two groups which are fairly discreet *as groups*, and which are brought together in sharp competitive struggle for the fruits of the economic process, antipathy will develop; and the sharper the conflict, the stronger the resultant antipathy. The tendency for race attitudes to correspond to economic relationships suggests a basic functional nexus between the nature of economic processes on the one hand and the configuration of race attitudes on the other.

A ROUGH INDEX OF SENSITIVITY OF RELATIONSHIP BETWEEN ECONOMIC PROCESSES AND RACE ATTITUDES

The foregoing theory of historical relationship is given empirical reference in an analysis of the degree of correspondence between two indices. The historical analysis has suggested how the pattern of economic processes strongly influences the pattern of race attitudes. This second study suggests how fluctuations in economic conditions within the process have their counterpart in corresponding fluctuations in the intensity of race attitudes.

Changes in the purchasing power of the per acre income of the cotton producer are used as a rough index of the annual fluctuations in economic conditions in the cotton belt. Fluctuations in the number of lynchings of Negroes by whites in the cotton states are used as an overt index of race tension. The supporting data of the study are given in Appendix A.

The study shows that, in the main, when the purchasing power of the per acre income of the cotton producer goes down, there is a tendency for lynchings to increase either immediately or in the ensuing twelve months; and when the per acre income of the cotton grower rises in purchasing power, there tends to be a decrease in the number of lynchings. The long-term trend toward higher cotton prices and fewer lynchings is not used as a basis for the study, because this would give a specious indication of a type of interrelationship which is denied by the experience of 1926 to 1932, when both trends moved downward (see Figure 8, page 394). Many forces are at work to influence the course of the trend in lynchings; but the study reported in Appendix A shows that in spite of all other factors, there is a striking tendency for variations in lynchings to follow the annual deviations in the per acre income of the cotton grower, particularly as these deviations are translated into changes in the purchasing power of the growers' income. When the economic situation grows more desperate, the despair finds expression along lines of deeply grooved social antagonisms. There appears to be a functional nexus between the two sets of phenomena, and it is therefore fair to conclude that there is in this fact some degree of corroboration of the hypothesis that economic conditions and race attitudes are interrelated, at least in the American South.

This fact may puzzle some persons who were under the impression that lynchings are usually connected with crimes committed by Negroes; but as Appendix A points out, there is no necessary connection between Negro crime and white lynchings of Negroes. It is necessary to distinguish between the *causes* of lynchings, which are imbedded deep in the social process; the *occasions* for lynchings, which may be real or may be invented, since they have their principal expression in psychological attitudes; and the *excuses* given for lynchings, which sometimes have a connection with the occasions, but are rarely connected with the causes. As Raper has pointed out, Negroes are lynched in the American South not because Negroes have done something for which they must be lynched or otherwise punished, but because whites have a mind-set to lynch Negroes—just as witches were hanged in old Salem not because there were witches but because the Salemites had a mind-set to hang witches. And the basic cause of this anti-Negro animus is economic competition with a competitor who has "high visibility," just as the principal occasion (not excuse) for expressing that Negrophobia in lynchings comes in economic duress with attendant increase in tension.

Let it be emphasized that we are not implying that the economic process is the only factor influencing race attitudes; but we are driven to the conclusion that, in the general social process, race attitudes tend to conform quite faithfully to patterns of economic competition.

Lessening of race tension may be looked for, then, as the general level of economic and cultural life for whites and Negroes alike is raised. From the standpoint of better race relations, or even from the more limited point of view of the advancement of the Negro, it appears that raising the standard of living of lower-class whites is fundamental to any improvement in circumstances for the Negro. Since economic competition is the most important of the social factors causing race antipathies; and since race attitudes of paternalism also root in economic patterns; and since overt expressions of race tension come with fluctuations in economic conditions; we are justified in inferring that any comprehensive attempt to improve the condition of the Negro must include a realistic treatment of (*a*) the fact of economic exploitation of the Negro working classes by the white middle and upper classes; (*b*) the fact of economic pressure which frequently thrusts great numbers of whites and Negroes below the

poverty line; and (c) the fact of economic competition between Negro and white working classes, a competition which
is made desperate by the low wage level and rendered chron-
ically bitter by fluctuations in the economic process.

While it is not the task of the college to attempt to dictate
the patterns of economic life, it is the task of the segregated
college to make clear the causes of the major difficulties confronting the Negro. This is one more step in the progress
away from the superstition that all evil comes from devils
and toward the understanding of social forces.

III

PREJUDICE AT WORK

Attitudes toward Negroes are now chiefly determined not by contact with Negroes, but by contact with the prevalent attitude toward Negroes. —E. L. HOROWITZ

WE HAVE seen that race attitudes are fundamentally social in character, and that they are related particularly, though not exclusively, to the economic patterns in the social matrix.

We next turn to the closer examination of the ways in which the social pattern expresses itself in the lives of the various types of individuals who develop in it and help to shape it, as they are shaped by it. In Chapter IV we shall discuss more fully the sociological epiphenomena which accompany race prejudice, helping to perpetuate the phenomenon which is the soil out of which they grow. For the moment, we concern ourselves principally with the psychological aspects of race prejudice as they appear in individuals working through social processes, or social processes working through individuals, as the individual and the culture interact. And as in Chapter II, the writer makes no claim to originality. On the contrary, the strength of his case rests on the fact that he is merely restating in summary form what appears to be supported by the consensus of contemporary research.

Katz and Allport[1] report a study of student attitudes which reveals that racial prejudice is not so much a private attitude as it is an institutionalized or public response, fashioned for the purpose of maintaining status. Psychologically, this maintenance of status is a highly important matter to the individual. Just as the body is "anchored in space," so the ego is fixed in definite relationships to surrounding cultural components, such as a profession, a political party, a racial group, and the like.

This anchoring is our *status*. How can we characterize the ego formation which takes place in every individual more clearly than by saying that it consists of reaching a *status* in such and such respects? The stability of our status in these many respects forms the identity of our

[1] D. Katz and F. H. Allport, *Student Attitudes.*

persons. When this stability is obscured we are confused; when it is damaged we are deeply hurt; when the ties that bind us to a definite status are cut we toss in a strange and hostile sea with uncertainty and distress.[2]

The peculiar tenacity with which race attitudes persist from generation to generation, and the difficulty experienced in throwing them off or supplanting them with other attitudes, rests back upon the unsettling character of social change as it demands individual adaptations. Some psychological patterns change with less pain than others, depending not only upon the fixity of the idea in the mind of the individual, but also upon his relatively stable anchorage or equilibrium in his "social ground." It is not so much a matter of the objective importance of a given pattern, as it is the derived importance of that pattern as it affects the individual's status, which makes a particular shift difficult or painful. Thus it is that some social norms are transmuted with relative ease, particularly those which change as a result of technological advance in the tools of civilization. But this relative mobility recedes to a point of seeming absolute fixity in the set of attitudes and stereotypes clustered around race relations. Any proposed disturbance in racial norms, or in conduct controlled by racial norms, is particularly and emphatically upsetting to the individuals concerned. One loses status; the ego is adrift in a sea of shifting relativity; the mental processes become confused and the emotional responses uncontrolled. This is due to the fact that contemporary American culture (especially, though not exclusively, in the South) has so emphasized racial status as a guarantee of individual status, that racial norms assume a primary position in the hierarchy of individual values; and to the fact that this primary emphasis upon racial status has led to a social experience in which deep emotional attitudes are attached to the social norm, and the mental processes are used to rationalize and to fortify the entrenched position.

Race is therefore made a symbol of cultural status, auto-

[2] M. Sherif, *The Psychology of Social Norms*, p. 197.

matically classifying individuals and readily serving as a
means of directing and controlling the individuals so classified. In this sense "race" becomes a primary factor in controlling the social process, shaping the culture.[3] Consciously
and unconsciously, social patterns are shaped in accordance
with the demands of race attitudes. Social devices evolve.
They are devices for perpetuating a psychological state of
race antagonism rather than of interracial affinity. Once
started, the process builds up, the devices themselves functioning to buttress the attitudes out of which they grow, and
the attitudes likewise supporting the devices which consolidate their security of status.

Chief among these social devices which function to perpetuate race antagonism, and which are perpetuated by race
antagonism, is the double fact of economic competition between the poorer whites and Negroes, and of economic exploitation of the poorer Negroes by the upper-class whites.
Discussed in historical perspective and in contemporary expression, in the preceding chapter, the economic processes
may be here passed over with the comment that they provide
the day-by-day tools for the continuous renewal of race
prejudice.

The tenacious strength of these attitudes which are
grounded in economic processes is intensified, however, by
the perpetuation of the legend of the old Southern plantation.
Based on a sincere sentimentalizing of history, the "great
legend" is as definite a part of the thinking processes of the
average white Southerner as timetables are in the life of the
New York commuter. The South looks back to its past with
"a pathological nostalgia. That past, of course, culminated
in the Civil War."[4] What Schrieke calls "the sentimental

[3] E. B. Reuter, *American Race Problem*, pp. 31-44.
[4] B. Schrieke, *Alien Americans*, p. 104. Cf. the whole of Chapter V for
a brilliant analysis of the way in which the great legend functions. A word
summary: "In one of the cities of the South I saw a beautiful big old tree
right in the middle of a street. Although it blocks modern traffic—many
accidents occur because of it—it cannot be removed because its task is
perpetually and eternally to remind Negroes of the hanging of some coloured rebels from its branches many years ago. It is an ever-warning mon-

stereotype of the great culture" is a mental fixation among Southerners. It is the great, inclusive stereotype which sums up all the other attitudes which separate the races in antagonism and unite the whites in sentimental loyalty. There is surely a, large basis of fact with which the tradition started; and if time has lent its aura to sanctify normal exaggeration and to intensify idealized romantics, it is only because everything that was fine and noble and high-minded in the South has been so thoroughly identified with the system which went down to defeat in the Civil War. It is more than a rationalization, more than a defense mechanism, more than a sighing for the return of the good old days; it is a mass illusion which holds unquestioned sway over the willing minds of the inhabitants of Dixie.

The grandeur and dignity of the century-old manorial mansion on a wooded hill near the river bank, its wide porch and great white Doric columns, spacious halls, and luxurious rooms, the distinction of its approach through stately avenues of live oaks draped in Spanish moss, the exquisite beauty of its landscaped gardens, the extent of its rice and cotton fields limited only by blue horizon walls; the profusion of the Old South's proverbial hospitality, the medieval splendour and unalloyed mirth of its recreational life, the knightly magnificence and feudal providence of the refined but imperious and proud southern gentleman with his cavalier pedigree and his sensitive code of honor, the fragile loveliness and ravishing charm of the southern belle in hoop skirts; the solid satisfaction and loyal allegiance of the carefree, devoted slaves, including the affectionate, superstitious old mammy and the cheerful, humorous but irresponsible butler with his vanity over the standing of his "quality folks." All these traits were elaborated and recited world without end to glorify the superior social order of the past—the embodiment of the Golden Age.[5]

Here is the great stereotype as it has laid hold upon the mind of the South. One has but to touch one part of it— any part—to call up the whole pattern. The mention of Negro education in the modern day to a white Southerner

---

ument to white supremacy. That tree seems to me to be a symbol of what the Negro problem and the obsession about white prestige are to the South: it roots in the past, it cannot be removed, and it blocks the way." (P. 133.)

[5] *Ibid.*, p. 107.

will hardly bring up the image of a young colored man from Birmingham whose father is a steel worker, and who wants to fit himself for graduate study of medicine—rather will it start a train of thinking which sooner or later will lead to the great legend. Some of the irritation sometimes encountered is probably caused by this rude jostling of idealized history by the crude present. At any rate, here is a stereotype of untold power which operates as a contemporary influence that must be reckoned with. It prevents clear thinking about contemporary issues. It calls into play a complex of emotional attachments and fixations which will make it one of the primary factors to be dealt with for decades, even generations to come.[6] Within the general framework of this all-inclusive legend, several other stereotypes are at work.

Perhaps the most potent of these several psychological tools for the buttressing of race prejudice is the sex myth. This myth is an integral part of the pattern of race relations, inextricably woven into the experience of the individuals and groups concerned.[7] It is the constant thread of emotional intensity woven into social patterns as individuals are shuttled about by cross-forces of the economic struggle. The myth takes several forms. One of these forms is the superstition that Negroes, and particularly men, are much stronger in sex urge than whites. This idea appears to have emerged in America beginning about 1830, when the cotton gin was making slavery economically advantageous. It has been used from time to time to justify extraordinary methods, like lynching, to terrify the Negro, until the South is today the victim of its own terrorism, terrorized by the myth of its own conjuring. When a lynching takes place, it is not infrequently assumed by the general public that a sex outrage is back of it, despite the fact that actual statistics of reported lynchings

[6] It is interesting that a novel like Margaret Mitchell's *Gone With the Wind*, which involves the re-creation of actualities back of the great legend, should have been attacked by many Southerners as being unfair to the ante-bellum planter. Even this highly romanticized novel is too realistic, too gross, to fit the sentimentalized and idealized picture which tradition has conjured up and imagination has embroidered.

[7] Cf. W. D. Weatherford and C. S. Johnson, *Race Relations*, Ch. III.

show that less than 30 percent of all lynched persons have even been accused of a remote connection with a sex act of any sort—whether rape, attempted rape, "insulting a woman," slapping a little girl, or any other attitude which might be given the interpretation of having some relationship to sex; and less than 20 percent have been accused of rape.[8]

But the sex myth persists. It is used to give emotional potency to the notion of social equality. It is this insistence that there shall be no social equality which explains the persistence of a complicated and devious etiquette of contemporary race relations. Consider the curious refusal of white America to use the terms of address, "Mr.," "Mrs.," and "Miss" in addressing persons of color. In college circles, the terms of "Professor" and "Doctor" rank higher than "Mister," but whites regularly use the former terms in preference to the latter in addressing Negroes in academic circles. Academic jargon has not been freighted with the particular emotional content given to the forms of polite address which the old planter aristocracy reserved to itself and which, with emancipation, became the property of the entire white population. In themselves, the three simple words of salutation have little significance; but as symbols of cultural status, implying the acceptance of racial superiority of the Caucasian, they carry the whole complex of emotional meanings surrounding the racial conflict as based in economic conflict and as heightened by the sex myth.

The whole set of subsidiary social practices which have grown up around this central idea makes an interesting pattern. The Negro in the store is addressed as "Customer," the white as "Mister." The white patron is served while the colored patron waits "his" turn. Business firms with large mailing lists sometimes use the abbreviation "col" after the customer's name in sending out the bill, to prevent typists from making the mistake of using the tabooed terms of address. This fact has been responsible for a great volume of mail-order business, since it appears to make no difference

[8] See Appendix A for discussion of causes and excuses of lynching.

to the mail-order house whether the customer's money comes from white or colored patrons. The resultant thrust of competition has, in some instances, caused local firms to drop the "col" from the envelope; but in very few cases is the polite address prefixed to the colored customer's name. Comical, even ludicrous to the visitor from Mars, this matter of social etiquette is a serious business to the white citizen who has grown up in the milieu of racial antipathy and racial discrimination.

An important indication of a possible shift in racial etiquette is seen in the fact that many white newspapers, Northern and Southern, are abandoning the small "n" and capitalizing "Negro." The use of the lower case rests back simply upon customary practice; but the proposal to change to a capital "N" is sometimes met with editorial opposition. In view of the sensitiveness of Negro intellectuals on the point, it is encouraging to see some of the more influential white newspapers using the same courtesy of treatment for Negroes as they accord Caucasians or Englishmen.

The press has not, however, shifted its news policy to give a fair picture of the Negro to white readers. Bryant's study of twenty-eight newspapers, sixteen urban and twelve rural, in Texas, attempts to show the comparative amount of space devoted to social, antisocial, and neutral news stories about Negroes in the white press. Antisocial news included all news that pertained to criminal offenses. The term "social" was applied to those items concerned with the activities of individuals, organizations, and institutions relating to such constructive subjects as education, arts, business, or sports. The term "neutral" was applied to those items that could be placed in neither of these categories, such as records of births, human-interest stories, and news of a general nature. Using this classification, Bryant found that antisocial news comprised 81.6 percent of all Negro items appearing in the urban papers, against 11.8 percent in the social category and 6.6 percent neutral. The rural press emphasized the antisocial news by giving 59.8 percent of its space for Negro news to this type of story, relating social items in 24.5 percent of its stories about Negroes, with 15.7 percent neutral.

It would not be amiss to conclude in the light of these figures that the constant playing up of these types of news by the urban and rural press may cause such beliefs to be formed concerning the Negro's traits of character as: that Negroes are morally weak; that they have a natural disposition to sexual crimes and crimes of violence; that they are naturally addicted to petty thefts and emotionality. . . . Much space was given to items that might substantiate the beliefs among Southern white people [and others] that Negroes are superstitious, simple, ignorant, childish, clown-like, sincere believers in the power of the rabbit's foot, voodoo and fortune tellers of the most absurd type, . . .

making these racial, rather than individual, characteristics in the stories.[9]

A parallel study of the reporting of racial news in a Northern city brings results which confirm this same point. The Chicago Race Commission made a two-year study of the reporting of news concerning Negroes in the white Chicago daily papers, examining 534 articles classified under twenty-two headings. The items were classified also as to whether they presented Negroes in a favorable or unfavorable light, and whether these items appeared on a front page or in another section of the paper. "Most of the published information concerning the Negro and issues involving him magnifies his crimes and mistakes beyond all reasonable proportion," the Commission concludes, naïvely adding the explanation, "Ordinarily when misleading emphasis, misinterpretation, and distortions of fact occur, they are due to ignorance concerning Negroes which is fairly general among white persons, rather than to any inclination to injure a disadvantaged group."[10] It is not necessary to impute knavery to newspapers and reporters of news—they are merely reacting in accordance with accepted stereotypes, but in thus acting they are perpetuating and buttressing the stereotypes which direct them.

But the day-by-day pressure of vocational segregation and

[9] Ora B. Bryant, Jr., "News Items about Negroes in White Urban and Rural Newspapers," *Journal of Negro Education*, IV (April, 1935), 169-78.
[10] Chicago Commission on Race Relations, *The Negro in Chicago*, p. 172.

economic differentiation, fortified by the sex myth, expressed in social etiquette and supported in the news, is not always sufficient to achieve the end envisaged by the worse members of the dominant group or to give adequate release to the emotional interests which cluster around this important social action pattern. Accordingly, pressure groups are organized, most notable of which has been the Ku Klux Klan. The testimony taken by the Congressional Committee of 1870-71 which studied the growth and activity of the original Ku Klux Klan[11] is replete with testimony which demonstrates the economic origin of the organization, testimony which is all the more effective in proving the point because it is naïvely given. Repeatedly the witnesses asserted that the purpose of the first Ku Klux Klan was not to oppose the Federal Government or to make political capital of waning white strength, but merely to "frighten" the recalcitrant freedman into working with docility. "The planter merely wants his labor," said the witnesses.

The methods used by pressure groups vary. Whether (like the Klan) organizations of some standing, or (like a hastily gathered lynch mob) hysterical agglomerations of individuals brought together for the purpose and then disbanded, the methods of these temporary and long-term pressure groups range from boycott and blackmail through threat and intimidation to violence and murder. The white man's fear is the principal cause of overt activities by these pressure groups. One always tends to fear another whom he has wronged. Add to this the hatred for a class which is threatening to assume a new economic or cultural status. This fear-hate complex probably lies at the base of most crimes committed against Negroes by whites. It is relatively unimportant what the particular offense, actual or alleged, may be. The racial antagonism is latent, ready to respond to an "incident," expressing itself in overt activity. The occasion which sets off the

[11] "The Ku Klux Conspiracy," *Report* of the Joint Select Committee on the Condition of Affairs in the Late Insurrectionary States. (See above, page 45.)

activity is relatively unimportant, a matter of accident as far as the expression of the attitude of race prejudice is concerned. It is possible to find race prejudice unaccompanied by hostility; but the presence of pressure groups ready to react whenever a moment of instability or insecurity arrives, means that the existence of race prejudice is a constant threat of open hostility.

Nor is it necessary to wait for an "incident" to precipitate a crisis.

Formerly an instrument of popular justice in frontier communities, and still retaining something of its frontier character, lynching and the threat of lynching are now primarily a technique of enforcing racial exploitation—economic, cultural, political. . . . The whole spotted fabric of lynching has one thread running through it: the Negro must be kept in his place. . . . Rural whites may point out that it is about time for another lynching when they think the Negro no longer fears one.[12]

The upshot of this whole matter, from the standpoint of the analysis we are here making, is that the stereotype is a means toward its own credence and perpetuation. We have seen that the individual develops as a part of an evolving society which molds him and which he helps to mold.[13] We have seen that the basic economic pattern of activity, together with the attendant epiphenomena of the social process, interact through the group contacts of individuals who thereby build up attitudes which play a crucial part in determining actions of men and groups. Racial prejudice is a composite attitudinal pattern made up of emotional responses to a race name, a belief in typical characteristics associated with a race name, an evaluation of such typical traits, and the acceptance of a set of stereotypes which symbolize this complex attitude.[14] The accepted stereotype tends to become the censor

---

[12] Arthur Raper, *The Mob Still Rides,* pp. 22-23.

[13] "It seems that attitudes toward Negroes are now chiefly determined not by contact with Negroes, but by contact with the prevalent attitude toward Negroes." E. L. Horowitz, "The Development of Attitude toward the Negro," *Archives of Psychology,* No. 194 (January, 1936), p. 35. (Previously quoted.)

[14] Cf. Daniel Katz and Kenneth Brady, "Racial Prejudice and Racial Stereotypes," *Journal of Abnormal Psychology,* XXX (July, 1935), 191-92.

of all other mind-sets, the monitor of all ideology both individual and collective. The weight of public opinion tends to censure all behavior which varies from the accepted pattern, exerting coercive force upon the innovator.[15] The prejudice or stereotype thus becomes the arbiter of its own expression, master of its fate and of the fate of those who live under it, tyrant over the individual and collective life of the persons whose credence gave it existence. The tyrannical character of this old man of the sea has been experimentally demonstrated by Rice.[16] Fixed impressions, which may or may not conform to facts, do exist in racial concepts. They actively vitiate the judgment of persons who hold them.

The effect of race prejudice on individuals who hold it is to limit their powers of discrimination. It blinds a man to differences where these would otherwise be easily seen. Persons are treated according to a stereotype and not as separate and distinct individuals. This is a sort of mental laziness due to emotional attitude, which, being directed toward a class, is manifested toward the varying members of a class as if it did not vary.[17]

These stereotypes need not be logical or rational or consistent with each other. In fact, they characteristically contradict one another; but since the rules of logic do not operate in the realm of prejudice, this contradictory character of stereotypes does not mean that they cancel one another. It only means that they stock an arsenal of race controversy, enabling the prejudiced individual to meet any situation without thinking about it. "All Negroes are lazy," says a stereotype, but another popular expression, "working like a nigger," enjoys an equally wide vogue and enjoys it with the same individuals. "Negroes are irresponsible, undependable, irregular," says the stereotype; but there is no recognition of similar habits among non-Negroes who enjoy the dubious benefits of identical occupational experience and exhibit identical charac-

---

[15] Cf. L. L. Bernard, "Attitudes and Redirection of Behaviour," in *Social Attitudes*, pp. 53-54.

[16] S. A. Rice, "Stereotypes: A Source of Error in Judging Character," *Journal of Personality Research*, V (1926-27), 267 ff.

[17] E. Faris, "Natural History of Race Prejudice," in *Ebony and Topaz*, p. 94.

teristics. For example, the cultivation of cotton throughout the South has stamped much the same pattern of life upon white and colored tenants and sharecroppers alike. The two periods of activity—planting and chopping in the spring and early summer and picking in the fall—with the warm summer of idleness and the bleak, barren winter of shifting about on low rations, provide experiences perfectly calculated to produce individuals who can be characterized as "shiftless," "irregular," "lacking in forethought," "undependable." In the case of the Southern sharecroppers, whatever epithets of malediction can be appropriately attached to the members of either racial group apply with equal force to those of the same occupation in the other racial group. Hundley[18] describes the so-called poor whites as

the laziest two-legged animals that walk erect on the face of the earth. Even their motions are slow, and their speech is a sickening drawl . . . while their thoughts and ideas seem likewise to creep along at a snail's pace. All they seem to care for is to live from hand to mouth; to get drunk . . . to attend gander pullings; to vote at elections; to eat and sleep; to lounge in the sunshine of a bright summer's day, and to bask in the warmth of a roaring wood fire, when summer days are over.

The annals of race controversy do not contain many passages dealing more severely than this with the Negro.

It is this same species of generalization from individual cases which are not biological but environmental in nature which has resulted in constructing the stereotype which brands Negroes with these characteristics and calls it a racial matter. Its accuracy as a description of all whites of the lower economic strata is precisely as great as the accuracy of imputing these characteristics to Negroes who share the same set of experiences—and no greater. Character traits of this sort are to be understood not as biologically inherited racial traits but as the product of experiences of people—any people—under given sociological circumstances.[19] The method of making a

---

[18] D. R. Hundley, *Social Relations in Our Southern States*, pp. 263-64.

[19] "The lack of ownership in house or farm encourages shiftlessness as well as mobility. Possessing by law no right in his tenancy and no claim for improvements made, the cotton renter has acquired a shiftless attitude toward

living through cotton culture under the tenant system; the prevalence of a deficient diet; the wide incidence of pellagra and of hookworm; the striking similarity in culture patterns such as language and pronunciation, religious expression, "polite" habits, and the like, without reference to race—all these point to the general conclusion that certain experiences tend to nurture particular characteristics in a given geographical area which is dominated by a cotton-culture pattern. If the experiences had been limited to one ethnic group, the rest of the world might possibly have concluded with apparent justification that the particular culture patterns were racial; but when two racially diverse stocks, subjected to the same set of experiences, produce the same characteristics, it is astounding to find intelligent persons rationalizing the appearance of these characteristics in one of the two groups by claiming that they have merely learned to live like the other—to be specific, that "poor whites are jes' copyin' the niggers." If two allegedly different biological stocks under the same culture pattern tend to produce group characteristics which are strikingly similar, there is strong presumptive evidence that the characteristics are not racial in the sense of a biological inheritance, but cultural in the sense of the sociological milieu. Klineberg,[20] in his brilliant and definitive study of the influence of changing environment upon alleged racial characteristics has shown that habit patterns assumed to be foreign to the racial stock emerge in that race as the individuals are transplanted to a new culture pattern. Laziness is transmuted into determination and intense application when new environmental factors call out new response patterns. The uncritical and uncriticized currency which racial stereotypes enjoy is both a source of wide error in understanding racial groups and individuals and also the further cause of the undesirable attitudes of racial antagonism out of which the caricatures grow.

the place in which he lives. . . . With nothing to lose and all to gain the tenant may adopt a policy verging on exploitation and expropriation." R. B. Vance, *Human Geography of the South,* pp. 202-3.

[20] Otto Klineberg, *Negro Intelligence and Selective Migration.* See also *Race Differences* by the same author, esp. pp. 341 ff.

Nevertheless, the art of building acceptable stereotypes is assiduously cultivated. One of the most effective tools for constructing a stereotype is humor. It need not be overtly vicious; it can be pleasantly condescending in its race implications. But men do not readily take seriously a thing (or a race) at which they have learned to smile. The Negro is represented as droll, laconical, light-witted. "It's like the colored preacher who . . ." Quick to seize whatever small advantage is offered him, the Negro knows that if he is to express any clear insight, especially if it be a matter of criticism, or if it be concerned with philosophical pursuits and the like, he must couch his statement in a humorous and figurative manner. The white man will laugh—and accept the criticism or the idea. The Negro, adapting himself to the stereotype, occupies a position like that of the king's jester in the Middle Ages. By presuming to criticize or to think high thoughts, he is not stepping out of "his place" because he puts the matter in a humorous vein which cancels the implication of equality. In this case, the acceptance of the stereotype not merely as a control for the thinking of the white caste, but as a mode of expression used by the colored caste in self-defense, gives the notion a special degree of plausibility.

It may be said that there are discernible rules for the construction of acceptable racial stereotypes, pragmatic rules which can be deduced from observation of the stereotype at work. (1) The acceptable stereotype must always imply the superiority of the white caste. The more subtly this can be done, the more acceptable it will be for the upper classes; the stereotype tickles their vanity. The white lower classes demand a broader sort of formula, but with the same implication. (2) The effective stereotype must be vague and general, leaving much to the imagination. The more vaguely and generally suggestive it is of racial differences and of inferiority of the Negro, the better, because no reservations are implied. (3) The potent stereotype includes the possible appeal to fear as well as to superiority, combining the qualities of both (1) and (2) and seasoning with a bold dash of uneasiness. This type of race notion will be most effective if it applies to private lives, and particularly if it is connected with sex. (4) Elements of common experience should be included, but the gate must be left open for the wildest flights of imagination. A stereotype about the Negro's religious life may begin with the "accepted" notion that among Negroes emotion and feeling play a strong part (as, indeed, in the typical religious expression of untutored persons, white and black, in the South where the Negro learned his Christianity). It may then heighten this notion by harking back to the jungle ancestory (while forgetting the Druid worship of the British Isles in an earlier century which is equally pertinent to the present religion of Americans of Anglo-Saxon ancestry.) Out of the combination of religious emotionalism and voodooism emerges the stereotype of Negro religion. Being dependent not upon the laws of logic but upon the laws of psychology, the stereotype is one of the most efficient tools which race prejudice can command.

Equipped by experience with this conflicting and contradictory set of irrational rationalizations, the white child grows up in a world where the whole weight of social usage is calculated to produce in him a sense of distance from the Negro. Just what emotional content and intensity will be given to that sense of distance, may vary widely. He may hate, or he may have a genuine affection; he may have contempt, or he may feel benevolently helpful; he may be bitterly antagonistic, or he may even be a champion of fair and decent treatment for Negroes—but always and everywhere the pressure of social usage is forcing him to remember that there is a line between the two races, and that each race must keep its "place." This separation of the races also places its stamp upon the Negro child who grows up under it. It is intended by the dominant group that he shall find his place and stay in it. The effectiveness with which this pattern of social separation functions to determine both the actual and potential patterns of individual life is indicated in Chapter IV.

But as we turn to a closer examination of the pattern of

racial arrangements in the American South, let us keep our perspective by reminding ourselves that discussions not unlike the two foregoing chapters could be made for markedly similar attitudes of Gentiles toward Jews in the North and in Europe, toward Japanese on the West Coast, Indians and Mexicans in the Rocky Mountain areas and the Southwest, and toward French Canadians and Polish in certain parts of New England. While this book is concerned with one particular set of social arrangements between two racial groups in the South, we do well to remember that there are other situations not unlike the one we are here studying.

IV

THE CASTE SYSTEM

The Caste of Kin is the practise of the theory that blood is thicker than water; and the Sermon on the Mount can not invalidate God's own law of the Survival of the Fittest. —THOMAS P. BAILEY

IN THE preceding chapters, we traced the devious pattern of psychological development in our American race-divided society, seeing that the basic configuration tends to follow the lines of conflict in economic interests; that fluctuations in economic conditions tend to be accompanied by fluctuations in the intensity of race antagonisms; that in this process race becomes a symbol of cultural status as well as a symbol of struggle for status; that the struggle to maintain status is attended by the use of peculiarly effective socio-psychological devices which gain currency in the form of stereotypes; and that these stereotypes are used to support rationalizations rather than being themselves rationally examined for validity. We are now interested in carrying through an examination of the social system which is built up in accordance with these race attitudes.

CLASS AND CASTE IN AMERICAN SOCIETY

American society, not solely in the South, but particularly there, exhibits a culture pattern which combines the phenomena of class and caste. The class into which an individual is thrust is largely determined by his economic status, although "family" and other factors such as education and profession may have subsidiary parts to play in determining his class. The caste in which one is kept is determined by his external racial characteristics, and it is presumed that an individual cannot leave the caste into which he is born. Within either racial caste are found various classes, and movement up and down the social ladder of class within either caste is expected; but it is not expected that there will be any movement across caste lines in either direction. Caste is determined by birth; it may not change. Class is determined by "family" and by economic circumstance; it may change.[1]

This dual relationship of caste and class is suggested in Figure 2, which is to be taken as suggestive of relationship rather than as quantitatively accurate. The United States census reports do not recognize classes, so that it is not possible readily to define with nice precision the exact line of demarcation between the classes within each caste, and an

[1] After these chapters had been completed in their present form, there came into my hands an able socio-psychological study of *Caste and Class in a Southern Town* by John Dollard which is the most intensive study of its kind I have seen. Its principal value lies in the fact that it is based on a detailed, specific study of a single small town and its surrounding county.

But its strength is also its weakness. What it gains in specificity it loses in representativeness. While the picture Dollard gives is probably quite accurate for the town he selected (due allowance being made for the serious handicap he suffered in taking his stance in the town as a member of the white caste), at least three considerations detract from its value by making the study atypical: (1) the state chosen is one of the two or three lowest in per capita wealth, rather than being median for the South; (2) the town selected is a Black Belt town in which Negroes outnumber whites in a county which is 70 percent Negro, whereas a typical Southern town and county would show a much smaller proportion of Negroes than this; (3) the town itself is made up largely of middle-class whites and lower-class Negroes and the consequent absence of upper-class Negroes and upper-class whites, with a relatively small proportion of lower-class whites and middle-class Negroes, gives the picture of caste and class in this particular town an atypical skewness. Doob's appended chapter on the lower-class whites recognizes Dollard's deficiency, but does not correct it; because the total pattern of Southerntown is the pattern which Dollard gives and that pattern does not include the poorer whites and the better Negroes.

A single example will suggest the variety of points at which these limitations enter in. In the chapter on "Religion," Dollard was unable to point out that the religious pattern he describes is a class pattern, not a racial matter. His study did not include lower-class whites, whose religious expression is strongly similar to that of lower-class Negroes. Bourke-White and Caldwell in *You Have Seen Their Faces*, present photographic evidence of the similarity of culture pattern which marks the poverty-ridden and illiterate of both races. But Dollard's research site did not include representatives of all classes in both races, so that his findings are inevitably fragmentary and partial.

But when due allowance has been made for the foregoing, and when it is remembered that Dollard's research is that of a psychoanalyst with a strong Freudian bias, the general picture of caste and class structure which he finds in a field research is strikingly similar to that which I found in the study of mass data and historical processes. This mutual corroboration of basic data by independent studies, undertaken from quite different angles and with quite different methods, is striking evidence of the probable reliability of the general picture of caste and class in the American South.

arbitrary division of the diagram roughly suggests the class divisions as outlined. As pictorial devices for aiding the analysis of psychological patterns which accompany class and caste lines, Figures 2 to 4 should be useful. The principal population groups in the fifteen Southern states in 1860 are shown in the following tabulation of the United States census reports:

TABLE 1

POPULATION GROUPS OF FIFTEEN SOUTHERN STATES, SHOWING NUMBER AND PERCENT OF TOTAL POPULATION OF WHITES, SLAVES, AND FREE NEGROES AS REPORTED BY THE UNITED STATES CENSUS BUREAU, 1860

| STATE | WHITE | NEGRO | |
		Slave	Free
(1)	(2)	(3)	(4)
Delaware	90,589	1,798	19,829
Maryland	515,918	87,189	83,942
District of Columbia	60,763	3,185	11,131
Virginia	1,047,299	490,865	58,042
North Carolina	629,942	331,059	30,463
South Carolina	291,300	402,406	9,914
Georgia	591,550	462,198	3,500
Florida	77,746	61,745	932
Kentucky	919,484	225,483	10,684
Tennessee	826,722	275,719	7,300
Alabama	526,271	435,080	2,690
Mississippi	353,899	436,631	773
Arkansas	324,143	111,115	144
Louisiana	357,456	331,726	18,647
Texas	420,891	182,566	355
Totals	7,033,973	3,838,765	258,346
Percentage	63.1	34.5	2.4

The caste line in ante-bellum days in the South (line A, B, C, Figure 2) conformed to a sharp division between the whites and Negroes, while the socio-economic classes within each caste tended to shade off into one another, except that the line was sharply drawn between lower-class whites on the one hand and upper- and middle-class whites on the other. At the top of the social strata were the landed aristocracy,

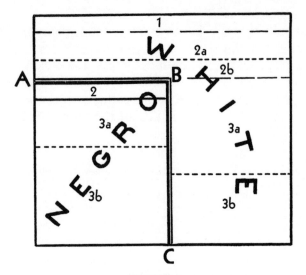

FIGURE 2

CASTE AND CLASS IN THE ANTE-BELLUM SOUTH (*ca.* 1860)

The two working-class groups (white 3a and 3b and Negro 3a and 3b) are divided by the caste line (B-C), while the supraordinate white upper classes (1 and 2a and 2b) rest securely upon this caste-divided working class.

Free Negroes are a buffer between the caste of slaves and the caste of free whites, in that the hope of individual manumission is often a substitute for general movement toward emancipation for all slaves.

Economic status on both sides of the caste line in a horizontal direction is more or less similar.

Legend: A, B, C = Caste line.

Negro caste (4,097,111) = 36.9 percent	White caste (7,033,973) = 63.1 percent
	1 —Upper class: planters; members of "old families"; bankers and financiers
2 —Free Negroes (258,346) = 2.4 percent	2a—Upper middle class: manufacturers and merchants; professional people
	2b—Lower middle class: small tradesmen; clerical workers
3a—House slaves and mulattoes	3a—Upper working class: plantation overseers; skilled workmen; owner-operator farmers; semi-skilled workmen
3b—Artisans and field hands	3b—Lower working class: unskilled workmen; tenant farmers; unemployed

the planters, the people with "family." This upper class enjoyed a position of relative security. The middle-class whites,
who were the small merchants, independent farmers of some
means, and the professional groups, were psychologically
identified with the upper class into which they hoped to climb.
They were the upper classes "on the make."[2]

Below these two classes of whites were the two great divisions of the working classes—lower-class whites and Negroes.
Sharply separated by the caste line, these two lower-class
groups enjoyed much the same economic level. But within
the Negro caste, a stratification also took place.[3] There was
a small group of free Negroes, many of whom were farmers
and small tradesmen, some of whom were themselves slave-
holders. These free Negroes, numbering over two hundred
and fifty-eight thousand in the Southern states, where they
made up 2.4 per cent of the total population, were almost a
caste by themselves. The position of the free Negro in
Figure 2 is symbolic of the double significance of these free
persons of color as the upper stratum of the Negro caste
and as a kind of buffer between the whole slave group and

[2] Frequently this great group of the middle class in ante-bellum society in
the South is completely overlooked, on the tacit assumption that there were
only three groups of persons—planters, slaves, and poor whites. Nothing could
be wider of the mark. At least three-fourths of the white population had no
proprietary interest in the Negro in ante-bellum times, according to H. W.
Odum, *American Epoch*, p. 54. Odum's chapter on "Middle Folk and Common
Man" discusses at some length the fact and nature of the ante-bellum white
middle classes. And B. Schrieke, *Alien Americans*, p. 119, has this to say
about the same classes: "The self-respecting plain countrymen, the back-bone
of the ante-bellum society, a great class of sober-living, thrifty, independent,
and, as a rule, strongly religious proprietors, who cultivated their lands themselves, or, if they owned a few slaves, worked the land together with their
Negroes. In their crude way of living they preserved many of the traits of
pioneer days. Compared with New Englanders they were fully a hundred
years behind the times in education and in all kinds of improvements. Most of
this class were self-sufficient farmers and grew but little cotton; others occupied themselves with cattle raising; others with the turpentine industry. In the
Mississippi delta this class was to be found largely as overseers, as patrolmen,
or as wood-cutters who supplied the steamboats with fuel. But, in the mountains, in some parts of the pine barrens, and on the borders north and west
they comprised nearly the entire population. Everywhere else they dwelt as
neighbours of the planters and well-to-do townsmen."
[3] E. B. Reuter, "The Changing Status of the Mulatto," in *Ebony and Topaz*,
pp. 107-10.

the upper strata of the whites. That the presence of the free
Negro did not soften the relationships between the white and
Negro lower classes is also indicated in the configuration.
The importance of this group of free Negroes should not be
overlooked. They comprised about 10 percent of the total
Negro population in 1860, and more than 6 percent of the
Negro population in the Southern states of that time were
free men of color. Legally free, their social status was fixed
principally by ritual observance. As long as the free Negro
in the South observed the etiquette of caste, there was relatively little conflict; but the legislation of the several states
indicates that the threat to the caste system which the presence of the free Negro brought was a matter of serious
concern to the white group—particularly in the states where
other crops (like tobacco in Virginia) loomed larger in the
total economy of the area than cotton. Thus, in 1860 Maryland had 83,942 free Negroes and 87,189 slaves. Virginia
had 58,042 free Negroes and 490,865 slaves, while Mississippi had 773 free Negroes against 436,631 slaves; Alabama had 2,690 free Negroes against 435,080 slaves, and
Georgia boasted only 3,500 free Negroes as compared with
462,198 slaves. As far back as 1827, Louisiana had found
it necessary to legislate in the effort to fix the status of the
free Negro through compulsory observance of proper etiquette: "Free people of color ought never to presume to
conceive themselves equal to the white; but, on the contrary,
they ought to yield to them in every occasion, and never
speak or answer to them, except with respect."[4]

Throughout the slave states, it is fair to say that the free
Negro occupied a precarious and anomalous social position.
Free, he did not "belong" with the slaves; yet, Negro, he
did not "belong" with the whites. Under pressure of the
white group, the free Negro gradually accommodated himself to the demands of the caste line. If he wished to live
in anything approaching peaceableness and equanimity, he

[4] Bertram W. Doyle, "The Etiquette of Race Relations," *Journal of Negro Education*, V (April, 1936), 203.

learned to conform to the code. And he also found that he
attained a position of leadership among Negroes and of influence among whites in proportion as he reverted to the etiquette of caste despite his freedom.[5] The patterns for
acceptable Negro leadership which were formulated under
this set of conditions have not readily been supplanted by
other patterns in more recent times, and the ante-bellum
stratification of the Negro caste as between slave and free
has left a definite impression upon the configuration of class
within the Negro caste right down to the present.

A second stratification was also present in the Negro caste
—thrust into the Negro group by the attitudes and practices
of white masters who tended to separate the house servant
from the field hand, and to distinguish between the mulatto
and the Negro of unmixed blood. While these divisions were
by no means watertight, there was a strong tendency for the
house slave to occupy a position distinctly superior to that
occupied by the field hand. Undoubtedly many mulattoes
found their way into the fields, and many Negroes of unmixed African descent were used in positions of confidence
and trust and as personal body servants; but there was a
marked tendency for the Negro caste to stratify along the
lines indicated in Figure 2.

The caste-and-class stratification of 1860 represented a
relatively stable configuration. The status of each individual
was clearly and definitely defined. He might with relative
ease move up and down between the economic classes in the
white caste, or he might with difficulty move from class to
class within the Negro caste; but caste was the unquestioned
pattern of life. Even for the free Negro, accommodation to
the dominant pattern proved to be the more satisfactory adjustment if he wished to avoid conflict. The caste line was
principally a simple, vertical division of the working classes
on racial lines, with no caste line bifurcating the middle and
upper classes. The two working-class groups might threaten
each other, and indulge in bitter competition; but the con-

[5] *Ibid.*

trols were in the hands of the middle and upper classes of whites who could use this situation to solidify their own status. Relatively speaking, the social order of 1860 was in a static state.

The psychological attitudes accompanying this social stratification were the familiar and expected patterns. With the reservation that many permutations and combinations of attitude are possible and probable within this general framework, we can suggest the general nature of the dominant sets of attitudes. We can see what they tended to be in the main, generally, and in the long run, during ante-bellum days. The following tabulation is therefore merely a schematic representation of the implications growing out of the discussions of Chapters II and III.

A. Characteristic interclass attitudes in the ante-bellum period. (Compare Figure 2.)

   1. The white upper-class attitude toward
     —white middle class: affable patronage not unmixed with conscious superiority and condescension;
     —white lower class: indifference, sometimes softened by paternalism, but usually merging into contempt or hardening into exploitative treatment;
     —free Negro: little contact or knowledge, but active uneasiness in many cases, with open tolerance in others, since no threat to status is implied in the small numbers of free Negroes, and the legality of manumission does not threaten the slave system; but insistence upon the observance of the etiquette of caste;
     —house slave and mulattoes: benevolent paternalism of the master-slave relationship, with insistence on reciprocal attitudes of acceptance in childlike conformity;
     —field hand and balance of slaves: owner-chattel relationship, the owner taking decent care of his investment and expecting good returns in labor.

   2. The white middle-class attitude toward
     —white upper class: conscious emulation not unaccompanied by envy and active jealousy, and occasional fawning;
     —white lower class: pecuniary interest in purchaser or laborer, but little interest in welfare of individuals involved, and resultant indifference to general fate of lower class;

—free Negro: little contact, but vague uneasiness in the fact that the free Negro occupied a class position somewhat similar to many middle-class whites; and resultant insistence on etiquette of caste;

—house slave and mulatto: appropriation of attitudes of white upper class (paternalism), with undercurrent of panicky insistence on rigid maintenance of caste and "social distance";

—balance of Negro caste: indifference or contempt.

3. The white lower-class attitude toward

—the white upper class: secret bitterness and public obsequiousness;

—the white middle class: active emulation and wishful rivalry, merging into resentment or antagonism;

—free Negro: antipathy rooted in jealousy;

—house slave and mulatto: jealousy, fear, antipathy, rooted in relative insecurity of poor white and increased by competition in most branches of work;

—field hand and balance of slaves: active antipathy, based partly on subconscious identification of slave with owner, with resultant "taking it out" on slave, partly on frank jealousy of relative security of slave whose owner "takes care of him," and partly on economic competition of slave and poor white.

4. The free Negroes' attitude toward

—house slave and mulatto: conscious superiority;

—the rest of the slaves: superiority sometimes softened by fellow-feeling;

—white upper class: secret emulation;

—white middle class: active emulation;

—white lower class: superiority complex.

5. The house slaves' and mulattoes' attitude toward

—free Negro: active emulation, sometimes seasoned with compensatory resentment;

—the rest of the slaves: complacent superiority, sometimes relieved by altruism;

—white upper class: observance of the etiquette through childlike acceptance of paternalism of owner, sometimes developing into childish dominance of household, but seldom leading to revolt;

—white middle class: aloofness and avoidance;

—white lower class: open contempt toward "po' white trash."

6. The field hands' attitude toward

—free Negro: secret envy and emulation, occasionally leading to a slave's buying his own freedom;

—house slave and mulatto: petty jealousy and rivalry;

—white upper class: acceptance of slave status, obedience with occasional revolt;

—white middle class: observance of etiquette, avoidance of conflict, resultant acquiescence;

—white lower class: resentment, antipathy, antagonism, open contempt, "bad blood."

During the twenty years which began with the outbreak of the Civil War, the basic configuration of caste and class underwent significant change. It had been "a rich man's war but a poor man's fight," according to the popular cry; and the poor white was determined to demand his rights. But the Negro also was pushing upward, aided by the Yankee who sympathized with his desire for rise in status; and the upper- and middle-class whites were forced to choose whether to admit the demands of the Negro caste or to unite forces with the lower-class whites against the Negroes and the Yankees. As Reconstruction proceeded, the latter alternative won out, and under the united defense of all classes of the white caste, the line held inviolate.

Instead of breaking, the caste line pivoted under the impact of Yankee and Negro attack to a position where it threatened the dominance of the white caste (A-B, Figure 3). This challenge to white supremacy was tremendously unsettling to the entire white caste, since it threatened to remove the "ground" in which the whole life of the several individuals had been developed. Complicating the matter was the fact that several groups of Northerners, from the carpetbaggers to the school teachers, presented a new factor in the situation, somewhat analogous to the mountaineers of the 1830s. Ranking as outcasts from the white caste, they were socially grouped with the Negro caste in much the same manner as the free Negroes of ante-bellum days had been denied status in the caste of free men. Some of these Northerners were not in the South for unselfish purposes. Others were moved by the high altruism of moral fervor, and to them the Movement for the advancement of the Negro took on something

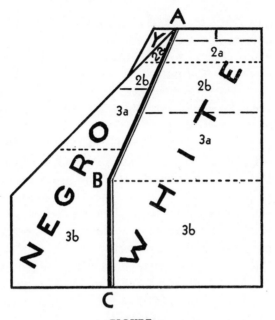

FIGURE 3

CASTE AND CLASS IN THE RECONSTRUCTION PERIOD IN
THE SOUTH (*ca.* 1870)

The effort to break the caste line *above* the Negro, rather than to break the caste barrier between the two working-class groups, brought a temporary retreat of white upper classes to yield parallel status without violating integrity of caste. There followed a resurgent counter-pressure to restore the dominance of the white caste. As compared with ante-bellum configuration, the pattern of reconstruction society was relatively unstable. Yankees living in the South were generally outcasts from the white caste, and often classified with Negroes.

LEGEND: A, B, C = Caste line; Y = Yankees living in the South.

Negro Caste (5,953,903) = 36 percent
Y —Yankees living in the South

2a—Upper middle class: preachers; political leaders; teachers; merchants
2b—Lower middle class: owner-farmers

3a—Upper working class: plantation overseers; skilled workmen; tenant farmers; semiskilled workmen
3b—Lower working class: unskilled workmen; unemployed

White Caste (10,555,427) = 64 percent
1 —Upper class: persons of "old families"; bankers and financiers; planters
2a—Upper middle class: professional people; merchants and manufacturers
2b—Lower middle class: small tradesmen; clerical workers; owner-farmers

3a—Upper working class: plantation overseers; skilled workmen; tenant farmers; semiskilled workmen
3b—Lower working class: unskilled workmen; unemployed

of the flavor and intensity of a Crusade. These several groups of Northerners, having joined hands with the Negroes in their common effort for the breakdown of the caste system, helped to confuse the issue because of the widely divergent motives with which they worked. In the main, the intergroup attitudes remained substantially what they had been before emancipation, particularly as far as the whites were concerned. There were great stirrings within the Negro caste, but the shackles of custom, tradition, and long conditioning in the observance of etiquette held the great masses of Negroes "in their place." It was a time of readjustment, of uncertainty, of emotional tension, when old attitudes were given new intensity and heightened significance although they retained their essential characteristics.[6] Fortified with new rationalizations, the old caste lines were transformed from dykes to breastworks—and when men have fought in defense of caste, they will not readily forget the race attitudes thus deeply ingrained in their personalities.

It did not take the white lower classes long to see that their hope lay in using the fears of the upper classes, to raise their status above that of the Negro, just as the upper classes had been using lower-class phobias to play them over against the Negro caste in ante-bellum days. Perhaps the ideas never were as clearly defined as this statement implies; but the

[6] The clear economic basis of race attitudes during this formative period was always recognized by the South and only grudgingly admitted by the North. Anxious to gloss over the conflict between the manufacturing North and the agrarian South, the North clung tenaciously to the notion that the issue was solely a moral one—that moral issue having been hammered out in the heat of the Civil War. But the South, attempting to disclaim any moral issue, tried to make clear the economic issue (which was, *ipso facto,* outside the pale of morality!). Thus, for example, a "prominent Mississippian" in the Chicago *Inter Ocean* for November 4, 1890, attempting to answer the charges of the North: "It is a question of political economy which the people of the North can not realize nor understand and which they have no right to discuss as they have no power to determine. If the Negro is permitted to engage in politics his usefulness as a laborer is at an end. He can no longer be controlled or utilized. The South has to deal with him as an industrial and economic factor and is forced to assert its control over him in sheer self defense." (Quoted in *The Disfranchisement of the Negro* by John Love, "Occasional Papers," No. 6, of the American Negro Academy, and published as a pamphlet by the Academy in Washington, D. C., 1899.)

intensity with which the lower classes identified themselves with the white middle and upper classes demonstrates that whether the idea was formulated or not, the attitude controlled.[7]

In Reconstruction days the class lines within the white caste tended to be less rigidly drawn, partly because economic fortune fluctuated so greatly that there was considerable interchange in personnel between the classes, and partly because the classes within the white caste were drawn together in common opposition to the threat of the Yankee and the Negro. The Negro caste had but two classes, middle and lower. An upper class of professional men and financiers had not yet emerged in numbers large enough to be statistically discernible, although many of the Negroes who had enjoyed the status of free men before the war started with initial advantages and constituted the nucleus of the Negro upper class which was gradually to emerge. Many more, in both the middle and lower classes, were embryonic members of the new upper stratum of Negro society which was to be fashioned in the structure then being raised. In general, then, the

---

[7] See Horace Mann Bond, *Education of the Negro in the American Social Order*, Ch. II, "Social Classes and the Beginning of Reconstruction." This is the way the matter looks to B. Schrieke (*Alien Americans*, pp. 122-23): "Emancipation seemed to put both farmers and mechanics in one class with the Negroes. Moreover, the freedmen were forced by economic necessity to try to invade occupations which had been reserved for lower-class whites. That was exactly why the latter had been opposed to emancipation and its consequence: equality. Even before the war, abolitionists had had to be careful in the presence of 'poor whites' lest they be molested by a mob; the lower-class whites hated the Negro and slavery, but feared emancipation more. In order to save their status, these whites (not yet class conscious and articulate and, until the agrarian movement of the eighties and nineties, not yet politically organized) now clung frantically to the resentful planters, lest they be degraded by the elevation of the blacks. The slogan of 'white supremacy' had especial appeal for the lower-class whites, whereas for the 'quality folks' it needed not to be claimed but could be taken for granted. The competition into which they were thrown, and their pent-up grudge against the Negro, embittered the poorer whites. So the struggle began to keep the Negro down. . . . The rise of craft unionism with its apprentice system helped to consolidate the white artisan's position. Industrial changes and the introduction of machinery made obsolete much of the Negro's skill and training. In agricultural pursuits, however, the competition between the Negro and the white man went on, and in the rural districts racial feeling remained the strongest."

pattern of attitudes in Reconstruction days looked something like this:

B. Characteristic interclass attitudes in Reconstruction days. (Compare Figure 3.)

   1. The white upper-class attitude toward
      —white middle and lower classes: substantially as before, except that insecurity of economic status melted the sharp divisions, and a new oligarchy began to rise on the ruins of the old;
      —Negro middle class: despairing and bewildered attempt to restore former subservience;
      —Negro lower class: resentment of new status of freedman, with tendency to vent pent-up emotions on Negroes, and with frequent attitude of fear;
      —Yankees living in the South: bitter contempt and resentment, with active opposition and use of terrorist tactics, ostracism being the mildest form of treatment.

   2. The white middle-class attitude toward
      —white upper class: a lessened sense of distance and an identification of interest in opposition to the Negro, the Yankee and the poor white;
      —white lower class: a sharpened cleavage on class lines, alternating in intensity with a feeling of kinship in the face of the threat to white supremacy;
      —Negro middle class: active opposition and rivalry, with constant attempt to break the morale of the Negro middle class, leading to use of terrorism with attendant hatred, bitterness, and antipathy;
      —Negro lower class: resentment of new and strange freedom, with determination to insist on restoration of much of slave status;
      —Yankees living in the South: ostracism, hostility, suspicion, and hatred.

   3. The white lower-class attitude toward
      —white upper and middle classes: democratic upsurge of rebellion, speedily replaced by acceptance of class differences because of common threat of rising Negro caste;
      —Negro middle class: antagonism based on jealousy carried over from ante-bellum days and intensified by new free status of Negro who was *ipso facto* higher in social scale than lower-class white unless caste line could be maintained inviolate;
      —Negro lower class: intensification of preceding patterns, a hearty

reciprocation of fear and antagonism leading to desperate espousal of terrorism;

—Yankees living in the South: exaggerated bitterness and hostility toward champions of Negroes who by their presence threatened complete loss of status by poor whites.

4. The Negro middle-class attitude toward
   —white upper class: active competition for status;
   —white middle class: active opposition and competition, both in economic realm and in special status;
   —white lower class: contempt, not unmixed with fear of reaction;
   —Negro lower class: variety of attitudes, most of which merely duplicated the corresponding range of attitudes within the white caste;
   —Yankees living in the South: comradery, coupled with gratitude.

5. The Negro lower-class attitude toward
   —white upper class: conflicting habit patterns, carrying over much of the old slave psychology of acceptance and acquiescence, even loyalty and affection, but mingling with it a ferment of discontent and rebellion, a blind search for new independence without means of realizing objectives;
   —white middle class: substantially same as foregoing;
   —white lower class: mutually reciprocated antagonism and fear;
   —Negro middle class: carry-over of antagonisms of slave days, accentuated in some instances by new rivalries and bickerings, softened in other cases by new feeling of racial identity in face of common opposition to whites;
   —Yankees living in the South: gratitude mixed with bewilderment, sometimes leading to naïve overconfidence.

6. The attitude of Yankees living in the South toward
   —white upper and middle classes: aloofness and hostility;
   —white lower classes: contempt;
   —Negro middle class: comradery and fellow-feeling, coupled with attitude of crusader and champion of a cause;
   —Negro lower class: benevolent paternalism, relieved by occasional comradery.

Gathering strength and power in the 1870s, and continuing through the succeeding half century, the movement to restore white supremacy was ultimately triumphant. This period of adjustment was characterized by the retreat of the Yankee, and by unceasing efforts of the white South to restore the caste line to a position of stability approaching that of ante-bellum days. But in ante-bellum times, the working classes had been conveniently divided against themselves by the caste line, thus providing a singularly stable foundation for the middle and upper classes which could always make one group behave by threatening to use the other. In the 1890s there was a temporary flurry of the agrarian movement which threatened to continue the rift between the white lower classes and the white middle and upper classes. As this flurry passed, the lower-class whites succeeded in identifying their interests with the dominant group which needed their vote to put through the Black Codes. The Jim Crow pattern of social control emerged, the caste line being so manipulated as to restore the supremacy of the middle- and upper-class whites, but also giving the lower-class whites "social" status superior to all Negroes. Whereas in ante-bellum times, a white aristocracy and bourgeoisie had rested upon a caste-divided working class; now, a united white caste demanded social superiority of the entire caste over all Negroes. The Atlanta Exposition speech of Mr. Washington in 1895 accepted this caste demarcation in general, but as the price of acceptance it bargained for a different pattern in economic affairs. The bargain was eagerly accepted by a grateful South with a sigh of relief which the Atlanta Constitution amplified into a song of praise and joy. The adjustments of the next twenty years consolidated and institutionalized the Atlanta Compromise, resulting in a duality of caste patterns (Figure 4). In economic matters, there is the "oneness of the hand" as expressed in the economic integration of the Negro (although this apparent integration still recognizes the color line sharply, resulting in an integration of encystment rather than of assimilation). In all other matters, there is the "separateness of the fingers" which is interpreted by the white caste to mean the inferiority of the entire Negro caste.

Part of the emotional difficulty of the South today grows out of this contradictory situation of two different caste patterns operating simultaneously. When an individual occupies one relationship in economic matters and another in "social"

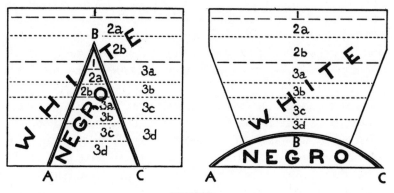

FIGURE 4

CASTE AND CLASS IN THE AMERICAN SOUTH OF THE 1930s
(1) ECONOMIC   (2) "SOCIAL"

Two caste patterns prevail, each governing etiquette and fixing status in its
sphere. In economic status (1), the Negro caste is integrated (as an encysted
group, not assimilated); but in all other respects (2) every Negro is judged
inferior to all whites in status.

LEGEND: A, B, C = Caste line.

Negro Caste (9,359,577) = 25 percent	White Caste (27,673,879) = 75 percent
1 —Upper class: financiers and bankers; intellectuals; persons of "family"	1 —Upper class: persons of "family"; bankers and financiers
2a—Upper middle class: professional people; merchants	2a—Upper middle class: professional people; merchants and manufacturers; intellectuals
2b—Lower middle class: small tradesmen; clerical workers	2b—Lower middle class: small tradesmen; clerical workers
3a—Upper working class: owner-farmers; plantation foremen; skilled workmen	3a—Upper working class: owner-farmers; plantation foremen; skilled workmen
3b—Semiskilled workmen	3b—Semiskilled workmen
3c—Lower working class: unskilled workmen; domestics; tenant farmers	3c—Lower working class: renter-farmers and tenants; unskilled workmen
3d—Unemployed; sharecroppers	3d—Unemployed; sharecroppers

matters, the etiquette of social observance becomes hopelessly complicated. For the white man who is sensitive about
the maintenance of the "proper" social distance (Figure 4
[2]), the closer and more nearly equalitarian relationship
of the economic status (1) is abhorrent. He tends to demand
that Negroes should all stay in the lowest economic brackets,
thereby simplifying the problem by making economic status
permanently identical with the old social status of slavery.
But for the Negro upper-class member, the situation is equally
abhorrent. He feels that his economic classification should be
reflected in his social status; and when he finds himself thrust
unceremoniously from the status of (1) to that of (2), he
feels that violence is being done to his personality. The
"social ground" in which he stands as a producer and consumer is suddenly taken from under him as a citizen, and he
is dropped to a status below that of the lowest white person,
with the trap door of caste clamped over his head, while the
white caste draws itself together to give its united weight to
the defense of the closed door.

This dual configuration is an interesting illustration of the
tenacity of a stereotype. The old social patterns which were
fashioned in ante-bellum days in accordance with the economic processes of that time became so thoroughly a part of
the group thinking of the white caste, that a shift in the economic pattern has not yet appreciably altered the social
pattern. The rigid enforcement of the caste line of separation
in both economic and "social" patterns makes possible the
modification of relative status in the economic sphere at the
same time that the inferiority of the old stereotype is maintained unmodified in all other relationships.

By the 1930s, the number of Northerners actively engaged
in furthering the cause of the Negro in the South had become so small as to be statistically negligible; the few Yankees remaining in the South are either merged in the Negro
upper class or absorbed by the white caste, in accordance with
the conformity of the individual Yankee to one or the other
group standard. The typical attitudes across class and caste

lines are tabulated below. One important modification needs to be borne in mind as this tabulation is read, namely, that the expression of a given attitude through contacts in the economic realm will tend not to be the same as the expression of that attitude in noneconomic "social" contacts. This is particularly true of race attitudes where Negroes in the upper- and upper-middle-class groups are involved. If it is an economic relationship (white seller, Negro customer, for example), the economic status of the Negro may be taken into account. But beyond this recognized economic realm, the old differences of caste inequality are enforced.

C. Characteristic interclass attitudes of the 1930s. (Compare Figure 4.) Interclass attitudes within each of the respective castes follow closely the same general patterns, with the upper class setting the pace, the middle class emulating, and the lower class envying. The picture is substantially the same in both castes.

    1. The white upper-class attitude toward
      —Negro upper class: puzzled appreciation, not unmixed with open tolerance as long as caste lines are rigorously adhered to;
      —Negro middle class: pleasant and paternalistic benevolence, which helps to preserve the self-respect of the white at the expense of that of the Negro;
      —Negro lower class: paternalism shading into indifference.

    2. The white middle-class attitude toward
      —Negro upper class: hostility and resentment of threat to status, sometimes softened into philosophical acceptance of status as long as sophistry of caste line preserves fiction of superiority;
      —Negro middle class: active opposition to Negro business and trade development which seems to undermine economic security of white middle class, resultant antagonism;
      —Negro lower class: indifference except to Negro as purchaser or laborer, merging into hostility, with latent oppression and terrorism.

    3. The white lower-class attitude toward
      —Negro upper class: undisguised antipathy and resentment, including unadmitted inferiority complex which must be vehemently denied in action;
      —Negro middle class: same as preceding, differing only in degree;
      —Negro lower class: day-to-day tolerance as long as caste line is rigidly observed, but latent terrorism lurking underneath calm exterior.

4. The Negro upper-class attitude toward
   —white upper class: extremely self-conscious race consciousness, with resentment over lack of social recognition of class status through superimposition of caste line;
   —white middle class: much the same as preceding;
   —white lower class: resentment that inferior class occupies superior caste position, with antagonism, contempt, fear, and acute race tension at all times.
5. The Negro middle-class attitude toward
   —white upper class: general adjustment to caste system and acquiescence in superior status of upper- and middle-class whites, with refusal to consider the plight of the lower-class white, and resultant effect that Negro middle class maintains position of dominance over Negro lower class by accepting caste division as its own limit;
   —white middle class: much the same as preceding, but confused by competitive conflict of two middle classes for business and income, though not for caste status;
   —white lower class: secret contempt, open indifference.
6. The Negro lower-class attitude toward
   —white upper and middle classes: the perpetuation of the slave psychology with its acceptance of inferior status, emulation of white aristocracy, and eager receipt of paternalism in exchange for observance of caste;
   —white lower class: antagonism, friction, resentment, an easy, day-to-day adjustment glossing over the deeper antipathies, and renewed competition for jobs stimulating latent race feeling.

Let it be repeated that these tabulations of attitude are not intended to be definitive or all-inclusive or infallible. It is readily granted that there are many exceptions to even these general attitudes, and that the permutations and combinations of attitudes are not limited to the mathematical possibilities of these tables. We are dealing here with the devious processes of human beings, and each individual tends to weave his own pattern of action. These individual variations sometimes amount, in the aggregate, to group exceptions to the generalizations which are here offered merely as a convenient means of suggestive analysis. One of the important sets of exceptions which should be noted here, and which will be discussed at an appropriate point later, has to do with the numerically small but potentially important group of individuals whose attitudes do not conform wholly to those of the class and caste to which they belong. Not a few of the present generation of white college students in the South, to cite but one example, will be molders of new patterns which will be at variance with the accepted race attitudes of their own social groups.

Let it also be pointed out that the variety of attitudinal patterns made probable by the cross-currents of caste and class sheds additional light on a phenomenon which is puzzling to many persons not intimately acquainted with the South. Many Southern whites can say with complete truthfulness that they feel no antipathy toward Negroes, that they know no antagonism or unfriendliness. But we have seen that antagonism is not a necessary concomitant of acceptance of caste; there may be other forms of prejudging (prejudice) than those which result from sharp conflict. Indeed, one of the most widely prevalent patterns of prejudice is this pattern of paternalism which expresses itself in kindliness and condescension. It is probable that this attitude is much more effective in perpetuating the caste system than are the more vigorous and explosive tactics of the direct actionists. It is no reflection upon the character or good intentions of a benevolently inclined white person to point out that his assumption of an attitude of benevolence results in cultivating a corresponding attitude of dependence on the part of the Negro. At best, this paternalistic "looking out for" particular Negroes is an enheartening relief in a difficult situation.

Individual white persons, particularly those who have a family tradition of former ownership of slaves, are quite likely to take a genuine and sincere interest in the welfare of certain Negroes. They are quite likely to extend to them a regard and affection which they would deny to many white people. Occasionally this may even carry over into formal and public action, such as burying a favorite servant in the family burial plot (white) in defiance of caste usage. Quite commonly, it means that the white person assumes a responsibility for the Negro at crucial moments of financial or legal trouble, or at times of sickness and the like. There is a carry-over of much that was good in the old master-slave relationship when paternalism is benevolent. But at its worst, this attitude can become a cloak for hypocrisy. The white person permits charity to take the place of justice; he "looks out for" the Negro who is faithful to him, but he wishes to be free from any involvement in the question of social justice for an oppressed race. Two baleful effects of this attitude of paternalism need to be put down to its debit: it tends to perpetuate the old plantation legend, by giving plausibility to the idea of the contented darky and the kindly master; and it inevitably saps the self-respect and undermines the independence of the Negro who is involved in it. Viewed from this angle, the benevolence of the well-intentioned white person who wants to "take care" of certain Negroes is on a par with the misdirected zeal of the social uplifter who is out to "do them good" rather than to work alongside Negroes for the solution of common problems. The attitudes and status of the members of the submerged group are in large part a reflex of the outlook and stance of members of the white group with whom they happen to associate. If in the white person's attitudes there is any recognition of difference in status, that is fairly certain to make its impress upon the Negroes concerned; and if the social stance taken by the white person suggests the posture of condescension, the caste system is being subtly and effectively maintained. This last is important; for stance is not so much a matter of where one stands, as how he stands. One can move from a former position of opposition to a new position of tolerance, but if the posture of superiority remains unchanged, the fact that the person stands on new ground does not alter the basic relationship. The important thing to note about the caste-class complex of psychological attitudes we are here examining is that, although many diverse, and sometimes contradictory, attitudes are included in the whole matrix, each of these attitudes does in some way recognize the caste line, and on the whole the attitudes of whites tend to insist on caste.

Despite the endless variations and nuances in attitude which socio-psychological measurement might uncover, it is believed that the main lines of psychological configuration corresponding to the socio-economic system of caste and class as that system was set forth in the data of Chapters II and III and more systematically described in this chapter, are substantially in accordance with the facts of experience. Let the interested reader retrace, step by step, the descriptions of Chapters II and III and the synthesis of this present discussion, and be for himself the judge of the extent to which the conclusions are warranted by the data.[8]

It appears, then, that prejudice is the reverse of the coin whose obverse is group loyalty. This fact permits it to pass current in respectable circles, and the image of virtue which is stamped on the face of the coin lets the attitude pass current for desirable social exchange even though its alloy of vices makes it ring false on the counter of justice. Loyalty to one's own kin and caste are exalted into virtue; and the corollary of antagonism to another caste is seen not as a vice but as the natural expression of the virtue. Race attitudes can therefore be defended with peculiar tenacity and complete self-righteousness. Stereotypes are built up and gain credence without regard to scientific verification or lack of verification, because they tend to bolster the caste division and to win continued acceptance for it. As these defense rationalizations grow, they fulfill a threefold purpose: (1) they become shorthand expressions of accepted social patterns; (2) they serve readily as rallying cries for the maintenance of caste, and of other components of the *status quo*; because (3) they obscure the real issues involved and appear to appeal to high motives and loyalties. There is an extensive literature which rationalizes the alleged racial differences which are the de-

[8] Readers sufficiently interested to make the comparison will find strong corroborative support for this analysis in Dollard's *Caste and Class in a Southern Town*. (See above, p. 72.)

fined boundaries of caste. Largely a product of the last two
centuries, this literature has, through the control of stereotypes, tended to fix the status and to control the relationships
of the two castes.[9] In particular, it has circumscribed the "social space" of the upper- and middle-class Negro, a fact
which has definite bearing upon the plight of the Negro college which is staffed and managed largely by persons of these
prescribed groups.

Judging the caste system by its operation, however, instead
of by its rationalization, certain pragmatic axioms of operation can be described. First, the white man's floor is the
Negro's ceiling. Wherever possible, the caste line is to keep
all Negroes below the level of the lowest whites. This is
the first, and deeper, meaning of "separate but equal." It puts
the emphasis on the separateness and insists that, if possible,
the separateness shall be obtained by keeping the Negro in the
basement of the social system. A trivial example may serve
to illustrate the point, an example which is all the more significant because its symbolic importance magnifies it out of
all proportion to its intrinsic triviality. It is not the policy to
issue a charter for a troop of Girl Scouts composed of Negroes unless there is already in existence in the same area a
Girl Scout troop composed of whites, with an area committee
(also of whites) to take charge. This not only avoids the
possibility of "Troop One" being a colored troop, an eventu-
ality which would be embarrassing at some later date if a
white troop should have to be "Troop Two," it also very
effectively limits the opportunities of the Negro girls to the
level already attained by white girls. As long as the white
girls have no troop, the Negroes may not have one. Here
is an instance where the white man's floor is not off the
ground, which means "ceiling zero" for the Negro.

The second, and more obvious, meaning of the "separate
but equal" notion is that wherever the Negro does win his
way upward, that progress must be interpreted as an improvement in condition but not in status—the caste line may

[9] See W. D. Weatherford and C. S. Johnson, *Race Relations,* Ch. III.

be dented but it must not be broken. To return to the simile of the white man's floor being the Negro's ceiling, we point out that when the Negro does break through to a new level, he finds that the whites have been busily erecting a new partition, so that he has let himself into a new and vaster prison house, more terrible in some respects than his former confinement, because he had hoped for larger freedom on the new level. Let a contemporary struggle for educational opportunities at the graduate level illustrate this point. In recent months, legal struggles have resulted in a court decision compelling the state of Maryland to admit Negroes to certain branches of its state-supported graduate schools because the segregated school system did not provide these graduate opportunities. Similar action is pending in several other states. It is interesting to note that, closely synchronized with the announcement of these legal rulings, several of the border states are taking a suddenly active interest in establishing "graduate schools" in connection with the segregated state institutions of higher learning. This is in addition to the long-term interest in education for Negroes at the graduate level which has been exhibited by many fair-minded persons throughout the South. It is the expression, conscious or implied, of the old insistence on the integrity of the caste line. It says, in effect, "If the Negro *must* have education which is equal to the white, it must be separate." This is the other meaning of "separate but equal."

A second pragmatic axiom of the caste system is the importance of etiquette in preserving the system. Observance of the etiquette implies acceptance of caste status. Failure to observe caste etiquette implies at least lack of sympathy with the racial division, and may imply refusal to conform to caste distinctions. This is what lies back of the refusal to use "Mr.," "Mrs.," and "Miss" as terms of address for Negroes;[10] and the contrary insistence that Negroes must use these terms in addressing all whites. This is what gives the

[10] Although these terms may be used in business proceedings on occasion, and omitted under other circumstances.

etiquette of eating such great importance. Whites who have been nursed, even suckled, by Negro nurses, in later life may refuse to sit at table with Negroes, not because they have any particular innate or instinctive aversion to the idea, but because the whole weight of social institutions and common opinion surrounds the idea with emotionally potent negatives. To break eating taboos is to defy caste. So, at all costs, etiquette must be observed. Personal knowledge of the writer supplies incidents in which grave bodily harm has been done to cultured persons of color who happened to say, "Yes," instead of "Yes, sir," to middle- and to lower-class whites. It is axiomatic that the etiquette must be observed as evidence of the acceptance of caste.

A third axiom of the caste system as it operates in America is that in making comparisons across race lines, no distinctions within either caste are to be permitted to operate disadvantageously to the white or advantageously to the Negro. Colloquially phrased, this notion is, "Any white man is better than every Negro." Thus, in Figure 4 (2), which suggests the contemporary social configuration, the caste line places *all* Negroes in a social position inferior to *all* whites, even though the economic class lines would operate to put all of the upper-class Negroes and some of the middle-class Negroes higher in economic status than most of the lower-class whites. In this sense, caste becomes the compensation mechanism whereby the poorer white achieves a status which his position in the economic scale denies him. It also operates as a psychological force of high potency in establishing and maintaining the Jim Crow system of providing public conveniences and public services. Since any white man is "better" than every Negro, it follows that no Negro should be permitted to go into railroad stations, cars, theaters, etc., on a par with any white person. To admit a Negro to the white coach would be to deny white superiority and to endanger white supremacy. Thus, in actual practice, the Negro who is cultured, refined, and in all ways (except ancestry) a desirable social companion, may not enter the church or the school or the theater with white persons of similar background and sensibilities; he may not purchase a railroad ticket except by going to the Jim Crow window and waiting until all white patrons have been served (which may be rather disconcerting if the train is pulling into the station); he must wait for "his" turn, keep in "his" place. As the caste system defines "his" turn, it is: after all whites; and as the caste system defines "his" place, it is: below all whites. From the standpoint of caste, and in the eyes of the legal and juridical system which expresses and perpetuates that caste, a moronic criminal with a white skin is superior to a Harvard Ph.D. of darker hue.

The situation is particularly embarrassing and irksome to white persons who, for one reason or another, wish to estimate individual Negroes on a basis of their own merit rather than as members of an arbitrarily defined lower caste. Many of the sons and daughters of the old slave masters resent the present caste insistence through which social pressure compels them to show an esteem and consideration for lower-class whites equal to that shown for "their" Negroes. Privately and informally, they may refuse to conform to caste demands in this respect, still treating certain Negroes with a consideration and genuine respect for the individual as a person which they would not readily admit in their attitudes toward certain whites; but formally and publicly, they will be forced to conform to the pressure of public opinion and to observe the dictum that any white man is better than every Negro. Another group of persons who are equally irked by the insistence of caste is a growing number of young men and women, mainly from the white colleges of the South, who have learned to distinguish between the well-bred Negro and the poorly bred colored person; and they would like to have their social conduct reflect their newer estimate of the New Negro. They feel the nonsense of the notion that the lowest criminally inclined white man is superior to the finest gentleman of color; and when the caste system demands that they conform, they do so with increasing restiveness. But the feeling of greatest frustration, of most poignant longing, of

deepest irritation over the arbitrariness of caste, is probably
reserved for the upper- and middle-class Negro. When a
white salesman wishes to sell a car, he may call an upper-class
Negro "Mister." But that same salesman might be the first
to object if his customer sat down next to him in a moving-
picture house. In economic relationships, the upper- and
middle-class Negro, while he is still rigidly hemmed in and
circumscribed, has forged ahead. Here is the spearhead of
the upward thrust of the submerged group. To a certain extent, a new status has been won by some Negroes in the economic realm (Figure 4 [1]). But "in things purely social"
the caste line is impregnable. (Figure 4 [2].) In social
status, the upper-class Negro lives under the shadow of the
slave system; and no rise in economic status has yet brought
the light to dispel that darkness.[11]

The anomalous position of the upper- and middle-class
Negro under the caste system is reflected in the maldistribution of professional services for Negroes. Since the caste system is somewhat more rigid and pronounced in the South than
it has yet become in the North, there is a marked tendency for
Negroes of the professional classes to gravitate northward
in an escape from the onus of caste. The 1930 census reports
show Illinois, with a total Negro population of 328,972, reporting 192 lawyers, judges, and justices; while the whole
tier of states constituting the Deep South (Florida, Georgia,
Alabama, Mississippi, Louisiana, Arkansas, and Texas) with
approximately half of the total Negro population of the nation (5,567,258) report only eighty lawyers, judges, and
justices for the entire area. New York and Illinois, with a
combined Negro population of 741,786, have 323 Negro
dentists; while the Deep South with its five million Negroes
has a grand total of 354 dentists. The contrast with reference
to physicians and surgeons is: Illinois and New York, 541;
the Deep South, 892 But in clergymen, the South carries
away the banner: Illinois and New York combined can muster
only 1,376; while the Deep South reports nearly eight times

[11] See Dollard, *op. cit.*, pp. 297-301.

that number—10,328. This last fact not only reflects the de-
cidedly inferior professional preparation of the typical clergyman[12] as compared with other professions, which accounts
in part for the tremendous disproportion of professional
religious services to the other three professions listed. It
raises a further question as to whether the type of activity
carried on by clergymen is more nearly compatible with life
under the caste system than the type of activity required of
other professions. Alabama, with its 1,653 Negro clergymen
in 1930, lists only four lawyers who cared to struggle against
the caste system in Alabama's courts. With the recent death
of one of these four, there are but three lawyers of color in
a state which has a Negro population of nearly one million
people. Are the hazards of law practice before Alabama's
courts and under Alabama usage such as to discourage Negroes from establishing themselves in that state? Or is it to
be assumed that the colored clientele is so adequately and
satisfactorily served by white lawyers that Negro competitors
are discouraged on that account? And is the Negro clergyman more free to practice his profession under the caste
system than is the Negro lawyer? If so, is this relatively
greater freedom due to the leniency of the caste system in
matters of religion, or to the lack of anything in religion as
it is preached and practiced which seriously challenges the
caste system?[13] Further light on these questions comes from
translating the data of Table 2 into the comparable units of
Table 3, which shows the comparative number of professional men of color in four primary professions in proportion to each 100,000 Negro population, comparing the
Deep South with the two Northern states. The number of
clergymen per 100,000 Negroes is almost identical in the two
areas—185.9 in the Deep South, 184.8 in the Northern

[12] Cf. W. A. Daniel, *The Education of Negro Ministers.*
[13] Trevor Bowen, *Divine White Right,* p. 152: "Many of the more active Negro
supporters of their racial cause contend that, behind the other worldliness and
conservatism on the race issue shown by many leaders in Negro churches, lies,
consciously or unconsciously, the desire to perpetuate present conditions, favorable to a continuation of their own leadership."

TABLE 2

DISTRIBUTION OF PROFESSIONAL SERVICES OF NEGROES SHOWING COMPARATIVE
AVAILABILITY OF SUCH SERVICES IN THE DEEP SOUTH AND IN TWO
NORTHERN STATES, AS REPORTED IN THE 1930 CENSUS TABULATIONS

STATE	NEGRO POPULATION	LAWYERS, JUSTICES, AND JUDGES	DENTISTS	PHYSICIANS AND SURGEONS	CLERGYMEN
(1)	(2)	(3)	(4)	(5)	(6)
Florida	431,828	10	45	96	1,488
Georgia	1,071,125	15	60	193	2,087
Alabama	944,834	4	45	116	1,653
Mississippi	1,009,718	6	29	71	1,408
Louisiana	776,326	8	45	107	1,295
Texas	854,964	21	100	207	2,308
Arkansas	478,463	16	30	102	889
Total, Deep South	5,567,258	80	354	892	10,328
Illinois	328,972	192	159	331	732
New York	412,814	120	164	210	644
Total, Two States	741,786	312	323	541	1,376

states, which would suggest that the proportion of clergymen
tends to be constant without reference to the caste system.
On the other hand, in the other three professions, the ratio
shows an inescapably significant disparity between North and
Deep South. Using the figures for the Deep South as basic
100 in each profession, the comparable indices for the several
professions in the two Northern states are: lawyers, justices,
and judges, 3,007; dentists, 596; physicians and surgeons,
394; and clergymen, 99.8. Herein is strong presumptive support for the hypothesis that the pressure of the caste system
pushes professional men northward where professional service is accompanied by professional status. Such fragmentary
evidence as is now available on incomes of professional men
does not indicate that differential in income is the primary,
or even a secondarily important factor, in determining the
place of residence of the Negro professional worker.[14] There

[14] Data are now in preparation by a national committee under the direction
of Ira DeA. Reid, which may throw some light on this aspect of the problem.

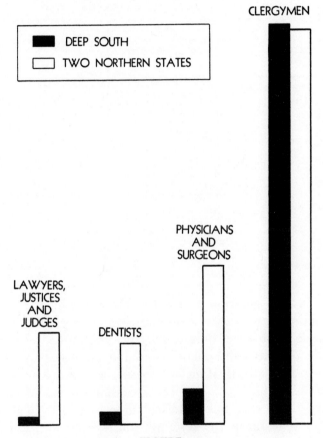

FIGURE 5

PER CAPITA DISTRIBUTION OF NEGRO PROFESSIONAL MEN

Showing the comparative number per 100,000 of Negro population in the Deep South and in two Northern states, as computed from tabulations of the 1930 census (see Table 3)

TABLE 3

Per Capita Distribution of Negro Professional Men, Showing Comparative Number of Such Men per 100,000 of Negro Population in the Deep South and in Two Northern States, as Computed from Tabulations of the 1930 Census

STATE	LAWYERS, JUSTICES, AND JUDGES	DENTISTS	PHYSICIANS AND SURGEONS	CLERGYMEN
(1)	(2)	(3)	(4)	(5)
Florida	2.3	10.3	21.0	342.2
Georgia	1.4	5.6	18.0	193.8
Alabama	0.4	4.5	11.6	165.7
Mississippi	0.5	2.9	10.6	138.4
Louisiana	1.0	5.8	13.7	165.8
Texas	2.5	11.7	21.4	270.0
Arkansas	3.4	6.3	21.4	186.7
Total, Deep South	1.4	6.3	16.0	185.9
Illinois	57.6	47.7	99.3	219.6
New York	28.9	39.5	50.6	155.2
Total, Two States	42.1	37.6	73.0	184.8

is also a nice question as to the extent to which this maldistribution of professional services is an instance of selective migration; but even though selective migration may be at work in this case, the operation of the caste system appears to work as a strong stimulant to this northward movement of the abler and better trained professional man. Moreover, the hypothesis that this maldistribution of professional services is a function of the caste system, does fit the data; and in any case, the conclusions rest back upon the evidence of mass data as given in the earlier part of this chapter, while this supplementary illustration of the skewness of the distribution of professional services merely corroborates the principal evidence.

The caste system is an established part of American life, with particularly clear legal and social definitions in the South.

V

PATHOLOGICAL RESULTS OF CASTE

And in hell he lift up his eyes . . . and he cried and said, Father Abraham, have mercy on me, and send Lazarus. . . . But Abraham said, . . . between us and you there is a great gulf fixed: so that they which would pass from hence to you cannot; neither can they pass to us, that would come from thence.   —JESUS

NOT THE least important aspect of the caste system is its results in seriously malconditioning the individuals whose psychological growth is strongly affected by a caste-divided society. These influences are not limited to the Negro caste. They stamp themselves upon the dominant caste as well. They strongly affect the general pattern of social life.

The conflicting welter of attitudes and opinions which the caste-class system nurtures inevitably brings unbalance in psychological processes, and personalities are warped. A divided society tends to drive its divisive and disintegrating forces into the vital inner processes of personality growth.[1] The baleful effects are not limited to either caste. It is a real question which personality is impoverished the more—that of the well-meaning paternalist or that of the object of such paternalism. It is likely that the victim of persecution is not more seriously warped in personality than are his persecutors. Hatred not only does something to the victims, it also

[1] For example, the element of fear which is more or less common to the entire white caste takes its toll of personality, according to E. B. Reuter, *The American Race Problem,* pp. 386-87: "In the American South there is a deep-seated and all-pervading fear of the Negro. One source of this fear is the treatment that the Negro has received at the hands of the whites. The slavery of the Negro, his economic and industrial exploitation, his moral degradation, and other historic facts of the Southern situation are fundamentally repugnant to civilized moral standards. The members of the dominant group are more or less conscious of the injustice that the Negro has suffered at their hands. There is in consequence an uneasy sense of moral guilt, as may be seen in the rationalized justifications of the historic treatment and of the existing situation as well as in the naïve apologies for behaviour not defensible on accepted moral standards. By a familiar psychological process sentiments and attitudes that the non-socially trained persons imagine that they would have had they been subjected to similar treatment are imputed to the Negro and the Negro thereby becomes possessed of behaviour tendencies menacing to the white man, to his domination of the social situation, and to the culture he represents. This fear complex . . . functions to create an external image which objectifies the psychological state; the Negro becomes the objective symbol of that subjective state rather than an objective social reality."

marks those who do the hating. The false pride which exists only while it has a dubious base in contempt for others is dearly bought. If we had presumed to study the educational problem for both racial groups, we should be forced to examine in some detail the various typical maladjustments of personality within the Caucasian caste which grow out of the caste system.

But we are concerned mainly with the difficulties which the caste system places in the way of normal, happy, useful, and well-balanced development of the personalities of persons in the Negro caste. Certain broad classifications may be helpful in describing the pathological results of the caste system as it impinges upon Negroes.

Denied equality of status, the Negro develops a diversity of attitudes. He may "laugh it off." He learns to smile in spite of hardship, to sing in the face of catastrophe and disappointment. This is more than whistling to keep up one's courage passing the graveyard. This is a definite psycho-hygienic technique for keeping a modicum of equanimity and sanity in the face of crushing circumstance. This is the attitude which gave birth to the "sorrow songs," the pouring out of the undefeated hopes and deep yearnings of the spirit in the spirituals which have been unequaled in American musical development for sheer poignancy and emotional meaning. At best this attitude leads to a high-minded and beautiful religious escape mechanism, in which the individual who is denied a just share of this world's goods looks to the hereafter for compensation and solace. He is not happy and carefree; but he goes on from day to day, living in the hope of a better day. "Nobody knows the trouble I've seen, Glory hallelujah!" He does not face the issues of life squarely; he sings his sorrow songs and waits for the future.

At worst, this flight from the world leads the individual to play the part of the clown, the buffoon, the jester. Caught in a difficult circumstance, he makes a clever remark, cuts a caper, executes a jaunty dance step, forces a hearty laugh at his own expense, or just acts "plain dumb." As the slave, when caught in some petty misdeed, grinned and pulled at his forelock to escape punishment, so some Negroes today escape the more troublesome consequences of adulthood in an inequitable and hostile society by refusing to appear as adults, masquerading as children. Many whites see this, and conclude that the Negro is happy-go-lucky, carefree, contented, and childlike. What they are really seeing is a very adroit piece of acting which has been so continuously used that it has become an established social pattern. The minstrel show has given wide currency to the stereotype; and the Negro has learned through experience that if he will accept the stereotype as a description of himself, he will frequently avoid serious clashes and emerge from difficult situations with his skin whole. One has witnessed this phenomenon, for example, in the conduct of a university professor, a highly educated man, who dropped into the vernacular, affected a slouching posture and a "dumb" face, as a reward for which he was dismissed by the traffic officer with nothing but a quick oath of anger mixed with disgust. Clowning is a definite social pattern used by Negroes to pull the leg of gullible whites. It feeds the vanity of the white; but it violates the self-respect of the hypocrite who is forced to debase himself to save his skin.

A third attitude may be called resignation, with varying degrees of sullenness or moroseness. Having the sense of inferiority impressed upon him from birth, and passing through many experiences which reënforce that early training, the individual ceases to have ambition or hope. His motto becomes, "Do what de man say." He resigns himself to mediocrity, or less. He does not strive to better himself, his condition, or his status. He learns that what he and his fellows think or desire is of no concern to the powers that control his destiny. Nothing can be done about it. Much of what looks to the outsider like laziness or shiftlessness is merely this defeatism and resignation which have been beaten into the individual by a niggardly society which has denied him the hope of being anything or anybody. It is a culture pattern which is most frequently found among the share-croppers *of both races*; but when the stereotype, "All Negroes are lazy" is used as a defense for wage differentials and other forms of discrimination, that stereotype gains a degree of specious acceptance out of the prevalence of this defeatist attitude which the Negro has learned as one of the culture patterns which the caste system encourages him to develop.

A fourth attitude, one which is much less common, and which is developed less by osmosis and social suggestion than by reaction and rebellion, is the attitude of revolt. Bitter, even envenomed, the individual becomes more and more antisocial, waiting for the chance to strike back at a world which has given him nothing but crusts and cursed at him for wanting more. He may develop pathological delusions of grandeur, fancying himself to be the Messiah. He may identify himself with a dream of the coming revolution and work for the growth of some radical movement.[2] Or he may strike out blindly against whatever members of society happen to be nearest and most obviously in his way at a particular time of emotional strain; and the jails have another "criminal" to whom they may furnish board and lodging.

Almost it might appear that the stereotypes of the Negro as intensely religious, as funny and ludicrous, as sullen and shiftless, or as a threat to society, have some founding in fact. But that apparent fact is not due to peculiar biological heritage, a function of dark skin and African blood. It is created by the society which prescribes the possible limit of development of persons born into the Negro caste, thereby making normal, well-rounded psychological growth very difficult for the average Negro. To be sure, many persons of color are clowns, many are erratically religious, many are sullen and indifferent to standards of decent life, and many are bitter and antisocial; but these are the inevitable results

[2] Cf. G. H. Dession, "Making a Radical," *Saturday Review of Literature,* XV (April, 1937) 11, for a critical review of Herndon's autobiography, *Let Me Live,* which points out the way in which the caste system operates to make radicals out of intelligent young men.

of the caste system for which not the Negro but the white race is responsible. By the attitudes of mingled fear, hostility, deprecation, discrimination, amused patronage, friendly domination, and rigid authoritarianism, the white caste generates opposite and complementary attitudes in the Negro caste. It is a touch of consummate irony that the dominant group should then argue that the characteristics which exhibit themselves in the submerged group are "natural," or "racial."

While the foregoing comment applies broadly to the whole range of personality maladjustments which the caste system nourishes, it is not implied that the four general types of difficulty mentioned in the preceding pages are the only types of pathological development to be noted. The variety of patterns is as great as the number of individuals involved. The crude classification here given merely provides a suggestion for the cataloguing and analyzing of the individual cases as these are met. For example: a young college graduate from a middle-class home, having studied the classics and having built up for himself a roseate dream of a future life of scholarly study which a year's graduate work at a leading university will bring to him, meets with rebuffs and discrimination at the university. The upshot of his year's experience is the adoption of an escape pattern which includes features of several types. He accepts a job as a domestic employee during the daytime; but he lives in another world of fantasy and "society" as soon as he can get home to his third-floor bedroom and change his clothes. He becomes a "Cinderella," enduring the days of drudgery for the sake of the evenings and nights of hilarity—but he never marries royalty to live happily ever after. Instead, he becomes a permanently divided personality, one part of his life being lived in acquiescence and conformity ("Yes, sir. No, sir!"), and the other half of his waking hours being spent in an escape from drudgery into a little world of likeminded escapists who treat one another with the elaborate social courtesy of overcompensation. He exhibits the escape mechanism of the religionist without the saving grace of high ideals, and the conformity of the quiescent at the price of personal integrity.

Long, in his discussion of "The Psychogenic Hazards of Segregated Education,"[3] suggests that the real harm of segregation lies in the "neglected field of pauperized and gnarled personality development."[4] When it becomes clear to the individual Negro that the limitations of caste definitely circumscribe the possibilities of his development and advancement, he tends to lose incentive. He develops a feeling of inferiority and frustration which may take any one of a number of courses. "The individual may take flight into unreality in order to escape a world of crass adversity where one must play an unpleasant rôle."[5] Or he may develop watertight compartments, impervious to reason, *bulkheads* of defense against unpleasant facts, sometimes resulting in an overdeveloped race pride and assertiveness. Another pattern of compensation and escape is that of *regression* in which the individual reverts to juvenile or childhood responses to evade the necessity of meeting the adult difficulty, such as bursting into tears and complaints instead of facing a problem. The *ostrich* escape from reality needs no comment, and the *mystical* fantasy that it will all come out all right in God's own good time is likewise a familiar pattern of flight. On the other hand, more vigorous attitudes of protest lead to equally serious psychopathic conditions of *projection*, in which one compensates for one's own shortcomings by blaming "the system" or other individuals; of *rationalization*, in which one gives specious and plausible excuses for failures to meet the rigorous demands of an inequitable situation; or of *catharsis*, in which one speaks one's mind without fear or favor, and feels that "telling them" is all that it takes to rectify the

[3] H. H. Long, *Journal of Negro Education*, IV (July, 1935), 336-50.

[4] *Ibid.*, p. 342. The importance of normal personality development is emphasized by the difficulty of realizing the same when one is a member of a segregated group. "It is the real self in contrast with the overlay of self-deceptions which minister to a distressed psyche in conflict with the prevailing mores."

[5] *Ibid.*, p. 344.

situation or justify the inactivity of the teller. Long has thus given a catalogue of some of the more obvious costs of the system of segregation in terms of the personality difficulties of the segregated. A similar and equally interesting list of the psychogenic hazards as they threaten the members of the dominant group might also be drawn up. With what difficulty the individual escapes one or another of these hazards, only those who have grown up in a caste-divided world can understand.

The difficulty with which an individual Negro avoids one or another of these pathological developments, or a combination of them, is illustrated by the predicament of an individual born into the uppermost group of his caste. He is

superior to the lower whites in class, but inferior in caste. In his own personality he feels the conflict of the two opposing structures, and in the thinking and feeling of members of both groups there is to be found this same conflict about his position. . . . If it ever came to an issue, the supraordinate white class would maintain the solidarity of the white group by repudiating any claims by any Negro of superiority to the lower-class whites. This would be true, even though the admission might be made privately that the Negro was superior to certain of the lower-class whites.[6]

Warner offers the hypothesis that the "instability of many of the individuals in this group (as compared, let us say, with the Negroes of the lower positions) may be due to the instability and skewness of the social situation in which they live. They are always 'off balance' and are constantly attempting to achieve an equilibrium which this society, except under extraordinary circumstances does not provide for them."[7]

An exaggeration or aggravation of the foregoing difficulty is found in the instance of the mulatto whose predicament is more anomalous than any other of the illogical social positions into which Negroes are thrust. From the first, the white caste assumed that, since it was superior to

---

[6] W. L. Warner, "American Caste and Class," *American Journal of Sociology*, XLII (September, 1936), 236.

[7] *Ibid.*, p. 237.

Negroes, then by corollary, mulattoes must occupy an intermediary position. In New Orleans, for example, a kind of third caste developed in ante-bellum days, and the dispersion of this caste into the two recognized castes of the post-Reconstruction period, under pressure of the Jim Crow process, marks one of the harrowing and difficult experiences of racial adjustment. So, too, in Richmond, Virginia, in the 1920s when an attempt was made to enforce rigorous "racial integrity" laws, a third caste was temporarily created to accommodate families which were, for a few months, legally cut off from the white caste to which they had belonged.

Johnson[8] estimates that about twenty thousand persons per year are passing over from the Negro caste to the white caste, giving up their former identity and moving into a new social setting. That is one way of resolving the internal conflict that divides the energies of many persons of mixed blood. Some additional thousands of persons live dual lives, passing for white during their working hours in order to find satisfactory employment and living as Negroes during the rest of their hours to find the companionship they prefer. Still others go from year to year facing a world which resents their presence and refuses to give them recognition, while at the same time that world implies that they are better than other members of their caste. The implication of the white man's assumption that he is better than the Negro is that the mulatto is midway between; but the caste system does not recognize this intermediate group, with the result that the standard of values based on relative pigmentation which the white arbitrarily thrusts into the Negro caste to divide it against itself, creates a special set of disquieting and unsettling factors which become the special problem of each individual mulatto.[9]

[8] E. R. Embree, *Brown America*, p. 46.

[9] "In some respects Negroes are more American than the Americans. Because of repression of self-determination, and little opportunity to rise to importance, their desire for recognition is confined to the group life. Hence appears a psychopathic tendency toward individualism. Negro society is rent asunder and torn into innumerable factions by senseless jealousies,

In attempted justification of this attitude toward mulattoes, the white caste points to the fact that the great majority of the leaders of the Negro group since emancipation have been persons of mixed blood rather than of pure African descent. This rests back upon the wishful thinking of the master class in slave times, when the assumption that mulattoes must be superior to Africans, plus the sentimental attachment of some masters toward their own children of color, led the whites to give superior training and advantages to mulattoes. Given superior opportunities, mulattoes naturally tended to make superior achievements. The assumption became father to the deed which in turn justified the belief. "The resulting sentiments and beliefs presently came to operate as an independent force making for the perpetuation and increase of the separation that, in the first instance, gave a basis for the body of belief."[10] The net result of this initial advantage of the mulatto is that, given an earlier start in the struggle for self-realization, he is a generation or so ahead of the bulk of the race. It may be expected that an increasing number of Negroes of unmixed African descent will emerge into positions of leadership in the present half century. But in the meantime, the caste system has, in accordance with its own self-secreted standards of value, thrust the divisive knife of pride-in-color through the vitals of the Negro caste, and raised the innocent and often unwilling mulatto to the anomalous position of a man without a caste in a world where caste determines status.

In summary, if any one psychological attitude may be said to characterize each of the two castes, suggesting the complex of interrelationships and shadings of prejudice which each caste exhibits, these two are to be selected: for the white

intrigues, and petty strivings. This lack of coherence and coöperation is a severe impediment to progress. Religion furnishes an outlet for gregarious tendencies but is torn into more bitter sectarian fights than even among whites. In politics race consciousness urges solidarity, but within the Negro community and within the groups of which it is composed discord disrupts unity, and distrust hampers leadership." B. Schrieke, *Alien Americans*, pp. 150-51.

[10] E. B. Reuter, "The Changing Status of the Mulatto," in *Ebony and Topaz*, p. 108.

caste, dominance; for the Negro caste, dependence.[11] Obliga-
tory observance of the etiquette of caste conditions the Negro
in an attitude of inferiority and nurtures the dependency
complex. As long as no member of the subordinate caste
openly breaks ranks or flouts the etiquette, things go with
comparative smoothness. "Interracial friction has been relieved by the simple process of reverting to the etiquette of
the period of slavery."[12] Under the caste system, however,
different individuals react differently, partly because they
come from different class levels within each caste, and partly
because they have diverse temperaments and experiences.[13]
It is this set of attitudes with which the student comes to
college, which help to make up the stuff of the educative experience he will be prepared to undergo. These basic attitudes on the one hand describe more or less definitely the
limitations of that part of the educative process which is to
go forward on the college campus; and on the other hand
they are a challenge to the educator who is interested in
using collegiate experience for the purpose of remaking
attitudes in the long-term effort to remake society.

[11] Psychological measurement of groups of white and Negro subjects has
revealed some significant differences between the two castes in a dominance-
submission scale. J. H. McFadden and J. F. Dashield ("Racial Differences as
Measured by the Downey Will-Temperament Test," Journal of Applied Psychology, VII [1923], 30-53), E. B. Hurlock ("The Will Temperament of
White and Negro Children," Pedagogical Seminary, XXXVIII [December,
1930], 91-100), and G. C. Sumner ("Environmental Factors Which Prohibit
Creative Scholarship among Negroes," School and Society, XXII [September
5, 1925], 294-96) describe differences between the two groups which are
less definite and conclusive than our study of the caste system would prepare
us to anticipate. No study in this area has yet established a clear-cut demonstration of differences in temperament on a dominance-submission scale which
can be traced unmistakably to biological inheritance, whereas the weight of
the class-caste system upon the persons involved is calculated to produce
reliable differences in temperament which are thereby explainable on environmental bases.

[12] Bertram W. Doyle, "The Etiquette of Race Relations—Past, Present,
and Future," Journal of Negro Education, V (April, 1936), 208.

[13] A. S. Beckham, "A Study of Race Attitudes in Negro Children of Adolescent Age," Journal of Abnormal and Social Psychology, XXIX (April,
1934), 18-29, shows that in an unfortunate circumstance involving personal
humiliation, some Negro children felt a stimulus to personal ambition, others
became antagonistic, aloof, or resentful. He calls the former "normal," the
latter "delinquent." It might be better to call the former "healthy," the latter
"pathological."

VI

DILEMMAS OF THE CAUCASIAN CASTE

In our greedy chase to make profit of the Negro, let us beware lest we cancel and tear to pieces even the white man's charter of freedom. —ABRAHAM LINCOLN

IF THE main outlines of the analysis to this point are correct, two important inferences may be drawn. The first is that segregation, as a social institution, will not be removed tomorrow, or the day after tomorrow. No matter how earnestly individuals or groups may desire its removal, the caste system, based on historical economic divergence and maintained by powerful social stereotypes, will be modified, if at all, very gradually. Not within this generation, certainly, will the folkways of a great area, involving the emotional stability and social status of nearly forty million people, be completely revised.

The second inference is a contrary thesis: in spite of the inertia of social institutions, there are indications that genuine transformation of the caste system is not only possible, but probable—if not inevitable in the long run. The marked differences in caste configuration at different historic periods, the decided modification of some of the overt expressions of race attitudes (decrease in number of lynchings, for example), and the noticeable growth of small groups of white and colored persons, each of which within its respective caste challenges the continuing changelessness of the caste system, all point to the inference that caste has been changed, and that it will be. The system of race-differentiation-for-subordination which is the caste system may not entirely pass away tomorrow; but it is being modified and may possibly be transformed in the long run.

Our interest in the discussion of caste, race prejudice, and attendant phenomena is not that of amassing evidence for an attack; but rather, we are here interested in understanding as completely and fully as possible the conditions under which the Negro college student is to be educated and the world into which he goes at graduation. This is merely an intelligently realistic approach to the question of the function and aim of the Negro college in the American social setting. To refuse to consider the problems we are here raising would be to blind ourselves to the most important aspects of our real job. And if there be persons outside the circle of our colleges who feel uneasy over this discussion, the answer can only be that if they object to the attempt to be intelligently realistic in analyzing a job, then they must plead either that the segregated college be unintelligent or that it deliberately fail to do its job. Both of these alternatives we reject.

To see the problems which confront the Negro in their fuller perspective, it may be well to begin by pointing out in this chapter that the dilemmas of segregation are at least as baffling (if not apparently as crucial) to the white caste as to the Negro.

THE PERPLEXITY OF THE WHITE CASTE

The Caucasian has the bear by the tail; he cannot let go and he dare not hang on. What is he to do?

Segregation is here. The individual is born into a segregated community. He has no choice in the matter. His elders, who were likewise conditioned, bring him up in a world which is separated along race lines, and he learns to follow the group mores, the folkways. His reaction to the folkways may be different from that of others about him; but willy-nilly he grows up in a caste-divided society, and inevitably he is affected by that fact. And it is not for him to say whether there shall or shall not be caste divisions in his world—here they are! To be sure, he may have something to do with influencing the course of future developments; but as far as today and the immediate tomorrows are concerned, caste is a fact of life, a stubborn, tenacious fact. The Caucasian has the bear by the tail.

He cannot let go. We have seen in earlier chapters how great a weight of social pressure is brought to bear upon the individual, to bring conformity to accepted race patterns. It is with tremendous difficulty that an individual white person tears himself loose from the habits of his lifetime, flouts the accepted codes of conduct of his group, "loses caste," and sets the current of his own life against the tide of society. We shall see later that much the same thing is true of the individual Negro. And in addition to these psychological inhibitions are the sociological "facts" which appear in large part to support the belief that it is best to hold on to the bear's tail.

THE PROFITS OF CASTE

Consider the money saved through segregation. Oftentimes it has been said that segregation imposes an unduly large expense by forcing the duplication of public services for education, health, and the like. If the services provided for the two castes were roughly equivalent in quality and extent, then to the degree that segregation called for a useless duplication of supervisory and overhead costs, the argument would carry weight. But as a matter of fact, this is not the case. Far from being an extra burden, the dual system (whether in education or in health services or whatnot) as it operates today is an actual means of saving rather large sums of money because only the first half of the "separate but equal" clause tends to be enforced. The Rosenwald study of expenditures for schools[1] shows that in eleven Southern states where records are available it would be necessary to increase expenditures on an average of nearly forty million dollars per year in the elementary and secondary schools for Negroes in order to equalize the educational opportunities for white and colored children. The Negro teacher receives only 47 percent of what the white teacher receives—another way of stating the clear saving in money costs. If the school properties for Negroes were to be put on a par with those for whites, $240,000,000 would need to be spent in fifteen Southern states on schools for colored children. Segregation in schooling spells enormous savings for the South. One important qualification of this general truth must be noted. The savings on the elementary

[1] The Julius Rosenwald Fund, *School Money in Black and White.*

and secondary level, through providing cheaper educational facilities for Negroes are enormous; but on the college level, where many of the white and Negro colleges are operating with small student bodies, quite below the level of efficiency, merging of the two sets of colleges would be a great financial gain.

The main outlines of what is true for schools could be repeated with reference to parks and playgrounds, paving and sidewalks, sanitation and sewage services, water mains and street lighting. The device of getting paid for *not* doing something antedates the Agricultural Adjustment Administration. Large sums have been saved by not providing public services and public conveniences in the sections of towns and cities inhabited by Negroes. Fire protection is notoriously ineffective in colored sections of towns, where narrow roads which are slippery or impassable in wet weather impede the heavy fire-fighting equipment, where insufficient water pressure in the mains increases the difficulty, and where jerry-built houses go up in a flash of fire which would beat the swiftest of fire departments.

In addition to the tremendous pressure of history and social usage, then, the financial pressure urging the maintenance of segregation is ample to insure the caste system a good long life. It would cost too much to equalize public services and facilities for the two races. The white South cannot consider it. To clinch the point, consider the fact that the South is relatively the poorest section of the nation. The average per capita wealth of the South is $1,785 as compared with $3,609 for the nation, and every one of the eleven states of the Union having less than $2,000 of per capita wealth is a Southern state. Not only would it cost tremendous sums of money for the South to equalize the public services for the two races but also, the South does not have the resources with which to bring the expenditures for Negroes up to the white level. In this case, therefore, equalization would mean the lowering of the level for whites in order to raise the level for Negroes to an intermediate position. But the South already suffers a decided differential advantage as compared with the rest of the nation. This is illustrated in per capita school expenditures which average nearly $100 for the nation, a little over $44 for the white South, and less than $13 for the Southern Negro. It is therefore simply impossible for the white Southerner to contemplate the end of the caste system with its money-saving inequalities. This set of factors supports one horn of the dilemma.[2]

This horn of the dilemma is sharpened and strengthened by another set of facts, having to do with the wage differential between the castes. Quite universally throughout the South (and in many places in the North as well), the practice prevails of paying lower wages to Negroes for work which is better paid when done by whites. This phenomenon has its historical roots in slavery, and it means that an uncalculated amount is saved in annual labor costs wherever the racial differential is observed. A hidden saving to the entrepreneur, which is equally important, is seen in the way in which the low wage level of the colored laborer acts to depress the wage level of the white worker as well. This, again, has its historical rootage in the "peculiar institution." America gained a position of dominance in the cotton markets of the world on the basis of a slave economy. As other sections of the globe came into the market, they were likewise forced to depress their costs of production to the level of a slave economy. With over half of the American cotton crop[3] being sold outside our borders, the world market sets the price for

[2] A possible exception must be noted, namely, public conveyances. It is possible that the cost of building two waiting rooms in railway stations, two sets of toilets, two ticket windows, etc., together with the cost of pulling two cars over the tracks instead of one, may tend to increase the expenses of the dual system of transportation. But over against this must be weighed the distinct savings realized through using the discarded "white" cars for colored patrons, through failure in many cases to clean the Jim Crow cars, through crowding colored patrons into the back seats of busses over the wheels in cramped and jostled quarters, and many similar devices. It might cost more to maintain separate but equal facilities for transportation than to maintain equal and unseparated facilities; but where separation becomes a device for executing inequalities, savings from the inequality of the service tend to offset possible extra expense.

[3] Cf. E. Q. Hawk, *Economic History of the South*, p. 517. The actual percentage of the cotton crop exported from 1925 to 1930 averaged 53.3.

American production today—and this is a market which is still dominated by the wage level of a slave economy so effectively established by America. The bankruptcy of cotton farming in America rests basically on this simple fact that, with the passing of a slave economy and the exhaustion of the soil, cotton costs two or three times as much to produce in the Southeast as it will bring in the world market.[4] The only possible way to meet the press of world competition, therefore, is to cut labor costs either through mechanization (as in the Southwest) or through further wage reductions. A rise in the wage level is thus doubly dubious, for it would necessitate raising the level of the colored tenant; and to destroy the caste division of the white and colored sharecroppers and tenants would be to run the hazard of finally destroying the cotton-producing ability of the South which has rested upon the perpetuation of slave-level wage costs. This is unthinkable, for while King Cotton may be a very ill sovereign, he is still highly revered by his subjects—barons and vassals alike. The cost of modifying the caste system would be at least the partial scrapping of the cotton economy which has made the South, and made it what it is. To persons who have grown up under the system of cotton culture, the adjustment would be extremely difficult, constituting a major revolution almost as difficult as the alteration of racial attitudes. Strangely enough, this inability to contemplate the passing of King Cotton is not peculiar to either racial group.[5] The cotton culture sys-

[4] Cf. *The Collapse of Cotton Tenancy,* W. W. Alexander, Charles S. Johnson, and E. R. Embree, pp. 34-46.

[5] Consider the argument of the three co-authors of *The Collapse of Cotton Tenancy,* and the implied agreement of an imposing roster of citizens, white and colored, to the effect that the future of the cotton-growing Southeast, while it is extremely dubious, must still be found primarily in cotton culture. The belated efforts of white and colored sharecroppers to make common cause against the cotton tenancy system are interesting as a development of interracial understanding in common opposition to a common difficulty; but they cannot be of great hope if the cotton industry itself is to pass off the scene. One cannot assume the rôle of prophet and declare that cotton culture will certainly leave the Southeast; but indications are strongly weighted in that direction. The burden of the argument in this direction in such an admirable book as the above-mentioned *Collapse of Cotton Tenancy* is inescapably headed to that conclusion.

tem, with its accompanying generations of habituation of both castes, has made mental slaves of an entire region— slaves to King Cotton and bondsmen to caste. The mental and emotional costs reënforcing the financial costs involved in giving up this pattern of life are so great as to make it next to impossible for the South to let go of the bear's tail.

THE COSTS OF CASTE

At the same time (and this is the other horn of the dilemma), the Caucasian is right in saying that caste does place a large cost burden upon the population—costs both monetary and other. The caste system costs a great deal, not so much in the items ordinarily mentioned, which we have just examined; but more in hidden costs which are sometimes overlooked. We have seen that many of the alleged costs turn out upon examination to be net savings; now we shall find that certain real costs which are spread upon the whole social group, or hidden in the normal processes, actually make the cost of caste tremendous. These are the reasons why the Caucasian dare not hold on to the bear's tail.

The cumulative interest charges on the alleged savings of the caste system are compounded with relentless regularity, and the collection is ruthlessly made in money costs and cultural costs. If the Negro has had poor educational facilities, poor playgrounds, inferior cultural opportunities, poor public services of all kinds, this fact has had its direct result in increased costs for corrective, penal, and charitable institutions and in a general lowering of the whole level of life for both racial groups. As a first example, take the case of health services for the Negro. Public and private health expenditures for Negroes have been kept low. Hospitalization either in hospitals for Negroes or in special wards of white hospitals is so inadequate as to beggar description.[6] Poorer housing

[6] The best recent summary of health problems and facilities amongst Negroes is the July, 1937 *Yearbook* issue of the *Journal of Negro Education* which is devoted to the question, with 326 pages contributed by thirty-four writers. Perhaps the best previous summary of the question was Louis L. Dublin's "The Health of the Negro" in the *Annals* of the American Academy, CXL (November, 1928), 77-85.

and lower income spell higher incidence of disease, with the inevitable corollary of contagion in both racial groups. Adequate reliable statistical investigations in this field have not been made, but shreds of evidence are available to show which way the wind is blowing. Figures reported by the health department of one large Southern state show that in 1929 one in every six Negroes who died in that state went through his last illness unattended by medical aid in any form, and that in 1934, this proportion had risen to 23 percent.[7] The proportion of the same predicament among whites was about one-third of these figures in each of the respective years. A second shred of evidence is the table of infant mortality. Since this particular form of death is, in the main, directly correlated with lack of adequate medical care and hospitalization, it is of particular interest to us:

TABLE 4[a]

INFANT MORTALITY, COLORED AND WHITE, IN TEN SOUTHERN STATES, 1928–34.
DEATH RATE UNDER ONE YEAR OF AGE PER 1,000 BIRTHS

(1)	(2) 1928	(3) 1929	(4) 1930	(5) 1931	(6) 1932	(7) 1933	(8) 1934
Negro	105.2	103.5	102.8	95.9	85.5	89.7	94.5
White	67.6	65.1	63.0	58.7	57.2	56.6	62.1

[a] Table compiled from U. S. Bureau of the Census Reports, "Birth, Stillbirth and Infant Mortality Statistics 1928–1934" and quoted in Mary Gover, "Trend of Mortality among Southern Negroes since 1920," *Journal of Negro Education*, VI (July, 1937), 279.

At no time during the period is the infant mortality rate for whites two-thirds as high as for Negroes. While the health situation for Negroes is undoubtedly much better than it was fifty, or twenty-five years ago, it is still deplorably bad. It is not merely in failure to provide adequately for the health of colored people through public-health services that the caste system impedes satisfactory progress of both races; but the

[7] Michael M. Davis, "Problems of Health Service for Negroes," *Journal of Negro Education*, VI (July, 1937), 440.

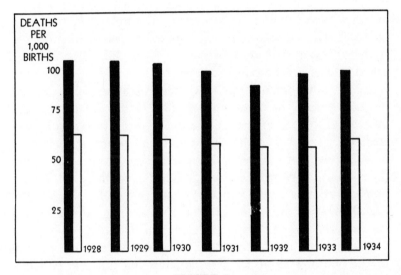

FIGURE 6

INFANT MORTALITY, COLORED AND WHITE, IN TEN SOUTHERN
STATES, 1928-34

caste system, in driving Negro professional men North,[8] tends to leave the great masses of Negroes in the South without what little medical help the race might be able to provide within itself. As Ray Lyman Wilbur puts it: "The health problems of the Negro are not his alone. They belong to the whole population. There is no possibility of isolating either the Negro or his diseases. . . . The disease organisms living in his body can perhaps more readily reach another Negro; but they soon can and do spread to all elements of the population."[9] The caste system may appear to save something in terms of lesser expenditures for Negro health; but who shall say that it is a net saving for society?

Again, while many qualifying reservations would need to be made before the point is ready for blanket defense, it may, in general, be asserted that the experience of 1929-36 made clear the general fact that laborers make poor purchasers unless they are paid an adequate percentage of what they produce. Consumers with empty pockets bring the kind of economic costliness leading to costiveness which has been called the Depression. We are not now disregarding all the historical factors, and particularly the destruction of property and capital in the Civil War, which also contribute to the poverty of the South. It is also worth emphasizing that the policy of the manufacturing North has usually been one of deliberately trying to keep the agricultural South and Middle West at a differential disadvantage, as a financial capital usually treats its agricultural hinterland. Yet, after all allowances have been made for other factors, it still remains true that the systematic and long-term payment of low wages (while it has brought a modicum of industrial activity and was the basis of the former cotton supremacy of the South in the world market) has led inevitably to the impoverishment of the region at the point where no people can afford to be impoverished—the buying power of consumers. Roughly

[8] See pages 98-102.

[9] Ray Lyman Wilbur, "Health Status and Health Education of Negroes in the United States: A Critical Summary," *Journal of Negro Education*, VI (July, 1937), 577.

one-fourth of the South is Negro; and with that one-fourth unable to buy the produce of North or South, the net saving of the caste system largely disappears. If to this is added the fact that low wages for colored workers depress the wage level for white workers, likewise reducing them to a meager standard of living, with very little extramarginal purchasing power in the hands of the working classes, whether white or colored, the total impact of the caste system on the economic process which sired it is that of impoverishing and stultifying the economic life of the region. The parasite exhausts the host.

There are other costs which do not as readily yield to quantitative description, but which are quite real. The cultural costs of caste, in terms of the general retardation of the region, need to be noted in passing. Incomparably the best general summary of the problems and opportunities of the South is Odum's *Southern Regions of the United States*.[10] This pioneering survey of the South presents with ample supporting statistical and quantitative data, and in its proper historical perspective, the picture of a chronological lag with its concomitant cultural lag, rooted deep in the history of the South. As we have seen, this history includes the story of the peculiar institution which was slavery and which is now caste. "The South holds the Negro back; the Negro holds the South back; and both point in recrimination."[11] One of the most vicious results of this mutual recrimination is the building up of the poor white myth to the point where it became a social stereotype, as effective in stigmatizing the unfortunate white victim of environmental circumstance as were the racial stereotypes in categorizing the Negro. The myth of the biological inferiority of the poor white was given additional credence by being dressed up in academic jargon and sent forth in "scientific" respectability by such writings as David Starr Jordan's *War's Aftermath*.[12] The myth had as much apparent

[10] H. W. Odum, *Southern Regions of the United States.*
[11] R. B. Vance, *Human Geography of the South*, p. 463.
[12] I am indebted for this citation and for the accompanying discussion of the poor white myth to Vance, *op. cit.*, pp. 464 ff.

justification as the corresponding legend of white biological supremacy. Both theories could point to the obvious cultural inferiority of their objects and rationalize this acknowledged backwardness into a theory of biologically inherited incapacity. Our analysis of the working of the caste system, based on economic processes, would support the belief that the cultural backwardness of both poor white and poor Negro roots not in "whiteness" or "blackness," but in poverty—poverty, that is, not merely in terms of money, but impoverishment of body, mind, and spirit through generation after generation of cultural starvation and deprivation. When the profit-and-loss account of the caste system is finally reckoned, on the debit side of the ledger must go this incalculable retardation of the entire Southern region through the drag of caste upon both racial groups. So serious is this retardation that present-day writers on the problems of the South are wont to point out that unless the whole South goes forward together, none of it can move. At long last, we are seeing that economic, aesthetic, intellectual, spiritual, or any other form of advance will come in full measure to any people only as the entire group share in it. The white South has known this for some time, and it is now becoming one of its accepted ideas. Somehow or other, the chains of caste which hold both races in the dungeon must be broken if either is to be free. To return to our metaphor—the Caucasian dare not hang on to the bear's tail.

Without wishing to prolong this phase of the discussion unduly, and certainly with no desire to excoriate or accuse a particular section of the nation, but only to attain adequate orientation for our own problem in this study, we consider one more sample of the way in which the dilemma of caste thrusts itself upon the white South. American democracy is probably as ineffective and as corrupt in a great many Northern centers as it is in much of the South; but in the South the primary reasons for the stultifying of democratic political processes is closely related to the institution of caste. When the accepted mores of a people are based upon the open disregard for basic statutes, it cannot be otherwise. The attempted national prohibition of intoxicating liquors convinced the nation that legislation without public backing is ineffective. So, too, with the processes of democratic government—one cannot maintain faith in an institution which is supported tongue-in-cheek. To be sure, the ignorance of large sections of the white electorate makes it easier for the demagogue to sway his following; but there is an effective whipping boy always at hand for use by the adroit politician. A candidate has only to sound the blast of white supremacy, no matter what the real issue may be, and his chances are better than before. Real issues seldom come to the front in such an atmosphere.

Moreover, there is strong presumptive support for the belief that, psychologically, the continued denial of basic political rights to one-fourth of the population is likely to work for the circumscribing of the exercise of the franchise by part of the other three-fourths. And the one-party system which the caste pattern demands leads finally to a political situation in which it is literally impossible to have an Opposition—with all the weakening of the Government and the stultifying of political life which that one-party system implies. Outside the party primary, which is always a family scrap within the party itself, it is as impossible to vote effectively for issues or men as it is in contemporary Nazi Germany. Generally speaking, one may vote for the Democratic candidates, or one may stay away from the polls. The "solid South," a political phenomenon based on caste and the maintenance of caste, is politically delivered to the Democratic party lock, stock, and barrel. But in a land where there is no free and actively critical Opposition, the process of slow attrition sets in, leading to decadence and misgovernment. The remarkable thing is not that the South has governmental inadequacies (so do other parts of the nation); but that with the dead weight of the caste system upon it, the South manages to be politically as articulate as it does. What could not be done if this impediment to intelligent political activity were removed!

With its social institutions stultified, its economic life impoverished, and its cultural life correspondingly weakened, the South develops and nurses a regional inferiority complex which is familiar as a culture pattern of any disinherited or expropriated minority. What Sinn Feinism is to the Irish, what Zionism is to the Jew, what the new Nationalism is to the several small nation-states carved out of Europe after the World War, so is "Dixie" to the Southerner. It is an object of emotional attachment and loyalty which frequently transcends rational processes and commits the individual to a quite irrational if not fanatical finality. It demands its own etiquette of observance ("War Between the States" not "Civil War"), writes its own version of history (as the North also does), takes self-conscious pride in the production of things Southern (in art, literature, industry), and produces the politically solid South. Resenting the continued smugness of the average Northern attitude toward the South, the latter has been accustomed to use the Negro as the scapegoat. Southern life has never gone to the completely illogical extremes of Nazi Germany; it has always been tempered with the fine graciousness of the old aristocracy; it has sublimated much of its inferiority by nostalgic recollection of the plantation myth; and there is therefore great hope in the contemporary effort of leading Southerners to transmute the vices of sectionalism into the virtues of regionalism.[13] But to bring about a genuine renascence, the South will need to free itself from the impediments of caste. If, in the end, it is unwilling or unable to shake off the confinement of caste, it runs the risk of cultural stillbirth.

The horns of the dilemma on which the white South is impaled are these alternatives of the indefinite continuance of the caste system which it has inherited and with which its whole life fabric is interwoven, or the realization of the values of the new life for which it is struggling. Caste must go if progress is to come. If there were any way in which the segregated college could be of help to the majority group in this

[13] Cf. Odum, *op. cit., passim.*

supreme effort to shake off the shackles of caste, this would be one of the greatest services it could possibly render. For the good of the white man, the Negro ought not easily to acquiesce in an outgrown social dichotomy. By acquiescing in the inequity of the caste system, the Negro becomes accessory to the act of economic, aesthetic, and cultural self-strangulation with which the Caucasian threatens himself. Dr. Washington long since pointed out that the only way to keep the Negro in the gutter was for the white man to stay there with him. If the Negro, however, were to refuse to stay in the gutter and were to help the white man in the latter's efforts to break the habit of generations, then the control of caste might be modified, complexes might be conquered, attitudes might be changed, both white and Negro might step out of the gutter. One of the principal objectives of the segregated college, then, might be this effort to discover ways in which the Negro can help the white man to modify the race attitudes which caste has engendered, and through that means to transform the institution of caste. It thus appears that what might have been looked upon as merely the white man's dilemmas of segregation are actually shared by the Negro.

VII

DILEMMAS OF THE NEGRO CASTE

Are we only to be permitted to defend general principles on condition that we draw no practical inferences from them?
—LORD MORLEY

THE dilemmas confronting the Negro, like those discussed in the preceding chapter, are not mere academic debates; they are not theoretical gymnastics but living dilemmas. The choices never come singly, and they seldom come simply; they tend to come intertwined and confused. There is seldom an opportunity to choose between the good and the bad; it is usually a choice between what appears to be a little better than something else which, if looked at from another angle, might appear to be almost as good.

Sometimes a shorthand statement of the dilemmas of segregation is offered in the thesis that it is a choice between "principles and expediency."[1] Actually, if such a clear choice were offered, the decisions would be much easier than they are. What happens is that there are usually excellent principles bound up in each of the several alternatives; and, conversely, no matter which way the decision is made, there are usually elements of expediency involved. Nor is it the whole truth to say that it is essentially a choice between immediate benefits as against long-term benefits, even though this is often apparently the character of the practical alternatives presented.[2] What begins as an immediate benefit may conceivably also be a long-term benefit in a relatively static society; and what begins as an attempted long-term objective may find itself vitiated and thwarted or rendered irrelevant in a relatively dynamic society. Morever, the Negro must always include the white man's attitudes and principles in his study of a problem. The white man's dilemmas become part and parcel of the Negro's larger dilemmas because the Negro's decisions and his attempts to implement these decisions are inevitably

[1] For example, Alain Locke, "The Dilemma of Segregation," *Journal of Negro Education*, IV (July, 1935), 406-11.
[2] Cf. *Loc. cit.*

executed *sub specie Caucasorum*. There is no one, single, clearly defined and universally accepted answer to the question of segregation. The dilemmas are real, genuine, perplexing, and long-lived.

It is therefore not uncommon to find earnest and able men of essentially similar point of view taking dichotomous attitudes on a particular issue, and both arguing with sincerity from accepted principles in defense of their conclusions and proposals. Because of the emotional overtones of the controversy, men have been known to indulge in vitriolic invective and violent vituperation, adding more heat than light to the point at issue. Nevertheless, in spite of all the difficulties involved, indeed, because of the complexity of the problem, the segregated college must concern itself with these dilemmas of segregation. The nature of its approach and the kind of concern the college expresses will be discussed in Chapters IX and X. In this chapter we shall state and examine a few of the typical antinomies of values which make up the dilemmas of segregation for the Negro in American society.

One more prefatory word before the listing of the dilemmas: although segregation exhibits certain constant characteristics, there are variations in the kind or form of segregation used. It may be *geographic* (separate parts of town for housing accommodations). It may be *mechanical* (separation of space in public conveyances such as trains and buses). These two may be grouped as *spatial* segregation. It may be *institutional* (provision of separate schools, or churches, hospital wards, etc.). It may be *functional* (setting aside of certain social functions to be performed by the segregated group, such as domestic service or barbering; or conversely, proscribing entrance of the segregated group into fields reserved for the dominant group). It may be *cultural* (preventing the segregated group from having easy access to cultural opportunities, such as libraries and theaters, and resulting in an arrested cultural development of the segregated group). It may be *temporal* (permitting the segregated group to reach a given level or enjoy a given advantage only after that level has been reached or passed by the dominant group). It may be *ceremonial* (allowing a Negro to enter as a guest in hotel dining rooms and Pullman cars when wearing the uniform of a servant or nurse and accompanying those served). But whatever the form of the separation or segregation, the general purpose is usually twofold: to preserve a sense of social distance between the two groups and to make that distance carry the connotation of the inferiority of one group to the other. These two characteristic purposes of segregation are forced upon the subordinate group; and this involuntary feature is the third definitive attribute of segregation. It is important to note that these three aspects of segregation (social distance, subordination, and compulsion) must generally be present if the social phenomenon in question is to be called segregation; for segregation implies caste, and caste demands involuntary observance of social distance and submission to subordination. When a religious group, like the Dunkards, draws together in a self-contained settlement, its members cannot be described as segregated. They make the withdrawal voluntarily with the implicit option of returning to society at will without any imputation of inferiority. When a group of Caucasians develops a residential area, agreeing not to sell lots in the development to Jews or Negroes, the Caucasian group cannot be called segregated, for it is the "in-group," shutting out the others. But when a group of Negroes voluntarily comes together in a social club, a church, or a residential development, the same line of argument cannot be applied. The option of integration with society is not there, as in the case of the Dunkards or the Caucasians. Whenever the Negro is separate, he is always segregated, no matter whether he calls it "voluntary grouping of congenial peoples" or "involuntary segregation of a distinguishable people." Lacking the actual alternative of participation or integration on a basis of self-respect, the Negro must always express himself in accordance with the formula of segregation; involuntary-social-distance-in-inferiority. It was this aspect of the problem which Miller must have had in mind when he wrote, "The right-minded

Negro does not oppose segregation as such, but on account of its compulsory character and the resulting hardships."[3]

Here, in this observation, is a key to a perplexity which puzzles many uninitiated persons in the consideration of segregation. "Doesn't the Negro like to live with his own people? What is it about his color that he is ashamed of? Why must he always want to make himself unhappy by crowding in where he isn't wanted?" These and many other questions are asked by well-intentioned white persons. They do not see that as long as caste is an accepted pattern of American life, then anywhere in American life that Negroes are brought together in an unmixed group they are under the cloud of caste— their being together implies an involuntary withdrawal from a "superior" group and the acknowledgment of social distance. Segregation or separation, in whatever form, thus symbolizes inferiority for the Negro. Of course Negroes are happy with each other. It is Caucasian obtuseness which assumes that the Negro's reluctance to accept the involuntary inferiority of caste is a subtle compliment to the dominant group, a hidden desire to be with the white. It is additional obtuseness which does not carefully weigh the psychological possibility that compulsory inferiority may generate a countervailing upward push. Thus, one Southern city which requires a Negro to hold a pass, identifying him and giving the nature of his errand, before he can enter the white section of town has a particularly tense racial situation on its hands; but it does not seriously consider the experience of another Southern city which has taken exactly the opposite track, permitting the widest possible individual and group freedom within the interpretation of the general framework of caste observance—with the result that white folk in this latter city are accustomed to remark with smiling emphasis, "We aren't *afraid* of 'social equality' here!" Lack of clear thinking about segregation is one of the primary causes of its more rigid and destructive expressions. As an accompaniment of the caste

[3] Kelly Miller, "The Causes of Segregation," *Current History*, XXV (March, 1927), 828.

pattern with its powerful stereotypes, this obtuseness of thought is not surprising. Failure of many Negroes to analyze the essential nature of segregation, and similar failure by many whites, accounts for some of the prevalent confusion of attitudes toward the practice.

One of the dilemmas which segregation thrusts before the Negro comes in the form of an offer of increased autonomy and freedom with an improvement of facilities, at the price of isolation and insularity, with probable postponement and possible surrender of claims to larger freedom and effective autonomy within the whole social body. Figuratively, the Negro is told that if he will hoe *only* in his own back yard, he can plant almost any crop he wants—provided he will consume it himself, and provided he will not ask permission to plant anywhere else. This is possibly better than not being permitted to plant for himself at all, being forced to hoe only in someone else's yard. Will it be best to accept the proffered compromise as half-a-loaf-better-than-none? Will accepting the half loaf mean that hope of receiving the other half is forever relinquished? Or will this turn out to be a step toward getting the full loaf? And will it be better not to worry too much about the indefinite future, concerning oneself only with the immediate decision in hand? Or will tactical myopia cheat one of the future?

Consider the vexed question of housing, as symbolic of many other forms of segregation. In 1925, a St. Louis newspaper proposed what it considered to be a solution of the problem of housing the migrant Negroes who were then pouring in from the South, many of them pushing into sections of town previously occupied by whites only. The pressure of population in the segregated areas was forcing Negro professional men to find housing in the better white residential areas. Considerable race tension was being aroused. Said the newspaper:

There is one obvious way to settle this vexing question, namely, by appealing to the self-interest of colored property buyers and renters, by offering them, in areas not preëmpted by white owners and tenants, as good accommodations as would be offered to white people for the same money. This would encourage colored buyers and tenants to take such accommodations. And it would be but simple justice, as well as in the general interest.[4]

Here, the dilemma is posed in one of its most seductive and difficult forms. The white man looks at the proposal and says, "What could be fairer than that? We give the Negro every opportunity the white man has. That's justice. All we ask is that he cease destroying our property values by moving into our neighborhoods—that's injustice." The Negro looks at the proposal and sees so many differing and conflicting things in it that he cannot decide what to do. The statement of the white man is ringing in his ears, and the sting of the implied accusation smarts: he can give only part of his energies to the effort to solve his dilemma satisfactorily because the rest of his attention is directed toward the actions and attitudes of the upper caste. So he asks himself: "How can this segregated section be 'as good' as any other section of St. Louis, as long as everyone knows that we Negroes are forced into it by being excluded from the rest of the city? It may have many of the physical and civic advantages of other sections—may, indeed, have better light and air or better sanitation and streets or better houses than some white areas—but it is still a segregated district; and under the caste system, segregation implies that the segregated group is inferior. Should we, then, accept this proffered compromise as giving us better housing facilities than those we now have? Or should we fight this segregation to the last ditch? If this proposal goes through, we can have better homes, if we'll stay by ourselves. Is it worth it? And would we gain anything by refusing? Wouldn't that doom us to indefinite continuance under the present highly unsatisfactory situation? Perhaps it will be best to take what we can get now, and wait for more later. . . . But that will be to accept an inferior status! Yet, of course, we are in that status already. . . ."

[4] State of Missouri, "Negro Industrial Commission Report," *Monthly Labor Review* of the U. S. Department of Labor, XX (May, 1925), 988.

And the discussion goes on and on, without an easy solution of the problem.

We have illustrated this type of dilemma with a housing problem—geographical segregation. We might have taken an institutional example in the contemporary debate over the proposed union of three of the six Methodist Episcopal Church bodies. The plan of merger recognizes a separate, autonomous group of Negro churches within the larger framework of white American Methodism. Autonomy within the Negro group is to be granted; representation in the General Conference is assured; but the line of demarcation between colored and white churches, North and South, East and West, is clearly and sharply drawn. "Let the Negro run his own affairs," plead one group. "Why must the white man always interfere?" From this angle, the proposal for autonomy of the Negro bishopric is a step forward. The Negro is to be permitted to hoe for himself. "But don't let him assume that he can run the Methodist Church," says another group. "The Negro churches are in on this merger on an equal footing with the rest of us; but that does not imply that the old barriers are down. The Negro may be getting increased power and autonomy in his own sphere; but let him not assume that this applies outside his 'proper' sphere." He must confine his hoeing to his own back yard. Two extreme points of view are also injected into the debate from the white caste. One, expressed by the Negrophobe, objects to the whole idea of having Negro churches in the merger at all; and objects, secondly, to giving them any control over their own affairs if they do come into the merger. The only way to keep the Negro in his place is to keep him there! The other, stated by the Negrophile, demands that the Negro churches not only be included in the merger, but that they come into their natural geographic conferences along with the white churches of the same areas, without any distinctions of any kind. They would want the Negroes to have full participation in the whole church rather than increased autonomy in a circumscribed area. With the controversy confusing the white caste, the Negroes within the Methodist Church, North, approach their answers to the problem of the merger with multiplied dissension and uncertainty. "Is it possible that we are to have a voice in affairs only when we have first been put into a special room beyond which our voice will not carry?" ask some. And others reply, "It's better to have a chance to speak out in meeting without fear or favor as we wish, even if that opportunity is limited to our own circle."

Additional examples might be adduced if it were necessary to emphasize the point. One of the dilemmas of segregation for the Negro is that autonomy and freedom are played against isolation and insularity. The Negro seldom gets a clear choice on a single issue.

A second dilemma closely parallels the first, but lies in a different area. The Negro may find an increased opportunity of cultural self-expression and creativity in some segregated field provided he is willing to run the hazard of cultural eccentricity and sterility. The dilemma offers the Negro an opportunity to attempt to make a creative contribution to advancing culture, provided he is ready to withdraw by himself and thereby risk stagnation and irrelevancy. Is it possible that American society will paradoxically accept the Negro and permit him to be integrated culturally in direct proportion as the Negro is most "Negroid" and least "white"? The spirituals and jazz have profoundly affected American culture. In these the Negro is integrated—or is he? It is Toynbee's[5] thesis that self-articulation, self-realization, by an individual or by a minority group, can come only in temporary withdrawal from society, a spiritual declaration of independence. In withdrawal, the minority achieves independence and objectivity to liberate subjective creativity. The new action pattern is hammered out and then offered to society. This "withdrawal-and-return" is the key to creativity. According to this point of view, if the Negro wishes to make a distinctive and valuable contribution to American culture, he must do it by withdrawing from the main stream of American

[5] Arnold J. Toynbee, *A Study of History*, Vol. III.

culture and projecting back into that main stream whatever fresh and creative materials he can construct.

In his thinking on the question, the Negro is, once again, forced to consider the attitudes of the dominant group. The caste system would interpret any withdrawal of the Negro as an acceptance of social distance and the status of inferiority. The counter-effort generated by the caste system pushes and pulls the Negro toward the cultural norms established by the dominant group with terrific concentric force, making eccentricity and nonconformity matters requiring almost superhuman courage and stamina. Experience suggests that the Negro artist or writer can get wide acclaim from the white caste if he interprets what the whites think are "Negroid" materials, that is, if he conforms to the stereotypes. But the popularity of Dunbar is waning; the authentic minstrel show is now an unheard-of thing. And the Negro is asking himself whether the game is worth the candle. The Negro sang the sorrow songs of slavery; but Stephen Foster, white, published them as folk ballads. The Negro of an earlier day developed a simple and effective piety; but Marc Connelly, white, wrote *The Green Pastures* and made the million. The Negro produced jazz and swing music; but the colored band uses the back doors and the freight elevators. The Negro makes his cultural contribution to American music, literature, and art; and he asks himself whether the net effect of that contribution is not the buttressing of the barriers of social distance. By every subtle psychological differentiation of himself from the majority group, the Negro may be increasing the sense of social distance even though there is heightened appreciation from the dominant group. Indeed, the increasing appreciation may possibly come as an expression of relief from the tension of a too-intimate cultural approach.

The reversion of the Negro to specifically "Negroid" themes and modes of expression is in a sense a tacit admission that the Negro is giving up the struggle for acceptance as part of a white world—he is accepting cultural segregation, a symbol of social status as well. So the Negro is impaled on the horns of the dilemma: he cannot make a creatively diverse contribution to the advance of culture unless he is willing to be eccentric and diverse; but if he becomes eccentric and diverse, he runs the risk of being shunted away. He may retreat into his chamber for creative work; but how does he know that the door will open when he wants to come out? And how can he be sure that this society which appears to have such fine contempt for him and his people will by some paradoxical alchemy be moved to accept the gifts he bears? Moreover, as he makes his differentiated contribution, he plays up to the differentiating trends—and to put the matter quite baldly, the Negro artist sometimes wonders whether the privilege of contributing to cultural advance is worth the price of caste he must pay. Are the spirituals worth the sorrow and suffering out of which they were born? And if they are, why should the artist have to pay, rather than the patron?

If the Negro turns to the opposite possibility, he is confronted with a similar quandary. Rather than try to make a distinctive cultural contribution by withdrawal-and-return, suppose the Negro makes his effort to share in the cultural growth and richness of American life by integrating himself as completely as possible in the cultural processes. Here he faces the possibility of the loss of anything distinctive and enriching; he must be prepared to give up the idea of a black culture for the sake of living at peace in an American culture which is almost completely white. Then, living as a black man in a white culture, and yet as an American though black, he is torn between the demands of the two worlds in which he lives. This is, of course, a common experience for him in his daily living, as far as his movements between the segregated and white sections of town are concerned. If the Negro adds to this the further strain of an ideational and psychological transition in the cultural sphere every time he moves from one area to the other, he has by that much increased his burden rather than lightened it.

The particular dilemma of segregation which is most widely

discussed in current literature is the question of a black economy. The Negro wonders whether he cannot gain for himself many of the advantages of economic opportunity which
the caste system now denies him, by using the fact of segregation to develop the economic powers of the segregated
group to the fullest possible extent. He also wonders whether,
as he builds this economic strength behind the walls of segregation, he is not thereby contributing to the inertia of the
social institution. He cannot find full economic opportunity
under the caste system unless he builds that opportunity for
himself within the walls of segregation; and he feels that if
he does build up a satisfactory economic life within the pattern of segregation, by that action he buttresses and strength-
ens the caste separation. Perhaps he looks ahead to a time
when the economic power of the segregated group becomes
strong enough to worry the economic powers of the majority
group; and he wonders whether, at that time, the very strength
of the black economy will be its undoing. He sees his dilemma
as the possibility of economic self-sufficiency through self-
denial with the risk of self-destruction and group frustration.
Very few of the persons thinking and experimenting in this
field are unrealistic enough to think that they can build up
the whole financial and industrial foundation and superstructure of an economic order to parallel that now in existence.
When they speak of a black economy, they usually mean the
development of commercial and business enterprise, largely
in the distributive and service fields, so that the buying
power of the segregated consumer may be used to support
segregated merchants and professional people. It is a "Buy
Black" campaign. Since the Negro lives in segregated areas,
let this grouping of consumers be used as the means of developing a Negro business class, a Negro professional group, Negro
theaters and amusement services, Negro political power,
and Negro property ownership.[6] But to this point of view
immediate retort is made: "A fundamental which Dr. Miller
entirely loses from sight is that the Negro as an American

[6] Cf. Kelly Miller, *op. cit.*, pp. 828-30.

citizen has no choice except to fight segregation to the last ditch. To accept it would be to brand himself as an inferior and to accept permanent impairment of his status as a citizen."[7] To which Dr. Miller gives his answer in equally vehement fashion: "The destiny of the Negro population in large cities is clearly foreshadowed. The Negro is to live and move and have his being in areas apart from the whites. About this it is needless to argue or debate, but merely to observe."[8] And Dr. DuBois adds that this obstinate fact of segregation is a thing not to be theorized about but to be utilized through the fullest possible development of every resource of human ingenuity, so that segregation will in the end defeat itself.[9] Since Negroes are forced together in compact communities of racial contiguity, DuBois would seize upon the lever of segregation to pry the lid off caste. He would use segregated consumers to support black merchants and traders, black dentists and doctors, black lawyers and ministers; and he would use black professional men to build up the strength of the black community. He would permit the Negro to eat in the kitchen only so long as he is forced to eat there—and he would urge the Negro to eat well and get strong while he is there. Less adventuresome, or more serene spirits disagree with DuBois, arguing that his attitude is fat for the fire, and the Negro will be roasted if he feeds the flames too much. So the ball of controversy is hurled back and forth.

One step removed from these foregoing quandaries is another dilemma. It is concerned not with specific proposals for thought and activity, but with the underlying problem in social dynamics of how a minority—any minority—may improve its condition and status. In American society, the Negro makes up one-tenth of the population. The general tendency is for the other nine-tenths to treat him as the tenth man—last in

[7] Herbert J. Seligman, "The Negro Protest against Ghetto Conditions," *Current History*, XXV (March, 1927), 833.

[8] *Op. cit.*, p. 831.

[9] W. E. B. DuBois, "The Segregated Negro World," *The World Tomorrow*, VI (May, 1923), 136-38.

everything which has to do with opportunity and advancement, happiness, and welfare. Philanthropic persons and agencies may soften the blow of discrimination, but the colored person bears the brunt of social injustice. What can he do about it?

This is not merely the problem of a 10 percent minority against a 90 percent majority. If it were that, it would be difficult enough. In addition, two-fifths of this minority group is scattered about through the North and West, mainly in urban centers, but without any cohesive unity for its attack. Piecemeal efforts, sporadic and disconnected, can hardly suffice. The remainder of the Negro population lives in the South. Now, the South itself has its problem as a submerged minority region in the total American scene.[10] The three-fifths of the Negro Americans who make up the 25 percent of the population in the South are thus a minority population group within a submerged or retarded geographical region. The question thus becomes: How can a racial minority which is submerged in a geographical area which is itself depressed, find a footing for advancement? If the Negro attempts to climb by himself, he has no footing. If he attempts to climb with the white, he is rebuffed. Often he is blamed for the predicament of both white and black. Many individual Negroes, seeing that their racial membership is a handicap to opportunity, scramble up and out by some legerdemain of personal achievement[11] leaving the masses of Negroes much as they were, escaping from the dilemma without solving it. It is a problem in social dynamics, a problem of minority group strategy. It is the real problem which underlies the practical dilemmas of the Negro's life. Upon its solution rests his hope of solving the dilemmas.

The urgency of these perplexities is increased by the personality problems involved. The psychogenic hazards of caste continually stalk the pathway of the Negro. What is he to do

---

[10] Cf. H. W. Odum, *Southern Regions of the United States.*
[11] Cf. Paul R. Williams, "I Am a Negro," *American Magazine,* CXXIV (July, 1937), 59 ff.

to be saved? He may attempt to find the antidote for the
poisons of prejudice, to preserve a "stern, calm, unostenta-
tious"[12] exterior in the face of a hostile world. He may learn
to look upon the white man objectively as a fellow-victim of
circumstances, not as an incarnation of evil who wilfully hates
the Negro, but as "a puppet in the hands of a monster tradition,"[13] who has relatively little control over his personal attitudes. The Negro can thus "sympathize with what is obviously the white man's weakness,"[14] and achieve a degree of
inner poise and calm which he maintains precariously in the
face of repeated cumulative emotional and intellectual shock.
This acceptance of stoical outward conformity as the price
to be paid for relative inner peace and poise is a step which
many educated persons of color take. But the psychogenic
risk is tremendous. Only superhuman or superlatively human
strength of character can carry this inner conflict and retain
integration of the ego.

Some resource for the struggle is found in falling back
upon the segregated community itself for emotional support
and integration. The firmness of one's actions and the clarity
of his decisions depend largely upon having some stable
ground for his personal life.[15] The Negro community represents "a little social world or moral order. . . . It is in this
world with its own public opinion and class differentiation
that the Negro acquires status, and controls are maintained."[16]
As a technique of personal survival, the individual Negro
learns to rely upon the assurance of his segregated community
life to restore the damage done to his ego in the unsympathetic contacts of the white world. The Negro church has had
an incalculable effect in rendering this particular service,[17]

[12] Bettie Esther Parham, "How the Conservative Negro Intellectual of the
South Feels about Racial Segregation," *Social Forces,* XIV (December, 1935),
269.
[13] *Ibid.,* p. 270.   [14] *Ibid.,* p. 270.
[15] Kurt Lewin, "Psycho-sociological Problems of a Minority Group," *Character and Personality,* III (March, 1935), 175-87.
[16] E. Franklin Frazier, "The Negro Community: A Cultural Phenomenon,"
Social Forces, VII (March, 1929), 420.
[17] George E. Haynes, "The Church and Negro Progress," *Annals* of the
American Academy, No. 140 (November, 1928), 264-71.

by giving "a social compensation for the restrictions of the segregated, handicapped life of Negroes in America," not only in providing an outlet for Negro talent in an appreciative atmosphere free from the hostility of white observers, but also in restoring the disintegrated personality and rebuilding self-esteem. In part this has been done through faith in postmortem compensation in a future life which will make up for all the ills of this world; but in any case, it has bolstered the faltering ego of many a man, "sustained the morale and lengthened the patience of the Negro."[18] In his church services, the Negro has felt that in the eyes of God he was not a despised, humiliated, and exploited object of the caste system, but that he was a child of God, a man of worth. He has been strengthened to face the world for another week without breaking down. In this, and many other ways, the segregated community has been the "ground" and support of the individual Negro. As long as there is white hostility toward the minority group, the Negro is therefore confronted with the dilemma of how to maintain himself as an integrated and normal personality without falling back upon his group for support—and at the same time, the very fact that the group upon which he must rely is a despised, humiliated, and segregated group with no respectable status in its own right, means that his "ground" is a shifting and insecure foundation. Here is the point at which the whole crushing burden of caste descends upon the head of each individual Negro, while at the same time the ground is cut away from beneath him. No wonder the melodic refrain of one of the sorrow songs is

Keep me from sinking down.

The individual not only needs a group to give him ground on which to stand; he needs what Lewin calls "space for free movement."[19] Both physically and socially, limitations of this freedom are important. The quandary arises from the fact that as long as his environment is generally hostile, the individual acquires this freedom at the risk of security. He faces the dilemma which offers him a choice between security and

[18] *Ibid.*, p. 270.   [19] *Op. cit.*, p. 180.

peace with inferiority, as one alternative, and as the other, relative freedom of movement with the probability of becoming a target. An eagle may soar—but the huntsman's eye is keen. Perhaps the disappointment of this yearning for larger space for free movement, escape from the cage of caste, helps to account for the many spirituals which sing of the coming day of compensation.

>   . . . gwine t' walk *all over* God's Heaven.

THE COLLEGE AND THE NEGRO'S DILEMMAS

Every one of the dilemmas of segregation walks onto the campus of the segregated college when the doors open in September. The segregated college is itself an anomalous expression of the demands of caste, and in its very structure and function it bears the imprint of caste and feels the stresses of segregation.

In the segregated college, the Negro student and teacher find increased autonomy and freedom, oftentimes with facilities for education considerably improved over what they might have obtained by refusing to accept segregated educational offerings; and they possess these goods in the isolated insularity of the segregated institution which is (quite unintentionally, to be sure) ignored by the main stream of American academic life. In the segregated college, the Negro student and teacher may find increased opportunities for cultural self-expression and self-realization; but they run the risk of cultural eccentricity, and (particularly where there is institutional inbreeding) cultural sterility. In the segregated college, the Negro professional worker finds opportunities for employment and advancement which might not be opened to him unless there were separate institutions in which he could teach and work (less than half a dozen Negroes have ever held regular staff appointments in mixed colleges); and at the same time, the Negro educator looks with decided disapproval upon the movement to extend segregation in education beyond the present limits.[20]

[20] Cf. W. A. Robinson, "What Peculiar Organization and Direction Should

The Negro college also shares the problem of how to advance itself and its cause when it cannot find solid ground on which to stand. It is mired down in the poverty of the region —the financial and cultural retardation of the whole area. It dare not advance too rapidly, even if it could, lest it incur the active resentment and hostility of a South which is hypersensitive over its own chronological lag and will not countenance Negro advancement more rapid than its own.

As part of the segregated group, the college shares the feeling of insecurity in the midst of a hostile situation; and it has a peculiar dilemma which is shared by other institutions which the Negro builds up within the framework of caste, namely: the stronger and better the college becomes, the more firmly is the institution of caste fastened upon the segregated group. Every brick added to fine buildings in the Negro college is an additional weight sinking the Negro into the mire of segregation; while at the same time, unless the Negro college does its work superlatively well, the Negro will not be able to cope with the differential handicap of American society. Without the segregated college, the Negro is sunk; and with it, he sinks. If the college attempts to correct this situation by trying to advance the Negro in condition and in status, the barriers of caste are thrown up and the institution may be thrown down.[21] Yet, if the college does not attempt to ad-

Characterize the Education of Negroes?" *Journal of Negro Education,* V (July, 1936), 395-96, for discussion of the resolution of the National Association of Teachers in Colored Schools calling for (a) equality of educational facilities wherever there is segregation now, and (b) no extension of segregation in schools beyond present boundaries. Robinson holds that the employment of Negroes as teachers, principals, professors, and presidents is scant compensation for the acceptance of caste: "Even in the Northern communities where the segregated school does not suffer all the intolerable features of the segregated school in the South, Negroes have come to realize by bitter experience that any apparent advantages such as jobs in the segregated schools or the relief of Negro children from the embarrassment of unsocial attitudes in the mixed schools, are too sorry an exchange for the acceptance of a social principle that forever thwarts their hopes of becoming real Americans." (P. 396.)

[21] Consider the Berea College case, in which the courts ruled that the college charter was subject to revision by legislative act, and therefore the attempt to educate Negroes and whites in the same college—which was the purpose of its founders—was abandoned after nearly half a century of coeducation of the races.

vance the Negro in condition and in status, it becomes part and parcel of the whole plan of segregated institutions, elaborate ritual, illogical laws, and irrational folkways which work to subordinate the Negro and keep him in his place. The dilemmas of segregation are the dilemmas of the segregated college, not merely by virtue of the attendance in it of students from a segregated people, but because the college is itself a focal point at which the several dilemmas of caste converge, and a strategic instrument upon which each of the castes seeks to lay its hand.

The crux of the Negro's attempt to obtain equitable educational opportunity is the separate Negro school. Not only does it permit and encourage gross discrimination, but as an instrument of social policy it connotes and enforces inferior status. The separate Negro school . . . is a symbol of the inferior social, economic, and political status of the Negro in American life in general.[22]

But the separate school for Negroes is an absolute necessity under present conditions of caste differentiation—not merely from the standpoint of the majority group wishing to preserve its integrity and superiority, but equally necessitous from the standpoint of the submerged group wishing to remove its handicaps. "Sympathy, Knowledge, and the Truth, outweigh all that the mixed school can offer."[23]

In presenting these dilemmas as peculiarly the special problem of the segregated college, we are not, of course, denying

---

[22] C. H. Thompson, "Education of the Negro in the United States," *School and Society*, XLII (November 9, 1935), 627.

[23] W. E. B. DuBois, "Does the Negro Need Separate Schools?" *Journal of Negro Education*, IV (July, 1935), 328-36. The context of the quotation is important for preserving the thought of the writer: "Theoretically, the Negro needs neither segregated schools nor mixed schools. What he needs is Education. What he must remember is that there is no magic, either in mixed schools or in segregated schools. A mixed school with poor and unsympathetic teachers, with hostile public opinion, and no teaching concerning black folk, is bad. A segregated school with ignorant placeholders, inadequate equipment, poor salaries, and wretched housing, is equally bad. Other things being equal, the mixed school is the broader, more natural basis for the education of all youth. It gives wider contacts; it inspires greater self-confidence; and suppresses the inferiority complex. But other things seldom are equal, and in that case, Sympathy, Knowledge, and the Truth, outweigh all that the mixed school can offer." (P. 335.)

that the rest of society may have an active concern in the solution of these problems. On the contrary:

TO AMERICA

How will you have us? As we are,
   Or struggling 'neath the load we bear?
Our eyes fixed forward on a star
   Or staring empty in despair?
Rising or falling, men or things,
   With lagging pace or footsteps fleet?
Strong, willing sinews in your wings,
   Or tightening chains about your feet?
                    —JAMES WELDON JOHNSON

TRANSFORMING AND TRANSCENDING CASTE

Whatever attitude the segregated college takes toward the institution of caste, it has a special set of responsibilities connected with the mental health and personality development of its students and staff. These fall into two general classifications: those connected with the problem of transforming the caste system, and those which have to do with the success of the individual member of the minority group in maintaining his own personal integrity in the face of defeat, or of partial achievement.

The cataloguing of dilemmas of caste has made clear the fact that there is no single answer to the problem of how to improve the opportunities of the Negro. Wilkerson[24] states that the submerged group must recognize that either it is permanently submerged, or there will be a period of conflict as the submerged group struggles for release and emergence. "The price of peace is permanent inferiority." He therefore urges that the tactics of conflict be used to force openings, and that after each conflict, the Negro tacticians concentrate on the terms of the compromise which determine the extent of the advance made. The Negro caste must "impel advantageous compromises. . . . The subordinate group can influence the level on which accommodation is made." Therefore he

[24] Doxey A. Wilkerson, "American Caste and the Social Studies Curriculum," *Quarterly Review of Higher Education among Negroes*, V, April, 1937, 67-74.

would have the college teach the attitudes of conflict-for-ad-justment-on-a-higher-level.

Replying to this argument, Wiggins[25] maintains that attitudes are the outgrowth of sociological processes and cannot, therefore, be changed by magic or preaching or exhortation. Instead of attempting to convert the student to a given attitude of conflict for accommodation on a higher level, he would fall back upon the critical analysis of the historical origins of contemporary society, expecting the processes of critical intelligence to bring their own results.

Somewhere on a scale which includes both of these extremes, the segregated college will find its mode of working. It is probable that different colleges will find themselves at different points on the scale of attitudes and that within a given institution, there will be variations. All we are now insisting upon—and this is the conclusion to which we are driven by the cumulative weight of the evidence—is that the college must concern itself directly with the problem of whether caste ought to be transformed; and if it ought, whether it can be; and if it can, how it may be. To have this concern may be to dig the pit of institutional suicide; but to have it and to refuse to express it would be intellectual stupidity and moral hypocrisy. Add this to the list of quandaries facing the segregated college, and consider it a summary statement of one of the two jobs of the college under the caste system.

The other function of the segregated college under the caste system has to do with the abilities of its students and graduates to transcend what is not transformed.

Reference was made in a preceding page to the fact that the young Negro must live in two worlds—the white world which dominates his movements whenever he is outside the segregated district, and the Negro community to which he returns at intervals. This fact makes it necessary that the Negro prepare to live successfully in both of these worlds, that he be a cultural hybrid, and a successful cultural hy-

[25] Forrest Oran Wiggins, *Quarterly Review of Higher Education among Negroes,* V (April, 1937), 77-78.

brid.[26] The precarious and unsettling nature of this dual existence is well calculated to produce instability unless proper psycho-hygienic precautions are followed. The crux of this problem comes in the contrast between the ideal and the real in the experience of the individual. Suppose that in his experience he is able to meet the demands of shifting from the black world to the white as, day by day, he shuttles back and forth. Yet, in both these worlds he is confronted with a reality which comes short of the ideal to which he aspires. And as he works to realize that ideal, he becomes increasingly and painfully conscious of the acute tension between the ideal and the actual. Both the actual and the ideal worlds are real to him,[27] and any warring between the two is a genuine conflict within him, a disintegration of his experience, which may lead to a bifurcation of personality because of inability either to bridge the gap or to sustain the inner tension, or may lead to a psychopathic flight into unreality because of refusal to meet the actual, or may result in complete surrender and disavowal of the ideal because of the pain of the tension of holding to both ideal and real when they are so widely separated in experience, or may lead to the development of abilities of the personality to include both the actual and the ideal in its purview, enduring the tension between the two, and transcending what is not transformed.

One of the functions of the college in this connection is the teaching of the ability to salvage excess ideality.[28] If ideals are high, it is inevitable—absolutely unavoidable—that they are not to be realized in completeness and fullness

[26] Cf. Charles S. Johnson, "The Development of Personality of Students in Segregated Communities," *Quarterly Review of Higher Education among Negroes*, V (April, 1936), 67-71.

[27] "The ideal is more than a repetition in inner image of the actual. It projects in securer and fuller and wider form some good which has been previously experienced in a precarious, accidental, fleeting way." John Dewey, *Human Nature and Conduct*, p. 23.

[28] I am indebted for this insight to T. V. Smith, "Ideals in the Life of Practise," in *Growth and Development: The Basis for Educational Programs*, pp. 119-22.

within the lifetime of the person holding them. Unfulfilled idealism is an inescapable concomitant of high ideals. The man who realizes his ideals, aims low. "No action can fully contain its appropriate ideal."[29] It is the nature of ideals to be ampler than the actions which embody them. While the ideal gives direction and meaning to the action, it also spills over that act, "leaving the actor nostalgic because of the excess of ideality over fulfilment."[30] And it is well that ideals are ampler than the activities which give them body. This excess amplitude of idealism is the guarantee of continued effort, of refusal to rest on the oars, of dissatisfaction with halfway measures and compromise. Without it, partial truth becomes accepted dogma, self-satisfied smugness becomes the substitute for righteousness and justice, and routine technique takes the place of spontaneity and creativity. As Langston Hughes puts it:

> Hold fast to dreams;
>   For when dreams go,
> Life is a barren field
> Frozen with snow.

The threat of personality maldevelopment under this stress between the ideal and the actual emphasizes the job of the college to cultivate in its students and staff the ability to transcend the actual while attempting to realize the ideal in transforming the stuff of life. If the college does not meet this challenge, it has failed in half its job. It turns out graduates who are cynical, beaten, and contented with mediocrity, or who are stupidly self-assertive in an ineffective kind of broadside bravado, and

as between the introverted vices of cynicism, pessimism, and audacity, and the extroverted vices of dogmatism, self-righteousness and insensitivity, I, as an educator, know not which to fear the more. They are

[29] *Ibid.*, p. 119.

[30] *Ibid.* "No dutiful act, I mean to say, ever gives full catharsis to the drive of conscience; no just act ever embodies justice without an embarrassing remainder; and no artistic creation ever fulfills the vision of beauty. 'I beheld in every book in my library,' observes Cabell, 'a human dream badly damaged at birth.'"

all born of the fact that the humblest has higher ideals than the mightiest can exemplify in action.[31]

One important means of maintaining personal integrity in the face of disappointing results from idealistic effort is the achievement of a certain objectivity of attitude about one's own life and the possibility of making one's contribution to civilization. The world was not made in a day; it will not be remade in a week. Institutions and customs have long backward and forward reaches into time. They are changeable, to be sure; and sometimes changes culminate with cataclysmic swiftness. Yet seldom do these changes come as the result of the activities of one person or by virtue of the influence of one life, or within the life span of the particular individual. The lengthened shadow of men of great stature is sometimes cast down the centuries to produce a cumulative change after their lifetimes; but Jesus and Socrates tasted the cup of bitterness at their own deaths. Not even the collective influence of a larger group appears to produce fundamental changes in customs and institutions in a short span of years. The experience of democratic societies founded on political or military revolution illustrates the manner in which a surface change is deceivingly sweeping, and only the glacial motion of the generations can fulfill the expectations of the revolutionists. It is well for the individual to know this.

It is well for the individual to know it, because the mores are not merely the summation of private attitudes of individuals. They are also unique functions of group relationships. They are changeable also; but they have tremendous qualities of inertia and vitality in themselves. Customs and traditions maintain their hold on men and nations long after the circumstances which brought them into being have been altered or removed. The changing of social patterns comes slowly, but irregularly; and the irregularity of movement gives occasional effects of suddenness. While the launching of the iceberg may give a startling impression of sudden mobility, the glacier's movement in the preceding decades or

[31] *Ibid.*, p. 120.

generations may have been almost imperceptible. Yet it was the slow movement of the generations which did actually launch the iceberg. The individual needs to know this.

He needs to know it because inordinate and unrealistic ambition, however idealistic and altruistic, if not grounded in a genuine understanding of the nature of social movement, and if not seasoned with an appreciation of the "tragic sense of life," not merely kills the individual but also kills his influence. Only the serene spirit which looks beyond tragedy and sees an increasing purpose, and then actively and persistently and indefatigably coöperates with that purpose, can survive the harsh disappointments and the immediate defeats of the idealistic venture.

If these sentiments hold good for the representative white college student, they apply with multiplied force to the Negro college student. Divided between two actual worlds, white and black, and torn between two real worlds, actual and ideal, inspired by hope born of great fear and disappointment, rooting his pessimism in deeper optimism, the young Negro looks to his college for help in meeting the tremendous tensions of life in a caste-dominated society. What can his college do? Was it on the academic anvil of the old Atlanta University that James Weldon Johnson hammered out his credo?

I will not allow one prejudiced person or one million or one hundred million to blight my life. I will not let prejudice or any of its attendant humiliations and injustices bear me down to spiritual defeat. My inner life is mine, and I shall defend and maintain its integrity against all the powers of hell.

VIII

ACHILLES HAD A HEEL

What matters most to the person who has been subjected to racial discrimination resides in his consciousness, becomes incorporated in his personality-pattern. Once there as personality ingredient this element continues to condition all future conduct. Re-education of attitudes is, therefore, the point of departure for those who desire to see themselves reasonably and rationally as members of racial groups.

—EDUARD C. LINDEMAN

FROM the standpoint of the segregated college, the analysis of American society is of greatest importance at the point where light is shed on the question of how and where to begin work to crack the crust of caste. Not alone for the sake of conquering caste, but even more because of .the larger opportunity for free and creative living for both races which will be possible in an America without caste, the question of where to begin work to make caste irrelevant is of major importance. Does this contemporary Achilles have a heel of vulnerability?

SOCIAL ATTITUDES AND SOCIAL REDIRECTION

The analysis of Chapters Two to Seven has shown that as social attitudes develop, they become an integral part of the personalities or characters of the individuals who share in the caste-and-class system, and, further, that as these attitudes develop they help to shape the system in which they grow. The crucial question now becomes: Is it possible, through the use of intelligence and forethought, to influence the development of the caste system and of the attitudes which are nurtured in it, so that the system and its attitudinal concomitants are radically altered?

Consider, for illustrative purposes, the case of the mulatto: how an attitude of the dominant caste, based on the assumption that the mulatto *must* be midway between the two castes in abilities, gave to the mulatto an intermediary status, which in turn tended to afford the very opportunities which would bring out and develop the latent abilities to justify the assumption which projected the development. In this case, the notion operated to affect personality development, and to effect a stratification of caste based on the combination of the notion itself and the personalities developed under the aegis of the notion. It would appear that an attitude which was in general conformity with the caste system played a decisive part in shaping social configuration and individual psychological patterns. Is it possible that attitudes which are *not* in general conformity with the basic caste-class social pattern may play a directive part in modifying the course of events?

Our first answer is only a partial one. It is possible to trace significant modifications in the overt expression of race attitudes. The lynching curve, for example, has gradually declined over the years (see Appendix A), from a known high of 153 in 1892 (there are no accurate statistics for the earlier years of the Reconstruction period when the annual lynchings sometimes ran into four figures) to a known low of eight in 1929, 1932, and 1937. Part of the decline in lynchings over the years is probably due to an easing of tension as the Negro caste relinquished its active campaign for equal rights and suffrage, and as the Jim Crow pattern of social control restored the confidence of the white caste in its own powers and calmed its fears. Part of the decline is also probably due to the fact that improved means of communication focus more effectively a vehement and growing anti-lynching opinion among Southern whites, as in the publicity given to the activities of the League of Southern Women against Lynching. Part of the decline is probably due to the growth of a national public opinion which condemns lynchings. Part of the decline may also be due to a slight improvement in the economic well-being of the lowest class of whites; for, since lynchings tend to occur most frequently in the poorer counties of the lynching states, a long-term actual improvement of the economic condition of these poverty-ridden areas should make possible a decline in the number of emotional outbreaks, even though the established social pattern lived on after the economic tension has been somewhat eased. Dr. Raper, a professor in one of the South's leading colleges for white women, points out that lynchings come, in reality, not so much from crimes committed by Negroes as from the state of mind of white people.[1] As the state of mind changes, then, it ought to be possible to discover changes in overt expression of racial attitudes, and to this change in attitude we must ascribe part of the decline in the lynching curve.

As to whether fundamental changes in the basic social patterns of race relations can be expected, no final answer can be given in advance of the experience of actually trying to make such change. It is not enough to point to other parts of the globe, like Hawaii, Brazil, Switzerland, Jamaica, Greenland, *et al.*, in which the American form of caste demarcation does not prevail. For the United States, the questions are whether this particular caste-divided society can be altered, with a subsidiary consideration of whether it ought to be if it could.

Consider the latter of these questions first. Perhaps the best recent formulation of the point of view that the caste system ought to be maintained inviolate is that given by Sir Arthur Keith[2] in his plea that race prejudice is not only natural but highly desirable. Hypothesizing a body-brain dualism, he deduces a duality in the evolution of the two. And on the basis of this hypothesis, he projects his interpretation of primitive man into the origins of the evolutionary process which has produced modern man. "Inside man's brain is another machinery—which automatically plays the part of breeder. This machinery is represented by what may be called tribal mentality."[3] This tribal mentality, persisting through the ages of evolution, is present in an attenuated but effective form in modern man, and is the basis of tribal affinity as evidenced in national and racial loyalties, as well as the basis of tribal antipathy as evidenced by national and racial antagonisms. Since race prejudice has played a part in the evolution of man since prehistoric times, "In the modern world we must listen to the voice of Nature. Under the control of reason, prejudice has to be given a place in the regulation

[1] See Appendix A.
[2] Sir Arthur Keith, *Place of Prejudice in Modern Civilization.*
[3] *Ibid.,* p. 13.

of human affairs."[4] Quite apart from the question of ultimate value judgments upon which the choice between a caste-divided and nondivided society will be made, it is interesting to see the pseudo-scientific artifices to which an anthropologist of Keith's standing is driven in the effort to defend the irrationalities of race prejudice. The antiquated and outmoded "faculty" psychology on which Keith is forced to rest his argument scarcely carries so great weight. Granted his hypotheses, his argument may be justified logically; but the hypotheses are themselves fathered by the wish to substantiate his preconceptions as apparent conclusions. If the case in favor of the caste system is to have a basis in science or in logic, it is not to be found here; but rather, in the relatively subjective area of value judgments. There is no objective, *a priori* basis on which to rest the case in favor of the caste system.

On the other hand (and this is the other point mentioned above), there is *a priori* expectation that changes can be made in a caste-divided society.[5] Not that these changes are inevitable, or easily possible—but rather that they are not impossible, is the hypothesis which we appear justified in advancing, on the following grounds:

1. The present caste system is itself the product of a proc-

[4] *Ibid.*, p. 55.
[5] "Race prejudice cannot only be mitigated, it can disappear. In many cases it has entirely disappeared and in other situations it is obviously increasing." It is modified very slowly. "The subjective emotions are only half, the other half being the external conditions and organized regulations. . . . There is, therefore, a double problem: the one psychological, the other institutional. . . . This is the sense in which race prejudice is appropriately called a natural phenomenon. It changes slowly, but it does change. . . . But to call race prejudice a natural phenomenon is not to assume that it should be endured or accepted. If we must call race prejudice natural we must also admit suicide, murder, and automobile accidents into the same class." E. Faris, "The Natural History of Race Prejudice," in *Ebony and Topaz.*
    While racial antagonisms have a natural history and are widespread, they are not instinctive and they can and do disappear. "Not only may physical circumstances change, but human nature itself changes. Prejudices cannot be argued away, but an investigation of the fundamental processes involved can contribute to an understanding of them as simple social phenomena, and, perhaps, provide a rational basis and point of view for new experiences." W. D. Weatherford and C. S. Johnson, *Race Relations,* p. 63.

ess of developmental change through which it has come to its present stage. It is not "God-given," but man-made—man-made in the sense that it is produced through the working of the social process in which individuals and groups constantly interact through social institutions.

2. A fundamental change in the basic configuration of the caste relationship will be possible only if a much more radical change is made in the existing psychological patterns which help to determine the actions of men when confronted with particular sets of conditions. The point of greatest plasticity is this point of individual social attitudes. "Social changes begin with changes in the conditioned attitudes of individuals. Attitudes change first, and thus the changing attitudes of individuals in any community is a sort of barometer, indicative of changes that will presently take place in social institutions and mores."[6]

3. Much more thoroughgoing differences in social attitudes than changes in race attitudes have been brought about through social conditioning, notably, the modifications in attributes of personality associated with sex. Mead has shown that "the personalities of the two sexes are socially produced."[7]

4. Sherif[8] has also shown the decisive part played by social norms, that is, by the stereotypes built up by a group of individuals to direct and control their common experience. These norms enter into the directing of the social process in a peculiarly effective, almost tyrannical manner, shaping men and events. Changes in these social norms guide changes in individual attitudes.

5. Psychological research discloses instances in which

[6] Robert E. Park, "Human Nature, Attitudes, and the Mores," in *Social Attitudes,* pp. 42-43.

[7] Margaret Mead, *Sex and Temperament in Three Primitive Societies,* p. 310. "Many, if not all, of the personality traits which we have called masculine or feminine are as lightly linked to sex as are the clothing, the manners, and the form of headdress that a society at a given time assigns to either sex. . . . We are forced to conclude that human nature is almost unbelievably malleable, responding accurately and contrastingly to contrasting cultural conditions." (P. 280.)

[8] M. Sherif, *The Psychology of Social Norms,* p. 203.

changes in the conditions of life have altered not merely such functional expression of the self as sex characteristics or race attitudes, but even such stubbornly "native" factors as the level of intellectual performance. Peterson, Arlitt, Burks, Freeman *et al.*, Klineberg, McAlpin, and Strong[9] furnish evidence to warrant the hypothesis that the level of intellectual attainment is vitally affected by environmental factors. Is it too much to hypothesize the possibility that less stubborn attributes of personality, such as race attitudes, may likewise be affected, at least in part, by proper guidance of social processes? Certainly, until extended experimentation has been made in the field, we may at least leave open the possibility of favorable results. The educator, however, cannot wait until research has brought in all the evidence. He can only make the best possible guess in the light of what we now know, project his program in the light of that knowledge in the direction of that guess, and watch his results.

The remaking of society demands the remaking of psychological patterns. The interplay of social forces impinging upon individuals, as influenced by conscious intelligent effort, in part determines what the impact of these social forces upon the individuals shall be. Certainly, in a day when the forces of racial bigotry are able to manipulate social processes to produce the attitudinal patterns conducive to the

[9] Joseph Peterson, "A Comparison of the Abilities of White and Colored Children," Comparative Psychological Monographs, Vol. I, Series 5, July, 1923.

A. H. Arlitt, "On the Need of Caution in Establishing Race Norms," *Journal of Applied Psychology*, V (1921), 179-83.

R. S. Burks, "Relative Influence of Nature and Nurture upon Mental Development: A Comparative Study of Foster-Parents-Foster-Child Resemblance and True-Parent-True-Child Resemblance," 27th *Yearbook* of the National Society for the Study of Education (1928), pp. 103-218.

Frank Freeman, *et al.*, "The Influence of Environment upon the Intelligence, School Achievement, and Conduct of Foster Children," 27th *Yearbook* of the National Society for the Study of Education (1928), pp. 103-218.

Otto Klineberg, "An Experimental Study of 'Speed' and Other Factors in 'Racial' Differences," *Archives of Psychology*, No. 93 (1928).

Alice McAlpin, "Changes in the I. Q. of Negro Children," *Journal of Negro Education*, I (April, 1932), 44-48.

A. C. Strong, "350 White and Colored Children Measured by the Binet-Simon Measuring Scale of Intelligence," *Pedagogical Seminary*, XX (December, 1913), 485-515.

success of the dogmas of Aryanism, we should not be too greatly inhibited in making the effort to direct social processes in directions which appear to the unjaundiced eye to be somewhat more desirable. Time alone can give the verdict as to whether the effort will be crowned with greater or lesser success. We can only say that there is no *a priori* argument against it. We are deterred only by the extreme difficulty of the undertaking.

IX

DETOURS AND DEAD ENDS
IN NEGRO EDUCATION

. . . this would have its positive value and it would have its negative value. While the negro child is interested in his own matters he will not be incited to wish for the white man's conditions of life or for his nature.

—H. W. ODUM (in 1910)

THE journey of Negro education down the road of progress toward self-realization in American democracy has not been uninterrupted. Detour signs have sometimes been posted by friends to warn of a bad spot ahead; and other side trips, marked by hands not so friendly, have sometimes diverted traffic into a cul-de-sac. In this chapter we shall examine a few representative ideas of Negro education which have been proposed from time to time, and which in one way or another have functioned as detours or dead-end streets.

OPPOSITION TO EDUCATION OF WOMEN PARALLELS OPPOSITION TO EDUCATION OF NEGROES

Perspective for the examination of the opposition to Negro education may be gained from a glance at the strikingly similar opposition to the education of women which characterized American educational thinking during the past century. The education of women, both in segregated colleges for women and in coeducational colleges with men, is so genuinely accepted as a part of the American educational structure today that it is difficult to follow with credulity the story of tl.e subterfuges and devices used to oppose the movement a generation or two ago. At almost every point along the line of progress, arguments have been thrown in its path and excuses used to lead it astray, which arguments and excuses have an interesting and instructive parallel in the history of Negro education. Practically every timeworn and moss-covered notion which has been brought out for use against the education of Negroes has also been used to oppose the education of women.[1]

The first argument used against the education of women

[1] Willystine Goodsell, *The Education of Women,* is the chief reference for this summary of the opposition to the education of women.

was the contention that there is a fundamental, inherited, biologically determined difference in temperament between the sexes which means that different kinds of education should be given to each. Woman is "anabolic rather than katabolic." She "normally represents childhood and youth in the full meridian of its glory in all her dimensions and nature," so that to educate her away from her true nature is to destroy the winsomeness of her childlike personality without giving her the strength of the male she is trying to imitate.[2] Women must therefore be kept in the sphere "where the blind worship of mere mental illumination has no place." It is a grave tactical mistake to encourage women to get out of their proper sphere.

Secondly, there is an inescapable inferiority of women to men in intellectual capacity, so that "women should be educated far more in body and less in mind," lest by education we should "spoil a good mother to make a poor grammarian." (This argument, of course, was elaborated long before the day of the modern intercollegiate athletic craze which dares to educate the masculine student in body far more than in mind, leaving the intellectual arena to the "sissy" and the "coed.") This intellectual superiority of men is a fixed, immutable fact, and "what has been decided among prehistoric protozoa cannot be annulled by any act of parliament."[3]

Thirdly, if women are to be educated, contrary to all the indications that such education will be a catastrophic event, then there must be adaptations of the curriculum to meet the differences in temperament and type. A leading principle should be "to keep the purely mental back and by every method to bring intuitions to the front; appeals to tact and taste should be incessant; a purely intellectual man is no doubt biologically a deformity, but a purely intellectual woman is far more so." Therefore, women should study nature, with emphasis on the "poetic and mythic factors," art, literature,

[2] Cf. *ibid.*, Ch. III; and for opposite point of view adequately supported, cf. Margaret Mead, *Sex and Temperament in Three Primitive Societies.*

[3] Goodsell, *op. cit.*, Ch. III, as also for quotations of next paragraph.

history "with the biographical element very prominent
throughout, with plenty of stories of heroes of virtue, acts
of valor and tales of saintly lives." But metaphysics, the
theory of knowledge and logic should have a minor place,
and physics and chemistry should be "kept to the elementary
stages." Further, "domesticity" should be "taught by example" so that it persists as the dominating ideal throughout
girlhood and young womanhood, blotting out the possibility
of a career illusion.

Fourthly, the demands of society upon the sexes differ, so
that education should be adapted to adjust woman to her
peculiar social rôle of homemaker and consumer. "The manly
economic ideal is the effective direction of production; the
womanly ideal is the beneficent ordering of consumption."[4]
This differentiation is "grounded in an eternal distinction of
nature which runs infinitely deeper than any question of
merely formal right." Therefore, in education, as in industry
and politics,

our aim henceforth should not be toward a stupid equality, with interchange of imitated functions, but toward differentiation—giving as far
as possible the direction and control of economic production to strong
and forceful men, and the superintendence and ministry of consumption
to wise and gentle women; giving for the most part the hard, dry task
of scholarly investigation and formulation to the absorbing and pro-
tracted toil of men, and the appreciation of results and the impartation
of established knowledge to the quick wits of women; giving strife and
turmoil, the compromise and diplomacy of politics to the firm will and
sound judgment of men, and the things that make a country worth
dying for to the warm hearts of women.

With an education designed to fit the sexes for their respective social rôles, a minimum of harm will be done through the
education of women, if, in spite of everything, some kind
of education must be offered to them.

Fifthly, vocational opportunities determine the fact that
it is a "waste of time and energy to fit women for many kinds
of work which can only be performed by men." "What a
woman needs to know and to do in order to meet the respon-

[4] Remainder of quotations, *ibid.*, Ch. IV.

sibilities that come to her in life is the basic element in determining what her education shall be." Since three-fourths of the women of the nation eventually become homemakers, the education of women should be concerned less and less with a multitude of things which have been injected into the curricula of women's colleges to give general "cultural education," and should emphasize more and more the things necessary to good homemaking, e.g., household arts, furniture, decoration, cooking, sewing, child training, and the like.

Sixthly, there are sex differences in mental traits which may not imply inequality, but which do establish an immutable barrier to coeducation or equality and similarity of education. For many years this was an established and uncontradicted assertion: "To aim by means of education and pursuits in life to assimilate the female to the male mind might well be pronounced as unwise and fruitless a labor as it would be to strive to assimilate the female to the male body by means of the same kind of physical training and by the adoption of the same pursuits." It is not assimilation leading to flat uniformity, but cultural variety leading to richness and diffusion, toward which we should aim; and biological necessity in this instance reënforces sociological desirability.

Here, then, are six arguments against the education of women: (1) biologically determined differences in temperament and (2) inherited inferiority in mental ability make the education of women beyond the elementary stages a dubious affair. But if they must be educated, then let the curriculum be designed especially for the needs of women as indicated in (3) the preponderance of intuition rather than reason in feminine psychological processes; in (4) the social demands that women restrict themselves to the arts of graceful consumption rather than invading the masculine areas of production and distribution; and (5) the actual fact that three-fourths of the women do become homemakers, so that education should fit them for continuance in their place. And if women, with their defense complexes aroused, object that they do not want to be given this special education designed to fit them for a peculiar place in society, then (6) it must be admitted that the whole idea of educating the two sexes in the same manner implies an effort to assimilate the two sexes, making them physiologically as well as psychologically alike, which is patently absurd and therefore explodes the whole affair.

As will become clear in the remainder of this chapter, if the word "Negro" be substituted for "woman," and "white" be inserted instead of "man," in the foregoing discussion, the whole description will conform with astounding accuracy to the arguments advanced against the education of Negroes. And, just as in the case of the education of women, one of the results of the debate was the drawing of a false dichotomy between vocational and cultural education, with an extraneous debate as to which should be offered to women, so, too, it has happened in the education of Negroes. What we have, then, is not an isolated instance of careful thinking and reasoning in the light of a particular situation; but rather, the striking similarity of the two patterns leads us to believe that both are examples of the rationalization of a dominant group, opposing the intrusion of a submerged group which is struggling for emergence on a new level, implying a new social status. Reduced to their least common denominator, the arguments against the education of women are summed up in the shibboleth, "Woman's place is in the home." The idea of place, status in society, is the controlling concept.

This same idea of place, status, is the controlling concept in the debate on Negro education. Not always expressed, it is nearly always implied; and it is so commonly the accepted basis for the ultimate decision that persons who enter into the discussion almost automatically impute to their opponents on any specific question an added opposition on the underlying question of caste. In at least five principal areas, the education of Negroes has been actively opposed, or led astray, or otherwise hindered in its onward march.

DETOUR NUMBER ONE

A system of segregated education postulated on assumed inferiority in intellectual capacity or educability.—The idea that the Negro is innately inferior to the white in intellectual capacity has dominated the thinking of educators and pseudo-scientists who have discussed the problems of Negro education; and only in recent years has scientific evidence begun to accumulate to the point where it begins to be possible to shift the discussion away from the preconceived notion of innate inferiority to the objective basis of scientifically determined fact. A quarter century ago, Odum gave a fairly accurate interpretation of the prevailing attitude when he wrote:

Text books are needed which are especially adapted in the negro *mind*, texts based on the most accurate and sympathetic knowledge of the characteristics of the Negro, which comprehend the peculiar needs of the negro children, which are carefully planned and graded to teach the things fundamental in their proper education. . . . But if any such results are to be hoped for, they must be obtained before the pupil goes beyond fourteen years of age; here the physical brain in the Negro reaches its maturity, and nearly all that can be done for a generation must be done by methods suited to children.[5]

This statement is by no means an isolated expression of the opinion of one man. In this instance, for example, it merely reiterates one of the resolutions passed by the Southern Educational Association in its 1907 meeting:

On account of economic and psychological differences in the two races, we believe that there should be a difference in courses of study and methods of teaching, and that there should be such an adjustment of school curricula as shall meet the evident needs of negro youth.[6]

Perhaps the most widely quoted monograph in this field was Brigham's *A Study of American Intelligence*, published by the Princeton University Press in 1923. This famous study of the army Alpha tests gave an apparently scientific sanction to the myth of Nordic superiority, listing all the races of men

[5] H. W. Odum, *Social and Mental Traits of the Negro*, p. 48. Author's own italics.

[6] Quoted in H. P. Douglass, *Christian Reconstruction in the South*, p. 297.

in order of their intelligence as revealed by the army tests. It became a fighting document for the Ku Klux Klan, and is still widely cited as an unimpeachable authority. Bagley's[7] answer, in addition to four major sources of error in the study itself (the assumption that the army tests were an accurate index of native intelligence, the assumption that they were fairly administered, the assumption that the representatives of the national and racial groups involved were typical of the groups from which they came, and the assumption that environmental factors have nothing to do with performance on intelligence tests), showed that Brigham's analysis was more nearly a measure of educational discrepancies than of any other single factor because the scores of the several national groups on the army tests had a positive correlation of .91 with the educational systems prevailing in the several countries of origin; and that Brigham's analysis was likewise more nearly an index of educational discrepancies as between white and colored groups in the United States than an index of comparative mental abilities, since the literate Negroes from Illinois "achieved a median score above the median scores of the literate whites from nine Southern States." Prior to this exchange of ideas between Brigham and Bagley, much of the discussion of comparative mental abilities had proceeded on a plane of controversy and assertion, with an occasional excursion into anthropology or psychology for corroborative evidence in support of the assertions of white superiority.

The literature of the subject of race differences in mentality today would fill a respectable library.[8] For the purposes of the educator, the implications of the investigation as it stands today are best summed up in the words of Klineberg:

The general conclusion can be only that the case for psychological race differences has never been proved. . . . The general conclusion of this book is that there is no scientific proof of racial differences in mentality. This does not necessarily mean that there are no such differences. It

[7] William C. Bagley, "The Army Tests and the Pro-Nordic Propaganda," *Educational Review*, LXVII (April, 1924), 179-87.
[8] See Appendix B.

may be that at some future time, and with the aid of techniques as yet undiscovered, differences may be demonstrated. In the present stage of our knowledge, however, we have no right to assume that they exist. There is no reason, therefore, to treat two people differently because they differ in their physical type. There is no justification for denying a Negro a job or an education because he is a Negro. No one has been able to demonstrate that ability is correlated with skin color or head shape or any of the anatomical characteristics used to classify races.[9]

As far as the educator in America is concerned, there is today absolutely no reason at all for supposing that a separate kind of education must be given to Negroes because of alleged intellectual inferiorities. That this is rapidly becoming the accepted judgment of intelligent whites in all parts of the nation is suggested by Odum's argument (a quarter of a century after the publication of *Social and Mental Traits of the Negro*) that the race situation in the South is increasingly dynamic and plastic, particularly because of "the general conclusion of the psychologists, sociologists, and anthropologists that evidence of inferior and superior races does not justify the world's previous appraisal and action to races."[10] With an air of finality and certainty, Odum in 1936 characterizes as a "tragedy of error" the false premises on which were projected the assumptions of race superiority of whites over Negroes and the notion that "races were inherently different rather than group products of differentials due to the cumulative power of regional and cultural conditioning."[11] In 1930, he says, "the picture was such as to justify the conclusion that, if the Negro be given a fair opportunity with his remarkable powers of adaptation and his attractive per-

[9] Otto Klineberg, *Race Differences*, pp. 343, 345.
[10] H. W. Odum, *Southern Regions of the United States*, p. 479. I have felt free to quote the earlier statements of Odum which contrast sharply with this more recent attitude, because he has now explicitly modified his earlier statement and one does no injustice to an individual or a group by thus indicating the direction of growth. While it would not have been difficult to get much more extreme statements of the earlier attitudes of opposition, I preferred to quote the moderate formulations of Odum as "classical examples," with the knowledge that he represents much that is best in the new South which is steadily moving away from its earlier prejudices, often expressly repudiating them, as in this case.
[11] *Ibid.*, p. 483.

sonality, he would become one of the most important of the basic elements of American culture."[12] It will be time enough to consider curricular adaptations and refinements of teaching method to meet inferior educability when it has been demonstrated that such inferiority exists. In the meantime (and, it appears, for a good long time to come) there will be nothing but good to come from the effort to provide the very best educational opportunities for all of the children of the nation without reference to race. The Negro child should not be given an education any better than that provided for his white neighbor, as some overweening sentimentalists would urge, saying that if the Negro is "not quite as bright" as the white, that is all the more reason for giving him a better education! But rather, if all the children everywhere are given first-rate educational opportunities, in the course of several generations we shall be able to see, with a little less racial myopia, what the actual facts of comparative mental abilities are.

DETOUR NUMBER TWO

A system of "moral education" postulated on assumed or alleged "moral" inadequacies of the race.—Second in importance only to the theory of racial inferiority in mental capacities and educability, and second to none in absurdity, is the notion that the Negro is a morally inferior being, made so by biological inheritance. The corollary derived from this second notion is that Negroes should be given a particular kind of "moral" education to fit them for life in civilized, white, "moral" society.

One of the difficulties we face in making an impartial and fair analysis of this attitude is that its actual force as an operative opinion controlling the trend of educational and social affairs is far greater than a casual reading of current literature on the subject would indicate. Perhaps it is fair to say that the vanguard of social thinkers in the South have

[12] *Ibid.,* p. 479.

abandoned the notion,[13] with the consequence that it is not
frequently written about in educational and sociological trea-
tises; but that the notion is so firmly fixed in the minds of the
masses of Southern whites, and not merely among lower-class
whites, that it is a vitally operative notion at the present time.
It is always dangerous to generalize from personal experience; but there are times when the cumulative experience of
casual personal contacts is a more adequate index of the
actual state of mind of a region than the more carefully
guarded and qualified statements which appear in print for
public perusal. In private conversation, men are likely to say
what they genuinely feel, and to express their dominant
thoughts. It is, therefore, of some significance that the writer
notices that in at least three-quarters of his initial contacts
with white Southerners, two questions are raised: What is
the I. Q. of the Negro college student? Is it not true that
the Negro has marked moral deficiencies, as measured by the
standards of American society? We have just discussed the
first of these notions. The widespread prevalence of the second notion, both in the North and in the South, suggests that
it may play a part as a controlling idea in shaping the kind
of educational opportunities offered to Negroes. On the basis
of such experience, therefore, we feel justified in going back
a quarter of a century for explicit statements of the idea
which, as an illustration of cultural lag, still plays a determining part in shaping the opportunities for the Negro even
though it may have been in large part abandoned by the
more forward-looking thinkers and writers.

The notion of moral inferiority of Negroes was given
classic expression in H. W. Odum's *Social and Mental Traits
of the Negro*.[14] As a pioneering attempt to introduce the

---

[13] Although it keeps cropping up in one form or another. Instance the argument that Negroes ought not to go to the Northern colleges because "the white
institution of higher learning being primarily devoted to intellectual work, the
Negro student who might need moralization as seriously or perhaps more
seriously than intellectualization would find himself at a disadvantage and
later an ineffective leader to his race." G. C. Sumner, "Morale and the Negro
College," *Educational Review*, LXXIII (March, 1927), 168-72.
[14] See also F. L. Hoffman, *Race Traits and Tendencies of the American
Negro*.

concept of impartial sociological investigation into facts about the Negro, written in the scientific spirit of open-minded inquiry, the book marks a milestone in the development of Southern sociology. It is in no sense an attack upon the school of thought in which Odum is a contemporary leader, to go back a quarter of a century to see the earlier ideas they held, many of which are now expressly corrected in later writings.[15] Characterizing that earlier period, Odum has recently written:

It came to pass, therefore, that the South was a puzzled South in the first third of the twentieth century, contemplating its plight, in so far as it ever did or could contemplate fully. It was as if there were fleeting moments of a first tragic consciousness that nowhere in all its borders and among its millions of black men and women had one ever had a fair chance to develop to full capacity. Conditioned by white environment, conditioned by his own limited environment, there was never an opportunity for natural development. . . . And equally startling was the barefaced reality that nowhere, perhaps, was there a white person who had an untrammelled freedom to develop, free from racial prejudice or imposed conditioning.[16]

We turn, then, to Odum's classical statement of the widely held notion that the Negro is possessed of peculiar, and inferior, moral traits.

The characteristics of the race of Negroes according to *Social and Mental Traits of the Negro* are:

. . . no home consciousness or love of home, . . . no pride of ancestry, . . . few ideals and perhaps no lasting adherence to an aspiration toward real worth. He has little conception of the meaning of virtue, truth, honor, manhood integrity. He is shiftless, untidy, and indolent; he would live "coolly in the shadow of his skin." The migratory, or roving tendency seems to be a natural one to him, perhaps an outcome of an easygoing indolence seeking freedom to indulge itself and seeking to avoid all circumstances which would tend to restrict its freedom. The Negro shirks details and difficult tasks. . . . The Negro is improvident and extravagant; lazy rather than industrious, faithful in the performance

---

[15] Odum in 1925 wrote, "What man of distinction does not blush to think of the youthful statements made, or early convictions for which he has proclaimed himself willing to make the great sacrifice, or make a fool of himself generally?" *Southern Pioneers,* p. 9.
[16] H. W. Odum, *An American Epoch,* p. 267.

of certain duties, without vindictiveness, he yet has a reasonable amount of physical endurance. But he lacks initiative; he is often dishonest and untruthful. He is over-religious and superstitious. The Negro suspects his own race and the white race as well; his mind does not conceive of faith in humanity—he does not comprehend it.[17]

Having posited this picture of the Negro, it was inevitable that persons accepting it should expect the Negro to be socially acceptable only when so educated as to correct these alleged faults; and if educated some other way, the Negro was expected to exhibit the faults in a perverted and exaggerated form. Thus,

The young educated Negroes are not a force for good in the community, but for evil. The Negro quickly outgrows the influence and control of his instructors; especially has this been noted in cases where the whites have taught them. . . . They sneer at the idea of work. They imitate the whites and believe themselves thereby similar to them. . . . They have not rejected vicious practices in their own lives nor condemned them in theory. . . . It is clear that their moral natures are hopelessly perverted. . . . The Negro schools taught under present conditions have not produced the desired results.[18]

Alleged "moral irresponsibility," principally shiftlessness and sex promiscuity, with attendant personal habits and group mores, were thus used as a kind of frame of reference within which to construct the notion of what would be an education appropriate for this inferior people.

Such a notion dies hard, particularly because it feeds the ego of the dominant group who propose it. Indeed, preached loudly enough and asserted over a long enough period of time, it gains currency among the subordinate group as well. The bogey of racial irresponsibility, conjured up out of the nightmare of Reconstruction and embellished with the fertile imagination of back-fence gossip and old wives' tales, continues to have a popular hold upon the masses of people long after respectable intellectual circles have relegated it to the limbo of erroneous superstitions. And, occasionally, the popular idea is laid hold upon by an intellectual who formulates

[17] *Op. cit.,* p. 39.
[18] *Ibid.,* pp. 41-42.

a sophisticated rationalization for it and seriously proposes it once again. Thus, Sumner[19] argues for a special kind of educational opportunity for Negroes on "moral" grounds.

Since individuals as well as races find themselves today at unequal stages of cultural evolution, it of necessity follows that the institution of equal education for all individuals or races is bound to result either in a serious retardation of cultural progress for those which have already attained a higher level of civilization or else in the too rapid advancement of those of a lower cultural level. The pragmatic way out of such a dilemma is apparently a system of unequal education. Thus for the vanguard of civilization there must be provided an education commensurate with its cultural status; for the rearguard an education likewise commensurate with its status.[20]

The thirteen objectives of the Negro part of this "system of unequal education" as Sumner proposes them, would be: (1) physical well-being; (2) simplicity in living; (3) "a reverence and belief in the reality of a higher power ever present to assist one in a righteous cause"; (4) "fondness for literature, art, and music of a cultural trend"; (5) industriousness; (6) contempt for loud talking and laughing, and for public ostentation and swaggering in trains, street cars, and other public places; (7) thrift; (8) honesty and absolute trustworthiness; (9) courteousness and friendliness; (10) "respect for hard-won sexual morality"; (11) race pride; (12) contempt for gossip and back-biting and chattering; (13) punctuality. The methods for obtaining these objectives are threefold: (1) rigorous discipline by parents and teachers; (2) compulsory courses in ethics "in all Negro schools"; (3) religion—"To a large extent the dynamic influence which morality had in the life of primitive man came from religion. Hence the paramount duty devolving upon the Negro church is that of giving divine sanction to the moral law."[21]

Sumner was stirred to make his proposal in 1926 because,

[19] G. C. Sumner, "A Philosophy of Negro Education," *Educational Review*, LXXI (January, 1926), 42-45.

[20] *Ibid.*, p. 42.

[21] *Ibid.*, p. 45.

having held the ideas for some time, he was encouraged by finding Cools giving them expression in public print. Cools complained that Negro education did not develop "sterling character," among Negroes and he accordingly proposed a list of fourteen virtues of civilized living which are very similar to those given in Sumner's (later) proposal, emphasizing the use of soap and water, application to hard work, and strict observance of sex purity.[22] The notion that somehow or other the Negro is more primitive in his emotional nature than the white man, and that if he is to live in a white man's world he must be civilized in his emotional controls and made more presentable in his daily habits, persists in the form of a serious proposal to set up an entire system of segregated education for the purpose of teaching the Negro these character traits. The suppressed minor premise of the reasoning process here involved is that no whites are in need of the cultivation of the graces of civilization; for if this is to be a serious proposal exclusively for Negroes and their education, it must be concluded that whites do not also need education in these virtues. If this corroborative minor premise cannot be maintained, then the proposal is not for a system of education based on racial differences in moral development, but for an educational effort to overcome inadequacies in moral training wherever they are found. And in that case, the serious proposal of a "new philosophy of Negro education" based on alleged moral differences between the races becomes patently absurd. The longevity of the notion may in part rest upon a tendency to think of all Negroes in terms of the less admirable members of the group, and to think of all whites in terms of the higher types of white men. The ability to discriminate between lower and higher levels of cultural development in both racial groups would enable educators to propose educational methods and techniques suited to the needs of every social group as well as every individual. To be sure, many Negroes may need to cultivate many of the

[22] Victor G. Cools, "Why Negro Education Has Failed," *Educational Review*, LXIII (December, 1924), 254-59.

fine virtues enumerated by Cools and Sumner; so also may many whites. Moral training may be a very good thing, and it should then be stressed in both white and segregated schools, not as a racial adaptation of education, but as an intelligent attempt to meet particular problems in particular schools. There appears to be little excuse for projecting a segregated school system on the basis of alleged exclusive moral inferiorities of the segregated group.

One further word may not be inappropriate at this point, however. It is the point of view of this study that many differences between individuals and groups are to be understood largely (if not exclusively) in terms of culture patterns, just as similarities are likewise produced in terms of the culture pattern of which they are a part. If it were assumed for a moment for the sake of argument that Negroes are inferior to whites morally, then it must at once be argued that the surest way not to overcome that inferiority is to shut the inferior group off by itself. Segregation is a condition and a guarantee of the perpetuation of the inequity which allegedly justifies it. To project a system of segregated education designed merely to meet the alleged moral inferiorities of Negroes, while at the same time denying the possibilities of cultural assimilation, is to indulge in cant and lay one's self open to the charge of hypocrisy. If there were to be any excuse for special efforts at "moral uplift" among Negroes by means of the segregated school system, that excuse would need to rest back upon the clear demonstration of two facts: that Negroes were now morally unfit to share in the cultural life of whites, and that whites actually intended to permit cultural assimilation when Negroes became "fit."

The real point of the proposal for moral education of Negroes is therefore like the sting on the scorpion's tail— it comes over last. The moral lapse is at least as great on the part of whites who assume the indefinite continuance of the segregated school with all that is implied in the indefinite perpetuation of separate institutions. It may be that the acceptance of the task of "moral" education of Negroes to a point where they are patently superior to the whites who would not be receiving this education (since, by proposal, this "moral" education is to be for Negroes only), would be one means of overcoming the basic immorality of the system of segregation on which the alleged moral differences must rest for their continuance. If so, then Odum, Sumner, Cools and the rest will have done a real service in calling attention to one possible line of development within the segregated system.

But it does not appear that we have here the most fruitful proposal for the projecting of a satisfactory system of education for the segregated school, simply because the difficulties which this proposal wishes to attack are themselves at least in large part outgrowths of the system of segregation. Backwoods communities tend to have standards of morality and conduct generally thought to be inferior to those of other communities which are in the main stream of life. Isolated mountain pockets harbor degenerate civilizations in the midst of American culture. So, too, segregation, cutting off one-tenth of the population from fuller participation in the cultural and civilizing influences of American life, and limiting culture contacts across race lines to the lowest and meanest forms of competitive struggle and mutual antipathy, instead of admitting mutual knowledge of racial achievements in the arts, music, literature, and the like, serves to work against the civilizing of both Negro and white. If we are to be serious about the business of "moral" education of the Negro, we are forced to be equally serious about the "moral" education of the white, and also to consider seriously the possible immorality of the system of segregation which may be partly responsible for the difficulties in which the two races sometimes find themselves.

To suggest a temporary special emphasis upon basic habits of decent living is one thing. Such a proposal hardly requires a separate school system for its execution, and scarcely justifies being dignified into a "philosophy of Negro education" in which form it would serve to crystallize and make permanent the devices designed for temporary purposes only. Quite another thing is this effort to posit a racial moral inferiority, and to project a special kind of education for moral delinquents on this hypothesis. It is an unconscious but very effective device for rationalizing the segregated system, and by giving it this apparent justification, to perpetuate the whole vicious system of educational inequities and cultural iniquities. The naturalness with which the term "unequal stages of cultural evolution" leads directly to the conclusion that "the pragmatic way out of such a dilemma is apparently a system of unequal education" only suggests the widespread and devastating use to which this theory of moral inferiority might be put if it ever regained the ascendancy which it had in the first quarter century after emancipation. Fortunately, the notion appears to have little vogue in intelligent circles today, where the forthright white Southerner is apt to use language like this from the Alabama Department of Education: "Any fair-minded appraisal of our policies in relation to the Negro must lead to the conclusion that these policies were not always such as to release the best impulses of either race. Even from the standpoint of our own self-interest as a white race without reference to altruism, our policies need improving."[23]

DEAD-END NUMBER ONE

An instrument of social control designed by the dominant group to "keep the Negro in his place."—When the notions of innate intellectual inferiority and of inherited moral delinquency or primitiveness are shown to be inadequate ideas on which to project the racially segregated school, the proponents of the separate school are forced to take their stand on a much more open and understandable platform. They frankly maintain that they want to keep the Negro "in his place" and that it is the function of the school to facilitate

[23] "Procedures in Large Unit Teaching, Suggestions for Improving Instruction," State of Alabama, Department of Education, Bulletin No. 9 (1937), p. 111. Issued by the Division of Instruction and authorized by the State Board of Education, 1937.

this process of subordination or subjugation. "How do you manage to keep the Negroes subservient?" asks the kindly eyed, anxious, elderly visitor from a Southern city as she is being shown around the campus of a segregated college. "Keep him in his place" is the refrain which runs through many of the proposals for the segregated school. Since the Negro is subordinate, and since he is to be kept in that relationship, then the school, as an instrument of social purpose, must help to prolong and to entrench the subordination. Here, we are out in the open, on clear ground of straight-forward debate. This is no rationalization of a hidden purpose, but a frank defense of an openly admitted social policy.

To be sure, not a little of the opposition to adequate schooling for Negroes comes from following the line of least resistance in trying to keep taxes low. Certainly, not all persons who argue for inferior schools for Negroes, or for schools designed to subordinate Negroes, do so solely, or even primarily, on the grounds of white superiority. They are anxious to cut public expenditures in order to cut taxes. This is an attitude known the country over. But in a caste-patterned society, this impulse, like many others, is grooved in the accustomed channels of race discrimination. The savings effected are inequitably apportioned between the races. When taxes are to be cut by paring school funds, the schools for Negroes are pared first, and deepest. Once again let it be repeated, that in the analysis of the South and its practices, no imputation of censure is intended. This analysis is merely part of a straightforward attempt to understand the task and difficulties of the segregated college as it faces the society which segregates it.

It is important, therefore, to bear in mind that the historical trend is toward less inadequate school facilities for both racial groups in the South. Public education is, as history goes, an affair of little more than yesterday. Only a century ago New York and Pennsylvania were earnestly debating how much of it they would have. The absence of cities and the presence of a landed aristocracy made the South lag be-

hind the North in the adoption of universal public education
of whites. Notwithstanding, North Carolina had before 1860
a system fairly comparable with most of the North. Georgia
adopted, just before the panic of 1837, a fairly good paper
scheme; but under the panic gave it up. Yet, by 1857, it had
made a genuine beginning toward a state system. The Civil
War stopped all this.

Under Reconstruction auspices, state after state set up
systems of free public education.[24] But these gains were later
largely rejected along with the rest of Reconstruction. The
whites, in their opposition to anything imposed by Reconstruction legislatures or Freedmen's Bureau activities, accepted in
theory Herbert Spencer's opposition to the idea of general
public education but actually retained skeleton outlines of
the new systems. Under conditions of post-bellum poverty,
the South was naturally slow in building up a comprehensive
and adequate support for free public education for white
children. The rural whites, being themselves uneducated,
cared little about the matter. In such a situation, the Negro
suffered, not so much because a well-formulated positive plan
to use Negro schools as an instrument of social control in-
tentionally made the segregated schools bad, as that negatively the caste system and poverty made it easy in a situation
where there was not enough money for both, to take care of
the white children first. In other words, the caste system,
working amid poverty, retarded the development of adequate
ideas of public education; and particularly, the fortuitous
presence of caste made possible the differential progress of
schools for the two races which has caused the segregated
school to be a means of perpetuating caste. The trend is toward adequacy, even though the trend is very slow.[25]

There are two general types of data which support the
assertion that the segregated school is often used as a means
of social control to keep the Negro "in his place." The pri-

[24] See W. E. B. DuBois, *Black Reconstruction*, pp. 637-67.
[25] For example, the average salary of teachers in the rural Negro schools of
Mississippi is reported to be the same as it was forty-seven years ago. (State
Department of Education information to author.)

mary data on the point are to be found in the school laws
of the eighteen Southern states with their open and frank
discrimination between the two races; in the financial policies
which provide, on the average, three and one-half times as
good facilities for the education of whites as for the education of Negroes; in the shorter term and the lower salary,
the inferior building and the antiquated textbook, the "step-
child" treatment of the Negro in the educational system. The
secondary data, with which we are equally concerned because
they describe the point of intelligent attack upon the situation, are the opinions and statements of educators and statesmen, sociologists and publicists, who explain, justify, and
promote the educational inequities designed to keep the Negro subordinate. The primary data are matters of common
knowledge which may here be summarized briefly merely to
carry the argument:

The latest accurate summary of comparative expenditures
available is the study sponsored by the Rosenwald Fund[26]
which showed that children of the 3,000,000 Negroes of the
Deep South have less than one-fifteenth of the opportunity
for education of the average American child. Georgia in 1930
spent an average of $35.42 for each white pupil in the state
and $6.28 for each Negro; the figures for Mississippi are
$45.34 against $5.45. While the national average expenditure in elementary and secondary education was $99.00 per
pupil, the expenditure for white children in the South was
$44.31 and for Negro children was $12.57. Negro public
schools in eleven Southern states for which records are available received in 1930 a total of $23,461,959, while the white
pupils in the same states received $216,718,221. Teachers'
salaries in thirteen Southern states in 1930 averaged $901
for the white and $423 for the Negro teacher. One of the
more glaring discrepancies is in Montgomery County, Alabama, where $28.00 per year was spent in 1930 for each
white child, as against $4.00 for each Negro child. The in-
vestment in public school property in fifteen Southern states

[26] The Julius Rosenwald Fund, *School Money in Black and White.*

is at the rate of $157 for each white pupil and $37.00 for each Negro pupil, an aggregate difference of $744,352,000 between the two sets of schools, which on a per capita basis means a net differential of $240,000,000.

Some justification for the poor schooling in the South is found in the relative poverty of the region. The Rosenwald study indicates that, as a region, the South has a higher "effort quotient" than the rest of the nation—that is, it is spending a higher proportion both of its tax dollar and of its total income for education than is the rest of the nation. Lacking a Federal equalization fund, it is inevitable that the South will have schools which are not as good as the rest of the nation. But this is not a justification of the four to one differential in average expenditure between white and Negro, unless we are to assume that the Negro alone is to carry the burden of Southern poverty.

Nor can it be argued that "the Negro pays no taxes and should therefore be content with what he gets." There are certain kinds of taxes which cannot be passed on to the consumer, notably income taxes. But in the normal process of things, most taxes are passed on to the consumer, which means that, as one who eats, wears clothing, and consumes the staples of life, the Negro pays taxes exactly as does anyone else. If he has not become a large property owner in the Deep South, that is at least in part due to the educational discrimination against him; and if this educational discrimination (which keeps him in his "place" of illiteracy, ignorance, and subservience) is to be used as a tool for preventing him from improving his condition so that he can be a large payer of direct taxes, it is captious to argue that the present failure of the Negro to pay such taxes is justification for the discrimination.

Now, as to the secondary data, the arguments which defend this practice of educational discrimination may again be summarized in the classical utterance given by Odum twenty-five years ago. Fortunately no longer supported by their author, these opinions nevertheless are the mental furniture of not a few persons, and must therefore be taken seriously as contemporary obstacles to fuller educational opportunities for Negroes:

Let the influences upon the negro child, at least so far as the school is able to effect his end, lead him toward the unquestioning acceptance of the fact that he is a different race from the white, and properly so; that it always has been and always will be; that it is not a discredit not to be able to do as the white. . . . This would have its positive value and it would have its negative value. While the negro child is interested in his own matters he will not be incited to wish for the white man's conditions of life or for his nature. . . . The negro child needs simpler exercises than does the white child. However, each should be designed with a special purpose in view. Negroes are rarely open to reason; here they need to see things in their details rather than in the total appearance . . . if it is possible to eradicate the criminal tendencies, it can best be begun in the schoolroom. . . . It would, of course, be impracticable to require separate texts for negroes above the grammar grades; but it is only in the formative period, when the pupil will be in the elementary subjects, that special texts are needed. Students whose ability and ambition carry them into advanced studies will most likely be intelligent enough to understand their position. . . . If the plan is properly interpreted no negro leader who aspires for his race to reach the best results will offer objections. There should be no objection on the part of the whites if they desire the negro to be trained for usefulness.[27]

In an address before the National Education Association, Department of Superintendence, the Superintendent of Schools of the city of Memphis, Tennessee, said in 1910:

Public peace and the safety of the state demand that the less developed race be subordinated to the more developed, under conditions as they exist in the South today. The Caste of Kin is the practise of the theory that blood is thicker than water; and the Sermon on the Mount cannot invalidate God's own law of the Survival of the Fittest. If these widely different races cannot blend their blood—and instinct and science say nay—the only real foundation for democracy, equality actual or potential, does not exist and cannot be created. . . . Southerners understand the apparent cruelty imputed to the God of Israel who is represented as commanding the extermination of non-assimilable peoples. But the more refined killing of today in the South is not the taking of a Negro's life but the impassive and relentless murder of a people's hopes. But

[27] H. W. Odum, *Social and Mental Traits of the Negro*, pp. 48-52.

better this than worse that might be. . . . Sometimes we must be cruel would we be kind.[28]

Running through the literature of this controversy is the recurring accusation that Yankee teachers in Negro schools were using the segregated school not as a means of subduing the Negro but as a means of advancing him. Undoubtedly founded in fact, this accusation has led to a bitter debate over the place of white teachers in the segregated schools, a controversy which may be taken as illustrative of the whole area of which it is a part—the larger problem of whether the segregated school shall be used as a tool of racial subordination or as a means of advancing the subordinated group. Ex-Governor Jelks of Alabama was one of those who proposed that the best way to deal with the problem of Negro education was to staff the schools entirely with Southern white men. Here is a perfect proposal for the end in view. These teachers would be able to control the pupils, giving them the proper sense of white superiority and Negro inferiority. They would not, on the other hand, "put ideas into the heads of the Negroes." And they would prevent the Negroes from getting together by themselves and concocting "big ideas" about themselves. This proposal is similar to the practice of Southern white churches in ante-bellum days, when it was the common practice to demand that colored churches should affiliate themselves with white conferences, and thereby be subject to white control.[29] It is interesting to note that Jelks's proposal was immediately rejected by the Negro religious press on the grounds that it would be unsafe to trust the daughters of colored citizens to the care of Southern white men. In reporting the controversy, Odum[30] rejects

[28] Thomas P. Bailey, quoted with approval by Odum in *Social and Mental Traits of the Negro*, pp. 299-300. It appears that Bailey thought that Darwin had a more genuine insight into the nature of God than Jesus; but it is extremely doubtful whether a careful reading of Darwin himself would substantiate Bailey's interpretation of Darwin's attitudes. "The fittest" in human society may be not necessarily the "whitest" or the "strongest"—they may be "the most ethical."

[29] See Trevor Bowen, *Divine White Right*, pp. 102 ff.

[30] *Op. cit.*, pp. 42-44.

the proposal on the grounds that it would take away jobs from the educated Negroes, and moreover, "most boards of trustees are careless in selecting teachers for Negro schools," so that no well-equipped white teacher could be induced to accept a colored school. Let it be noted that the grounds for rejecting the proposal do not include the idea that the school should be used for other purposes than those of keeping the Negro in his place. That was accepted without debate as being the admitted, legitimate objective of the school for Negroes. Indeed, the attitude taken on this question of the use of white teachers in segregated schools is as useful as any available issue as an index into the meaning of the school as an instrument of group control.

There are at least four clearly defined attitudes on the issue of the use of white teachers in colored schools. Two of these attitudes aim at the dominance of the whites; the other two aim at the advancement of the Negro. But one of the first pair and one of the second pair would use no white teachers—for exactly opposite reasons; while the remaining two would use white teachers—again for diametrically opposed reasons. *Attitude 1:* Let us use all white teachers, men who know the place of the Negro and will educate him to stay there. *Attitude 2:* Let us use no white teachers, but thoroughly and completely segregate the Negro, shutting him off by himself and thus effectually keeping him in his place. *Attitude 3:* Let us use all Negro teachers, to provide fullest opportunity for untrammeled advancement of the Negro without white interference. *Attitude 4:* Let us use some white teachers and some Negro teachers, to advance the welfare of the Negro and at the same time to keep some of the lines of contact and communication across race lines. Attitude 1 is illustrated by the proposal of former Governor Jelks of Alabama and by the practice of certain schools with Negro student bodies which still maintain an all-white staff. Attitude 2 is illustrated by the laws of the state of Florida[31] which make it "unlawful in this State, for white teachers to

---

[31] General Acts and Resolutions, Florida, 1913, Sec. 1, No. 70, Ch. 6490, p. 311.

teach negroes in negro schools, and for negro teachers to teach in white schools." Attitude 3 finds its expression in several of the educational institutions run entirely by Negroes, effectively demonstrating (even to the doubting Thomases) that Negroes are quite capable of handling their own affairs without white interference. Attitude 4 is illustrated by a number of institutions in which an interracial faculty is maintained, without distinctions and with a genuine rapprochement between the two groups.

It is not our purpose at this point to assess the relative merits of the several attitudes (see Chapter XII). We are now interested only in understanding the involved nature of the discussion growing up around two sets of considerations, namely, whether the segregated school shall be an instrument of white dominance, and secondly, whether there shall be white teachers in the segregated school. We have seen that two different groups of people would try to use the school as an instrument of subordinating the Negro, and that they would do it through antipodal processes, while two other groups would wish the schools to advance the status and condition of Negroes, again disagreeing on the means to be used. It is important to keep in mind, as we proceed with this study, that it is quite likely that a great many of the moot questions raised from time to time are answered in very different fashion by persons who actually may be in agreement on the basic issues involved; and conversely, that agreement on a particular issue may be quite incidental to fundamental cleavage in objectives and underlying philosophy. Each time, it is well to ask: Why is this particular attitude taken? Why is this particular answer given? Is there a deeper concern back of the reason given? Does the statement reveal the underlying issues?

We next turn our attention to a situation in which the agreement and disagreement on specific issues is even more confusedly entangled with cross-currents of agreement and difference on underlying issues. It is a variant form of the education designed to keep the Negro in his place, and yet this very form of education is also proposed by earnest champions of Negro advancement as the means to an opposite end.

DEAD-END NUMBER TWO

Vocational education, designed to steer the Negro into the lower-income brackets of the economic system.—The whole problem of vocational training for Negroes is greatly complicated by entangling threads of controversy. Sufficiently involved with extraneous issues as it is applied to the education of white children, the question of vocational education becomes hopelessly confused with other issues when the preparation of Negroes is discussed.

It is not easy to unravel the tangled threads of controversy and to construct the several patterns of educational philosophy which might have been woven on the several looms if bobbins had not been hurled about and shuttled back and forth sometimes in one loom, sometimes in another, sometimes empty, sometimes with inappropriate thread. The truth of the matter is that the racially distorted warp provided by American society made it almost a foregone conclusion that the weavers' efforts would be at least partially frustrated. The shuttle might be thrown by a black weaver; but the white foot upon the treadles determined the resultant pattern. Shifting his position, the black weaver might again thrust his shuttle, only to find that the foot on the treadle had reversed the warp, and his new throw merely undid his previous effort. Soon, the dextrous black weaver might learn to thrust his shuttle quickly in behind the white weaver's shuttle, weaving the two threads together in a common cloth. Resenting this, the white man might insist that the black weaver set up and operate a loom of his own; but the warp for the segregated loom was to be threaded through the heddle eyes according to the white man's idea of what would be an appropriate pattern for black weavers. Rebelliously, the black weaver might insist on designing his own patterns, only to be met with the reply that if he wished to weave in peace, or possibly, to be permitted to have a loom at all, he had better be content with weaving what was allowed. And finally, the white weaver, at long last may have learned to his dismay that the pattern which he had been demanding that the black loom carry was actually producing a kind of cloth which the white market wanted—which meant that the pattern must therefore be appropriated for the white looms, leaving the discarded patterns of yesterday's white weavers to be copied without hindrance on the black looms of today.

Whatever thread may have been put into the shuttle, the pattern was determined by the warp as it had been drawn through the heddle eyes and as it was manipulated by the treadles; and these controls were managed by the white caste. The shuttle in its flight might carry either the thread of vocational training or of classical education; but the warp in its racial heddles was manipulated according to the preconceived designs of the caste system, permitting the shuttle to pass back and forth only in strict conformity with the patterns of caste. Thus, if it appeared for a time that vocational training might be better fitted to the perpetuation of the caste system than some other form of education, there would then be relatively less opposition to the black weavers if, whatever their actual operations, they called their thread "vocational education." And if black weavers learned that they would be less disturbed when they wound their bobbins with acceptable thread, their conformity becomes understandable—they needed clothes for their educational nakedness. So, too, if the white weavers coming down from the North to instruct Negroes imported their own warp and prescribed patterns for their educational looms which differed somewhat from those approved by Southern whites, this may be understood as not merely a desire to clothe nakedness, but to clothe it in garments of respectability if not of splendor, that there might be no reflection of low caste upon the wearers. And again, if Southern whites insisted that these fine silks which came from the Northern looms (and many of the black looms which were modeled after the importations) were woven in patterns which clashed with the accepted mores of the region—if they objected strenuously to the incongruity of the use of fine silks in the bobbins when the Southern-designed warp was made of coarser stuff and called for woof to match it, they need not be accused of diabolical motives. They were merely insisting on the integrity of the social fabric as life had taught them to weave it.

If this metaphorical description seems involved or confusing, it is not less so than the controversy which it symbolizes. Like most questions which get themselves mixed up with race issues, this problem of vocational training of Negroes has seldom been discussed as a separate issue on its own merits. Usually the discussion, while on the surface it has been concerned with the merits of vocational education, has carried just beneath its surface a vexed and vexing undertone of caste and social status. For purposes of analysis, we are forced deliberately to oversimplify the discussion, with the advance warning that the argument has not actually been as clear, as pointed, or as single-minded as our analysis must make it appear; for it is our hope that such an overly simplified analysis, while it may do incidental injustice to a particular point of view as held by a particular individual, will serve to describe the whole field and to clarify the actual issues. Our ten representative or exemplary points of view do not necessarily correspond to the whole of each of the positions carefully formulated by the various protagonists. They may be taken as several foci around which the discussion has revolved; and as such they serve not so much to characterize particular individuals or groups as to locate shifting positions of individuals and groups at various times and under differing circumstances.

1. Whatever training or education the Negro is to be permitted to enjoy must be such as will in no way unfit him for useful continuance in the lower economic brackets only; and as long as the educational opportunities for Negroes do

actually make them better workmen "in their place,"[32] it will be all right to let them have that kind of education. Such schooling can be looked upon by industrialists with the same impassive objectivity as a program for the development and exploitation of natural resources. This would be one extreme point of view, about as far removed from enthusiastic support of Negro education as it could be and yet be within the area of tolerance. It has, however, been used not infrequently as a lever for prying reluctant consent for educational facilities from the dominant group. "As a rule, Southern people are not antagonistic to negroes so long as they remain segregated."[33]

2. The Negro ought at least to be permitted to fit himself for useful service in the industrial and agricultural areas in which he has always been used. If he is to be limited to these occupational opportunities, he ought, in decency, to be permitted (or even encouraged) to train himself well for the adequate discharge of his function. This would tend to raise the standard of living of the Negro, improving his condition though not affecting his status. This opinion is well voiced by a "prominent North Carolinian":

I believe that the Negro should be educated and that industrial education is what he most needs. But he must not overlook the fact that he has other shortcomings besides those of economic inefficiency. His present condition is not due to a low earning capacity alone, but also to low standards of living. We must guard against any kind of one-sided development and bear in mind that the right ideal of Negro education is twofold: to increase the Negro's industrial efficiency, and at the same time and with the same speed raise his standard of living. The true type of industrial education not only makes the Negro a better workman, but also causes him to build a better home and live a worthier life.[34]

So this point of view, definitely championing the right of the

[32] Cf. B. Schrieke, *Alien Americans*, p. 165: "Sometimes with the help of the local Negroes . . . who know how to create goodwill, the state agent will succeed. Introduction of domestic science in the school program will be advocated by the trustees as a means of keeping the Negro in his place."

[33] E. Q. Hawk, *Economic History of the South*, p. 506.

[34] Quoted in "Negro Education," Bulletin No. 38 (1916) of the Bureau of Education, Thomas Jesse Jones, I, 83.

Negro to industrial education, while limiting his vocational opportunities largely to the jobs for which this type of training would fit him, would attempt also to enrich the quality of life on the restricted economic level.

3. Whatever else may be said about the vocational opportunities for Negroes, either actual or potential, the clear fact is that the great masses of colored people come from the farm and will have to find their futures there, while most of the remainder will find employment in industry as skilled and semi-skilled workers. It is sheer romanticism to think that the Negro is to find wide opportunity outside the lower economic levels for at least the first two or three generations after emancipation; and it is both stupid and wicked to think that he should not be well trained to take full advantage of the openings which he finds. "Let down your buckets where you are."[35] Recognizing the caste system as an inevitable part of the social framework of the South, this point of view proposes to make all the headway possible within the limits of that framework, by first frankly disarming the opposition, and then vigorously pressing the issue on noncontroversial grounds. The famous formula of the Atlanta Exposition speech, "In all things that are purely social we can be as separate as the fingers, yet one as the hand in all things that pertain to mutual progress,"[36] was designed to do exactly what it did—disarm the opposition. It accepted the caste system as the prevailing social pattern. Therefore, by logical corollary (as drawn by Washington's critics), this attitude inevitably attacked any form of education which aimed to advance the status as well as the welfare of the Negro.

The schools planted in the South by the Northern white people have remained—not always through their fault to be sure—in a certain sense, alien institutions. They have not considered in planning their

---

[35] The famous slogan of Dr. Booker T. Washington grows out of an incident which he frequently used to illustrate his point. A disabled ship, floating for many days without provisions or water, frantically signaled a passing vessel for aid. "Let down your buckets where you are," came the reply. The ship had drifted into the wide mouth of the Amazon, and fresh water was available for the asking.

[36] Booker T. Washington, *Up from Slavery*, p. 221.

course of instruction, the actual needs of either the Negro or of the South. Not infrequently young men and women have gotten so out of touch during the time that they were in these schools with the actual conditions and needs of the Negro in the South that it has taken years before they were able to get back to earth and find places where they would be happy and useful in some form or other of necessary and useful labor.[37]

The attempt to make ' rogress too fast would jeopardize the hard-won gains of the present. Any open challenge of the caste system would permanently alienate the white South upon whose consent future expansion and progress must depend, even though the progress itself were made possible by the enterprise of Negroes.

The higher and normal schools can greatly aid the Negro people in raising among themselves the money necessary to build up the educational system of the South if they will prepare their teachers to give the masses of the people the kind of education which will help them to increase their earnings instead of giving them the kind of education that makes them discontented and unhappy and does not give them the courage or disposition to help themselves.[38]

4. Even though the caste system were nonexistent, industrial training would still be the real opportunity of the Negro. "Blind worship of the professions" has given the Negro a false sense of values and a false contempt for genuinely productive labor.

Negro education, because of the overemphasis on the classical and non-productive training, fosters and perpetuates a low standard of living among the black people. . . . The more crying need of the group is for skilled producers of wealth and not for mediocre parasitical professional men. All other needs must be recognized as subsidiary. With an efficient producing class functioning, there will be no black man's problem as such. . . . The need of the black man—to make his a self-respecting group—is for skilled workers of hand and brain, mechanics and efficient business men.[39]

[37] Booker T. Washington, "Observations on the Negro College," *World's Work*, XXI (April, 1911), 14235.

[38] *Ibid.*, p. 14237.

[39] Victor G. Cools, "Negro Education and Low Living Standards," *Educational Review*, LXXII (September, 1926), 102 f.

The logical conclusion of this point of view is one from which its proponents do not flinch. The Negro, "from the kindergarten to the college should be *required* to spend one-third of his time in mastering a trade."[40]

5. While there is undoubtedly a place for industrial and agricultural training in the educational program for Negroes, there is an equally important place to be occupied by the classical and liberal training of the kind usually associated with liberal arts colleges. Just as the educational system for whites includes both types, so, too, education for Negroes ought not to be one-sided. Whether a well-rounded education will unfit the Negro for subservience in the caste system, or whether it will increase his happiness and effectiveness within the caste to which he is confined, is of relatively little importance. The important thing is to give him fullest educational opportunities; and the effort to limit him to one particular type of education on the grounds that only one kind of employment is open to him, is therefore in error. Equally vicious would be the attempt to give him purely classical education without any opportunities for practical training for occupational efficiency.[41]

This middle-of-the-road attitude has been maintained by relatively few persons, and by them with some difficulty. The centrifugal force of controversy tends to drive contestants toward one or another extreme position. In a caste-divided world, where the perpetuation of caste is the sole guarantee

[40] *Ibid.*, p. 107. Author's own italics.

[41] Talcott Williams is quoted in Augustus Field Beard, *Crusade of Brotherhood*, p. 288, in support of this inclusive educational aim: "Granted," he says, "that the Negro race requires an industrial training and natural selection, the Negro must be provided with higher education which will prevent him from being a mere stratum at the base of industry. If the Negro group is to be more than a caste, it must develop its aim, its aspirations, and its future by the aid of a wide training which puts it in touch with the past, and this training must be at hand close to the Negro population. Neither college nor industrial training can be spared. If the republic is at length to fuse and assimilate all within its sovereignty, it can only be as all enjoy the possibility of every advantage open to any. The final object of all American effort is a more perfect union, and can only come by closing no door to any man." It should be noted that the argument as to the kind of education to be offered is here clearly stated as resting upon the question of caste.

of the status which the system defines, men are not easily permitted the luxury of impartiality or indifference to consequences. A proposal must be "right" on the caste system—rightness depending upon the point of view of the particular judge.

6. More important than anything else to the Negro, as a human being, is the key to unlock the cultural riches of the ages. It is all very well for men to be able to make money and support themselves; but the real purpose of education is not that of training moneymakers; it is rather that of cultivating depth and breadth of spirit and understanding, so that the educated man is possessed of something far greater than money can buy. The caste system may deny him respect and status: he walks ahead, serene in his own self-sufficiency. The economic system may deny him adequate sustenance and compel him to live in poverty: he welcomes lady poverty as gladly as St. Francis of old. The object of education, therefore, is to give to the student, white or Negro, not merely the bases of literacy, but the means of possessing his own soul and spirit in quietness and self-respect.[42]

7. Since there are those who doubt whether the Negro really has the full mental and moral potentialities alleged to be the possession of whites, let education for Negroes be so designed that it will demonstrate, beyond any doubt, the full stature of intellect and character which Negroes do possess. Some Southern whites would seek to shut the doors of opportunity in the face of the Negro, alleging that he is not able to enter through those doors in any case. Let Negro education, therefore, champion the cause of the oppressed by furnishing the living refutation of the arrogant superiority of the whites.[43] Industrial education and training may be included as side lines in this educational program; but the heart and kernel of the whole business must be the classical, liberal arts course, with a distinct religious emphasis. Given true

[42] Cf. Beard, *op. cit.,* passim.

[43] This point could be documented by citations from the speeches and writings of dozens of the early Yankee teachers from several different schools; there is no point to be served by singling out any special individual or school.

culture and high religion, the Negro will walk the earth as a
man. The chains of ignorance and superstitution will fall
from him, and he will be a free person before whom the
prejudices of races and the barriers of caste must fall. The
attack, however, is to be not upon the social system but upon
the individual victims of that system. By preparing Negroes
for positions of leadership and of respectability, the educational system will thereby indirectly and inevitably undermine the system of caste.

8. While there may be some value in a program of industrial education when that is a part of a larger and more
inclusive effort to lift the level of life for Negroes generally,
and to provide opportunities for the highest cultural development in particular, it is equally certain that a program of
industrial education launched by sufferance of the dominant
group, which sufferance is purchased by the relinquishing of
any claims to civil rights or to the benefits of higher education, is too dearly bought. "Adjustment and submission," involving the surrender of political power, civil rights, and
opportunities of higher education, are the goods which have
been offered in exchange for the doubtful prize of freedom to
develop industrial education as best we may. Indeed, the very
success of the program of industrial education rests back
upon the training of leaders, teachers, and professional men
—and this necessitates genuine colleges. Moreover, "the way
to truth and right lies in straightforward honesty," rather
than in indiscriminate flattery; and the way of the Atlanta
Compromise leads inevitably to degradation.[44] If Negroes are
to claim their rightful place as men, free and equal with all
other men, they must begin by refusing to compromise at any
point, refusing to accept inferior status, refusing to accept
education which implies inferior status or which accompanies
inferiority or subservience. They must state "plainly and un-
equivocally the legitimate demands of their people," in words
which will be clearly understood:

[44] For full development of this point of view see "Of Mr. Booker T. Washington and Others." W. E. B. DuBois, *The Souls of Black Folk*, Ch. III.

It is wrong to encourage a man or a people in evil-doing; it is wrong to
aid and abet a national crime simply because it is unpopular not to do so.
The growing spirit of kindliness and reconciliation between the North
and the South after the frightful differences of a generation ago ought to
be a source of deep congratulation to all, and especially to those whose
mistreatment caused the war; but if that reconciliation is to be marked
by the industrial slavery and civic death of those same black men, with
permanent legislation into a position of inferiority, then those black men,
if they are really men, are called upon by every consideration of patriotism and loyalty to oppose such a course by all civilized methods, even
though such opposition involves disagreement with Mr. Booker T.
Washington.[45]

This point of view would use education not to meet the industrial and agricultural demands of capitalism, but to advance the human rights of the Negro.

By every civilized and peaceful method we must strive for the rights
which the world accords to men, clinging unwaveringly to those great
words which the sons of the Fathers would fain forget: "We hold these
truths to be self-evident: That all men are created equal. . . ."[46]

9. Since the Negro is primarily an industrial and agricultural worker in the American economic structure, education
of the Negro should be designed to break the caste line separating him from other workers, uniting the entire working
class in one great, united effort to overthrow the expropriators
and to establish an equalitarian society. There can be no "true"
education, whether technical or cultural, which does not have
as its primary objective this effort to unite the workers of both
races and thereby to advance toward the revolution.[47]

10. With the march of technological development, the field
of industrial labor calls increasingly for skilled rather than
unskilled labor. That means better pay for those whom industry employs; it also implies slightly higher social status.
This, in turn, means that the jobs must first be given to whites,
Negroes being employed only as a last resort. It therefore
follows that vocational training which aims to fit the Negro

---

[45] *Ibid.,* p. 55.
[46] *Ibid.,* p. 59.
[47] Cf. James S. Allen, *The Negro Question in the United States,* esp. pp. 1-12,
140-50.

for advancement with the advancing industrial technology is inimical to the prior interest of working-class whites. Vocational education, therefore, is to be opposed because it would tend to raise the Negro out of his place and put him in the place rightfully to be reserved for the white working man.[48] That would not only increase race tension and conflict between white and colored working-class populations; it would have its repercussions throughout the whole social structure. It would undermine the very existence of caste which is the only guarantee of stability in American society. Vocational education for Negroes is therefore to be shunned. To be sure, it would, if universally and exclusively adopted, tend to steer the Negro into occupations which would confine him to the lower-class brackets; but at the same time, it would tend to raise him to the upper rungs of that section of the ladder, a position which ought to be reserved for white workmen. Instead of vocational education, therefore, let the less practical academic education be given the Negro. Its apparent respectability will divert his attention from the fact that by accepting the husk of academic respectability he is missing the kernel of vocational preparation.

Thus the wheel of argument has come full circle, and we find ourselves back at the starting point, arguing for exactly the same end—the preservation of status in the caste system—but seeking to obtain it with opposite means—the denial, rather than the provision, of industrial and agricultural training for Negroes. The manner in which these cross-currents of controversy are intertwined is suggested in Figure 7.

The conclusion to which our discussion brings us is that at any particular time and under the then-prevailing circumstances, the attitude of particular individuals and groups toward the problem of vocational education for Negroes will be

---

[48] Cf. B. Schrieke, *op. cit.*, pp. 177, 181: "Although there are still people who regard all Negro education as nonsense, the majority will not deny it to the coloured man. But what education? Academic instruction? Little use. Vocational training? That spells competition, conflict! What is feared is the change of status. The Negro should keep in his place."

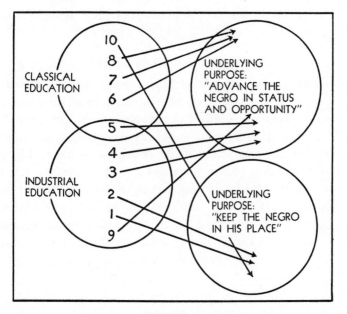

FIGURE 7

CROSS-CURRENTS OF CONTROVERSY

A schematic picture of the manner in which divergent attitudes toward caste may become attached to the same, or to divergent ideas of "proper" education for Negroes. Numbers refer to the ten attitudes toward industrial education listed in pages 198-206. Arrows indicate the manner in which different attitudes toward industrial and classical education are linked with attitudes toward Negro advancement.

determined largely by their beliefs as to the probable effects of the proposed education upon the status of the Negro within the caste system. A somewhat similar hypothesis regarding the heated arguments over the place of liberal education in the program of education for Negroes may also shed light upon that problem.

DEAD-END NUMBER THREE

A slavish imitation of prevailing educational patterns in American colleges.—One of the fallacies regarding the education of Negroes which has enjoyed wide currency both in the past and at present is the assertion that the colleges founded for the education of the freedmen attempted to give the higher reaches of advanced learning to illiterate, uncouth ex-slaves without first laying the solid foundations of basic literacy and self-control. Holmes[49] establishes the fact that "the persons administering [the early colleges] were content to perform the task at hand rather than to enroll students in college before they could meet such entrance requirements as were considered respectable at the time in question." This situation is held to be "typical of all the better colleges for Negroes."[50] The institutions were named "colleges" and "universities" by their founders who expected them to grow up to their ideals ultimately. These far-visioned educators gave them "adult names at the baptizin'," but they "did not take illiterate Negroes from the cotton fields and offer them at once the curriculum of the New England College."[51]

A second fallacy is the belief that all the institutions of learning established by the Yankee school teachers were designed exclusively for "book learning" and had no direct relevance to the actual life problems of the students. From the beginning, the American Missionary Association, one of the pioneer organizations which has remained in the field vigorously prosecuting its work for nearly a century, has em-

[49] D. O. W. Holmes, *The Evolution of the Negro College*, p. 98.
[50] *Ibid.*, p. 100.
[51] *Ibid.*, p. 100.

phasized not merely the necessity of fundamental training in the crafts and trades along with adequate training in the intellectual pursuits, but it has also endeavored constantly to relate its educational offerings to the life problems of its students. One of the first, if not the first institution to offer industrial training to the freedman was the institution founded at Talladega, Alabama, under the auspices of the American Missionary Association. With crude surroundings and rudimentary beginnings,

the missionary teachers from the North performed a labor of love which only devotion to a cause can inspire. Talladega was not an exception but a type of all the educational effort for the Negro in those critical years during and immediately following the Civil War. The teachers had to be persons possessing great faith in the possibilities of humanity and willing to lose themselves in their task and to endure hardships, social isolation, insult, and often personal danger. They lived with their students and taught them lessons in living outside of school hours often more valuable than the lessons learned in the classrooms.[52]

And yet, in a sense, both of these fallacies gained currency partly because they had some founding in fact. Next to religion itself, the most valuable possession the Yankee missionary carried with her was a high-minded, naïve faith in the value and efficacy of culture. The mark of highest breeding and of respectable social station, this stamp of the educated man, was now to be put upon the freedman in compensation for generations of ignominy, enslavement, and debasement. The effort to educate the Negro took on the character of a high and holy crusade, to which the best products of the finest New England and Midwestern homes gave themselves, reckless of self, station, and purse, sometimes even of life as well. In many instances they were motivated by the chauvinism of Civil War hysteria, and were met by the equally vigorous resistance which Southern whites carried over from the days of conflict. During the hectic days of Reconstruction the Yankee idealists carried on. In such an atmosphere of mutual hostility and opposition, it is understandable

[52] *Ibid*, p. 98.

that the missionary teacher may sometimes have urged that the education of Negroes must incorporate and express all the things that were held to be the finest and best in the classical colleges of the New England tradition; and that anything which smacked of inferiority or which was "of the earth, earthy," was to be scorned as fit only for "poor whites." There was the further consideration that many whites, both North and South, expressed doubts as to the higher intellectual capabilities of Negroes, so that it became a matter of supreme importance for the missionary teacher to lead her students as rapidly as possible into the more abstract and abstruse reaches of book learning in order to prove the case for the freedman.[53] Reconditeness then became synonymous with education. Instances are known of the employment of teachers in the early days of Negro education solely for the purpose of "going down there and demonstrating that Negroes *can* do calculus." There is some basis of fact for the contention that the education of Negroes was not always well balanced, not always carried forward with particular reference to day-by-day needs of students and graduates.

This evidence, however, is more than outweighed in importance by the verdict of history as to the whole movement of Negro education. Book learning there was, to be sure; and it was often of the highest standard possible at each successive stage of development of the school or college. But

the question of industrial training has not been forgotten. . . . The Association's theory was to make industrial training a contributing force to Christian education. It did not accord with the modern Southern theory of Negro education that it should be distinct from other

[53] "The prophetic men who were directing the Association believed that what experience had proved to be wise and efficient influences for Christianizing and civilizing white people ought to be equally good for black people. Indeed, the evidence already before them seemed to be sufficient to justify this judgment. The Association had gone far enough to confirm the opinion that the black people could be enlarged in thought and mind by the same influences and methods of discipline which had proved their power in other peoples; this much against the opinions of Southern people, who held for the most part to the essential incapacity of their former slaves for anything beyond elementary improvement." So Augustus Field Beard characterizes the early aims of the American Missionary Association in his *Crusade of Brotherhood*, p. 146.

education and compose about all the needs of these poor people destined
to be a permanent peasant class, and no more. At the same time, it was
plain enough that the vast majority of this people—as indeed all peoples—must live by bodily labor. . . . Hence, with the planting of permanent schools leading up to higher education, plans were at once made
for such industrial training as seemed to be practical in nearly all
schools for girls, and, wherever possible, for boys. . . . Labour was
honorable and to be honored.[54]

A sober and unbiased reading of history does not support
the notion that the early schools for Negroes were fantastic
concoctions of the grammarian's impracticality. They were
straightforward, conscientious efforts to train the "mind, the
conscience and the heart," and they were rooted in the immediate problems of the students. But they were modeled
after the New England colleges. By far the most serious
indictment of Negro education lies in the argument that it has
been imitative, almost servile in its fastidious duplication of
the educational patterns of the dominant group, thereby
tending to prolong the subservient attitudes of the subordinated group. Once again, it is understandable that many of the
persons engaged in the education of Negroes in the earlier
decades should have insisted that the educational opportunities for Negroes should be in every respect as good as those
for whites. It was then a very short step from that to the
insistence that schools and colleges for Negroes should be
exactly like those for whites. Differentiation implied inferiority. Therefore, equality could come only through exact duplication. Thus began the historic process from 1860 to 1930
which culminated in the accreditment of some of the better
Negro colleges on exactly the same standards of accreditment
as were used for the white colleges of the South—a process
dominated by the idea that colleges for Negroes must be as
nearly as possible exact replicas of the best colleges for whites.
Anything else implied inferiority. Conformity to the stereo-
typed pattern of the liberal arts college therefore was placed
at a premium. Innovation was frowned upon. Imitation became the norm.

[54] *Ibid.*, p. 163.

Highly educated Negroes denounce persons who advocate for the Negro a sort of education different in some respect from that now given the white man. . . . They are anxious to have everything the white man has even if it is harmful. The possibility of originality in the Negro, therefore, is discounted one hundred per cent to maintain a nominal equality.[55]

Undoubtedly this imitative character of Negro education has brought it many good features. The educational patterns hammered out by centuries of experience could not have been altogether wrong—at any rate, they were the best then known. Men ought not to be condemned too strongly for doing the best they know how to do, even though that best may occasionally appear to be a rather poor second best from the point of view of historical perspective.

From the standpoint of its effect upon the caste system, however, this imitative character of the Negro college is not an unmixed blessing. Looked at from one angle, it appears to be a direct onslaught upon the inequities of caste. Does it not aim to give the Negro the finest and best educational opportunities of the cultured gentleman? Looked at from another angle, it appears to be an astute device for prolonging the subservience of the colored man. Does it not teach him, by direction and by indirection, to copy the doings and thinking of the white race at all times? "The chief difficulty with the education of the Negro," writes one of the principal critics of the contemporary Negro college, "is that it has been largely imitation resulting in the enslavement of his mind."[56] No matter what packages of cultural materials may have been accumulated, or even assimilated, by the Negro student, if he still bows down before the idol of white supremacy, he is not a free man. If the net effect of the imitative college has been to make black scholars merely lengthened shadows of white superiority, then the Negro college can be seriously indicted as a tool of oppression or condoned as an excellent device for social control, as the predilection of the observer inclines him.

[55] Carter G. Woodson, *The Miseducation of the Negro*, pp. xi, xii.
[56] *Ibid.*, p. 134.

It is more than a question of weighing positive and negative effects and striking an average of probable value; it is a fundamental question of the intended and the actual effects of the typical college for Negroes. In all its characteristics, the Negro college tends to be a respectable copy of the white college. This may serve to give the Negro whatever status comes from being "just as good" or "just like" the dominant group; but at the same time it robs him of that subtle and precious ability to estimate himself in terms of his own worth rather than in terms of imitative standards of accomplishment. It is an instance where the progressive adequacy of the attainment serves to underscore its ultimate inadequacy.

To educate the Negro we must find out exactly what his background is, what he is today, what his possibilities are, and how to begin with him as he is and make him a better individual of the kind that he is. Instead of cramming the Negro's mind with what others have shown that they can do, we should develop his latent powers that he may perform in society a part of which others are not capable.[57]

If we are told that it will be difficult to develop these values of originality and imagination without incurring the accusation of differentiation in order to discriminate, we must reply that the difficulty is the measure not of the hopelessness but of the challenge. If we are told that education designed actually to meet the needs of the Negro as a Negro in American society will be as likely to cultivate the subtle nuances of psychological inferiority in him as the imitative duplication of white academic patterns has done, we must take this as a warning of evils to be avoided rather than as a prescription against the adventure.

[57] *Ibid.*, p. 151.

X

A CONCEPTION OF A
FUNCTIONAL COLLEGE

*Social institutions . . . , the pattern of social arrange-
ments, are the finally controlling influences in shaping
minds.*   —JOHN DEWEY

IF THE weight of caste is ever to be eased so that the Negro may draw a free breath and come into his birthright as an American citizen, and particularly if the Negro college is to play an active, though subsidiary, part in thus transforming the caste system and opening broad avenues of opportunity to all people, critical intelligence and humane understanding must be brought to bear upon the present institutions of higher learning for Negroes. A special effort must be made to probe beneath the surface controversies and specious interests to the deeper questions of national and racial well-being. We have seen that race attitudes support the caste system out of which they grow. We have seen that the important questions to be asked about Negro education have to do both with the bearing of the college upon the caste system and with the possibility of using the segregated college to build for optimum living for all people. The question now becomes: What kind of a college might best meet the demands of the present social opportunities which segregation thrusts upon education? How shall we conceive the idea of a college functionally designed to discharge its social purpose?

Look first at the fact that unless the college is actually designed to meet its social opportunities, there is relatively little likelihood that best results will follow. A cursory examination of American collegiate practice suggests (a) that the actual practices of typical colleges are such as to deny to the students their rightful opportunities to mature as social beings during their collegiate experience; (b) that there is a strong tendency of collegiate life to destroy nascent idealism and blunt ethical sensitivity, thus defeating efforts to grow in social-mindedness; and (c) that in the light of the two foregoing deficiencies, looked at from the standpoint of social functioning, the long-standing and periodically recurring debate between classical and vocational education is irrelevant and misleading.

COLLEGE DENIES ADULTHOOD

The assertion that the actual practices of the typical American college for white or black are such as to deny to the students their rightful opportunities to mature as social beings during their collegiate experience is most ably elaborated alike by Kallen and McConn.[1] The collegiate quandary is not an easy one to solve. The American college receives students who are in most cases still boys and girls. It graduates men and women. During the four years of residence, they are supposed to mature from late adolescence to adulthood. This problem is peculiar to American education. In the European systems, the transition from adolescence to adulthood is accompanied by a change of institutions. The American college, coming as a continuation of the high school and a preview of the university, faces a special range of problems and difficulties. That the colleges are not entirely successful in meeting this difficulty may in part be due to the lack of clear recognition of this peculiarly American problem.

Social infantilism, says Kallen, is imposed upon biological maturity in the colleges. The college, indeed, is a pat instrument for the prolongation of social infancy, in that (*a*) it selects automatically the individuals who do not have to begin earning their own living and taking care of themselves financially; (*b*) it provides academic classical education which has no relevance to the serious concerns of life, making the college and the college student tangential to the main currents and realities of life; (*c*) it ignores the upsurging sex life of the maturing student; (*d*) it permits active participation as a social adult not in the serious purpose of the college, but only in the extracurricular area, the relationship of the president and the dean to this area being like that of the policeman to the corner gang; (*e*) it sets the undergraduate apart as a

[1] H. M. Kallen, *College Prolongs Infancy*, and Max McConn, *College or Kindergarten?*

privileged character, not amenable to the ordinary laws of peaceful conduct to which all workers of the same age are responsible; (f) it concentrates his thinking upon invidious irrelevancies, for "College is not a republic of letters, but a plutocracy of fraternities, sororities, clubs, and 'activities,'" training the undergraduate in a false standard of values. "The American undergraduate makes the impression of a self-centered and selfish creature, absorbed in trivialities, comfort-loving, reactionary, and irresponsible; in a word, infantile."[2]

Approaching the matter from the opposite angle, McConn nevertheless agrees with Kallen in the insistence that college is a super-kindergarten. Kallen tends to emphasize the responsibility of the college in permitting itself to be an impediment to the student in his efforts to mature. McConn tends to lay the greater responsibility upon the children and parents who assume that the college is a kind of safe place to put young people after they are out of prep school and before they are ready for business and marriage, where they will be safely cared for until they are ready to "come out." But both writers agree that the academic set-up is based on the contention that life begins at Commencement, not before.

Now, the prolongation of infancy through collegiate life is serious enough in any college. There may be a place for the super-kindergarten as a depository for the children of the plutocracy, to keep them from premature plunges into adulthood (premature as their mothers see it, at any rate). Those who can pay for it may be permitted the luxury of a

[2] Kallen, op. cit., p. 25 and again: "But so long as colleges are managed as they are managed, and teaching continues as and what it is, it is impossible that students should not be in one form or another, collegiate—that is, adults conducting themselves like children. For social adulthood consists in self-support and self-management, in moral responsibility and intellectual integrity. These are associated with physiological maturity but are by no means identical with it. Physiological maturity comes as an instinctive ripening, in the course of nature. Social adulthood is a learned mode of behaviour in the social environment; a system of habits acquired, not a state of body grown into. This is why bodies may grow up and grow old while minds and hearts remain infantile. And this is why adulthood cannot be learned in colleges as they are now any more than swimming can be learned on dry land; the medium is too different, too alien." (P. 28.)

collegiate country club for their children; and some institutions may properly address themselves to the honest effort to provide this service. As McConn rightly argues, a limited number of these homes for older children will be eagerly welcomed by parents who can pay the bill. And from the standpoint of social welfare, it will be a good thing to have the gentlemen and ladies of tomorrow well groomed and trained, and safely guided through their last perilous years of adolescent irresponsibility. Good social policy supports the idea. But to contemplate the indefinite continuance of the super-kindergarten as the sole, or even the dominant, collegiate pattern is unthinkable. The idea is particularly uncongenial to the administrator of the Negro college.

To be sure, there are Negroes who have enough of this world's goods to enable them to patronize at least one or two of these efficient finishing schools for the gentry; and as long as their children are denied entrance to the "best" white finishing schools, it may be that one or two intelligently managed gentlemen's colleges for Negroes need to be developed. McConn's serious proposal for the development of such schools can well be considered by not more than two Negro institutions. But the possibility that many of the institutions for Negroes may, into the indefinite future, think of themselves as standing *in loco parentis* and of the students as being *in statu filiorum,* does not square with the functional idea of a college which is attempting to transform the caste system.

One of the principal methods by which the caste system perpetuates itself is that of permanently keeping the Negro from achieving psychological majority—he must forever stay in his place as dictated by the dominance-submission pattern of the old master-slave paternalism. If the defendants of the caste system wished to devise an educational institution which would perpetuate the invidious distinctions of white superiority, they could fasten on no better educational device than the collegiate pattern which lies at hand. Keep the Negro student concerned with the trivia of academic life. Do not let him have any part in the main business of college. Let him think only of himself as a yes-man whose job it is to learn the answers to professorial questions—answers also given him by the professors. Talk to him about good citizenship and social responsibility, but do not let this talk go beyond the realm of the classroom and the chapel rostrum.

In short, follow the dominant pattern of American collegiate life and you will have a perfect tool for the perfect job of keeping the Negro permanently in submission and acquiescence. You will assist in breaking whatever remnant of aspiration toward social maturity there may be in him. You will turn out graduates who, for the four most impressionable years of their lives (next to the two following birth), have learned one lesson and learned it well. They know that they are not expected or permitted to take serious concern in the important affairs of their own lives. They are to accept the social environment and make the best of it for themselves. From time to time they will gain increasing rights and powers to control their own restricted area of student social affairs and extracurricular activities. This will serve to emphasize the axiom of the caste system that if they will only be content to hoe in their own back yards, they may cultivate whatever vegetables or weeds they wish, but they must not presume to climb any fences. What difference will it make in such an institution whether they are offered the classical curriculum, technical training, or vocational education? Regardless of the subject matter of their courses of study, they are learning, and learning well, the basic lesson of unquestioning conformity to the dominant social pattern. For the finally controlling influence in shaping minds is the pattern of social arrangements, the form of social institutions.[3] And the college, which is the society, the social order, of the student for four years, shapes the student mind not so much by what it teaches as by what it practices.

In his disarmingly frank and fascinatingly real picture of undergraduate life as he knew it in student days, Canby writes:

[3] John Dewey, *Individualism, Old and New*, p. 128.

College *life* (not studies) for us was at least ninety per cent of our felt experience, and therefore ninety per cent of the college as we knew it. Thus it became our real education, for every hard-lived life is an education, and no education educates unless it is lived. . . . The official idea of education differed sharply from ours and was formulated, whereas ours was instinctive. . . . With this (official) *collegium* we students had a compulsory acquaintance, which varied from the bum's consciousness of a policeman just around the corner to an amiable arrangement by which so much required knowledge should be paid in small change into the dean's office in return for an adequate minimum of marks.[4]

This, then, is the first great weakness of the nonfunctional college—it works on the philosophy that life begins at Commencement; that by deduction, students in colleges are in preparation for life; and that by conclusion, they are not to engage in the serious concerns of living while in college. What happens on Commencement Day, when the academic umbilical cord is severed, is of secondary concern to the college. If for four years the student has been nurtured and developed and has come through unscathed, he is ready for graduation. The college can do no more for him. It has already done enough to him, in projecting a social infant into an adult world, where he is the prey of all the social forces of caste and class.

COLLEGE DISCOURAGES IDEALISM

The average young Negro who actually arrives in college has a genuine and understandable feeling that merely to have matriculated is in itself a great achievement. Only one in 500 ever gets to college. For those who do enter college, matriculation represents, in the majority of cases, the culmination of dreams and hopes and aspirations of an entire family, sometimes of a whole community. Great dreams and expectations are built up. Since many parents of the present generation have themselves had rather limited educational opportunities, the feeling of achievement is heightened as the son or daughter goes off to college. If high hopes mean anything, the Negro

---

[4] Henry S. Canby, *Alma Mater,* p. 59. Italics are author's own.

student is well equipped at entrance. He differs from the white college student in this particular only in degree, but he does come equipped with great aspirations. As T. V. Smith says of the white college students, so, *a fortiori*, we may say of the Negro student:

Our students have already, and indigenously, more high ideals than we know what to do with. Our job is not, however, to deplenish ideals. Our task is a tempering of ideals, so that the narrow limits of action will not so sour the excess thereof as to render action meaner than it must be. Our task is, in all conscience, more how to develop a strategic diversion of the excess, than to discover some ideal-fulfilling action. No action is likely to fulfill more than it frustrates the life of the spirit. Action is necessary but action is not enough.

Our task is the more difficult because our effects upon students will be more a function of our unconscious philosophy of life than of our prescription for their philosophies of life. What we *are* will speak to our students more eloquently in this vague field than any curriculum we advertise, or anything we say about it. Our only recourse here is to look to our own philosophies of life.[5]

By a familiar psychological process, high anticipations serve to exaggerate disappointments, and also to increase the likelihood of personality difficulties growing out of disappointment of ethical idealism. This is particularly true of the young Negro who at last arrives at college, too often with a naïve faith that the college will equip him with the full panoply of the educated man and send him forth a knight errant to battle for truth and right and justice. Anticipating these outcomes, however vaguely he may formulate them in his own mind, the student thereby creates within himself an inner tension, demanding the prerogatives and rights of the anticipated status and achievement in advance of the actualization of his dreams. In response, he gets a degree of sympathetic understanding from college administrators and teachers, but he seldom gets the substance of things hoped for. It is not merely that he is put to work on assignments, some of which are dull and some of which are not. Nor is it merely that he

[5] T. V. Smith, "Ideals in the Life of Practice," in *Growth and Development: The Basis for Educational Programs*, p. 121.

soon learns, as Canby did, that the real excitement is something other than the official college, and he transfers his active interest to "college life." It is that, given no meaningful participation in the determining of the main business of the college itself, he therefore welcomes the cheap and easy substitutes of campus trivialities to compensate for his disappointment on the real issues. He comes like a young Lochinvar out of the South or the North, to ride in the lists. He is put to scrubbing armor and grooming horses—which would be significant if the knights themselves ever entered the tourney. He soon learns from the older lackeys who have "been around a while" that nobody ever really does anything except drill and train and exhort. No wonder he loses interest in the main business. No wonder he works as little as he can and still "get by." No wonder he fills the vacuum of his life with the things which he and his comrades in service have discovered are interesting and exciting. Student absorption in academic trivialities is a direct function of the denial to students of active participation in shaping and administering the important things of collegiate life. Here in college, as back there in the home town, the student learns that all he is expected to do is "Do what de man say."

Here, also, is a tool for the perpetuation of caste. If the student does, by some accident, manage to nurse some sparks of idealism through the long winters of campus indifference, it is his own doing, not that of the college. In its effect upon the caste system, the college is then a negligible factor as far as the idealism of its graduates is concerned. Equally serious is the fact that the inner resources of the student have been torn down and depleted rather than built up and fortified. He came with hopes and aspirations. He was denied opportunity to express them in significant ways. He leaves, cynical and disillusioned, feeling that the world owes him a living and that he is out to collect his due. He may carry a pleasant afterglow of collegiate memories with him into the harsh outer world which will fortify him in moments of loneliness and fits of depression, but nostalgia is scarcely an adequate substitute for robust idealism. And unless the Negro college can meet this challenge—meet it directly, consistently, and continuously—its contribution to the advancement of the Negro and to the easier adjustment of the races will be negligible. "If the college can pour into the coming age an American Negro who knows himself and his plight and how to protect himself and fight race prejudice, then the world of our dream will come and not otherwise."[6] And the college which treats its students as older children rather than as younger adults, which arrests the development of their nascent idealism by refusing adequate exercise of the students' aspirations in significant enterprises and activities, is not meeting the demands of its social function in these terms.

The question which naturally emerges at this point is: What stands in the way of the college to prevent its meeting these two fundamental needs of the student—opportunity for maturing into social adulthood and opportunity for growth in idealism with adequate care for excess ideality? Many things stand in the way—things which are diverse for different institutions and situations; but one thing will tend to correct both evils. Let an honest attempt be made to conceive of the college as playing a normative and directive part in transforming life (in the case of the Negro college, of transforming also the institutions of caste and class) and as fortifying its graduates for the uneven struggle for personal integrity and satisfaction in an inequitable world. Let the college honestly seek to discharge its social function, and it will be forced to reconsider its theories and its practice. It will need to lengthen its ropes and strengthen its stakes.

THE MISLEADING IRRELEVANCY OF SIDE ISSUES

The misleading irrelevancy of the debate between classical and vocational education is indicated in the preceding chapter, where we saw that ten different attitudes toward industrial training had conflicting and contradictory reference to the

[6] W. E. B. DuBois, "The Field and Function of the American Negro College," *Fisk University News,* Vol. VI (June, 1933).

underlying issue of racial advancement. The interesting feature of this phenomenon to which we now revert is that the advocates of both the classical and the vocational courses of study have implicitly admitted this fact while explicitly denying it. The admission has come in the defense of their courses of study not on the grounds of their respective primary curricular offerings but upon the grounds of their alleged secondary and tertiary associated learnings.

The classical college course offered its students learning, primarily learning from books about books. Enrichment of the study with laboratory and field opportunities did not change the fundamental bent of the liberal arts course. The primary objective was the mastery of a body of subject matter, and the whole system of teaching and examining was directed to make sure that whatever portions of knowledge the teacher and examiner had decided in advance that the neophyte must retain at examination time, must, perforce, become the primary matters of collegiate (official) concern. This educational objective demanded teaching methods appropriate to it. Since the primary purpose of the college was to impart a known body of knowledge to young minds, the logical manner of attack was that of first agreeing upon the particular body of knowledge to be conveyed and then, dividing this subject matter up into convenient departments of study, get the youngsters to gorge as much as possible and regurgitate it at examination time. In all too many cases the invited guests have not thought highly of the roast beef and boiled potatoes of official diet, and have turned their attention to the spicier viands of extracurricular activities. Ingenious devices have been invented with the hope of making the main courses more palatable, or of increasing the appetite and capacity of the student—devices varying from the cafeteria style of Harvard's Eliot to the "Take it all or choke" demands of the comprehensive examiners who seem to think each undergraduate is a kind of H. G. Wells and Hendrik Van Loon rolled in one. And be it readily admitted that, from the standpoint of getting the students to develop from academic gourmands to intellectual and aesthetic epicures, many of these devices have been quite effective. The current growth of cramming agencies on the peripheries of leading campuses indicates that, at long last, students are taking this business seriously enough to pay good money for aid in last-hour gorging. That not a few great scholars and high-minded men of magnanimous character have come out of this system of academic forced feeding is readily admitted. And it is likely that, for the American scene, where college students normally come at a more tender stage of development than is common in Europe, this is to be preferred to the cold indifference of continental university officialdom. But good results from the subject-matter-centered college are accidental rather than inevitable. They come in spite of the college and because of the astounding resiliency of the human spirit.

The announced objectives of the colleges have been "training for leadership," "training in Christian character," "intellectual growth," and the like;[7] but the testimony of collegiate practice indicates that the real objectives, as distinguished from the catalogue pronouncements, have been those of imparting predetermined quantities of subject matter under threat of examinations with an effort to get a reasonable modicum of memory work on the part of the student and, where possible, to add to this the appurtenances and graces of civilized living, with occasional serious attempts to add lessons in morality or to cultivate habits of critical thinking.

Not for a moment would we question the real value of knowledge, the mastery of subject matter. If the choice lies between knowledge and ignorance, there is no alternative. But we do vigorously question whether the way to optimum knowledge is the road down which the liberal arts undergraduate has customarily been led. The ability to pass examinations, proving that one can remember reasonably well for the examination period a modicum of information formerly handed out by the professor, does not necessarily indicate that the

[7] See Mowat G. Fraser, *The College of the Future, passim;* and also H. S. Tuttle, *Social Basis of Education,* Ch. I.

student has knowledge. Certainly he has learned something, but probably the thing he has best learned is how most successfully to pass the examinations—how best to "get by." That is what "passing" means.

Moreover, as the friends of vocational education are never tired of pointing out, the liberal arts course is impractical. From the standpoint of the actual bread-and-butter needs of modern life, it is of relatively small value. It butters no bread, does not even bake it. Designed to serve in an earlier day when all serious books were written in Latin and the best available literature were the classics, retained at a later day as an adornment of the gentleman of leisure, the classical learning is offered now on a wide scale in America because of a belief that democracy demands that the best should be open to all. Yet, while the classical course of an earlier day may have functioned as culture in the life of the graduate,[8] it becomes increasingly clear that hardly a decimal of America's flood of baccalaureate degree holders can be accused of "cracking a book" for cultural or serious purposes after graduation. In college they were "educated," and they have their diplomas to prove it. But with Commencement, they began a new life, and what they knew on the campus was left behind.[9] They no longer have assignments to be filled or examinations to be passed. In college, they learned how to get through college. Being out, they have no further need for the campus techniques. What college graduate of five years' standing can readily recall the content of half a dozen of his courses unless he has had subsequent reason to keep himself freshly informed about them for professional and business reasons? What percentage of classically trained men will be found, ten years after graduation, reading Aeschylus or studying the stars (ruling out the preachers and teachers for whom the classical course is actually vocational training)?

Faced with this demonstration of the irrelevancy of classical education, the champions of the liberal arts course have

[8] See Everett D. Martin, *The Meaning of a Liberal Education*, Ch. IV.
[9] See John R. Tunis, *Was College Worth While?* pp. 57-67, 97-113.

not been silent. They have admitted quite frankly that much or most of the knowledge which in four years is dinned into the youngsters under compulsion of examination-to-come is subsequently forgotten. They have admitted, with some reluctance, that the classical course may not actually train a man or woman so that in life after graduation the holder of the parchment avidly pursues truth for the sheer joy of intellectual pursuit. But they have maintained that there were other values in the liberal arts course which justified it.[10] These other values were the habits of critical thinking,

[10] See F. W. Kelsey, *Latin and Greek in American Education,* for a judicious and well-balanced discussion of the issues involved. The following extracts, typical of the more vehement defense of classical courses of study, are taken at random from *The Value of the Classics,* a report of a conference at Princeton University in 1917, edited by A. F. West and published by the Princeton University Press: "For ages it has been the view of most of the master thinkers that the human mind does not develop well without exercise and that it is developed most highly by mastering knowledge which is both difficult and valuable." (P. 21.) "Thus he develops habits of analysis, habits of discriminating choice of words, habits of accurate apprehension of the meaning which another has sought to convey by written words, which lead to power of expression and to power of clear thinking." (P. 49.) "The best foundation for professional training is mental habits formed in school and college." (P. 50.) "This habit of close observation, of attention to detail, of looking for fine distinctions and shades of difference, and the alertness of mind awakened in an individual by these habits, prove of inestimable service to him. . . ." (P. 57.) ". . . of particular value in impressing upon the mind the great importance of precision in the expression of thought." (P. 71.) ". . . in widening his intellectual horizon, in adding to his all-around efficiency in dealing with men, and in teaching him accuracy of expression." (P. 72.) "The first test of education is the creation of an intelligent citizenship, inspired by love of country, by obedience to its laws, by willingness to serve them whenever and however such service may be required, and by abhorrence of everything detrimental to the public good . . . the leadership of mind and spirit is nurtured in the discipline which is found in liberal studies . . . in the cultivation of the powers of concentration and reasoning which experience has shown is best derived from the study of the classics." (Pp. 75, 77.) ". . . necessity of education for leadership in a democracy for which classical studies always have been and always will be the foundation." (P. 79.) "The first and dominant object of all education is to teach the child to use his mind. . . . Those who have been taught to use their minds can apply them to any subject and go as far as their individual limitations permit." (P. 102.) ". . . knowledge is essential to progress, and it has to be acquired by the cultivation of the faculty of independent reflection, which implies the power of selecting, combining, and testing the essential facts of the subject in hand." (P. 116.) "It is well to have this conception of duty and patriotism looked upon as a matter of course, as something not to be disputed, and there can be no doubt that early saturation of the boyish mind with the classics had much to do with this outcome." (P. 121.)

of the well-calculated mastery of the disciplined mind, which the assiduous study of the admittedly difficult classical course supposedly developed. Just as right exercise of the body developed the muscles and built up the tone of the body, having its beneficent effect in increased effectiveness for daily living, so, by analogy, the exercise of the "muscles of the mind" built them into stronger and more effective tools for intellectual operations. The "mental training and mental discipline"[11] which the classical course afforded constituted the real, the basic defense of the liberal studies. In addition, the student, during his course of study, was thrown in constant contact with high-minded, scholarly teachers of upright character; and by the contagion of example, as well as by all the subtle influences of daily living, he was trained in the appreciation of the finer things of life. If, therefore, the advocates of vocational and technical education questioned the primary value of the classical curriculum, the defenders of the liberal studies might, for the sake of argument, grant this contention; but they fell back upon the associated learnings, the development of desirable character traits, the value of the disciplined mind, as the final justification of the classical course.

An added degree of specious plausibility was given to their contention by the fact that most of the prominent men of learning, most of the great contributors to public welfare, most of the outstanding statesmen, in so far as they had been educated at all, were men trained in the classical courses. The possibility that, since the classical course was about the only course available up to the turning of the century, most of the mature leaders of the nation would have been educated in that course if they had been in college at all, did not dampen the enthusiasm of their defense.

Finally, the matter degenerated to the nasty level of statistical wrangling, where the defenders of the classical course argued that the boys who had been trained in the classical course stood much higher than the nonclassically trained

[11] Kelsey, *op. cit.*, p. 46.

boys in subsequent academic work.[12] The possibility that since campus opinion rated the classical course higher than the newly intruding technical and vocational studies, the men of ability gravitated largely to the "line of greater resistance," was overlooked or brushed aside as irrelevant. Thus, while many of the defenders of the faith in classical curricula refused to desert the citadel of knowledge-for-its-own-sake,[13] yet, under the insistent pressure of the twentieth-century demand for practical justification of everything, the classical curriculum found its contemporary apologetic not in terms of the subject matter covered but on the basis of the habits and attitudes professedly acquired in the process.

So, too, with technical, industrial, and manual education. The controversy has not been waged from one side only, and these newer types of education have had to look to their laurels. They began by maintaining that education of the hand would actually serve many of the purposes which the book learning was calculated to meet.[14] But from the start, they also stressed the value of the associated learnings. Manual training, in particular, was singled out as a happy method of training both heart and hand at once. It had a good disciplinary effect. It promoted habits of industry, independence of character, originality, and it stressed the development of masculinity as opposed to the effeminate character of book study. As the movement achieved the dignity of a new nomenclature, Bonser justified the industrial arts by saying:

The appropriate development of the curriculum in elementary and secondary schools with industrial arts properly coördinated provides reorganizing standards of value, and motivation for parts of nearly every other subject; and in the elementary and secondary schools the coming into a participating and appreciating experience of this body of thought

---

[12] The second half of the report of the Princeton conference on *The Value of the Classics* is devoted to marshaling the evidence on this point.

[13] They quoted Emerson: "Let us not forget that the adoption of the test, 'What is it good for' would abolish the rose and exalt in triumph the cabbage."

[14] See Charles Bennett, *History of Manual and Industrial Education up to 1870*, for full historical resume of the defenses offered in the early stages of the movement.

is of more importance than the development of mere technical skill in the manipulation of materials.[15]

Not so much in the primary curricular offerings of the technical course or the industrial and manual training, but much more in the alleged learnings of habits and attitudes, was justification found.

As an advancing technology left a relatively static technical training stranded on the mud flats of irrelevancy, vocational education tended to emphasize its secondary defenses more and more. In the early days of the movement, a Rousseau could maintain that training of the hands is a good thing because, when the Revolution came, he who had a trade would not be unwanted in the new society. But when the Industrial Revolution, followed by the Gargantuan growth of finance-capitalism, ushered in an age of intense specialization and rapid advance in technical processes, the handicraft idea of technical training was left without a friendly wave of industrial employment to moisten its keel. Accordingly, the defense of the landlubber academies was that at any rate their seamen knew the ropes and could take orders, even if they had yet to get their sea legs. The habits and skills of industriousness, thrift, application to the job, quickness and deftness, manual dexterity, perseverance, and personal integrity which were learned in the trade school stood the graduate in good stead as he found himself in the job to which he graduated. Not by the primary skills, but by the associated habits and attitudes, is technical and vocational training to be judged.

Now, within the circumscribed limits of the segregated institution of education for Negroes, this debate has been a tempest in a teapot. Enough of the debate was summarized in the previous chapter to indicate how seriously it has been taken. The point stressed in the previous chapter was that although the surface debate had to do with the choice be-

[15] Frederick G. Bonser, "Fundamental Values in Industrial Education," Technical Education Bulletin No. 10 (Teachers College, Columbia University, 1914).

tween two types of curricula, the real choice lay deeper in
the question of the relationship between the particular curricular offering with its peculiar teaching methods and philosophy on the one hand, and on the other, the underlying
issue of race advancement. We now add a second comment,
namely, that both the classical and the vocational schools of
thought have themselves suggested the real basis on which
they should be estimated, and in neither case is it the primary
curricular materials, but rather, in both, it is the indirect and
associated learnings which are held to be vitally important.

It appears, therefore, that two conclusions are justified on
the basis of the analysis thus far carried through: (1) the
important things about courses of study (as hitherto conceived) are not so much the primary materials to be mastered
as the attitudes and habits to be acquired; and (2) the real
question as to the type of education to be provided for Negroes does not hinge on the content of the curriculum narrowly defined, but on the broad bearing of the educational
procedure upon the efforts of the Negro to realize life goals
in American society and therefore also the bearing of education upon the caste system. If these two conclusions are accepted, we are permitted to proceed to another: (3) for the
Negro college, decisions as to educational procedure should
be made on the basis of the probable bearing which intended
student learnings of habits and attitudes will have upon the
caste system and upon the life of the Negro under it. To this
last may be added another, which academic and racial mod-
esty might discourage the Negro college from assuming, but
which genuine altruism as well as genuine self-interest insist
upon: (4) if it becomes possible for the Negro college to
contribute to the larger solution of problems of race relations, that, too, becomes part of the inclusive social function
of the Negro college.

Always and everywhere these four somewhat specialized
aspects of the social function of the Negro college are to be
kept in full relationship with the more inclusive general social function of the college. That is to say, the modification

of caste and the achievement of optimum living under the caste system during the interim of modification, while they are the most crucial aspects of the social function of the segregated college, are not the whole of the job by any means. The whole of the life of the Negro and the white man in the American South and North is significantly modified by the fact of caste; but caste is not the whole of life for anyone, white or Negro, North or South. An institution, then, which was so conceived as to work toward the modification of life so that every individual might have fullest opportunity to develop his richest and highest capacities, and which included the whole of life in its purview, might be called a functional college. A segregated college for Negroes, to become socially functional, would face the necessity of grappling seriously with the whole of American culture, a dominant feature of which is the caste system.

THE SOCIOLOGICAL APPROACH TO EDUCATIONAL PROBLEMS

This notion of the attempt to make the college socially effective is not new. Kilpatrick[16] demonstrates a truth that is often overlooked, namely, that the fathers of America had serious hope that education would be a principal factor in shaping social life. He also shows how this hope of a socially effective education continued and blossomed in the nineteenth century when the movement for universal free education was spreading. Today, the demand that this social function be thought of in terms somewhat more inclusive than the hopes of political democracy which defined the limits of these earlier desires for socially effective education, only serves to increase the challenge that in our own day we must reaffirm the avowed basic purpose of American education. There is therefore nothing new in the proposal that American education shall be conceived in terms of its social function. Nor is there anything new in the proposal that education for the Negro shall be so conceived. The novelty of the proposal, if any, comes in the insistence that a realistic attempt to imple-

[16] W. H. Kilpatrick, *Teacher and Society*, Ch. I-III.

ment the idea of a socially functioning college demands a complete realignment of the collegiate procedures and programs. The old dog must learn new tricks instead of going through the old tricks in response to the new commands.

To be sure, this proposal to implement the functional notion with appropriate instruments is, at least in major emphasis,[17] a departure from the orthodoxy of contemporary educational and social practice of the American college; but its heresy lies only in the serious proposal that faith should be expressed in works. Whatever educational heresy lies in the idea is connected with the proposal that the college engage frankly in making its major purpose the alleged objectives which, in self-defense, it has for some time claimed as its own, namely, the acquisition of desirable habits and attitudes, all else to be instrumental to this end. Subject matter becomes an important secondary consideration. Whatever social heresy there may be in the proposal grows out of the fact that the Negro college will openly and directly do what it has admittedly been attempting since its foundation, namely, make a serious effort to transform the caste system and to enable its graduates to transcend what, in their own lifetimes, they may not transform. Whatever fruitfulness there lies in this functional notion grows out of the fertilization of one proposal by the other—that the attitudes and habits which are to be the actual as well as the avowed educational objectives are to be conceived in terms of their bearing upon this intended transformation of caste and upon this individual fortification. The shape of the proposed social structure determines the manner of erecting the educational scaffolding, of fashioning the educational tools, of selecting the academic personnel, and of carrying on the actual construction. The functional notion of the college overcomes the structural and operational weaknesses of the nonfunctional ideas by insisting that the intended functioning is to be the controlling concept, and that all decisions as to method and procedure are to flow from this basic notion.

[17] See H. S. Tuttle, *Social Basis of Education*, p. 5.

THE EDUCATIONAL TASK IS THE TASK OF SOCIAL
RECONSTRUCTION

Despite the fact that this idea of a thoroughgoing socio-logical approach to educational problems is not new, there still exists a good deal of doubt in educational circles that the educational task is the task of social reconstruction. In the circles of the Negro colleges, in particular, this doubt is tenacious, and with good reason. Not merely does it echo the prevailing doubt of many professional and business leaders in the white group, but it represents the continuing effect of the example of Dr. Washington who is widely held to have been the greatest, as he was undoubtedly the most influential, Negro American yet to emerge from the group. Perhaps the best critical summary of his social philosophy is that of Curti[18] who writes:

Washington's social philosophy was, in fine, more typical of middle-class white Americans, whom he wanted his people to be like, than it was of the Negro as such. It is true that in appealing to former slaves and their offspring to eschew militancy and conflict with the whites in the effort to improve the status of the race, he capitalized the black man's way of getting along by laughing, dancing, and singing. . . . Washington made simplicity, earnestness, frugality, and industry the great desiderata. One searches his writings in vain for any appreciation of the aesthetic and cultural values of the African background. . . . In other ways Washington was like the average American. His insistence on looking at the bright side of things, his devotion to getting ahead by self-help, his conviction that everyone had his future in his own hands, that success came to him who was worthy of it, and that the greater the obstacles, the greater the victory over them—all this characterized the thought and feeling of most Americans. Equally typical of the dominant psychology of the middle and upper classes was his denial of any conflict or cleavage of interest between worker and employer, white or black. His was the gospel of coöperation.

If, in spite of his positive contributions in helping Negroes adjust themselves to a system, Booker T. Washington failed to criticize fundamental weaknesses in that system, his failure was hardly a personal one. He was merely accepting the prevalent American doctrine of self-help and the belief that the best man gets ahead, and, considering his back-

[18] Merle Curti, *Social Ideals of American Educators*, pp. 302-4, 309.

ground, it is not strange that he failed to see that this holds even less true for the humble Negro than for the average white man. The limitations of his social thinking were not, primarily, those of a Negro— they were those of the class which, on the whole, determined American values and governed American life.

The elongated shadow of this man of great stature who stood at the dawn of the new day and projected his influence into the future gives these middle-class ideas of personal success on the basis of merit a special tenacity and holding power in the minds of the Negroes of America. DuBois and Woodson may attack with great vigor; but the idea is firmly rooted. Only slowly and with great pain is the dominance of the middle- and upper-class white ideology being wrested from the minds over which it has held sway these generations.

Today there are voices, voices from all quarters, clamoring for a more realistic appraisal of the task of the Negro college under the caste system. DuBois and Bond have been cited briefly above. So, too, with Woodson:[19]

Can you expect teachers to revolutionize the social order for the good of the community? Indeed we must expect this very thing. The educational system of a country is worthless unless it accomplishes this task.

We should not eliminate many courses now being offered, but we should secure men of vision to give them from the point of view of the people to be served. We should not spend less money for the higher education of the Negro, but should redefine higher education as preparation to think and work out a program to serve the lowly rather than to live as an aristocrat.

Our study of the impact of caste upon the Negro leads us to see greater educational possibilities in the attack upon caste than in conformity to it. This means a double attack: an attack upon the "internal" problems of the Negro group, whether these problems are a result of segregation and discrimination or not, in the expectation that much can be done to raise the level of living and of insight and self-expression within the confines of caste as it now exists; and an attack upon the burden of iniquitous inequity which caste lays upon America, in the hope that white and black alike will one day

[19] Carter G. Woodson, *Miseducation of the Negro,* pp. 145, 149.

be able to walk the earth with dignity and without fear, working together for the greatest welfare of all. There will be a third objective of the functional college which is mediary between these two, and which represents a passing or transitional stage: the cultivation of individual ability to live above the difficulties of caste, to transcend what is not immediately transformed.

Our educational methods and procedures for the functional college must be elaborated and fabricated with these three purposes—or these three aspects of a single purpose—in mind. In short, the functional college under the caste system is one in which all that happens in the lives of students and staff is directed, as far as may be possible, with a view to making life under the caste system as fine and noble and humane and dignified a matter as it may be, while at the same time working to transform the environing system of which caste is a dominant feature to permit larger opportunities for normal living, and enabling individuals to reach beyond the limitations of the system and to lay hold on satisfactions of normal and happy living which the confinements of caste seek to deny. We do not imply that this transforming and transcending function is the whole of the functional college conception; but we do affirm that the whole conception of the Negro college is functionally modified by the adoption of this notion of the task of higher education for Negroes under the caste system in America. "We are concerned not merely with an educational program but with a program for the reconstruction of our future culture."[20] And we must therefore reorganize and reshape the college, which is the society in which the student learns, since "social institutions . . . the pattern of social arrangements, are the finally controlling influences in shaping minds."[21]

But if there is disagreement over the question of whether education should concern itself with the social process, there

[20] L. K. Frank, "General Education Today," *Social Frontier,* III (April, 1937), 209-11.
[21] John Dewey, *op. cit.,* p. 128.

is even more disagreement over the nature of the concern to be expressed. It appears that there are at least half a dozen different attitudes toward the social process which education may strike—and much depends upon which of these is selected. Without in any way indicating that these categories are distinct and discrete, in fact stressing the point that they are a series of foci for emphasis within an inclusive pattern of possibilities, and remembering also that any one college may include within its ranks believers in several different programs, and that a given college may actually combine two or more seemingly contradictory patterns in its practice, we may classify the actual practices under six convenient logical headings to facilitate analysis. The principal attitudes toward the social process which higher education commonly takes are:

Attitude 1 assumes that it is the purpose of the college to be the "citadel of culture," the ivory tower of academic serenity in a materialistic world.

This is the dominant pattern of the classical college[22] and the recognizable prototype of many liberal arts colleges today. That it has much which appears to commend it is suggested by its longevity and its wide prevalence. As far as its social attitude is an index of its pose of unperturbed serenity, we are justified in calling it *irenic*.

Attitude 2 assumes that it is the purpose of the college to serve the bread-and-butter demands of its hardheaded clientele, putting the individual demands for vocational proficiency at the head of its lists of objectives and subordinating long-range ideas of social concern to the more immediate and practical demands of job proficiency.

Not a few of the liberal arts colleges which still cling to the irenic stereotype also permit themselves to be classified under this heading of *mercantile*, for they persist in recruit-

---

[22] "I suppose that the analogy which best describes the relation of academic life to the country at large is the medieval state, in which the monasteries, supported by the community and enriched by predatory king or baron, provided harborage for men violently opposed to the world that permitted them to exist." Canby, *op. cit.*, p. 141.

ing students with statistically supported notions of the cash value of the Bachelor's degree. Many of the metropolitan trade and professional schools fit into this category, selling vocational proficiency for cash.

Attitude 3 assumes that it is the purpose of the college to conform to the demands of contemporary society, enabling each individual to find his niche and to be effective in it.

This is the so-called "sociological approach to education," typically characterized by the curriculum based on job analyses and the guidance based on a study of existing vocational openings, using social measurement and outlining of trends as the basis for projecting the educational process. Social demands as thus discovered become the basis for educational adjustment and accommodation. Many trade and professional schools belong in this group of the *accommodative* or *conformist* schools. From the standpoint of their social philosophy, many liberal arts colleges also tend to follow the breezes of the day rather than to retreat into the ivory tower or to challenge the dominant temper of the age.

Attitude 4 starts with a set of preconceptions and postulates about the kind of society which ought to prevail, analyzes the present society in the light of these principles, and then projects an educational program calculated to move society in the directions it has projected.

Popular with Fascist and Communist regimes abroad, this educational pattern is also found within the United States where it is most effectively practiced by a few labor colleges, certain graduate schools of business and commerce, and certain colleges maintained by the more vigorously orthodox religious groups. It is currently presented in its most persuasive form in *The Higher Learning in America* in which President Hutchins advocates the restoration of metaphysics as the central and organizing principle of education. There is another, and increasingly articulate, group of educators who wish to set up the democratic way of life[23] as the determinant

[23] See, for example, W. B. Bizzell, "Liberalism in Higher Education," *School and Society*, XLIV (November 21, 1936), 663-70: "There is one com-

from which all procedures and plans are to be deduced. The several forms of this *authoritarian* or *dogmatic* school share the common characteristic that each starts from an assumed body of doctrine from which all educational and social principles flow.

Attitude 5 believes that education ought to engage in the free and untrammeled study and discussion of the social process and of social issues, leaving to the future, however, whatever outcomes there may be from the continuance of this descriptive and analytical process.

In this *descriptive-analytic* camp we find a large section of "Progressive Education," men whose naïve faith in laissez-faire education is not yet shaken by the waning of this same notion in other quarters. In many respects, particularly in its effects, this attitude is the actual equivalent of the irenic retreat. It observes the social drift—but merely observes.

Attitude 6 begins with the tentative projection of desirable change in society on the basis of study and analysis, and moves by the evaluation of projected results and measurement of the consequences following adoption, using education as the means of critical analysis and as a tool of social reconstruction.

This *instrumentalist* or *experimentalist* approach to the problems of social change might conceivably be superimposed upon the pattern of almost any of the other five, but its adoption would mean the abandonment of much that was characteristic of the college, and the transformation of the residue. The experimental character of this approach is not easily maintained. Tentative programs tend to become per-

---

promise, however, that our public educational system can not make. It can not compromise with the theory of the Totalitarian State. Democracy is irreconcilable with any theory of government that fosters regimentation and restricts private initiative. . . . Education by its very nature is individualistic. . . . Education should recognize that individualism and collectivism represent two opposing tendencies in human society. . . . I traveled during the past summer in several countries where education is completely regimented and individual initiative is greatly restricted. I returned with the feeling that our educational institutions must resist such schemes with all the moral power that they possess." (P. 669.)

manent. The experiment tends to crystallize into the new orthodoxy. Instrumentalism is in constant danger of degenerating into dogmatism. Something of the objective impartiality and intellectually critical detachment of descriptive analysis must continually be incorporated in the experimental process to keep the experimenter humble and the process fertile; but something of the enthusiasm of dogmatic fervor must also be obtained, without the crystallized finality.

Of the colleges for Negroes, it is probably safe to say that any given institution probably represents an amalgam of several of these notions, depending in part upon the educational ideas which were dominant at the moment of the institutional founding, in part upon the racial and geographical origins of the founders, and in part upon the accidents of history. It is probably safe to hazard the tentative opinion that whatever normative and socially directive effort there has been in Negro education has been more nearly of the character and temper of the dogmatic than the spirit and purpose of the experimental. This last guess that Negro education has been more dogmatic than experimental applies with equal force to the believers in race advancement and to those who use education to keep the Negro down. Also, in Negro education, there has been a good deal of accommodative and conformist education under the aegis of sociological defenses. Not a little of materialism has masqueraded under the names of classical idealism on the one hand and of social adjustment on the other. Tentative gropings in the direction of descriptive-analysis have often been short-lived, leading to reversions to dogmatism. Experimentalism is just coming over the academic horizon; but it is being earnestly and intensively discussed in faculty "bull sessions" on segregated campuses. It is this instrumentalist approach to the problem of college and society which appears to hold greatest promise in shaping the idea of the functional college.

To be sure, there are weaknesses of the instrumentalist approach. Beside the robust reds and blues of dogmatism, its pale banners of tentative experimentation look sickly in the breeze. One looks with envy and nostalgia upon the effort of a Hutchins to bring order out of academic chaos by the legerdemain of metaphysical dictates. One is strongly tempted to adopt the dogmatic attitudes of the militant believers in democracy as they rally themselves to do battle with totalitarianism. The sureties of the dogmatists are values of strength which the instrumentalists in their most enthusiastic moments only faintly echo. And the assurance of dogmatic certainty either about ultimate goals or about immediate steps is a value for activity not lightly to be surrendered. Men still tend to believe that when one is right, one may be dogmatic; and conversely, that when one is not dogmatic, it is implied that he is uncertain that he is right. As a rallying cry, the hypotheses of experimentalism do not readily yield themselves to popular appeal. As an anchor for fearless adventure they leave much to be desired. Consequently, they make imperious demands upon their adherents, calling for inner resources which the certainties of some other approach might not demand. The quality of mind and spirit, the ability to carry on in the face of doubt and misgiving, to see an experiment fail and yet learn from the failure and to pick up the pieces and set to work again, the temperamental adjustment of critical loyalty to an evolving ideal—these are fruits of the spirit not born on every tree. The great weakness of the instrumentalist approach to social reconstruction (a weakness due in part to its newness in a hostile society) is that it makes these large demands upon its adherents. If many are called, few will be chosen.

The second weakness of instrumentalism as the educational pattern for social reconstruction lies in the requirement that the experiment must be embodied in some form or other. The institutionalizing of the experiment once it is projected means that in the very act of institutionalizing, it has been robbed of its tentativeness and plasticity. The momentum of a process once launched, the difficulty of gaining wholehearted support for an experiment without permitting supporters to erect the hypotheses into a new dogma, plus the time requirement for the period of the experiment, raise large demands and conjure formidable objections.

Particularly, the possibility of opposition to the experiment, not from within the ranks but from a hostile society, must be considered. Is it likely that the Negro college which frankly rejects the accommodative technique and tries to be normative will be smiled upon by the caste system? The disquieting experience of Berea College under the Kentucky laws serves as a reminder of the possibility of disaster ahead. Let that be admitted. But let it also be pointed out that if the college is to attempt this social function, the instrumentalist approach will be far better than the dogmatic, which would be certain to arouse a counter-dogmatism and engulf itself in the wave of its own eliciting. Certainly a frank, open-minded, straightforward attempt to train men and women so that they can grapple intelligently with the problems of life which most concern them is an attempt which ought to commend itself to men of good will everywhere. The narrow person of ill will would be opposed to any sort of move, but he should be less excited about undogmatic opposition. The undogmatic, experimentalist approach should commend itself strongly to intelligent persons of both races who have at heart the welfare of the masses of the people.

The consideration which makes the instrumentalist approach most appealing as we formulate the idea of the functional college is the fact that this idea appears to be best fitted to do the job which needs to be done in the light of the caste system. Of the six attitudes which might be taken, only one other makes a serious bid for acceptance by the functioning college; that one is the dogmatic. The irenic, mercantile, and accommodative are each well calculated to perpetuate the caste system. Each in its own way might prepare the individual for life under the system—the irenic by enabling him to possess his soul in serenity while worlds fall in shining ruin about him; the mercantile by enabling him to wrest a living from an inequitable society by superior training and hard application; the accommodative by teaching the methods of saving his own skin through conformity—but none of the three would generate one iota of effective influence to transform the system of caste. If any features of these three are to be included in the functional college, it will be on the basis that the particular qualities appropriated from the particular school of thought have value in preserving the integrity of the individual under the impact of caste. The analytic-descriptive attitude does not afford the promise of the instrumentalist approach because it aims merely at observation, classification, analysis, and study. It does not contemplate action; and if the college is to become anything like a normative influence, it must do more than observe. The descriptive-analytic method surrenders all the values of the positiveness and assurance of dogmatism without promising compensation in terms of effectiveness for action. But it does possess one great virtue which the dogmatic approach does not, namely, the belief in scientific method, with the accompanying distrust of authoritarianism and its deductive procedure. It is the inclusion of precisely this factor which makes the otherwise appealing dogmatism inappropriate for our purposes.

It is the characteristic of dogmatism to start with all the answers to all the questions subsumed in its own presuppositions, and then, like some gigantic spider who spins her web from her own bowels, to weave the gossamer structures of its self-secreted system for the ensnarement of the unwary. No one doubts the tremendous popular appeal that dogmatism has. It is the stock-in-trade of every political campaign, of most religious enterprises, of practically all business and economic activity. Most important for us, it is the backbone and strength of race prejudice and of the caste system. Without dogmatism, the barriers of race would not have one leg to stand on; and without dogmatism, caste would be meaningless. If this, then, is the method of the opposition, why should we not meet the enemy with the enemy's tactics?

Wilkerson[24] advocates just this fighting with fire. DuBois[25] in some of his speaking and writing shares some limitations of the dogmatic spirit, although such a work as *Black Reconstruction* takes on the authority of authenticity by the sheer weight of documentation and the evidence of meticulous and comprehensive research. The more temperate approach of the descriptive-analysts is suggested by Wiggins[26] as the proper alternative to the dogmatic attitude; but we have already noted the reasons for believing that instrumentalism is more promising than descriptive-analysis. Perhaps it might be put this way: the processes of descriptive-analysis must be included as a part of the experimental process of instrumentalism; and the allegiance to the enterprise which sees it through to its conclusions must likewise be found in instrumentalism, but without the blind and uncritical adherence of dogmatism. Instrumentalism calls for critical loyalty to an evolving ideal.

ACCURACY PLUS ARDOR

In the end, the case for the instrumentalist approach to the problems of caste rests upon the pragmatic results of such an approach, primarily in the results of such an approach upon the minds and attitudes of students. If the student learns well the methods and spirit of the instrumentalist approach to life problems, he will see through the weak sham of bellicose dogmatists, and be unappalled at their bluster.

[24] Doxey A. Wilkerson, "American Caste and the Social Studies Curriculum," *Quarterly Review of Higher Education among Negroes*, V (April, 1937), 67-74.

[25] See "The Field and Function of the American Negro College," Fiske University Commencement Address, 1933, for a characteristic expression of the dogmatism which DuBois hurls back to meet the arrogance of the white caste. An extract: "We do not advocate segregation by race, [we] simply accept the bald fact that we are segregated, apart, hammered into a separate unity by spiritual intolerance and legal sanction backed by mob law, and that this separation is growing in strength and fixation; that it is worse today than a half century ago and that no character, address, culture or desert is going to change it, in our day or for centuries to come." It may be that what is said here is true; but the spirit of dogmatism immediately stirs up a countervailing assertiveness on the part of the dominant group which may conceivably serve to defeat some of the things for which the speaker hopes.

[26] Forrest Oran Wiggins, in *Quarterly Review of Higher Education among Negroes*, V (April, 1937), 77-78.

The caste system loses its terror for him. He knows a stuffed shirt when he sees one. He can smile amusedly at the Ku Klux Klan parade. He can understand what drives the unfortunate white man to believe in the superiority of his own race; and he comes to look upon the white man not as an individual who wilfully hates the Negro but as "a puppet in the hands of a monster tradition."[27] He is freed from the tyranny of the dogmatism of caste because he understands how weak dogmatism really is. At the same time he is building up the strength for the countervailing effort which is to hammer out the tools and guide the processes for transforming caste. He has learned to use the critical and analytical powers of the scientific method, but he has not lost the crusading zeal of the great reformers. He has found that study and activity are actually associated aspects of a single process. He knows that the way to get things done intelligently is to do them intelligently. He gives allegiance both to the increasing search for scientifically verified truth and to the crusade for a better world. He begins to realize that unless there is actualization of insight, then the insight is something less than true; just as he also sees that the misdirected attempt to get things done without knowing well what is to be done, invites disaster. He learns the twin virtues of accuracy and ardor. He learns them because they become the patterns of his life during the four years of college living, if the college is designed with this function in view. The functional college, aiming to affect the caste system and to build effective individuals, selects the instrumentalist attitude toward the social process in the expectation that this is the most hopeful way to develop in its students the ability to see through the sham of caste and to meet it intelligently and without fear or despair, but with tenacious faith.

In this instrumentalist spirit and method, the segregated college may face the caste system with high hopes. If the

---

[27] Bettie Esther Parham, "How the Conservative Negro Intellectual of the South Feels about Racial Segregation," *Journal of Social Forces*, XIV (December, 1935), 268-72.

segregated college is successful in its attempt, it may well be that the device of segregation which was designed by the majority group to be the means of subordination and control, the means of keeping the Negro in his place, will be used by the Negro as the tool for achieving a larger destiny. The dominant group gave the Negro the crutch of segregation and bade him run with it. But if that crutch is used instrumentally, it may become the means of vaulting the barriers of caste and of overcoming the inequities under which the Negro suffers.[28]

THE TASKS BEFORE THE FUNCTIONAL COLLEGE

Seriously assuming its social function, and using this functional concept as its central organizing principle, addressing itself to its task in the spirit and with the methods of instrumentalism, what will the college do?

First of all, there are many things it will *not* do. It will not assume that education, and colleges, are alone at work on the problems of liberation. A long, clear look at the actual situation will lead the college to be somewhat modest about the areas it hopes to include. There are many other institutional and social forces to which the college looks as allies; and there are areas of social improvement which are quite beyond the province of a single college or of the whole group of segregated colleges, if not beyond their purview. The college will therefore begin by delimiting its field of endeavor quite sharply. Or perhaps it would be better to say that the college will begin by finding its own center of emphasis, shutting nothing out of its purview, but concentrating on what seem the most promising and significant areas of attack within the realm of its own possibilities. That does not mean within the realm of its present operations; but it does mean within the realm of what appears to the sane judg-

---

[28] "This educational segregation should be recognized not merely as a fact imposed upon the Negro by the prejudiced white race, but should be utilized as an agency for developing the best powers and possibilities of Negro youth, partly under their own auspices." Kelly Miller, "Reorganization of Higher Education of the Negro in Light of Changing Conditions," *Journal of Negro Education,* V (July, 1936), 491.

ment as a genuinely possible enterprise. The scientific judgment should guide the crusading spirit, just as surely as the crusading spirit should lend its enthusiasm to the carrying out of projects which the scientific judgment regards as profitable points of attack.

Secondly, the functional college will jealously guard itself against all attempts to fix and to crystallize its form, methods, or objectives.

It is impossible to foretell definitely just what civilization will be twenty years from now. Hence it is impossible to prepare the child for any precise set of conditions. To prepare him for the future life means to give him command of himself; it means so to train him that he will have the full and ready use of all his capacities; that his eye and ear and hand may be tools ready to command, that his judgment may be capable of grasping the conditions under which it has to work, and the executive forces be trained to act economically and efficiently.[29]

Resistance to all forms of institutional hardening of the arteries becomes one of the major concerns of the functional college, in order that the institution may keep abreast of the times in which it hopes to be functional. Nor is keeping up to date enough. This kind of education aims to be normative, contributive, rather than adaptive or dependent;[30] and to do that, it must keep ahead of the times. Education tends too frequently to be like a man running after a streetcar, who just misses the car at each stop.

The positive side of the foregoing negative is equally important. If the college is to guard against institutional inertia, it may well begin by stimulating institutional effort toward progress. As the college turns from passive to active adaptation, leaves behind the adaptive and conformist attitudes and takes upon itself the experimentalist and instrumentalist approach, it cultivates the qualities for social functioning. This cannot happen accidentally; it can come only by willing it so—by wedding the authoritarian assurance of dogmatism to the scientific accuracy of descriptive-analysis, to synthesize the two in the ardent accuracy of instrumental-

[29] John Dewey, *My Pedagogic Creed*, p. 7.
[30] See A. J. Todd, *Theories of Social Progress*, p. 521.

ism. This is an expensive process. Control of the events of men and nations comes only by intensive and persistent effort along the lines of (*a*) increasing the areas of positive knowledge which rests on empirical evidence; (*b*) cultivating the powers of critical intelligence; (*c*) overcoming fear which casts its pale shadow across the native hue of resolution; and (*d*) bringing critical intelligence and social insight to bear upon each other and upon the problem of caste, to the end that social intelligence is cultivated, in the harmonious interaction and mutual support of social sentiments and critical intelligence. This inclusive goal for the functional college demands inclusive methods and techniques expressing an inclusive vision.

Perhaps the two best formulations of the notion of the social function of the segregated college have been offered by Dr. W. E. B. DuBois and by Dean Horace Mann Bond.[31]

The American Negro problem [says DuBois] is and must be the center of the Negro American university. . . . You are teaching American Negroes in 1933, and they are the subjects of a caste system . . . and their life problem is primarily this problem of caste. . . . Unless the American Negro today, led by trained university men of broad vision, sits down to work out . . . exactly how and where he is to earn a living and how he is to establish a reasonable life in the United States or elsewhere, the university has missed its field and function and the American Negro is doomed to be a suppressed and inferior caste in the United States for an incalculable time.

And in a somewhat more temperate but no less incisive statement, Bond puts it:

. . . the contemporary college needs to have a mission, although it may not have a missionary on the lot . . . we need to make ourselves conscious of the social forces at work in the world around us, and construct our

[31] DuBois, *op. cit.,* and Horace Mann Bond, "The Liberal Arts College for Negroes: A Social Force," an address delivered at the University of Louisville Municipal College Centennial Celebration, April 30, 1937. See also "The College and the Social Process," report of a conference on the subject at Talladega College, Talladega, Alabama, April, 1933, obtainable from the college. Bond's excellent book *The Education of the Negro in the American Social Order* is a full and definitive survey of the whole complex of problems indicated by the title; but his Louisville address is his best formulation of the idea of social function of the college.

programs largely in accord with those forces. . . . The contemporary liberal arts college for Negroes needs to align itself with social forces and derive its mission from them, if it is to make a notable contribution. . . . There is nothing mystical in the effect of the sturdy missionary teachers on the Negroes they taught; their impress was revolutionary, but so was their faith and their message. . . . It is my belief that the college of liberal arts for Negroes has, almost ready-made, its imperative mission defined as a distinctive social force in American life.

The fundamental difference between the functional college and the nonfunctional is not so much the area or province of operation, but the functions to be discharged within the accepted province. To be sure, the socially functioning college cannot permit any kind of arbitrary limitation upon its province—that delimiting is simply a matter of pragmatic possibility, and is more in the nature of an emphasis than of a delimitation. For, to be fully effective, the functional college must exclude from its over-view nothing which is pertinent to its principal objective of affecting the flow of the social process. In contradistinction to the somewhat formal and academic conceptions of education which center on subject matter and emphasize the learning of knowledge, this functional education, while it will include much of the subject-matter learnings of the older education, will go beyond subject matter to the fundamentals of conduct, the mainsprings of progress. "From the standpoint of the individual, education has two social functions: (a) it must develop in him a deep respect for the human personality, an intense love for it, and a keen desire to promote its welfare; (b) it must develop in him the capacity, the social intelligence, to promote the common welfare."[32] The learnings which are now looked upon as associated with and concomitant to the primary learnings of knowledge and skills—these attitudes of mind and spirit, these predispositions of personality, these leanings of social outlook, are to be the primary objectives of the college. Knowledge and skills are still very important; but their importance is that of essential tools rather than of ends in

[32] Frank E. Baker, "Has Education Failed?" *Social Frontier*, III (April, 1937), 199-201.

themselves. The unoccupied provinces of knowledge are to be explored and colonized; but the quality of life in the new colony becomes the important question rather than the mere settlement of the region willy-nilly.

HOW AIM AT SOCIAL ATTITUDES?

"If human nature is in important respects socially contributed nature, then to deal effectively with men and women means to deal with the social forces which they embody."[33] Social attitudes cannot readily be developed in the presence of anti-social practices. The medium cannot be completely alien to the process. But in a college where large numbers of persons are denied responsibility in important affairs, they are disinherited in large or significant areas of thought and of action, and antisocial attitudes are inevitable. No matter what the intended functioning of such a college, its actual results are seen in the production of persons who, because they have been denied responsibility, have become irresponsible. This social irresponsibility is a function of social disinheritance. Denied desired privileges and their concomitant responsibilities, the disinherited take steps to secure the privileges without accepting the responsibilities. The sharing of responsibility and of concomitant privilege, that is, removal of the disabilities of disinheritance, is the first step toward the projecting of campus experiences calculated to nurture the twin attitudes of individual responsibility for promoting the general welfare and of individual exercise of personal privilege in the light of the common good. This cannot, therefore, be a haphazard or indirect process. It comes only as it is aimed at deliberately and followed after assiduously. It demands, in short, that the college itself become the medium congenial to the production of the desired habits and attitudes.

This total adaptation of the entire life of the institution to the primary purpose in view was the great strength of the

[33] Max C. Otto, "Philosopher of a New Age," *The Social Frontier*, III (May, June, 1937), 230-32, 264-66.

medieval monastery. Within the cloister, the brothers were enabled to pursue truth, goodness, and beauty because the whole of their lives, protected by the encircling walls, was ordered with these ends in view. But in many American colleges, a vicious bifurcation of life into the alleged intellectual and the nonintellectual, the curricular and the extracurricular, overlooks this fundamental unity of experience. Having surrendered the outer walls and breastworks of the extracurricular life, the college is forced to defend with desperation its inner citadel of intellectual contemplation, transposing its irenic contemplation into vehement dogmatism. A better defense of the intellectual life is seen not in an irenic retreat but in the robust attack upon the whole job. And in the end, this inclusive job demands that the whole of the life of the student and of the teacher be included within the conscious effort to relearn the lessons of better experience. Social attitudes are aimed at in the attempt to establish a better campus society as a means toward building a better social whole.

Attitudes, of course, are not all. They are primary, in the sense that the warp is primary to the woof. The pattern of attitudes determines the pattern of personality. But attitudes are part of a larger aggregate. Mind itself is the organized aggregate of its meanings, and meanings have specific content. The functional college, then, not only aims at the building of socially desirable habits and attitudes, but also it aims to equip the student with skills and techniques appropriate to these attitudes, and to ground the whole composite of abilities in as rich and diversified and meaningful a factual and informational background as the situation demands and permits. This threefold hierarchy of educational aims, although it insists that socially desirable attitudes and skills form the warp of the fabric of personality, also insists that the woof of specific content must be carefully chosen; and it further insists that the interweaving of warp and woof through the actual experience of the learner is the real educational process.

The procedure for setting up the notion of the functional college, then, is that of (1) analyzing social needs so as to select socially desirable attitudes of life and the habitual practices which embody these attitudes, of (2) implementing these habits and attitudes with appropriate techniques and skills, and of (3) outlining opportunities for acquiring a full and rich informational undergirding for purposeful living along the lines of (1) and (2).

WHAT ATTITUDES SHALL BE CULTIVATED?

Words are abstract symbols into which meaning is put according to the intentions of the speaker and the experience of the listener. The two meanings, of speaker and of listener, may not coincide. It is therefore with considerable trepidation that an attempt is made to set down in words the actual aims of the functioning college, partly because language is not adequate to convey what is essentially a matter of a whole pattern of life; and partly because, in the nature of dynamic things, the character of the functional college means that a precise formulation of objectives ought to be regarded with some distrust and misgivings. But as a suggestion of the sort of thing toward which the functional college should aim, we are obliged to formulate our present objectives—or rather, to indicate our present sense of direction.

The selection of these attitudes which are our educational objectives is to be based on a study of the caste system, and of the needs of individuals who live under it, and of the possibilities for changing it. What qualities of mind and spirit are needed for the effort to live meanwhile as best we may amid caste and yet so live as also to transform caste and to transcend its limitations? How is the Negro to live unobstructed as a normal American citizen? How can the attitudes and habits of mind and spirit learned in college promote this objective?

One way to indicate our collegiate objectives is to suggest a scale of values, and to indicate that what is wanted is movement on this scale away from the less desirable and toward the more desirable. We do not start with a false notion of perfection or of prefectibility; but we attempt to find out where we are on a scale at the present moment, and in which direction we are moving.

As an example of this method of defining of objectives, consider the plight of the student who enters the segregated college, as far as his own sense of independence is concerned. Under the impact of the caste system, he has been taught for eighteen years that he must be dependent. He must not stand on his own feet; he must rely upon the accommodative processes of adjustment to the demands of the supraordinate white caste. To be sure, not all freshmen in the Negro college will be fully grooved in this accommodative pattern. Many will have been saved from it in part or in large measure by the effective working of home or other influences. But by and large, as far as the caste system has affected them, the Negro students will come to college with a dependency complex fairly well developed. It would be gratuitous to point out that this is the corollary of the superiority or dominance complex which the white college freshman carries with him. Now, in the white college, it is difficult enough to take the self-assertive and (at least superficially) independent freshman, and to help him to build attitudes of coöperation and qualities of social-mindedness. But in the college for Negroes, the job is doubly difficult, for the student must be brought from dependence to independence before the plant of developing interdependence can have any soil in which to take root. Our scale, then, looks something like this:

——Sense of Direction——→		
Dependence	Independence	Interdependence
A	B C	D

A student at "A" may be moving in the direction of "B," and another student at "C" also may be moving toward "B" —one is progress, the other retrogression. But movement from dependence to independence is progress not so much because independence is more desirable than dependence from the point of view of social welfare, but primarily because it is a step toward the achievement of interdependence. It is movement in the better direction. It would be an oversimplification of objectives merely to say that we are working to develop a sense of interdependence on the part of each student. It is more nearly correct to say that we wish to correct the violence done to the student's personality through the fact that the caste system stamps a dependency complex upon him, and that we seek to move away from dependence, through independence toward interdependence. The student has been told by a caste-divided world that he does not count; he is a cipher. The college aims to help that student put the integer of personal purpose in front of the cipher of himself, in order to contribute the value of this integrated selfhood to the sum of social well-being.

Our method of defining objectives, then, is that of studying the impact of caste upon the student, and of attempting to discover the correctives for the violence done to his personality, which correctives should be designed not only to restore the individual to self-possession and normalcy but also to build needed stamina and insight for the struggle against the system of caste in the effort to promote the common good. We must constantly be on the alert for apparent dichotomies of values which, upon closer examination, appear to present the possibilities of indefinite extension of possible progress on a single scale rather than to be mutually exclusive realms of conduct. It is not, therefore, a question of dependence or independence; neither is it a question of independence versus interdependence. Nor can we set dependence over against the other two. It is a matter of growth from less desirable attitudes through desirable to more desirable; and in our defining of educational objectives, we must leave the end open for unlimited growth and extension of possibilities. When we name a quality of mind or an attitude of life as being a desirable educational objective, we are therefore saying by implication that this particular quality or attitude appears, from the viewpoint of its possible bearing upon the caste system and upon the life of the Negro under that system, to be more desirable than something else, and movement from the less desirable toward the more desirable, as thus defined, constitutes educational progress.

If we bear clearly in mind that we are not giving a definitive statement of the aims of education, but rather, that such definition can actually come only in terms of the methods we adopt—with this precaution clearly stated, we may content ourselves at this point with a general statement of the sense of direction which is to guide us in the selection of definitive methods. We want to move away from the caste system with its segregation and its inequities, toward an ordering of life in which all persons, without reference to race or color, may enjoy the normal privileges and opportunities of American citizens, it being understood that the price of privilege is the acceptance of responsibilities. Our educational procedures are therefore to be designed with this intended movement in view.

Another way, then, of stating the educational objective which, as an illustration, we put on our scale of movement a moment ago, is to say that we are aiming at the development of social intelligence, by which we mean the acceptance by the individual of the obligation to think *for* oneself but *of* others. We look for growth in independent, critical thinking in the effort to promote the common good. And a part of this growth is evidenced by advancement in the ability to make decisions about one's private life in the light of the social implications of personal decisions. To put the matter in the vernacular: We do not want "yes-men"; nor do we want "no-men"; what we want is "I-think-in-the-light-of-the-common-good" men. The acceptance of the obligation to think critically about the welfare of all is evidence of growth toward interdependence.

Less useful than this indication of the intended direction of growth is an enumeration of the "qualities of mind" which we should like to see developed. We might speak of healthy-mindedness—the avoidance of psychogenic hazards and the cultivation of normal and healthy mental attitudes and processes. We might ask for clear-mindedness—the ability to detect and to avoid logical fallacies and specious argument, together with the ability and desire to use logically sound and generally objective reasoning processes. We might speak of tough-mindedness—by which we should be suggesting that we wished to be ready always to face issues clearly, squarely, and without flinching or pulling our punches, no matter how vitally the matter in hand touched upon our personal affairs or our inner lives. We should also insist on social-mindedness —the constant effort to consider all matters in the light of the general welfare, and the instrumental use of lesser ends for larger goals. But in all this, we should merely be listing words, general ideas, to which practically everyone in America subscribes; and at the end of our listing of educational objectives we should find ourselves pretty much where we were before as far as actual suggestions for educational procedure and program are concerned. We should know that healthy-mindedness will come best if our personnel procedures and general campus life are adequate, if not optimum. We should be able to see a connection between clear-mindedness and teaching methods and the stuff of the curriculum. The mention of tough-mindedness should stiffen our resolve in the realm of educational standards and academic practices. Social-mindedness as an educational objective should imply some modifications and development of administrative policies, curriculum content, off-campus relationships, campus life, and religious outlook. But when we have said all this, we are not much nearer the goal of intelligent academic procedure. Enumeration of desired qualities of mind gets us nowhere. It appears that a better way to our educational objectives might be that of describing the methods we propose to use, letting the method be a functional or operative definition of educational aims.

By contrast, the authoritarian, or dogmatic method of procedure would have led us to draw up a list of the exact qualities and attitudes at which we intended to aim, and to use these as our authoritative criteria in projecting the educational program. Not so with the experimental approach. In the nature of the case, the impact of caste upon various individuals will vary somewhat, and the cultivation of attitudes and habits of mind and of life will therefore need to be carried through with the various individuals in terms of the needs of these several persons as seen within the framework of the general good. If we are to adopt the instrumentalist approach in any thoroughgoing manner, we are justified in letting the selection of our instruments be its own definition of our objectives, for it is our belief that methods used have much to do with determining results obtained.

If, then, we refuse to make a nice definition of the exact qualities of mind and spirit we seek to nurture, we are justified in that refusal by our assumption of the much more difficult task of proposing the implements of work and the actual manner of attack. In so doing, we are observing the principle that the realm of the general and the universal (often thought of as the realm of ends and objectives) is in reality the realm of means and of instruments. Always and every time the realm of the end, the objective, is that of particulars, not of universals.[34] And in so doing, we are giving the experimentalist definition of objectives—we select our general sense of direction, and define our methods, and let the ends and results come out of the process itself. At the same time, we are not adrift at sea without chart or compass. We know where we are; we know our ship well; we select the best possible crew; we get our bearings; and we set sail on a voyage of discovery, knowing quite well the general location of the area we hope to explore, but not knowing with any degree of exactness just what we shall find there. We go also not merely as explorers, but as colonizers; and as we go, we draw ourselves together in our Mayflower Compact which helps to shape the nature of the future colony.

The next chapters attempt to deal with three aspects of our venture as a functional college. They constitute the instrumental definition of our educational objectives, since these methods define the manner and direction in which we intend to move, and therefore what we hope to accomplish.

[34] See J. L. Childs, *Education and the Philosophy of Experimentalism*, p. 225.

XI

EDUCATIVE ADMINISTRATION

Ye know that the rulers of the Gentiles lord it over them, and their great ones exercise authority over them. Not so shall it be among you. —JESUS

WHAT kind of administrative policies will best serve the educational aims of the functional college? And what administrative procedures and practices will best implement these policies?

Perhaps the dominant method of collegiate administration of the past generation is that of the despot—sometimes benevolent, but typically despotic. A board of trustees, or a college president, or a faculty, or some modified combination of the three, makes the rules, sets up the courses of study, determines both the goals and the procedures, and judges the students according to these arbitrary standards.

This Procrustean administrative policy is directly correlated with the old classical curriculum. The two are perfectly adapted to support each other. They demand the same responses from students, operate through the same sort of mental processes, inculcate the same attitudes. The classical curriculum assumes that the professor knows all that the student is to learn; and that the process of teaching is that of getting the student to master the subject matter which the teacher already knows, and to prove such mastery at an examination in order that the teacher may certify that the student has "covered" the curricular ground. The student is encouraged to think; but his thinking is thoroughly canalized in advance by the arbitrary nature of the curriculum and of the teaching process. He is to think—but to think only about the things prescribed by the college, and to think only in the directions which the examiners judge appropriate. Under the occasionally exceptional professor, the student may be encouraged to deviate from the established pattern of responses; but the effort to graft the figs of intellectual and social maturity upon the thistles of academic dictatorship generally prove inept and unfruitful. The classical curriculum, and the Procrustean administrative policy which is suited to it, both aim in the general direction of conformity. "Passing on the social heritage" comes to mean "defending the *status quo* inherited from our forebears," and education degenerates into ancestor worship of the most slavish type— all the more insidious because gilded over with fair pretense and supported by good intention. An expression typical of many which might be cited is this:

It is well to have this conception of duty and patriotism looked upon as a matter of course, as something not to be disputed; and there can be no doubt that early saturation of the boyish mind with the classics had much to do with this outcome.[1]

In its essence, the authoritarian or dictatorial administrative procedure is that of the military. Terse and luminous statement of the derogatory effect of military methods and military discipline is given by General Robert E. Lee: "The training that makes soldiers is not the best for citizens. Military education is an unfortunate necessity for the soldier but the worst possible preparation for civil life."[2]

The methods of militarism are the methods of the commander, the manipulator, the dictator. Men are not people, they are pawns. Persons are not valuable in and of themselves; they are "effectives" to be used efficiently in the attainment of "objectives." And the objectives are determined not according to the probable welfare of the individuals involved, nor even in accordance with the probable welfare of the group or nations involved, but primarily in accordance with the rules of the game of military science, just as a college sets up its idea of education and demands that each aspirant conform to the prescribed courses according to the academic rules of the game.

If the essence of militarism is this dominance of the com-

[1] Henry Cabot Lodge, in *The Value of the Classics*, p. 121.

[2] William E. Brooks, *Lee of Virginia*, p. 319. As college president, Lee refused to permit military training to be included as a part of campus life in the institution which now bears his name.

mander, the corollary is absolute obedience by the commanded. Mussolini's best slogan is "Believe, obey, fight." The supreme military virtue is obedience; and obedience must be not to conscience nor to intellect, but to arbitrary authority.

> Theirs not to make reply;
> Theirs not to reason why;
> Theirs but to do and die.

In animals, this is called stupidity, or mulishness. Let it be said of militarism, then, that it makes mules of the men and asses of the officers. There are exceptions, shining and glorious exceptions, which are a tribute to the resiliency of the human spirit rather than to the success of the military method. But Lee was right. "The training that makes soldiers . . . is the worst possible training for civil life." The college managed on the autocratic principle of the military dictator, demanding that the student cultivate the military virtue of blind obedience to discipline—that college is giving perhaps the worst possible training for civil life. It is not training its students to think for themselves when it teaches blind obedience, absolute submission. Its graduates will be conformists. As a social institution, that college is ancillary, not normative. In the matter primarily before us, such a college supports the caste system by cultivating in its students the habits and attitudes best calculated to perpetuate the subservience of the Negro.

LAISSER-ALLER AS AN ALTERNATIVE

At the other extreme of academic method is that of the libertine. In place of military discipline, self-expression is advocated. Instead of dictatorship, anarchy. Instead of the doubtful military virtue of unquestioning obedience, the equally dubious unmilitary virtue of unquestioning revolt.

This method of academic procedure is, of course, a natural and expected reaction against the long dominance of the military method. Self-indulgence follows a long period of repression. Involuntary self-abandonment follows on the heels of involuntary submission. The military method with its arbitrary insistence on obedience breeds the spirit of revolution. The wave of cynicism and of disillusionment which followed the first World War demonstrates the point. Militarism not only begets more militarism, it likewise breeds a bastard revolt. Dictatorship stimulates the very counter-revolution which it seeks to suppress. Force generates counter-force. The excrescence of one disease is the culture medium for the growth of the virus of another malady equally hideous.

Very few of the so-called progressive schools have actually succumbed to the influence of *laisser-aller*; but from the conservative camp the critics have flung the accusation that the progressives have gone too far. Occasionally a school which had taken Freud too seriously has furnished an example which, properly caricatured, served to build up the stereotype. Relaxing curricular standards and administrative discipline to permit the unimpeded blossoming of the native potentialities of the child has, in some cases, been a step toward a kind of sentimental assertion that there was nothing of value in education unless it came from the abandonment of everything that smacked of arbitrariness and external discipline. And while these excesses have come from a few persons on the lunatic fringe of progressive education, the carping critics have eagerly tarred the whole movement with the brush of libertinism.

As a practical alternative to the methods of the dictator, libertinism has had very little effect in the circles of the Negro college. But as a theoretical Charybdis, it has served to keep the administrator close to the Scylla of autocracy. For the Southern Negro, the word "radical" has been closely associated with undesirable meanings since Reconstruction times when radical politics and anti-Negro sentiments were coupled in the activities of the lower-class whites. Moreover, the "safe," conservative Negro has more readily won the confidence of the dominant group of whites. The result naturally has been to make it rather difficult for progressive notions to take firm root on the segregated campus. In the cases where *laisser-aller* has been seriously discussed as an alternative to autocracy, the argument has been that the college serving a minority group may well hesitate to adopt a policy which would probably turn out a stream of graduates who would mainly succeed in stirring up the antagonism of a resentful majority. Such a policy would be aimed, consciously or unconsciously, at the promotion of conflict between the racial groups; and by sheer numerical weight of nine to one, not to mention the incidental features of economic and political advantage, the majority group could, and probably would, crush an aggressive minority more ruthlessly than Nazi Germany bears down upon its Semitic minority. So the argument has run; and so has it been decided.

THE USUAL COMPROMISE

The normal practice of college administrators and of academic people generally is that of finding some middle ground, some safe course. In educational administration, this means steering cautiously between the actual Scylla of autocracy and the bogey Charybdis of *laisser-aller*, adhering to the course of paternalism. As actually worked out, there is more of the grandmother than of the father in this paternalism. Students are managed, controlled, directed as effectively as under the dictator; but the method is that of wheedling, cajoling, pampering, coaxing, indulging the student's whims to get his acquiescence. This is the perfect product of compromise. It has all the weaknesses and none of the strengths of the two extremes. As militarism demands subservience and as libertinism breeds irresponsibility, so paternalism combines the two in a dependence which is acquiescence plus indifference. Paternalism gets the obedience of militarism without its Spartan self-discipline under orders. Paternalism gets the purposelessness of libertinism without its life-giving freshness. Paternalism is the dross and dregs of the other two, a perfect product of compromise.

Colleges today are paternalistic—not all colleges, but many. As authoritarian autocracy was the dominant pattern of the past generation; paternalism is characteristic of the present. A glance at the charts of administrative organization in American colleges suggests that paternalism is the dominant pattern. Kinder,[3] in his careful discussion of prevalent administrative practices underscores the point. His study is descriptive; it mirrors contemporary collegiate practice. It is not an indictment of the study, then, to point out that the idea of student participation in the determination of college policies does not cross the pages of the account. It is not in the book because it is not in the colleges.

To be sure, there is a thing called "student government," which is credited with working more or less well in a great many colleges. In some instances it is working with sensational success, if judged by the standards of its own objectives. But with a few notable exceptions, students do not share directly or indirectly in the actual process of making the policies of the college. They come to an institution which is made by the trustees, president, and faculty. The students may, in some cases, be invited to share in applying the policies worked out for them; but seldom are they included in the construction of the ideals, the elaboration of the objectives, the determination of policies. This kind of academic lock step is more stultifying than the high-handed methods of the dictator, more destructive than the abandon of the libertine. The student lives under the illusion of free participation in a creative process, but he does not realize the full satisfactions which come only through genuine sharing of responsibility and of decision making. The student is led to believe that he is something of a free agent, participating in the determination of his educational progress; but he finds that his actions (if not his thinking) are determined by the faculty and the administration. So, at long last, the administrators and faculties find themselves pulling the puppet strings, hopefully repeating democratic phrases, often deceiving themselves into

[3] J. S. Kinder, *The Internal Administration of the Liberal Arts College.*

thinking that the democratic dream is being actualized through the paternalistic process.

This notion of the college is closely correlated with a particular belief about the relationship of the college to the social process. It expresses the conviction that, as far as the college is to be concerned with society, its purpose is that of promoting and interpreting the fundamental purposes of "the existing social order."[4] It is a direct carry-over from feudalism. It is closer akin to the spirit and temper of Britain than of America. It illustrates the cultural lag of academic institutionalism, the American college having derived from its European (and particularly its British) antecedents, in this respect.

For as Löwe[5] has pointed out, English society is built not on liberty, equality, and fraternity, but primarily upon an inclusive fraternal spirit which compensates for the lack of genuine liberty and real equality. This fraternal spirit is fostered by the pleasant and serious aura of the church as it sanctifies the class stratification of society; and a semblance of free movement from class to class perpetuates the illusion of a much wider interfusion of classes than actually exists, thus taking the sting out of class differentiation. At the same time, relentless social pressure, backed by the necessity of

[4] See, for an example of many similar utterances, "The Obligation of the University to American Democracy," by S. P. Capen, Chancellor of the University of Buffalo, *School and Society*, June 22, 1935, pp. 817-22, which clearly advocates a compromise of democratic principle on the basis of academic expediency. Since the university is to advance the fundamental purposes of the "existing social order" in which it is located, then in a democracy, the university must include in its teaching the idea of change through experimentation with open minds, "liberty of opinion and utterance." The university must therefore try to exemplify true democracy. But "the external framework of the government of most universities is the product of an earlier day; of a pattern more oligarchical than democratic," so that the university "in its operation will be government with the consent of the governed." (P. 821.) This citation does not imply that there is not actual democracy in the operation of the University of Buffalo, nor does it single out Chancellor Capen as having sinned above all others. It does exemplify the strong tendency to rationalize an undemocratic set-up on the basis of academic difficulties, and it also illustrates the manner in which administrators can conscientiously permit themselves to speak of the essence or spirit of democracy as expressing itself in spite of an undemocratic institutional structure.

[5] Adolf Löwe, *The Price of Liberty: A German on Contemporary Britain.*

maintaining the tradition of the monarchy to preserve the sentimental unification of the Empire, insists upon conformity to class. The pressure of social conformity, to which individuals yield under the compulsion of this paternalistic spirit of fraternity, paradoxically makes possible a rather large degree of individual liberty or freedom from governmental control as such.

A large-scale society can stand the strain of freedom of action on the part of its members only if the individualization of those members is kept within definite limits. The individual must pay for this freedom by being turned to a certain extent into a type. The price of liberalism as a social principle is the sacrifice of self-indulgence.[6]

Thus is exhibited the compatibility of "spontaneous social agreement" with a "class-society based on modern industrialism."[7] In other words, a paternalistic pleasantry on the part of the upper classes is matched by a filial loyalty on the part of the lower classes, with a resultant psychological integration of diverse elements which makes the whole social unit function with a high degree of apparent spontaneity which in reality is an expression of social pressure. The English university and the American college may differ in a great many respects; but in the form and spirit of their governments they are strikingly similar. Both in England and in America, academic administration is aimed at teaching the student social conformity, with varying degrees of intellectual conformity as concomitantly taught.

This discussion has peculiar point when applied to the segregated college. The Negro student, for the most part, comes to college definitely conditioned by a society which is consciously managed in order to produce in him the complex of dependency. He is perfect material for the paternalistic administrator. The administrator, in his turn, has the standard pattern of the American college as his prototype, and therefore readily falls into the habits of paternalism. In the earlier stages of Negro education, when the fervor of Civil War patriotism still warmed the veins of the Yankee mission-

[6] *Ibid.*, p. 23.
[7] *Ibid.*, p. 25.

aries, not a few of the schools for Negroes launched ambitious programs of military discipline, which in many cases
have lived through the decades with astonishingly little modification, and in other instances have softened into the patterns of paternalism. There is, however, a rapidly growing
feeling that militarism and paternalism have both seen their
day on the segregated campus.

One means of hastening the demise of these inimical procedures is a straightforward analysis of the results of the
methods as employed, in their bearing on the caste system.
The student who is to be kept in dependence must be kept
under the direction of a dictator or the dominance of a paternalist. Conversely, the student who is to grow into social
maturity will do so only with the greatest of difficulty under
an administration which is either dictatorial or paternalistic.
If libertinism were the only alternative to these two, the
predicament of the administrator in the Negro college would
indeed be embarrassing. But there is a fourth possibility.

DEMOCRACY AS ADMINISTRATIVE POLICY

American academic thought has inherited a valuable legacy
of democratic idealism from the struggle to establish our
republic. In the contemporary world scene, with the emergence of a bloc of nation-states committed to the Fascist and
totalitarian ideal, the hope of a democratic way of life confronts a serious alternative. As long as the only practical
alternative offered by national practices was that of the monarchy, democracy rested content in the belief that the tendency to movement from monarchy toward democracy was
irresistible, and that only time was necessary for the realization of a world made safe through democracy.

The American college, sharing the pleasantly roseate optimism of this hope in democracy as the ultimate way of life,
was thereby made less uneasy in its own violation of the
democratic principle. This ability to be at ease while violating basic conviction was not limited to the campus; but it did
find safe anchorage in the academic harbor. Democracy was

the great ideal, the far-off destiny toward which all human-kind irresistibly moved. The college could teach about that ideal and hold it up before its students, while reserving to their post-collegiate experience the first initiation into the actualities of a representative republic. The division of the learning process between study and activity made it possible for the college to rationalize its bifurcation of democratic practice and theory. Democracy came to have about the same relevancy to daily life on the campus as that other great ideal to which men habitually pay lip service, the Kingdom of Heaven. Democracy became the Great American Myth.

Under the stress of active threat to the democratic ideal from Nazi, Fascist, and Communist quarters (each with its own variant of that attack, to be sure), the long-time de-fenders of the faith in democracy are galvanized into activity. Much of that activity is vocal in the earlier stages, but one senses the emergence of a school of educators who are about to demand that the democratic way of life should be en-throned as the new dogma, and defended against all comers at all costs.[8] What we need to fear is precisely this dogma that the democratic way of life is its own warrant and jus-tification. The crystallization of the dogma, and its uncritical defense and espousal, might well lead to the new tyranny,

[8] Boyd H. Bode, *Democracy as a Way of Life,* carefully guards against this pitfall by insisting that the relationship of the democratic ideal to the achieve-ment of desirable goals is functional. Democracy is the best, if not the only appropriate, method for achieving the ends envisaged. The closest Bode comes to uncritical advocacy of democracy as dogma is in the following quotation which does not appear as one-sided when left in its context: "Each way of life, then, has its own distinctive point of orientation. If we start with the official German conception of race, it is logical to . . . lay claim to more territory, more room for power, more absolute right. . . . [So also, it appears that] Communism will tolerate no other form of social organization than its own. . . . If civilization is to survive, there must be a change of base. Democ-racy must enter the lists, not as a symbol of a vague humanitarianism, or of a cumbersome parliamentarian procedure, but as a distinctive way of life." (Pp. 112-13.) In Bode's use of the ideas of democracy, there is very little of the tendency to elevate method to dogma; but the same idea is currently ban-died about by lesser men with a kind of naïve assumption that there is a "democratic way of life" just as surely as there is a Fascist or a Communist way; and that what we should do is to discover what are the characteristics of this democratic way, and teach them to school children so that democracy will be safe from the threatened destruction by one or the other of its rivals.

more terrible than the old because entrenched in the citadel of democracy. The dictatorship of a democratic majority is a long sea mile from the actuality of democratic living. We do well to mistrust the uncritical spread of the notion that embattled democracy must now defend herself against the threatening hordes of totalitarianism by hurling dogma to meet dogma. The best defense of democracy is not to be found in the vehement championing of the dogma but in the serious practice of the method. Like good music, democracy needs not defense, but rendition.

We distinguish three different meanings of the democratic ideal, two of which we reject while accepting the third. The first of these rejected ideas is that of the democratic dogma, the great myth, discussed in the preceding paragraph. The second form of the democratic ideal which we find inadequate is the conception of democracy as a structural framework— whether political democracy or industrial democracy. The weakness of the institutional idea of democracy as exemplified in this structural conception derives not so much from any inherent shortcomings in the democratic ideal itself as in the partial and imperfect realizations of the ideal so generally found in its institutional or structural forms. Further, these imperfect realizations have come to be used as means of defining the ideal which they so imperfectly embody. Since practice falls short of the ideal, societies tend to dilute the ideal to conform to practice, thereby pragmatically reducing the tension if not healing the breach between the two. Thereby, also, the ideal itself is discredited, without appreciably altering the quality of the actual. Consider an example, the belief in majority rule.

Judged from the standpoint of an oligarchy or of a plutocracy, the doctrine of majority rule is an advance. In that light it can be called a useful forward step. But judged in the white light of the democratic ideal, with its insistence on liberty, equality, and fraternity, the notion of majority rule falls so far short of the desideratum as to be at times almost a travesty of the ideal. At best it is a poor compromise, substituting an approximation of plurality of opinion for a consensus of considered judgment. The idea of the protection of all minority and individual interests and the careful safeguarding of the welfare of all groups within the whole, are foundations of the democratic ideal; simply to follow the dictates of the majority vote may as truly be a means of denying these basic demands as of giving them body.

Democracy as a mere structural framework is therefore not an adequate conception with which to guide our collegiate activity, because we should be limited by the force of political custom and the accumulated parliamentary practice of the generations, and we should therefore find it very difficult to break away from the inadequate forms and procedures in which democracy has tied itself up as it has tried to give expression to the ethical urge toward an egalitarian society. If, therefore, we made the mistake of identifying the democratic ideal with the alleged democratic political and industrial procedures, we should merely chain the college to dominant practices which are far short of the democratic ideal. Not as defined in the dogmatic myth and not as defined by the contemporary political framework, do we accept the democratic ideal.

It is in the sense of democracy as a method that we accept it. Particularly, our insistence that the academic method must be suited to the ends envisaged, demands that some form of democratic procedure must be devised for the segregated college if that college is to do its part in cracking the crust of caste. The educational job thus demands the democratic method—a method much more democratic than either the popular myth or the prevailing structural forms of democracy. The cure for caste is democracy, real and genuine democracy. The practice of democracy in the segregated college is therefore elementary. The primer of administrative practice begins with belief that all men are created equal. That does not mean that we attempt the untenable notion that all men are identical, either in degree or in kind. Democracy does not mean the equality of abilities of all men; it means the parity of the unequal. These inherent inequalities are probably considerably less than the operation of our discriminatory society makes them appear—greater opportunity commonly going to the more favored individuals. Moreover, there is no proved racial disparity of these innate abilities. When, therefore, we say that democracy implies the parity of the unequal, we are recognizing the fact of individual differences in abilities, not the allegation of racial differences. Failure to begin with this notion of the parity of all men means that the college will be governed, consciously or unconsciously, by an alternative idea, namely, that men of differing abilities and interests and temperaments and ancestry and belief are not to be on a par. And that is the essence of caste. If, in the administration of the segregated college, we permit anything except genuine democracy, we are surrendering to caste, and surrendering the most vulnerable sector of our line. The attack upon caste demands the use of the democratic method.

Democracy as method is therefore not to be confusingly identified with democracy as structure. Political democracy, which in practice actually does not even mean "the consent of the governed," but merely the consent of the plurality or of the majority, elaborates an institutional structure which defeats democratic aspirations by denying the wishes of the minority and overlooking the welfare of the several members of the social body. Industrial democracy, which is coming to mean the sharing of control and profits by workers and employers exhibits this same fundamental deficiency. It relies upon the opinion of the majority of voters rather than upon a considered attempt to discover what is the genuinely best thing to do for the welfare of all persons involved—workers, owners, and consumers. The interchange of thought and action between all persons and groups involved in the decision, with the open and agreed purpose of forwarding the development and welfare of all and of hindering none—this is democracy as method. This is the basic idea with which we shape the administration of the segregated college, expecting thereby to build the kind of academic experiences which will nurture the attitudes and habits ultimately necessary for the modification of the caste system. Functionally, democracy of this operational kind is demanded for the transformation of caste by the college. The college cannot cure a disease with which it infects its students. The only education which can help to build a society without caste is education without caste. That means the use of democracy as administrative method.

THE MEANING OF DEMOCRACY AS METHOD

The roots of liberty lie in conscious social concern for the welfare of each individual and of the several groups making up the social whole. This emphasis upon the value of individuality is not to be confused with individualism. Indeed, the achievement of this goal of individual and group welfare is hindered by the anti-social or asocial assertion of individualism. The socialization of the individual is the prelude both to individual self-realization in a democratic society and to the realization of the values of democratic society itself. The price of liberty is the socializing of the individual. There is no substitute for the self-controlled individual who seeks the common good. All other attempts to achieve the common welfare, through external and therefore essentially arbitrary control of the individual, are foredoomed to defeat. Men do not gather figs from thistles. The operation of democracy is therefore much closer to what has sometimes been called mutualism than to what is currently labeled democracy. Each for all and all for each—that is democracy.

Such mutualism demands equality. It does not, of course, blandly assert the idea that all persons have an equal natural endowment at birth. The idea of individual difference is too well established in the popular mind to demand any defense at this point. But what is asserted, and without equivocation, is that there must be equality of consideration. In distinguishing between natural equality and equality of consideration, we are not subscribing to the doctrine of racial inequality in natural capacities. We are merely agreeing with the apparent fact that, as things are now in our kind of society, some children are born into the world with greater capacities than others; and at the same time we are reminding ourselves that it has not yet been shown that there are differences in the capacities of individuals which are determined according to their biological racial inheritance. (See Appendix B.) Acceptance of the fact that individuals do now show differences in ability does not in any sense imply acceptance of the notion of racial inequalities in these individual differences. Indeed, the demand for equality of consideration is our way of asserting that whatever specious plausibility the doctrine of racial inequality may now possess is due in an important degree to the arbitrary limitations of the caste system. The doctrine ought not to be permitted to create the circumstances for its own defense. There is an empirical court of appeal. Into the closed system of logic-tight compartmentalization which defends caste, we bring the idea of equality of consideration, with the knowledge that under this kind of freedom we have nothing to fear.

Our equalitarian formula must initially mean at least equality of consideration, in order that it may mean something more than this in the end. Only after long sustained treatment of a most humane type—certainly not before—can we pass intelligent judgment upon the more recondite question as to whether men are by "race" naturally equal.[9]

This equality of consideration must express itself throughout the entire administrative procedure. Each person is "just as good" as the other. An idea or suggestion must be considered on its merits, without reference to its point of origin. The president's thinking may be fuzzy at some points; a student's fresh approach may give him some novel insight. No matter who propounds the idea, it must be given all the consideration which its intrinsic merit warrants. Equality of consideration of individuals implies equality of consideration of all ideas and suggestions, whether critical or constructive.

The inevitable correlative, from which there must be no shrinking, is that each individual or group within the college

[9] T. V. Smith, *The Democratic Way of Life*, p. 103.

must constantly be on the alert to make a genuine contribution to the welfare of the whole. Enjoyment of social privilege implies acceptance of social responsibility, just as surely as the denial of opportunity would imply the correlative irresponsibility of the disinherited.

A second principle through which this equality of consideration expresses itself is the reliance upon consensus. The notable weakness of the majority-vote process can be corrected by the use of a more inclusive technique. The cure for democracy, in this case, is more democracy. As long as a majority is permitted to force its will upon minorities, and even to do violence to personalities or to the group integrity of a minority, the principle of equality of consideration is violated. The majority may be wrong, as for example, in the dominant treatment accorded to racial minorities in America. Democracy must insist on the protection of minorities. There must therefore be an attempt to discover an inclusive consensus of judgment as the basis for action rather than the use of a mere numerical majority to establish the preponderance of judgment. Consensus becomes the ideal toward which our sense of direction carries us, and we judge the success of our administrative processes in part by the extent to which we actually do tend to get a genuine consensus of intelligent opinion.

This consensus must never be forced. In the nature of the democratic process, nothing but free and frank discussion without any inhibitions or prohibitions can be the prelude to decisions of importance. The more important the matter to be decided, the greater must be the effort to make sure that all persons vitally concerned have shared in the process of making the judgment. In a democratic college, each individual member of the student body, the faculty, and the administrative staff is encouraged to think and talk about matters of importance; and there is a genuine attempt made to formulate the policies of the college in the light and under the critical surveillance of this inclusive process. The judgment on which action is projected must then be based on the widest and most inclusive consensus obtainable through the methods which most clearly and usefully express the consideration of the entire group for the welfare and integrity of each individual member, and which in turn receive from each individual his best thought about the welfare of the group. The consensus must be inclusive. It must be openly arrived at in an atmosphere of freedom. It must be as fully debated and considered as the importance of the issue warrants. Failing such consensus, there can be no genuine democracy, no genuine equality of consideration of the welfare and the contribution of each person.

THE PROBLEM OF AUTHORITY

The problem of authority cannot be discussed by itself, but must be considered in the context of democratic procedure working by means of consensus. Any group which acts in concert or in harmony does so under the guidance of some form of authority, implicit or explicit. The army squad responding to the commands of the second lieutenant, and the Quaker meeting finding its common "concern" are both responding to authority. The difference in the consensus of the two groups does not lie in the absence or presence of authority, but in the nature of the authority and in the quality of the allegiance to it.

Obedience to an authority which is something less than the consensus of the whole group of persons concerned, is a basic violation of the principle of equality of consideration. One man, or a group, or the majority, makes a decision: the rest of the people obey. It is theoretically possible to obtain a consensus on the basis of acquiescence to the dictates of a leader or of a minority. But this agreement of silence is a violation of genuine consensus in two respects: first, the decision is made by a noninclusive process, thereby insuring only the consideration of the thinking of the few; and secondly, the obedience of the masses requires continuance in passive acquiescence, thereby violating the idea of equality of consideration.

But a consensus which is based upon critical thinking of all persons vitally affected by the matter under advisement, which is the result of a genuine effort to bring out and to weigh and consider divergent points of view, and which expresses a basis for action which is defensible in the light of the several points of view expressed and in the light of the general welfare, gives a totally different quality of authority. Each person has been consulted about the decision which is to affect him. He has shared in making that decision, presumably sharing in it up to the extent of his developed abilities. As long as he could give logical defense to a divergent point of view, clearly and convincingly maintaining that the proposed course was inimical to the general welfare or a violation of the rights and welfare of individuals or minority groups, just so long was there no consensus. The fact that consensus was achieved meant that, as nearly as human fallibility permitted, the decision was made so as to promote the general welfare and made in recognition of the interests of the several individuals and groups included. Obedience to this kind of authority is, in essence, obedience to one's own best self arrived at by the best available method known to man. The process of critical thinking in the light of the group criticism where all persons and interests are vocal, means that to a significant degree the decisions must always express what the several individuals have admitted and accepted as the best course of action. True, this acceptance or admission may sometimes have been made reluctantly, under the compulsion of clear logic and against the urge of illogical or less inclusive motives. But the surrender of the illogical and the less inclusive to the more logical and more inclusive is in itself a means of liberating the higher impulses of the individual by enabling him to learn the methods and values of constructive self-criticism.

This process, if continued and persisted in, should tend more and more to reduce the frequency and the importance of instances in which the surrender to the group judgment is made unwillingly or grudgingly. It should tend to build up the kind of free give-and-take which makes it a matter of sporting spirit and even of high joy to see one's own opinion shifting through the process of group discussion until one sees eye to eye with one's fellows (who may also have shifted their ground). Obedience to the authority of a group consensus in the formulating of which one has shared, is antipodal to obedience to an external arbitrary authority.

In this respect, the democratic method differs fundamentally and radically from the militaristic and the paternalistic. The democratic method also differs from *laisser-aller*, in that it has an authority which the last-named lacks. Without arbitrariness, the democratic method enables the individual to check himself and control himself in the light of the common good. If the sacrifice of self-indulgence is the price of liberty in a democracy, the kind of liberation of one's best self which democracy gives in return is ample compensation for the cost.

The final consideration in this matter, so frequently overlooked by men of great power who like to make decisions for others without consulting or considering these others, is that nondemocratic procedures tyrannize over the dictator, the despot, and the paternalist just as much as they dominate the lives of the victims of these tyrants. He who has not learned to think in the light of the common good, and to subject his thinking to the frank and unflinching criticism of friend and foe, is a slave to his own fears, his own smaller desires, his own petty self. Liberation of self comes only as one aids others in achieving fuller liberation.

THE EXPERT AND THE MASSES

There is an authority of the masses on general matters of common concern, an authority which has to do not so much with the fine technical points of executing the ethical judgment, as with the discovery of the ethical judgment itself. There is another kind of authority, the authority of the expert in technical matters and details, an authority based primarily on possession of knowledge and training applicable to the execution of the ethical judgment of the masses. The basic judgment on ethical considerations should rest with the widest possible range of persons involved in the proposed decision; but every effort should be made to employ the services of trained technicians in carrying out the consensus.

This reverses the order sometimes advocated. A curious self-flattery which has marked otherwise great men from Plato's day to our own, has led certain ones to advocate that there should be a select group of intelligentsia who should do all the thinking and making of decisions, while the common people are to be trained to obey. But this government of the wise men, the philosophers, experts, technicians, is once again a fundamental violation of the principle that each person in a democratic process must make his contribution to the important decisions. Government by the experts is self-defeating, carrying the seeds of its own disintegration in the fruits of its efforts; but society cannot tolerate a wasteful process merely because in the end it will defeat itself. We have at hand the means of correcting the evil of the dictatorship of the self-selected experts. That correction lies in the appeal to the greatest mass of the common people for the basic ethical judgments about the kind of world they want to live in. This process of canvassing the group mind must attempt to use the methods of intelligence, arriving at the kind of consensus we have earlier defined. The experts are to share in this process, but their opinions are to be considered on their merits, rather than as coming from an authority. The authority of status and the authority of expertness are abrogated in favor of the authority of the wisest and most considerate course arrived at by group intelligence and group sympathy. The effort of the college, then, is directed toward the development of specially trained individuals who may or may not be experts in a given field, but who in any case certainly have had special training in the process of understanding the meaning of group welfare, of sharing in the making of decisions with all persons and groups vitally concerned.

This does not mean that there is to be no leadership. Quite the contrary. We have said that the democratic method demands that every person and group vitally concerned with the decision shall be free to make suggestions with the assurance that such suggestions will be considered on their merits. This involves a fundamental readjustment of our concepts of leadership.

THE PROBLEM OF LEADERSHIP

There is a valid contrast between the leadership of prestige based upon authority or status and the leadership of knowledge based upon facts.[10] There is also a valid contrast between expert opinion which is offered as an aid in the achieving of values selected by the social whole, and expert opinion which attempts to impose an arbitrary set of values upon society in violation of the integrity of its members.

Primarily on the grounds that a useful division of labor can best be achieved through the employment of specialists to carry out, facilitate, and implement the processes approved by social consensus, we justify the use of experts. These experts themselves share in the process of discovering the consensus, but they do not dominate the process or dictate the results. Experts employed for socially desired ends become a part of the democratic method, helping to save that method from the pitfall of wasteful inefficiency. This problem of efficiency calls for additional comment a little later.

In the democratic process as we are here defining it, how does leadership emerge? Kilpatrick[11] has distinguished at least four types of leadership which can function in the democratic process. Instead of the one type of leadership demanded by dictatorship, or the leaderless phenomenon of *laisser-aller*, or the static dominance of paternalism, the dem-

[10] Cf. *ibid.*, p. 174. "The former conception goes along with the notion of a journey aimed at a definite place, with a few who love the goal, know the way, and confess the duty of conducting the many willy-nilly to the glorious destination. The latter conception is that life is worth living in its own right. . . . We need, therefore, leaders in the process rather than guides to a distant goal."

[11] William H. Kilpatrick, lectures in course at Teachers College, Columbia University, Summer Session, 1937.

ocratic method calls forth a rich variety of leadership types for different situations and different parts of the project.

There is leadership of concern, of feeling strongly about a matter. This may come from any person who experiences or observes a situation. Not uncommonly it will come from one who feels that an injustice is being done to him or to others. In the early stages of any movement or development, this type of leadership is more important than any other. It wakes the community to the consciousness that "something must be done." This type of leadership is peculiarly called forth by the democratic method, with its insistence that any voice which speaks seriously about matters of common concern must be heard.

Secondly, there is leadership in thinking about the matter, of seeing into it and around it, of weighing possibilities and considering consequences. This is peculiarly the province of persons who have had experience or training which not only has developed in them the habits of critical thinking and social sensitivity, but also has widened their horizons and deepened their experience so that they are able to grasp the significance of the question before them, see it in its social setting and follow out its ramifications. In the typical college, there will likely be more of this type of leadership among the faculty and administration than in the student body; but there will not infrequently be genuine contributions from the students in this area of leadership. The democratic process as it operates in the functional college should be the laboratory for training students in this field of leadership.

There is a third area of leadership which has to do with managing people, getting a group rallied behind an accepted project, making a concern effective in action. This requires a dynamic kind of activity. It is often a matter of personality. It involves the ability to work out a satisfactory strategy for enlisting the active interest of the entire group in the project. It calls for the gifts most frequently associated with leadership in nondemocratic processes; but in addition it calls for the exercise of these attributes of personality in such a way that they serve, not violate, the democratic method. This type of leadership must not be used, for example, in prejudicing the findings previous to the discovery of a consensus. Its place is distinctly that of seeing that the consensus, when it emerges, is given every fair opportunity for success; that lethargy and indifference, or unintelligent opposition, do not unduly inhibit the project. It is not to be used to "put over" a project in abrogation of the democratic method: a few instances of such short-cut methods to administrative ends would go a long way toward defeating the whole democratic program.

The fourth kind of leadership derives from superior knowledge, wider experience, or more intensive study concerning the problem under discussion. Any one of these three named factors may lead to a degree of expertness in the particular field, giving a type of leadership (not authority, necessarily) which is valuable in helping the group discover ways of meeting its problems constructively. One may expect this type of leadership to emerge all along the line of the academic set-up.

All four of these types of leadership emerge from the situation itself, rather than from alleged leadership abilities innately possessed by certain individuals. Without a propitious situation, any of these leaders are voices crying down the wind; but if the societal setting is congenial, the leadership flowers. The democratic process aims to call forth the widest range of inclusive thinking and criticism, the deepest insights, the richest meanings available, from each and every person or group. Thus democracy elicits leadership.

EFFICIENCY AND THE DEMOCRATIC METHOD

A program involving the democratic method encounters the problem of efficiency from its very outset. One of the strongest cases to be made out against democracy rests on its apparent waste of time and energy. Why should a great number of persons be called into conference to decide petty matters which can just as easily be settled by one or two intelligent administrators who have authority to act? Is it not an inexcusable waste of time and energy to make these few well-trained, able persons sit through long hours of conference with students who know little or nothing of what it is all about, or with faculty members who are jockeying for departmental and individual advantages? So run the questions.

And the answers are that there is no need to waste the time and energy of the few well-trained persons; that the student body often includes insights and experiences which are essential to an intelligent consensus, that if some faculty members are concerned with personal and selfish matters the cure to selfishness lies in saddling them with more inclusive duties and interests which impel them to widen their bases of judgment and to be more catholic in their outlook. It is inevitable that, in education as in industry, the man who is denied a voice in the government of affairs ceases to have an active interest in that government, except as from time to time he is able to bring pressure upon it to yield some differential advantage to him. The next stage of the degradation of the disinherited is the loss of interest in the work itself. In the end, then, the denial of the democratic process means the loss of interest in the work as such, together with a developing antagonism to the few who have been set in positions of administrative responsibility. Having no part in determining the conditions of work and study, no voice in creating the college, the individual learns to disregard all larger questions of collegiate welfare, and to concentrate on carving out a comfortable niche for himself. The concentration of administrative responsibilities and procedures in the hands of a few administrators and experts tends, in the end, to create a situation in which the alleged efficiencies are offset by the actual deficiencies and inefficiencies in the operation of the college.

The equality ideal must mean this highly important thing that every man shall be entitled to understand and progressively to create the ends for which his energy goes. And this means of course that he is entitled to the kind of character that can create and appreciate purposes that outrun the moment.[12]

It is not enough to point out that the allegedly efficient but undemocratic program defeats itself. The positive answer to the dilemma of efficiency and the democratic method lies in the fact that the only efficiency worth having is that which serves the purposes of the democratic method in its efforts to develop the personalities of all in terms of equality. Alleged educational efficiency which serves to buttress any disregard of personality by shutting the student or the teacher out from participation in the fundamentally important process of college policy is not efficient at all, as far as the purposes of the functional college are concerned. The problem of getting things done with dispatch and effectiveness must be solved by making sure that the things which actually get done are these fundamentals of growth in attitudes, habits, insights, appreciations, and the equipment of these with knowledge and skills and techniques appropriate to them, looking toward the modification of any and all hindering institutional arrangements and toward maximum richness of living for the individual. The administrator who looks for efficiency must therefore first answer the question: Efficiency for what? Is he to be more effective with his push buttons, telephones, stenographers, committees, speeches, and programs, only to find that the mill he has been so busily turning lacks grist? The problem is not simply the conventional warfare of efficiency and liberty. It is the deeper problem of scrapping entirely an erroneous notion that efficiency in itself has value. What we are looking for is effectiveness in doing well the functional job of civilization itself. Smooth running of academic machinery may or may not be related to this fundamental job. Efficiency has meaning only as it does actually relate to this underlying purpose.

That these general considerations hold with even more definite force in the segregated college is immediately clear with the statement of the proposition. A college which serves

[12] T. V. Smith, *op. cit.,* p. 105.

primarily the members of a minority group which, in American democracy, knows from first-hand experience the way in which alleged administrative efficiency serves the best interests of the dominant group, or even of a fraction of that dominant majority, begins the democratic effort with the initial support of its clientele. This is a point at which the segregated college has an advantage over the white college. For Negroes are, perhaps, more fully aware than whites of the glaring inadequacies of efficiency for efficiency's sake. They know that no matter how well oiled the machinery, or how rapidly the wheels go around, the net result for the Negro is still a minus quantity. Efficiency has meaning only as it relates to fuller life for people; and Negroes will not readily be interested in any other kind of efficiency. But let the segregated college once show that its efforts are genuinely geared in with the realization of the deepest yearnings and highest aspirations of America, both Caucasian and Negro America, and the clientele of the segregated college is in a position to give intelligent and sympathetic support to the enterprise.

Some beginning in effective use of time and energy in the operation of the democratic process can be made by an intelligent division of labor in the execution of policies. If the policies are selected and elaborated by an inclusive process, there is every reason to use a division of labor in carrying out the policies, with the delegation of duties and responsibilities to selected persons and committees, these administrative units to function subject to the general consensus of the college. It may well be a mistake to bring the entire faculty together to settle the location of a drinking fountain, or to waste the time of the whole student body in an argument which concerns only a fraction of those enrolled. That is not merely inefficiency; it is stupidity. But it is equally stupid to think that all the fundamental decisions of policy and procedure must be made behind closed doors and then announced to the college, whether this is done in the name of efficiency or under the aegis of any other shibboleth.

WHAT PRESCRIPTIVE LIMITATIONS?

There is certain to be some uneasiness in those academic circles which are not now democratic, as they consider proposals such as these for a more democratic procedure. "Where is this thing going to stop?" they ask. "Do you mean to include everything in the democratic process? Are you proposing that the students sit in judgment upon the fitness of the teachers or that they determine the president's salary? Are you advocating that the faculty shall hire and fire both themselves and the administration? Do you want to run the risk of having the students setting up rules and regulations to govern the social life of the staff and faculty? And will the governing board, the trustees or the overseers, permit this democratic phantasy to be realized anyway? Don't you have to begin by setting some pretty definite limits beyond which this thing is not to go?"

Fortunately, we are not here obliged to answer these questions for any particular college or for any particular board of trustees or any special faculty or student body. The problem of practicability, as well as that of practical steps to be taken in each situation, will need to be answered in concrete terms to fit each collegiate situation. But in general, some kind of suggestive answer to these questions can be given.

First of all, these questions imply a lack of faith in the democratic method. They ask for some kind of check on rash and immature judgment, some guard to academic dignity and decency, some guarantee that the democratic process will not run amuck. This doubt is a natural one, born of inexperience. One who has never flown in an airplane confesses to some quickening of the pulse on taking his first ride.

These doubts also reflect the fact that, as most American colleges are now established, legal responsibility for the welfare and progress of the institution rests upon a governing board (usually the board of trustees); and a governing board is naturally loathe to surrender control over policies while it is held legally responsible for the college. To meet this hesitancy of the governing board of the college, it will probably be well for the functional college to launch its democratic developments with the understanding that important modifications of policy which appear to be approved by campus consensus are to be subjected to the critical review of the board before final adoption as policy. Unless there is a fundamental disharmony between the board and the campus, this reference of basic proposals to the board is only one more means of insuring the fullest and most inclusive discussion of the matter; and in most cases this advice ought to work to remove any possible misunderstanding or misconception. It is a misconstruing of the true nature of democracy to contend that such reference to the board violates the prerogatives of the campus. On the contrary, refusal to include the board means exclusion of persons vitally concerned in the decision. In the few instances where irreconcilable cleavage between campus and board may appear the situation will be no worse— as far as democracy is concerned—than it would be without the democratic effort. And if the board of trustees of a liberal college begins by authorizing the shift in administrative procedure which this chapter outlines, that board thereby commits itself to the effort to see the experiment through to a satisfactory conclusion. The bogey of the recalcitrant board is therefore something to conjure with before the venture is launched, not after.

Nor are we very much worried by the allegation that this democratic procedure fails to provide sufficient checks and balances, or that it needs some authoritative point of reference to guarantee it against hasty and ill-considered action. One such check is inherent in the proposal that action is to follow inclusive consensus rather than being based on a majority vote. If the consensus is to include the men and women who, under the autocratic or paternalistic regimes, make the decisions for the college, the democratic method still gives their opinions and ideas full and complete access to the council table. They still share in making the consensus. The difference is that they are not free to act without consulting the minds of their colleagues who may be vitally concerned with the decision. All the values of the present checks and balances are retained; but the autocratic character of the undemocratic method is corrected. Far from lacking sufficient checks and balances, the democratic method adds to the difficulty of arriving at decisions and of projecting actions. The real objection comes from the other direction, in the observation that the necessity of discovering consensus before action may be taken means that there is grave danger of a stalemate in the face of some crisis. The objection that inclusive consensus brings insufficient checks upon the process of decision making falls to the ground, and in its stead is conjured up the difficulty of getting any degree of movement at all in the face of the necessity of striking a completely satisfying mode of action to which every student, teacher, and administrator agrees.

Here is a real objection, and one which cannot be met in theory. The answer must be an empirical one. As the college works its way into democratic processes and procedures, it will need to take whatever measures its own experience suggests as necessary to avoid a stalemate in the face of a crisis. Some method of breaking the deadlock may have to be devised, provided the situation is critical enough. But for all matters which do not involve an immediate or impending crisis—and how many crises come in an academic year when everyone on the campus knows what is going on?—it would appear that the cumbersome process of inclusive consensus promises values of collegiate solidarity and genuine intelligence which tend to outweigh the bogey of the stalemate.

Furthermore, common sense suggests that some division of matters be made so that the general machinery for considering matters of general importance does not get clogged up with numerous petty affairs. A pragmatic line can be drawn between matters which appear to involve the consideration of policies and those which are merely concerned with the carrying out of the policies on which the campus is agreed. A second distinction can be recognized which sifts the matters of policy with reference to the inclusiveness of their applica-

tion. Only those persons who are more or less vitally concerned with the results of the decision to be made need to be
included in the discussion. If all matters are run through these
two sieves before being presented formally to the democratic
machinery of the campus, much can be done to expedite matters without violating any of the fundamental considerations
of the democratic method.

Jealous care must be exercised at all times to avoid the
possibility that some arbitrary or biased ruling may at some
time keep a matter of vital concern hidden in the administrative portfolio or pigeonholed in faculty committee or em-
balmed in student loyalty to tradition. The democratic venture on the campus which starts off by arbitrarily delimiting
the province in which the democratic method is to function
("no discussion of budget or curriculum or fraternities," for
example) makes itself a hollow pretense, a timid excuse for
a robust adventure. And it will likely get the results it de-
serves—jaundiced and juiceless. What limitations? No arbitrary limitations in advance of experience, but rather the es-
tablishment of such operational safeguards to effective and
inclusive action as appear to be needed in the light of developing experience in the democratic method.

A principle which may help to guide the acting and thinking
of groups perfecting democratic operation on their campuses
is the suggestion that participation in decision making may
be shared in accordance with the ratio of ability-to-learn to
the value-of-what-is-at-stake. This would be an important
consideration in the elementary or high school where it would
act to delimit the province of pupil participation. The relative immaturity of the elementary school pupil distinctly limits his ability to share in the more intricate or more momentous decisions of major policy and program. It does not,
however, limit his ability to share in the decisions which to
him at that stage of his development are momentous and
meaningful. His ability-to-learn is, to an important extent, a
function of his felt interest in the matter to be studied. The
basic ethical insights and the attitudes appropriate to a more

enlightened society can readily be learned by younger children; but the intricate decisions of how to execute these judgments and implement these insights may not as readily be
learned by adolescents.

The principle that the student may share in the making of
decisions in accordance with the ratio of his ability-to-learn
to the value-of-the-matter-at-stake is just as important on the
college campus as in the lower schools; but here its force is
positive, not negative. By the fact that the functional college
expects its students to develop in social maturity, that college
is obligated to give its students the impetus of adult status,
and to hold them to the standards of adulthood. Adults may
vary in the degree of their maturity. Students and staff and
faculty will not all be on an identical level of social maturity.
But they are all capable, to a greater or lesser degree, of participating in the discussion of matters of importance to them.
The combined intelligence of the college faculty, staff, and
student body ought to be sufficient to correct the error of a
few inexperienced freshmen. And the arbitrary prescription
which would shut out any person from participation in decision making—any such arbitrary prescription—vitiates the
fraternal ideal of genuine democracy. Brotherhood cannot
be limited without ceasing to be brotherhood.

Before leaving this section, we must return to the fears of
those who wish prescriptive limitations to be laid down in
advance. These are they who ask, "Are students to sit in
judgment on the fitness of teachers? Is the faculty to set the
president's salary? Are the hiring and firing of personnel to be
decided by some conglomerate group including freshmen and
sophomores?" These and allied questions strike home at the
point of personal security and status, where it is least easy
for the individual to be objective and impersonal as a participant in democratic processes. Two of our principles apply
helpfully to the quandaries of our hesitant friends: (a) that
there is to be an operating division of labor between the process of making policies and the procedure for administering
policies; and (b) that all persons concerned are to share in

the making of policies in accordance with the ratio of ability-to-learn to the value-of-the-matter-at-stake.

With these principles in mind, it becomes immediately clear that wherever a change in policy is involved in an issue which arises, the deliberative body which arrives at decisions through inclusive consensus is not merely the final court of appeal. It is the only ethically approved arena for such decisions. The democratic machinery must be used, and the fullest consideration demanded by the situation must be given, whenever changes in policy are involved.

Conversely, it is equally clear that the jurisdiction of the deliberative body does not extend into the area of executing the policies. The administrative personnel which, in a democratic college, includes many students and faculty members along with administrative officers, must carry out the policies of the deliberative body; and the actions of all administrative persons and committees are subject to the surveillance of the deliberative body, as far as the policies of the college are involved. But the deliberative body does not presume to dictate either to students or to others who are charged with administrative responsibilities, the precise details through which the policy is to be executed. That would be to violate the democratic regard for the integrity of administering persons. At the same time, persons and committees charged with administrative duties may, if they wish, ask the advice and counsel of the deliberative body; but the responsibility for carrying through rests with the persons (students, staff, and faculty) who have been selected to carry out the policies of the college. Basic matters of general and specific policy, such as questions of tenure, salary schedules, freedom of teaching and freedom of administering, may on occasion be reviewed and discussed by the deliberative body with profit to all concerned. But when it comes to applying the policy in specific situations (the promotion of Professor A or the tenure of Dean Y) democratic *administrative* procedures must be used to carry out the policies. The campus *deliberative* body limits itself to the process of such review of administrative action as may from time to time be demanded by the situation. Persons and committees charged with carrying out policies may, if they wish, solicit this review—but the deliberative body does not determine administrative procedures.

If, for example, in the dismissal of an officer of instruction or of administration, or of a student, any person on the campus feels that there has been a violation of a college policy or the abridgment of individual rights or lack of consideration of the general welfare, full and frank review of the situation is indicated. Error is always a possibility of human nature. But it is presumed that there will be a minimum of instances in which such review of specific cases and situations is desired; for in a college where long habituation accustoms all persons to think of the larger implications of their actions and to govern themselves in accordance with the general welfare as agreed upon in their inclusive councils, there ought to be a minimum of antisocial intent and a gradually growing ability to use social intelligence. It would appear reasonable to believe that in such a college there would be many fewer instances both of administrative high-handedness and of individual recalcitrance, than in the typically paternalistic or autocratic institution. The atmosphere of hostility and of suspicion out of which violations of integrity come is dispelled by mutual understanding and intelligently critical loyalty on the democratic campus.

THE PROBLEMS OF CONTENTIOUSNESS AND CONTUMACY

There are some who feel that the necessity of arriving at a consensus may give the whip hand to the obstinate, the contentious, the loquacious, the opinionated, the articulate, the argumentative. If this were the case, a serious stumbling block would lie in democracy's path.

Let it be noted at once, however, that the practice of filibustering is not an invention of the Quaker meeting. Indeed, the filibuster flourishes under precisely those conditions which the method of consensus seeks to avoid, namely, the making of decisions by marshaling opposing forces and mustering votes to carry a majority in spite of all minority points of view. For example, in the United States Senate, the filibuster is the only defense which a determined minority can find in its last-ditch stand. Minority members use obstructionist tactics to win their point through sheer fatigue and exasperation. And back of the filibustering senators are constituents with fairly settled convictions who do not come face to face with the other side of their living conditions. Thus it happens that legislators, mindful of the coming elections, are forced to entrench themselves in defense of absolutist positions rather than being permitted to modify their opinions and votes in the light of the best available critical common thought.

Indeed, in advocating the advisability of the method of consensus for the college campus, we are not necessarily implying that it is a good prototype for political democracies. The college does not usually have in its student and staff selected representatives of constituencies back home, who are forced to resort to obstructionist tactics. It is important to note, however, that the success of the idea of consensus on the campus can be seriously impaired if either students or staff (or any bloc) so act as to make irreconcilables of themselves or their fellows. In general, the old-style curriculum which sets students and instructors over against each other, and the old-style autocratic control which automatically keeps the student from intelligent participation in campus government, lie at the bottom of student rebellion and professorial contumacy. A curriculum designed to enlist teachers and pupils alike as fellow-students, and an administration designed to elicit the active participation of all members of the campus family set the stage for the success of consensus and for the self-destruction of any nascent minority disregard of general welfare. Differences of opinion and thought there will be, and ought to be; but the discovery of common purposes and the effort to realize the common good through the method of consensus promises to avoid the dominance of the long-winded and the die-hards.

Under the method of majority rule, minorities know that

they are always to be outvoted, so that loquaciousness and contention become their defense; but under the method of consensus (at least in the intimate society of the small college campus), the minority is encouraged to defend the reasonableness of its position and encouraged to make such defense with the knowledge that, in the end, their assent can be withheld if justification for veto action appears. The minority member is thus enabled to concentrate his energies on the effort to think through the merits of the matters in hand instead of being forced to muster his wits for the desperate effort to block steam-roller parliamentary processes. The method of consensus gives him a margin of psychological security in the possession of a veto power which he can use if necessary. He therefore finds it possible to become much more tolerant and mature in his attitudes. In practical experience, democracy on the campus does not sell out to the filibusterer when it adopts the method of consensus. Rather, by such action it lessens the likelihood of contentiousness and contumacy, placing a premium upon group intelligence, fair-mindedness, and the effort to understand differing points of view. A sense of security for each minority interest is assured by the fact that the majority cannot ride ruthlessly over its minorities. The majority, in turn, is forced to be considerate. Both majority and minorities are forced to recognize that contention leads only to deadlock, and that reasonableness, group thinking, and, in some cases, compromise are the only answers.

Thus, the device which is intended to provide a wider ethical base for group decisions brings as a by-product a more nearly harmonious and ethical adjustment between the members of the group. Contumeliousness, which is so often a byproduct of the denial of minority rights, tends to be dissipated by the recognition of minority voices. In the end, the most effective cure for obduracy born of disfranchisement and disinheritance is the widening of the franchise and the sharing of the inheritance. If democracy adopts the method of substantial consensus, it at once curbs the high-handed ruthlessness of its dominant groups, and makes possible an ethically defensible process. Such an ethically defensible process cuts the ground from beneath irritable minority contentiousness and paves the way toward reasonableness.

As for the few congenitally contumacious die-hards, their position is at least as tolerable for all concerned under consensus as under majority rule. They cease to be heroes and martyrs, demagogic defenders of minority sensitivity, because the majority is forced to consider the just claims of minorities, thereby stealing the thunder from their storm clouds. The power and influence of the chronic objectors are reduced to a minimum quite below that enjoyed in the process of majority rule.

HOW INCLUSIVE A CONSENSUS IS NECESSARY?

Without attempting to answer this question for democracy in the large, we must answer it for democracy in the segregated college. We have spoken of the desirability of consensus; but are we to assume that this agreement is to include not merely the persons who live and work on the campus, but also that campus objectives must be squared with the opinions and prejudices of the society which engulfs the college?

The only possible answer is the pragmatic one. We counter the question with another—under the American caste system, what likelihood is there that a caste-ridden society will accept a casteless college? It is sheer moonshine and cobwebs to speak of the immediate possibility of consensus of the functional college with its culture. The purpose of the functional college, indeed, is to escape from the present compromising relationship by which the code of caste dominates the college, in order eventually to affect society. It follows that there must be at present a fairly sharp cleavage of objective between the functional college and the caste system.

If, then, we accept the idea that the college is to strike its own campus consensus without conforming to a wider social pattern, in the hope that the wider social pattern may eventually become more congenial to the college; the next question

is, does this same idea apply within the college? Can we assume that there will be times when a group of the few (who
claim to "see things clearly") or the majority (who admit
they "agree on what is best") or the administrators (who are
sure they "know what it is all about") should take things in
their own hands and press on, hoping for a developing consensus as time passes?

The first answer is that every effort must be made to use
all the resources of intelligence and fellow-feeling in the hope
that some larger measure of genuine consensus can be brought
on the campus. It is perfectly possible that good and sincere
men and women will differ on fundamental issues after months
of discussion and study; but this likelihood is greatly reduced
if the democratic process actually functions. Far-visioned leadership will attempt to look ahead and see problems emerging
long before they become acute, when they can be discussed
somewhat objectively and without too much personal or
vested interest. It is very possible that a concerted and continuing effort to catch progress by the forelock may enable
the college to keep a jump or two ahead of crises, and thereby
to insure an atmosphere for discussion which is much more
cordial to consensus than the strained and tense atmosphere
of a critical moment. Even with an unsuspected crisis upon it,
the college ought to be able to marshal its forces of intelligence and restraint so that a *modus vivendi* of a temporary
sort can be found, pending a more leisurely exploration of
possibilities and a less hurried final decision. It is to be hoped
that most critical situations can be met without abandoning
the principle of consensus, because this is the foundation rock
of the idea of genuine democracy. In colleges where the particular tradition and sponsorship support the possibility, a
high and genuine religious experience may at times be useful
in resolving a difficulty. Democracy has much to learn from
the Quaker meeting.[13]

Whether, in the end, some means for breaking the dead-

[13] The Chinese, I am told, also make extensive use of the method of consensus, although I am not informed as to the underlying religious or institutional bases of the practice.

lock must be devised, is a question which cannot be answered in advance of the event. One would hope that intelligence and human sympathy, plus self-control and the mellowing influence of time, would provide a specific even for the virus of dissent. Certainly it is to be expected that dissent will flourish, and that orthodoxy will accordingly be forced to become heterodox in the effort to achieve consensus. This is in accord with the democratic belief in the value of individual integrity. Social uniformity is not a desideratum; but individual variation with social harmony is to be desired.

We cannot dismiss this section without returning to the first question raised. If the college is to adopt an attitude in which the surrounding culture only partly agrees, does not the college thereby violate the idea of consensus which is fundamental to democracy? Is this not merely another way of introducing minority—or majority—rule? We think not. Consider the case of one person who strongly disagrees with a proposal which is before the college. If he believes that he is right, there is some possibility that he may change the outlook and judgment of the entire college group to an important degree. The fact that he begins with a point of view quite different from that of his colleagues of the staff and student body does not violate the principle of consensus—it is essential to the democratic process. In much the same manner, the segregated college begins by differing markedly from its surrounding culture. The college, however, is under moral obligation to consider these excluded persons and interests which encircle it, and to take only such steps as are calculated to be fair to them as well, and in the long run to serve the inclusive interest of all persons. If, then, its efforts are directed so that they are calculated to affect the thinking and acting of persons in the surrounding culture so that a larger degree of consensus may be hoped for, this is only another recognition of the essential principle that in the democratic process there must be complete freedom for all groups to present their suggestions and make their pleas.

The program and activities which flow out of the more

limited consensus of the college ought to be calculated to work toward a more inclusive consensus if possible. Otherwise the seeds of inner decay are already sown within the smaller group, and having attempted to use undemocratic methods on the "out" group, the "in" group will find (a) that if it is successful in its effort to realize its objective of modifying caste, the methods used will have become part of the new structure, so vitally affecting the new pattern that the lack of democracy in the procedure has killed the possibility of democracy in the new pattern; or it will find (b) that if it is unsuccessful in the attempt, it will have lost both its hope of victory and the tools for achieving it at some future time, because undemocratic attitudes and procedures will have entered into the practices of the group which attempted to be undemocratic in its "out-group" relationships. It is not possible permanently to have one ethic for the "in" group and another for the "out" group. Sooner or later, one partakes of the other; and either the higher ethic must be pushed outward to include the wider fellowship; or else the attitudes toward the "out" group will corrupt the inner ethic. The guarantee of democratic freedom, therefore, is the practice of democracy, of inclusive consensus, both within the group and in the attitudes of the group toward the larger whole. Permanent results derive from practice consistent with objectives.

IMPLEMENTING THE DEMOCRATIC IDEA

Inherent in the democratic method is the implication that the particular machinery fabricated to express the democratic notion will vary with each special situation. Any attempt either to impose a preconceived process upon a campus or to transplant a program from one campus to another without making significant modifications to fit local conditions, is a violation of the integrity of the local campus and of the guidance of common sense. But in order that persons interested in exploring the possibilities of democratic procedures on their own campuses may have something definite to use as a point of departure, there is included in Appendix C a discussion of one variant of the many democratic methods which might be put to use. In no sense is this a standard pattern, or an ideal. It is merely one of several attempts now being made to give tangible expression to the democratic urge in the segregated college. Its inclusion within the covers of this book is justified on the grounds that here is one definite, working embodiment of the democratic ideal; and however imperfect it may be, it is a practical answer to those who have doubts that the democratic ideal can be brought out of the theoretical realm and actually put into practice. The persons who happen to be concerned with this venture would be the first to disclaim its perfection. They would plead that their efforts be judged not so much as to whether they indicate that their college has "arrived," but rather as to whether it appears that the college is moving in a desirable direction.

THE EDUCATIVE EFFECTS OF DEMOCRATIC ADMINISTRATION

The functional college will select democracy as its administrative policy not on *a priori* grounds but on the probability that democratic methods will bring desired educational effects. To the extent that the administrative procedure actually produces the fruits appropriate to its nature, it appears probable that in the democratic method lies more hope than in any other.

The rejected methods of autocracy and paternalism keep the student in a state of conformity or else gall him into ineffective blind revolt. They may attempt to indoctrinate him with a form of social conscience; but they fail to provide the day-to-day experiences calculated to provide full opportunity for these ideas to take root in his habitual nature. Failing to make his social sensitivity a real part of his daily experience, they have the ultimate effect of destroying his faith in social idealism, and leaving him somewhat cynical or indifferent, if not embittered. So, also, the program of *laisser-aller* is principally a reaction against the dominance of paternalism and regimentation; its educative effects do not commend it to the administrator of the segregated college.

The democratic method, on the other hand, ought to provide opportunity and encouragement for growth into social maturity. If the deciding factor in shaping minds is the shape of the social institutions in which the minds operate, then a campus society which demanded the reactions of socially mature persons from all of its residents might be a constructive factor in producing the desired results. The continual use of the processes of intelligence to construct a consensus which represents the combined judgment of all persons affected by the decision and which is formulated by the individuals, thinking in concert and searching for the best means of serving the common good and of meeting the needs of the individuals involved, is a societal gymnasium in which students and staff alike practice the habits and arts of the democratic process. They learn to think critically about matters of common concern—not by thinking about some remote problem of classical antiquity, and not by studying some one of the "mental disciplines" to "improve the mind." They learn to think critically about matters of common concern by thinking critically about matters of common concern. They learn to protect the rights of minorities by protecting those rights. They learn to combine the objectivity of the scientific approach with the enthusiasm of fellow-feeling by making that combination in the reconstruction of campus society. They learn how to live without caste by living without caste. The educative effects of democratic administrative procedures promise to be in harmony with the educational aims of the functional college.[14]

[14] Cf. Jean Piaget, *The Moral Judgment of the Child,* for discussion of psychology of learning involved in this chapter. Piaget argues (experimentally) that two moralities operate on the child. One is based on the relation of constraint and authority. Respect is unilateral. The other is based on equality and mutual respect, the relation of coöperation. This second is "an equilibrial limit rather than a static system." The development of desirable and autonomous rationality in the child comes as the fruits of reciprocity rather than of restraint. And finally, the attempt to socialize the autonomous individual judgment can be successful only in an atmosphere congenial to the enterprise. "It is only through contact with the judgments and evaluations of others that this intellectual and affective autonomy will gradually yield to the pressure of collective logical and moral laws." See esp. *op. cit.,* pp. 402-14.

WILL THE FUNCTIONAL COLLEGE UNFIT THE STUDENT FOR LIFE?

The caste-controlled world into which the student goes at graduation, and from which he never quite succeeds in withdrawing during undergraduate days, makes harsh and imperious demands for conformity. Will four years in the functional college unfit the student for life in the caste-controlled society which he faces at graduation? The answer is twofold: in one sense, yes; and in another sense, no.

The student will be unfitted for that kind of conformity which means acceptance of the inequities of caste. To some educators, this result is little short of a calamity. They wish the college, whether a segregated institution or not, to take on the color of contemporary social processes and to serve the dominant purposes of the nation.

Education will promote national weal and security, provided educational objectives are adjusted to the natural social evolution. . . . Social adjustment of education must be a training that recognizes a measure of natural law in society and also the value of institutions that have been developed through the centuries of race experience. . . . Education must . . . embody matters of social attitude as well as those related to effective procedures. . . . Overemphasis on social reform to the neglect of sound procedures will certainly lead to a bog of sentimentality. . . . In the highest possible development of the individual lies the way to the social adjustment of education. . . . No man is wise enough to warrant his being a social or economic radical.[15]

Fortunately, no responsible head of a college for Negroes has expressed himself in print in similar vein on the question of the segregated college and the caste system. But outsiders waste no opportunity to tell the Negro college that its purpose is that of training its students to conform. From the platform of one of the largest and most influential of the schools for Negroes, a visiting speaker volunteered frank words like these:

[15] C. C. Williams, "Social Adjustment of Education," Inaugural address of the President of Lehigh University, *School and Society*, XLII (October 19, 1935), 521-26.

I want to give you niggers a few words of plain talk and advice. No such address as you have just listened to is going to do you any good; it's going to spoil you. You had better not listen to such speeches. You might just as well understand that this is a white man's country as far as the South is concerned, and we are going to make you keep your place. Understand that. I have nothing more to say.[16]

To persons who share the general frame of mind of President Williams and the special limitations of the late Governor Oates, the idea that the college will unfit the Negro for conformity to caste is abhorrent. For precisely opposite reasons, the idea commends itself to the educator in the functional college. Between the two is a great gulf described by a set of value judgments about the worth of human personality and the means of recognizing that worth. The first answer to the question of the probable effect of college upon the Negro is: yes, the functional college ought to unfit the student for conformity to caste, for this is one of its objects.

But the second answer must immediately be added, and in fact cannot be separated from the first nor the first from the second. The functional college will unfit the graduate for conformity to caste, but it will also equip him for the task of transforming caste and of transcending what is not transformed. Here is a sane and balanced program. Having learned to live without caste in the college, and having learned the constructive attitudes and habits of social reconstruction through democratic processes, the graduate should be saved from a blind and bitter revolt leading to despair and conformity in the end; and he should also be freed from many of the psychogenic hazards which beset the path of the Negro. Thus integrated personally and thus socially oriented, he can work in a straightforward, courageous, unashamed, and unapologetic manner to change the culture of which he is a part. He should be able to transcend the failures of today and tomorrow and to live in the hopes of continuing increments of

[16] Governor Oates of Alabama, at the Commencement exercises of Tuskegee Institute in 1894. Quoted in Horace Mann Bond, "The Influence of Personalities on the Public Education of Negroes in Alabama," *Journal of Negro Education*, VI (April, 1937), 174.

partial success, knowing that the mills of the gods grind slow but they grind exceeding fine. For he will know that his method is appropriate to any ethically defensible results, and on this basis he is ready to trust the outcome.

ONLY APPROPRIATE METHOD BRINGS PERMANENT RESULTS

When an attempt is made to alter a collective attitude, such as a race prejudice, there results a conflict between the old and the new attitudes. Each group, being interconditioned in favor of its own attitude, looks with disfavor upon that of the other. Rationalization of the attitude of each individual is reënforced by the suggestive reciprocal support of his fellows. Conflict results, the more bitter and the more intense as the conflict proceeds.

When such redirection of attitudes cannot be achieved on a rational or scientific basis, but defense rationalization continues on an emotional level, persecution and struggle, possibly revolution and civil war may ultimately eventuate. Although such a solution is often hailed as a triumph for democracy, the net result, as Martin has pointed out, is usually not a rational redirection of attitudes at all, but rather the putting of another set of irrational, but rationalized, attitudes into a position of dominance, giving rise to new dogmatisms, new intolerances, and persecutions. Apparently the only way in which such collective conflicts, as well as individual conflicts, can be successfully and hygienically solved is by securing a redirection of behaviour toward a more feasible environmental objective. This can be done by the rational reconditioning of attitudes on a higher neuro-psychic or intellectual and symbolic plane to the facts of science, preferably through free discussion, and with a minimum of distortion through propaganda. This is not an easy way to mental and social sanity, but it appears to be the only one that actually arrives at the goal.[17]

It may be that the gentlemen who most fear the kind of intelligent attack upon the problem of caste which it is advocated the functional college should make, will, in the end, recognize that the kind of attack upon caste which is contemplated in the use of the democratic process promises to give the only permanent resolution of the embittered difficulties of the caste

[17] L. L. Bernard, "Attitudes and the Redirection of Behaviour," in *Social Attitudes*, pp. 72-73.

system. The college which is wisely guided will lose no opportunity to make clear that its inclusive aim is that of raising the level of opportunity and of life for all persons of both races and all classes, and that its attack upon caste is only a means of breaking down the artificial barriers to fuller life which prevent Negro and Caucasian alike from entering into fuller life. The democratic method will not guarantee fullness of life; but it is difficult to see how fullness of life can be gained for the great masses of the people in any other way.

XII

TOWN AND GOWN: THE WIDER CAMPUS

Coöperative activities for community improvement form the vision of the best education yet conceived.

—WILLIAM H. KILPATRICK

BETWEEN the typical college and its surrounding village or city there is a peculiar sense of social distance best summarized in the classic phrase which characterizes the town of Oxford and Oxford University—"town and gown." There are subtle jealousies between college and community which cannot be attributed to differences in income or in standards of living, but which root in a kind of "irritated deference" which the town shows to the institution which it fosters. The academic alien within its gates is the source of notoriety to the city, and by that very fact the college is also a thorn in the civic and commercial pride of townspeople who might have preferred to be known instead for their solid business and professional achievement.[1] There are special variations of the college and community relationship in each locality; but typically and generally, there is a sense of social distance between the two, varying all the way from amused tolerance to mutual hostility and recrimination.

THE DOUBLE DIFFICULTY OF THE NEGRO COLLEGE

Difficult as it might have been for the typical New England liberal arts college to achieve a *rapprochement* with its community, how much more troublous was the situation of the doubly alien institution for the education of Negroes which sprouted where the trampling armies of the Blue and the Gray had lately been. The traditional social distance of town and gown was multiplied by the acrimony of war and the bitterness of Reconstruction. Not a few of the schools for Negroes were started in old Union army barracks or forts,

[1] For a delightfully fascinating discussion of the "irritable but fostering mother" of the college, and the manner in which town and gown have historically held one another at arm's length, see H. S. Canby, *Alma Mater,* esp. pp. 5-22 and 155 ff.

or under the auspices of the army of occupation, the Freed-men's Bureau.

For the most part, the white South did not welcome the Yankee schoolma'ams who came down to "uplift the Negro."[2] The favorite form of resistance was the simple device of os-tracism, although in many cases there were open threats of physical violence, of the burning of buildings, and a few actual lynchings of white teachers.[3] Here was more than the tradi-tional social distance of town and gown—this was the active animosity of the conquered and embittered South toward an arrogant army of occupation. The military army of occupa-tion had served its brief period and was gone; but this educa-tional army in petticoats stayed on, to the lasting irritation of the white South.

Nor were the Southerners irritated without cause. Some-times an extreme case gives a flash of insight into a large problem. So with the words of a speaker before the National Teachers' Association in 1865. Moved by his patriotic fervor as a Yankee Unionist, and expressing all the chauvinism of an unyielding victor, he said of the Southern whites, "We must treat them as Western farmers do the stumps in their clear-ings—work around them and let them rot out!"[4] It was too much to expect that the defeated South should welcome with open arms these Yankee intruders who were, to them, un-wholesome and dangerous meddlers. It was also expecting a good deal of human nature to look among the Yankees for a mellow understanding of the plight of the broken followers of Lee. From the start, in nearly every case where Northern

[2] Margaret Mitchell's lone comment on the Yankee teachers in the 1,037 pages of *Gone with the Wind* is a single paragraph which expresses the dilemma of the Southern whites who did not know which they hated worse—the carpetbaggers who were frankly there to despoil the South, or the teachers who were there to put ideas into the heads of Negroes.

[3] See, for example, the reports of the lynching of William Luke (white) at Cross Plains, Alabama, in 1870, as given to the Congressional Committee in-vestigating Ku Klux Klan activities (*Report* of the Joint Select Committee on the Condition of Affairs in the Late Insurrectionary States), Vol. VIII on Alabama. Permitted to leave a last letter to his wife and children, Luke wrote, "God knows I have only sought to educate the Negro."

[4] Sue North, "Damyankees in Negro Schools," *American Mercury,* XXXV (June, 1935), 199.

teachers and missionaries came into the South to plant their
alien institutions of education for freedmen, the white South
drew its skirts closer about itself and whispered darkly of the
"things that went on out there in that nigger school." For
persons unacquainted with the temper of Reconstruction days,
the story of these early struggles to establish schools and
colleges for Negroes is available in detail elsewhere. Those
who know the story will need no documentation of the fact
of antipathy, active and open antipathy, between white town
and Negro college.[5]

Seventy years ago, there was this wide gap between the
Negro college and the white town. It has persisted. Inter-
estingly enough, there has often been a correlative gap between the Negro college and the Negro community. This gap
did not always appear at first, when the freedman tended to
express a naïve and exuberant faith and confidence in the
Yankee school teacher whose tutoring was to be his open
door to opportunity. But as the institution grew up from its
rudimentary beginnings and began to achieve fuller collegiate
stature, and as class demarcations within the Negro caste became sharper and more exaggerated, the town and gown
problem of the New England college had its counterpart in
the gown and overall problem of the segregated college in
the South. In some instances, the white missionaries permitted
themselves to step into the psychological position formerly occupied by the masters of the slaves; and the perpetuation of
the master-slave pattern of relationships described the emerging gown-overall situation. In other places, the teachers refused to accept the psychological pattern which had survived
legal emancipation; and oftentimes this was a source of some

[5] Let one rather extreme example suggest many others. A certain white
teacher arrived in a Southern town to join the force at a school maintained
under Northern auspices in the 1870s. Soon after his arrival he read the following paragraph about himself in the local newspaper: "We had always considered soap-eyed Steward the meanest looking man we ever saw, but the
other day we met him in the company of a long-legged, white-eyed, red whis-
kered sorrel topped cuss from Connecticut who beat him twenty points. This
fellow has come down here to evangelize the niggers. He looks every whit fit
for the gallows."

misunderstanding and difficulty among the colored community which expected the Yankees to "look out" for it as the masters had formerly done. Legal emancipation did not necessarily bring with it in a single stroke of destiny the freedom from a tyrannical slave psychology. The ways of the emancipated Northerner were therefore foreign to the understanding of many a freedman of the town.

This was not the case with the students. They knew—or quickly learned to know—the meaning of the living friendliness and austere discipline of the missionary. Student and teacher were drawn together in a bond of common friendship as they looked out upon a race-divided community, one half of which bitterly resented the presence of the college and the other half of which soon came to sense an invidious distance between its own social status and that of the newly emerging Negro intellectual. Almost inevitably the more successful schools under Northern auspices became boarding schools in which teachers and pupils lived together in accordance with their own views, in little self-contained worlds, independent of the white and colored communities.

Then began on many campuses a strange warfare within the college—the conflict between an àcademic tradition of collegiate aloofness and the altruistic outreach of Christian idealism. The history of many of the segregated colleges is marked by this struggle between the educators who transplanted to the South the New England college with its interest in learning and its consequent traditional aloofness toward the community, and their missionary colleagues who were powerfully concerned with the social uplift and religious salvation of a people so recently emerged from slavery. This internal struggle was carried on in the presence of the caustic hostility of the white community and to the bewilderment of the colored community. The fluctuations in administrative attitude and institutional practice, as one or another faction within the college got the upper hand, often served to increase the tension and sense of social distance between the less privileged members of the Negro community and the

college which fully expected to serve their needs but sometimes failed to establish lasting rapport with them.

These three groups, white town, colored town, and segregated campus, have carried on a triangular sparring contest
through three-quarters of a century. The situation was soon
complicated by the emergence of a fourth group which for
the segregated college more closely corresponded to the social
elite of the New England college town. This fourth group is
the Negro intelligentsia.

WIDE VARIETY, BUT FOUR CONSTANT ELEMENTS

Both in degree, and often in kind, the relationships of the
three community elements toward the college vary in the
widely differing situations throughout the South. Historical
accident accounts for some of these differences. Local peculi-
arities have determined others.

One community may have very few whites, and these may
be either quite antagonistic, or somewhat friendly and tolerant. Another community may have its strong Klan element.
A third may have a solid group of Negro upper- and middle-
class population, making a strong town contingent for the
segregated college, particularly with reference to the off-
campus social contacts of the college staff; while in a fourth
situation, the practical absence of these upper strata within
the Negro caste leaves the college in comparative social isolation in the presence of the mutually estranged white and
black communities.

A college set apart in rural seclusion will have a sense of
its immediate community relationships that differs markedly
from that prevailing in another institution which enjoys the
gold-fish privacy of life in a Southern village. Still different
will be the campus psychology of a college which is relatively
submerged in the shuffle and bustle of a large urban center.
There will be noticeable differences of college-community understanding in the county seat agricultural town as contrasted
with the college which is surrounded by mills and industrial
life. And the older, more urbane centers of life and tradition

of the Old South will extend a brand of hospitality not found in the younger and cruder cities of the New South where a newly emerging upper middle class of whites sets the pace. There will also be a significant shading of attitudes as the observer of college-community rapport moves from the somewhat more tolerant border states into the Deep South.

These several lines of variation of pattern can be detected merely in analyzing the town and gown relationship with reference to the community. If the analysis is made from the campus angle, the variations are found to be equally wide and significant.

For example, there is a wide variety of pattern indicated in the single factor of control. In 1932, twenty-five colleges, enrolling 2,633 students at the collegiate level, were under the control of Negro denominational churches. Thirty-four institutions, with 5,609 students, were under the auspices of Northern church boards. One institution, enrolling 154 students, was sponsored jointly by Southern white and Southern Negro churches. Thirty-five public colleges, depending upon legislators and state officials for their support and progress, enrolled 9,438 students in college classes. The independent

TABLE 5

TABULATION OF COLLEGES AND ENROLLMENT, ACCORDING TO CONTROL (1932)[a]

	TYPE OF CONTROL				
	Negro Churches	Northern Churches	Southern White and Negro Churches	Public	Independent
(1)	(2)	(3)	(4)	(5)	(6)
Number of Colleges	25	34	1	35	14
Number of Students	2,633	5,609	154	9,438	5,084

[a] Based on D. O. W. Holmes, *Evolution of the Negro College*, Teachers College Contributions to Education No. 609 (1934), pp. 187-89.

colleges, fourteen in number, enrolled 5,084 students. Yet, within each of these several categories, the discriminating observer can discern wide variations in community attitudes of the individual colleges, and of divergent factions in individual campuses.

No one would wish to imply that the general situation is identical in all segregated colleges. On the contrary, what has happened is that in the particular expression of the problem, each college and its community have developed their own particular set of relationships through an historical evolutionary process. But, by and large, making full allowance for all the differences and variations, it is fair to say that there are four elements which mark the recurring foci of the problems of the Negro college in relation to its community, and these four are the campus, the Negro upper-classes, the Negro lower-classes, and the white population.[6]

Two of the three off-campus groups are typically estranged from the college. The white population is nearly always one of these estranged groups. And not infrequently, if the college has established a rapport with one of the Negro groups (upper or lower class), it will not have won the other. Only the practical absence of one of these three groups in the immediate community will usually permit the campus to enjoy the illusion of peaceful and harmonious relationships with either or both of the other two.

[6] Canby, *op. cit.*, in his analysis of the New England college recognizes three categories in the situation as he knew it in undergraduate days. The student typically resisted the teaching of the instructor, more or less reflecting the attitudes of his parents and of the town. "Hence there was a split in the college itself, so that in my days not a duality, but a trinity—town, gown and sweater—would have best described our community." (P. 20.) On the parallel problem, probably it is unsafe to generalize about the undergraduates of the present-day segregated college. In some instances, they might fall psychologically into the lower-class group; in some they would be typically identified with the mentality of the Negro upper classes (our "town"), and in others they would share the outlook of the teachers ("gown"). Rarely, if ever, will a student be found who sympathizes with the white mentality, although many will be dominated more or less by their acceptance of white estimates of race worth. Several carefully conducted field studies might shed considerable light on this aspect of the problem. For a suggestive beginning of such study see Thomas E. Davis, "Some Racial Attitudes of Negro College and Grade School Students," *Journal of Negro Education*, VI (April, 1937), 157-65.

An extreme instance of chauvinistic white antagonism was the special legislation of the state of Kentucky in 1905, aimed directly at Berea College, designed to compel the separation of the races in its student body. President William G. Frost rallied his campus with the statement, "The perverseness and blindness of our fanatical neighbors imposes upon us new burdens, but we refuse to be discouraged."[7] Examples of more friendly attitudes of the white South toward the college which educates Negroes can be found in the presence of prominent white Southerners on many boards of trustees, and in the contributions to endowment and building projects which in some instances are coming from Southern whites. Since the relationship of each particular college to its own immediate community is a matter for its own study if it wishes to be intelligent about its larger educational task, little good would come from a long-distance survey of the several institutions in these pages.

The seriousness of this complex problem especially for the aims here most in mind is suggested by the fact that the college which wishes to make progress toward more cordial and constructive relationships with any one of the three off-campus groups around it will almost automatically tend to estrange one or both of the other two groups in the effort. One cannot run with the hares and hunt with the hounds, especially when the hares themselves are running in different directions. The recognition of this division of the town into hostile camps gives a partial explanation, if not a complete excuse, for the failure of the segregated college to make friends with the white townsfolk. This quadrangular division of college, white caste, and bifurcated Negro caste, lies across the path of any project for community service or betterment which the college may undertake. It hems in the institution which wishes to widen its campus horizons and become active in the inclusive social scene. There will therefore need to be strongly compelling reasons if in the face of these odds the college is to be induced to venture from its traditional aloofness.

[7] From Servitude to Service, p. 66.

THE WIDER CAMPUS

1. *The functional basis.*—The college cannot be content with merely maintaining its traditional aloofness from the community unless it deliberately wishes to be nonfunctional, relatively irrelevant and negligible. The functional college must include the community as an integral part of its curricular overview. It is failure to take this inclusive view of the curriculum which has prevented not a few segregated colleges from exercising the normative and directive function in social change and improvement to which they give lip service.

Probably very few of the segregated colleges have ever yielded completely to the temptations of irenic beatitude. The world has been too much with them to permit it. The vigorous struggle to maintain the institution in the face of early opposition from the white South, matched by the complementary effort to reach out a helping hand to the Negro South —two aspects of a single great effort to give reality to emancipation—served to keep the early colleges free from ostrich-like serenity. But the colleges can hardly be blamed if, on occasion, as the pressure from the white South somewhat subsided, or the lot of the Negro South somewhat improved, they have drawn a deep breath and relaxed a bit. It seemed good just to be let alone for a time—and to let others alone. To be sure, many colleges have maintained community services as an integral part of their progress throughout their development. If, now, the colleges which currently have been taking a respite from active efforts at community betterment, wish once again to address themselves to the more inclusive enterprise, they can do so with the consciousness that they are only taking up a task which has always been an important part of the tradition of the segregated college.

2. *The educational principles.*—Experience in this realm of community activity suggests that certain important educational principles must be observed if the project is to bear good fruit. Comprehensively stated, these principles may be summarized by saying: the community must be an end in it-

self, not a means to campus ends; but it is precisely as an end in itself that the community serves educational (not institutional) ends.

There must be no attempt at institutional aggrandizement —the idea of making a big splash in the community puddle may be a bright one for the bad boy who merely wishes to attract attention to himself and does not care whether he gets favorable or unfavorable responses; but the student who participates in a so-called community service project, the clear purpose of which is to enhance the prestige of the college, learns inimical and false attitudinal lessons. He learns that people are less important than institutions. He learns that a seemingly altruistic effort must have a selfish core if it is to be thought worth while. He learns that the well-educated Negro is to have an interest in the less-educated Negro only in so far as that interest serves his own purposes.

Suppose this student graduates and becomes a doctor. He may take an interest in the church of the town where he settles—but only because such an interest gives him valuable social standing and consequent professional contacts. He may take an active part in getting his fellow-citizens to exercise their right to the franchise—but only because he expects to get his own share of political patronage and spoils as he builds up his own political power. He sits in his office and listens for approaching footsteps on the stairway, not because he is interested in the health of his community and the welfare of the people who live in it, but because every patient who climbs those stairs to interview him means another three dollars for his bank account. The student who participates, in college days, in a community enterprise which is designed to enhance the prestige of the college rather than to serve the interests of the community, will learn the lesson well—but it will be the wrong lesson. In the community service program herein advocated there must be nothing of institutional aggrandizement.

On the other hand, there must be in the community outreach of the college no element of overweaning paternalism

which tends toward community impoverishment and the cultivation of the attitudes of dependence. These are the stuff
out of which the caste system is made, the attitudes on which
it thrives. The functional college will avoid them as the
plague.

The basic conception underlying the whole wider campus
program is the idea that activity is an essential part of the
learning process. If we learn by doing, then, for example,
the way to learn how to build a community without caste is
to build such a community. Through the long, slow, devious,
and discouraging processes of generations of endeavor, the
college sets about to rebuild its relationships to its community.
Its students and staff participate in that enterprise, and therein
learn to know the satisfactions of high achievement in the
struggle to promote the common good. Herein is provided
one key to the problem of how to care for the excess ideality
of the student in the provision of worthwhile activities which
can be seen in the perspective of the total task. Herein is seen
a primary means of cultivating those habits and attitudes
which we judge to be the *summum bonum* of collegiate experience, the components of character which keep the graduate true to the ideals for which his college along with every
true ethical outlook does and must stand and in which he is
given practical training and experience as an integral part of
his undergraduate experience.

To the extent that the college successfully bridges any one
of the three gaps separating it from community groups, its
graduates will have learned how to bridge similar gaps in
their own living. To the extent that the college succeeds in
bridging all three gaps simultaneously, the student will enjoy
the experience of participating in the realization of a community in which caste has become irrelevant, and in which
men and women of both races are therefore able to enjoy a
more abundant life.

One of the necessary indices of success in the elimination
of those invidious psychological forces which so frequently
exert their disintegrative effect upon the social whole is the

actual physical mingling of peoples. The arbitrary physical
segregation of peoples in public conveyances and public meetings has its purpose in the furtherance of a sense of social
distance between the groups thus separated. The college
which wishes to bring classes and castes to a better understanding of each other in order to release all men and women
for finer living cannot overlook the leavening influence of
congenial meetings of members of disparate groups. The in-
termingling of town and gown often leads to the surprising
discovery on the part of wearers of the gown that individuals
whom the caste system had arbitrarily compelled to accept
the classification into which they were born, gladly welcomed
congenial opportunities to surmount the caste barriers, and
to know the larger freedom of transcending these arbitrary
social limitations. An incidental value also realized is that
the eyes of many an unsuspecting townsman, white and colored, are opened to the fact that the wearers of the gown are
intelligent human beings who are quite friendly and lovable
as one comes to know them.

No single individual in the South today is responsible for
the caste system which all have inherited. No one institution
is to blame for the presence of arbitrary artificial distinctions
which set groups apart from each other. The heritage of history can neither be defended nor disregarded. The caste
system is here. But both individuals and institutional groups
can choose to live above these distinctions until the lines become increasingly irrelevant. They can learn the ways of intelligence and of coöperation, the ways of humanity and
broader understanding, the ways of peacefulness and happiness. They can do these things if only they are enabled to meet
one another on a basis of mutual respect and appreciation.
Nowhere else in all the Southland does there exist a platform
on which the castes may have such mutually respecting contacts. Nowhere except in the segregated college is there an
adequate forum in which all may speak.[8] And these platforms

[8] A few churches, white or Negro, now and then manage to achieve the dignity
of practicing their profession by refusing to permit the intrusion of caste dif-

and forums will be found in segregated colleges only as the colleges discard their traditional easygoing aloofness and functionally address themselves to the remaking of their relationships to the community.

There are other points at which the caste system is being seriously challenged in the South today.[9] There are white churches which are shining exceptions to the denominations they represent. The Southern Interracial Commission and the Student Christian Movement are leavening influences of real value. Much is also heard at the moment of the challenge of the labor movement to the color line.

In the labor movement, or rather in some quarters of that movement, attempts are being made to reach across the caste line and to unite white and black workers in a common struggle against the white upper and middle classes. Thus far, scant success has accompanied these efforts. History is tenacious. Yet, without in any way disparaging the effort to unite white and black workers it may be pointed out that the kind of unity which can grow only in the soil of antipathy ultimately bears the fruits of its own disharmony and defeat. A movement which is based upon the divisive and factional emotional impulses of hatred, even though it be a common hatred, has continuing potency only as long as it has an ogre to hate. And if it succeeds in devouring the opposition, its cultivated appetite then perforce turns it inward upon its own members. Having learned to live carnivorously, it becomes cannibalistic. This does not deny the close connection between the more amicable adjustment of race differences on the one hand and the more just and equitable ordering of economic processes and the apportionment of the fruits of labor on the other hand. It merely calls attention to the instrumentalist position that means, to an important degree, shape results. The build-

_____

ferences into their services and meetings. These sporadic attempts to realize the inherent genius of the inclusiveness of Christianity are interesting and instructive. They are salutary for the segregated college.

[9] For a useful and instructive treatment of the gamut of interracial agencies and forces now at work see Paul Baker, *Negro-White Adjustment*.

ing of a brotherly world can come only as men as brothers build a brotherly world.

The free and congenial meeting of persons of both castes and all classes, who come together on a basis of mutual respect and appreciation for the pursuit of common goals, affords a high level of social integration which avoids the dubious benefits of the strategy of the class war. These pages are not the place in which to carry through a debate more fully; but certainly the intelligent Communist might be supposed to be willing to grant the possibility that good could come from the effort to bring white and black together upon a common platform of free and friendly discussion and acquaintance. Only a stubborn preference for ideology and the propagation of dogma could prevent placing human values first.

The foregoing paragraph does not deny the bearing of economic processes upon race attitudes. These pages have repeatedly affirmed the fact that the economic betterment of each racial group is hindered by its competitive manner of beating down the other. Chapters II and III documented the idea that race antagonisms are inextricably bound up with economic conflict and exploitation. There is at least this much truth in support of the effort to unite white and black workers: unless both go up together, neither will climb far. Having granted all this, we go on to affirm an aspect of the problem which our Communist friends sometimes overlook. To organize the struggle for economic justice and racial amity on the divisive and disintegrating principle of class antagonism is to jeopardize the larger social values. In a nation like Czarist Russia, the movement away from Czarist capitalism to Soviet state capitalism represents a net gain in social and human values; but a movement in America (however much we have failed to live up to our democratic principles) away from the ideal of inclusive democracy and in the direction of the dictatorship of the proletariat should be regarded as a last resort rather than as a desirable first attack. There are other, more immediately possible, and more promising modes of work, strategies which make use of American traditions and are conceived in terms of the American scene. It may be possible, for example, for a nation-wide inclusive enthusiasm for the realization of the abundant life to furnish the potent organizing and fusing principle which will incidentally make possible the dissolution of the economic bases of caste barriers.

It would appear, then, that before the functional college accepts the Marxist dogma of the desirability of the class war, it might better exhaust the possibilities of resolving the class struggle in other directions. The college may take its cue from the positive possibilities rather than from the negative note of the class struggle. Class struggle is a fact; it is the basic fact of race difficulties; but the effort to resolve the struggle can be positive rather than negative. That means, of course, that if America is to marshal the ethical and institutional resources necessary to prevent class struggle issuing in class war, it will be imperative that every opportunity for the training and cultivation of ethically sensitive and socially intelligent leadership be fully utilized. The functional college must therefore provide optimum opportunities for members of divergent classes and castes to discover their mutual enthusiasms for a more just, more fair, more abundant life. The idea of the wider campus, including the college and its three community groups, is a fertile idea with which to approach this larger problem.

The details of this college-community enterprise will differ widely between institutions. Local conditions will dictate tactics and procedures; particular resources of personnel or locale will suggest techniques and programs. The democratic process operating in each functional college will, of course, be extended to include the community participants in the college-community program. Each enterprise will find its special groups of interested persons to be enlisted. Variety of enterprises will therefore more and more bring in all the different interest groups. The programs will at first probably be exceedingly tentative and more or less exploratory. Much good experience has been accumulated in these seven decades during which the segregated colleges have been at work on this college-community problem. With this accumulated experience the functional college will be able to avoid many unnecessary errors and to employ many proven techniques. But changing circumstances make changes in programs and procedures necessary. Clarified objectives may necessitate shifts of emphasis or program. The one constant factor for the segregated college, its constant point of orientation in a developing program which is empirically determined and experimentally prosecuted, is the desire of the college so to modify its relationships with the communities about it that the general trend of results is toward a modification of the caste system in the direction of larger and fuller opportunities of living for all persons, Negroes and whites included.

One of the curious facts of social movement is that objectives are sometimes most easily attained not as direct aims of an aggressive effort but as by-products of some tangential activity. It is, for example, a real question to be seriously considered, whether the pursuit of other types of goods, the honest and true pursuit of these, may not afford one of the best means of transcending caste. Much of the self-consciousness of racial adjustment can be melted away in the warm enthusiasm of support for a common cause. Both the frontal and the flank attack on caste need to be made—and it is possible that the real victory will come in the use of some Trojan horse quite unrelated to racial concerns. This is an aspect of the attack on caste which must constantly be borne in mind and translated into action as strategic opportunities are discovered.

These are the educational principles which guide the segregated college as it addresses itself to the college-community problem in an effort to educate its students so that they can both transform and transcend the limitations of caste. About these basic principles we can be fairly sure. They are derived directly from our study of the educational demands of the social situation. They will be modified in the light of evolving experience in the enterprise itself; but as we see the issues today, these principles appear generally well defined and fairly clear. The writer is less sure about specific procedures.

3. *Procedures.*—Even though one is more sure about principles than about procedures, he is not relieved of the obligation to suggest the general type of procedures which are appropriate to the program. Recognizing, then, that this part of the discussion is quite tentative at best, one lists exemplary procedures which, under proper circumstances and with appropriate adaptations in the light of local conditions, will be useful.

There are first to be considered a group of institutional practices, matters which the college as an institution fosters and promotes, in coöperation with the community. These procedures are an integral part of the college program, not tacked on as a side issue or an afterthought, not relegated to some stepchild "extension division," but enjoying exactly the same status in the academic set-up and the educational and administrative planning as any other important part of curriculum planning and teaching procedure.

With the exception of a few of the larger cities, the South lacks adequate library facilities for Negroes. Book collections, designed to meet the recreational and cultural needs of the community, may well be made available. Wherever conditions are favorable, the college may consider extending these services out through the surrounding territory by means of a traveling book service.[10] At some point conveniently accessible to the townsfolk, there will be an attractive reading room with periodicals and books available for all ages and for a wide variety of vocational, avocational, and recreational interests. If the college campus is centrally located with reference to the community, the circulation and reading-room services may well be located on the campus, preferably in the same building as the college library itself, and in surround-

[10] The experience of the New Jersey Library Commission under the leadership of Miss Sarah Askew, State House, Trenton, New Jersey, is helpful in completing plans for county-wide library services.

ings which imply a dignity and status on a par with the library facilities of the college. And if circumstances permit, these library services may well be extended to both racial groups.

Another means of extending and sharing its cultural facilities more largely with its communities is the development of cultural programs (lectures, music, dramatics, forums, art exhibits, etc.) calculated to be of interest to the citizenry. For decades, groups of singers and musicians from Negro colleges have been welcomed in churches and schools, white and colored. The professors and teachers, the dramatic groups, the whole range of cultural and artistic talents gathered together on the campus should be made at least as available as choirs and orchestras. White audiences in particular need to know that the Negro not only sings spirituals well when well trained, but that a professor of political science can shed light upon world developments, regardless of whether his skin is pink, brown, or ebony. But the enterprise which starts out with the objective of race recognition will miss its mark. The cultural resources of the college should be made available to the larger community, simply because the community may care to avail itself of them, not because it affords an opportunity for Negro recognition. If students and staff participate in a program with a true community-betterment objective, the important learnings in terms of attitudes and habits will minister to the ability to transform the caste system rather than merely to demonstrate against it. Race advancement is often a by-product of service to humanity rather than a result of demonstrative effort aimed at race aggression. As the community must be considered as an end in itself, not as a means toward lifting and enhancing the self-esteem of the college faculty members, so also the community must not be made a mere means even to so good an end as race advancement. The natural and inevitable developments accompanying the normal growth of a sane and constructive policy of community service along cultural lines without reference to race advancement, will have a significance for racial recognition and interracial understanding quite out of proportion to the doubtful benefits of some other, seemingly more direct but ultimately less effective, approach.

A word on dramatics is not out of place at this point. As acting for the fun of acting becomes recognized as a means of community-college recreation, dramatics can be one of the finest means of building up satisfactory and satisfying relationships. The productions need not all be pitched at the professional level. Wide leeway will need to be made for the growth and development of good amateur performances. One of the most effective means of influencing character development is that of expert casting and conscientious coaching and directing. One of the most direct means of changing attitudes of actors and audiences alike is the effective staging of good drama. It need not be propagandist drama; in many cases it will be much more effective if it is not.[11] Good religious or folk drama, pageantry and pantomime, will be in the repertoire of the college-community dramatic and artistic program. Much the same sort of thing might also be added about music and the part which musical enjoyment can play in a program of cultural enrichment and recreational service.

These library and cultural services, both on and off campus, may well be part of a developing adult education program which serves the adults of the community as effectively as the younger adults who are resident students. Numerous short conferences and institutes may be a part of the larger program.[12] The idea that the learning process is as continuous as life itself, and that formal education may therefore be as continuous as life, lies back of this desire to project ade-

[11] The so-called "Negro" productions of classical plays like Macbeth under the auspices of the Federal Theatre Project, illustrate the way in which the effort to "race-angle" dramatic productions can so pervert both the dramatic and the racial results as to nullify the one and caricature the other. Racial self-respect is not served by turning Macbeth into a voodoo orgy. Good art and good propaganda are, in the end, synonymous; and the effort to make art serve propagandist ends merely means that the art ceases to be art and the propaganda either is unconvincing or carries conviction on the wrong issues.

[12] See the highly suggestive report of activities at Prairie View State College, Texas, by John P. Cade, "The College: Obligations and Relations to the Community," *Quarterly Review of Higher Education among Negroes*, IV (April, 1936), 91-96.

quate adult education. Wherever students can be successfully utilized in this program, they will get much from it; but the type of the work done and the results obtained will depend largely upon the use of a specially trained and highly competent staff.

One educational device frequently overlooked by the college is its athletic and sports program. As long as the college is content to permit its intercollegiate athletic program to loom larger in the public consciousness than anything else done on the campus, so long will the fundamental objectives of collegiate life be underrated and misunderstood by the Philistines. Under the stimulation of fat gate receipts, big-time football has come to occupy an unique place in American life—an uniquely ugly place; and the bug of commercial profit in athletics has bitten the presidents and coaches of the colleges for Negroes just as vigorously as it has affected their compatriots in the white colleges. Fortunately, very few of the segregated colleges have yet been able to invest great sums in huge stadia; they have not given undue hostages to fortune. It is still financially possible for the functional college to use its play-life for wholesome amusement rather than for commercial purposes. The development of a sense of fair play and of good sportsmanship on the part of spectators as well as players is a contribution as fundamental as any the college can make to its community. The people have never learned to play together. But the kind of fanatical partisanship and bad feeling which the big-time athletic contest sponsors does not meet the need. Almost it might be said that athletics, as frequently developed in the colleges, tend to pervert and obstruct the real social objectives of academic life. Pigskin poisons the ivy.

The college will not necessarily eliminate all intercollegiate contests. There is probably a highly legitimate place for the intercollegiate contest as the capstone for a fully developed and well-rounded intramural and intra-community sports program which enlists a very high percentage of citizens of the campus and community in active participation in vigorous sport. But the philosophy of athletics which uses it primarily as a means of milking the public for funds to pay bonded indebtedness on the big stadium and to support the lesser sports activities of the college has two great objections which completely disqualify it from admission to the genuine college.

The first objection to commercial sport is that this perversion of the athletic life of the college tends strongly to poison the academic life, the educational process, by introducing the element of commercialism at the point where it receives the highest emotional enthusiasm and approval of the spectators. Nothing is quite as important for the average undergraduate as the big football game. And the average undergraduate knows pretty well what prices are paid for the players who represent Alma Mater in the arena. No wonder the typical alumnus demands, "Winning teams, or else—" His self-esteem, bound up in the success of the hired gladiators of the college (that college in which he learned to have this violent enthusiasm for Commercial Sport with a capital "C" and "S") makes him a howling wolf on the trail of the losing coach if the season is relatively unsuccessful. The net effect is to bring great pressure upon the teachers, the registrar, and the administrators, to relax academic standards, or to wink at financial subsidies, to permit teams to win for Alma Mater in spite of the fact that they do not represent the college. The logical and honorable development of this attitude is to go the whole distance and frankly to put this brand of intercollegiate athletics on a commercial basis, as the Southeastern Athletic Conference has done. In that case, of course, the contests cease to be intercollegiate, and become games of hired professional teams which merely bear the names and carry the colors of designated colleges, as the knight used to carry his lady's colors in the lists. They also make money for the colleges. The only honorable alternative to this development appears to be the complete abandonment of gate receipts and the frank announcement that athletics at *this* college are given back to the amateurs who are bona fide students.

It will be objected that gate receipts are necessary to support the athletic and intramural sports program, and that it is unwise to charge these noneducational expenses to tuition, endowment, or other income. But such an objection serves only to make the issue doubly clear. The college is an educational institution, not a business enterprise. If athletics, intercollegiate or intramural, cannot be classified as educational, then what part can athletics have in the college at all? The only basis on which any activity can be attached to the college is its demonstrated educational value. Anything which serves genuine educational ends may rightfully be included in the institutional budget, and the assertion that athletics as now conducted are not rightfully a charge on the educational budget merely means that athletics as now conducted are not a genuine part of the real college. Athletics must be educationally rationalized, or else excluded from educational institutions. The alternative is clear. To save athletics for education, we must use sports for educational ends. Without the pressure of high finance, and with free access to the games, the emotional bubble will break, the big-time football hysteria will pass.[13] The larger conception of education, with the notion of the wider campus as we have been discussing it in this chapter, makes possible a sane rationalizing of athletics in terms of educative possibilities.

Such a rationalizing of athletic policy also corrects a second evil of the present unbalanced sports program. It permits play and sports programs to be used educationally, to develop both the bodies and the characters of a great number of participants. Both as spectators (free) and as participants (on the same basis as students) persons from the town are included in the play program of the functional college. If men learn to play together, foolish ideas of differences in class and caste vanish. The honest heat of spirited competition on diamond

[13] Johns Hopkins University (Maryland) and Talladega College (Alabama) have taken this step. Several years ago, Emory University (Atlanta) withdrew from intercollegiate competition, suggesting a third way out—a road which the individual college is forced to take when sister institutions do not restore amateur standards and renounce commercialism in athletics.

and court can melt many a difference and cancel many a hesitancy. Ingenious guidance and expert management of this inclusive play program will perhaps go farther than any other
single device to extend to the community the meaningful
services of the college—but the college must first be sure that
it understands the educational meaning of the service which
it extends.

The list of institutional activities which look toward larger
and more genuine service to the community might be pro-
longed indefinitely.[14] But in the end, each college will find its
own program and put its own procedures into operation in
its own wider campus. Some will develop one or more neighborhood houses or social centers as outposts for collegiate
activity. Others will think it wiser to concentrate upon
strengthening the existing religious, educational, and social
institutions of the community and letting the college and
townsfolk work together through institutions which do not
run as great a risk of being tainted with paternalism. Some
will take over a conveniently located rural area as a special
demonstration and experimental project; others will find
their outlet through organizing the farmers in a coöperative
marketing project which ties in with a coöperative mer-
chandising effort similarly organized in the city. Some will
emphasize credit unions and consumers coöperatives; others
will build strong hobby clubs and concentrate on an annual
hobby horse fair. Some will develop reading clubs and discussion groups; others will take a leaf from the Des Moines
adult forums. Some will provide leadership training courses
for community persons interested in the young people of their
churches; others will work on the curricular and other problems of the rural schools of the state. Community health
problems and the extension of the school's hospital and
medical services may engage one institution while another
may find it more immediately feasible to throw open its

[14] See, for example, William L. Graham, "The Relation of Paine College
to Its Community," *Quarterly Journal of Higher Education among Negroes,*
IV (April, 1936), 129-33, for an account of a carefully worked out program
of community service undertaken by a segregated college.

lyceum and lecture series to the townsfolk in an effort to begin a kind of community mental hygiene effort. The list of possibilities is limited only by the imagination and ingenuity of the college and its community. Enough has been said to indicate that there will be a wide variety and richness as well as a strong emphasis on high quality, in the community services envisioned and projected by the functional college. So much for the institutional practices. We must look also at the problem of student participation in this community-wide program.

Some colleges, as they address themselves to their communities, will need only to do a little better and more intensively many of the things they are already doing. Others will need to make a rather fundamental adjustment in their educational philosophies and institutional procedures before they can become functional in this area of community and campus contacts. But in every case, if the whole program is to have highest educational significance, it must enlist the students in active participation both in the planning and in the execution of the projects.

Kilpatrick maintains that

it is not sufficient merely to study the problems of life: if education is really to go on best, we must somehow carry the thought processes appropriately through into fitting action. On no other basis does thought find adequate means either for projecting its proposals or for testing its solutions. And even more, only on the basis of thoughtful action can habit and skill and appropriate emotional attitudes be built. In a word, an education which stops short of action is a thwarted education, aborted, held up in midair. Thought and action are inseparable aspects of a developing movement; any pursuit of either apart from the other degrades both.[15]

This is the true educative effort. Herein lies the hope that the college may train students who, not merely while under-

[15] William H. Kilpatrick, "Education in the Social Process and the Lessons for the College" in *The College and the Social Process*, p. 28.

In the Introduction to *Youth Serves the Community* by Paul R. Hanna, Kilpatrick also discusses the philosophy of education which leads to the conclusion that "coöperative activities for community improvement form the vision of the best education yet conceived." (P. 20.)

graduates but also in their continuing education after graduation, will study and work at the problems of community
betterment. Herein lies the hope for developing, through
actual experience, the habits, attitudes, skills, and techniques,
implemented and made effective with appropriate knowledge
and information, upon which the college must depend in its
effort to modify the caste system.

However it be effected, and you who know the situation will be more
capable of suggesting than I, the superiority of education possible from
actually doing things over merely studying about them is immense.
True, we may have to change our social order in order to make a real
education possible, but as now appears we can never have a satisfactory
educational system until school and life so interpenetrate as to make it
impossible to tell which part is which, only the varying aspects being
distinguishable. Meanwhile, we must do the best we can under existing
conditions to approach as nearly as possible to the ideals we hold.[16]

The student who participates actively in the process of solving the problems of the wider campus learns that all the world
is his campus and that his study and work go right on through
life.

The functional colleges, each severally attacking its own
problems in democratic fashion, will discover for themselves
those curricular and methodological developments which best
suit their own purposes. A beginning will be made in some
colleges where upper-class students customarily engage upon
a special project, by relating the student's project to his participation in this larger program. There will be a close correlation of formal study and active participation in the community program. The colleges which have primarily a liberal
arts bent will utilize their cultural resources to leaven the
community, and the student will use his own study and activity as one integrated means of furthering the larger objective.
The colleges which have a strong technical, vocational, trade,
or agricultural bias will likewise insist that the student bring
his study and work out of the classroom and the school shop
and put it to work in terms of community needs. The institu-

[16] Kilpatrick, *op. cit.*, p. 29.

tions which have reoriented their curricula on the sixfold
basis of health, home, vocation, avocation, citizenship, and
religion will find their community programs and the student
participation in these programs strategically canalized in these
six channels. The curricular and methodological implications
of the wider campus program, and of student-staff participation in it, will not fully dawn upon the college until several
years of working and experimenting and rethinking have built
a rich background of factual and conceptual data which fundamentally reorient the institution and the people in it.

WIDER OUTREACH IS NOT MERE "SOCIAL UPLIFT"

This discussion may well be terminated with a note of warning. Throughout the chapter we have been insisting that the
college must address itself intelligently, seriously, and imag-
inatively to the solution of the delicate and perplexing problems of relationships with its community if it wishes to be
more largely functional in directing the social process toward
a diminution of the importance of caste and an allaying of
the pernicious effects of the caste system so that men may
grow to fullness of stature unimpeded by socially undesirable
obstructions. We need also to recognize that in thus addressing itself to the concrete situation, the college must save itself
from myopic immersion in a too narrowly circumscribed area.
The community of the college is actually the world community. The particular bit of life which clusters around a given
campus is to be used as a means of understanding the wider
social whole. To limit the horizons of an institution to the
immediate locality in which it happens to be planted is to impoverish the students and the college, and to damage the
community by making it a special object of concentrated solici-
tude rather than a coöperating unit in world reconstruction.
Books and articles, reports of field studies, systematic study
of analogous and contrasting situations in other parts of the
United States and in other nations and continents, analyses
of the students' own home towns, the use of supervised in-
terne periods between junior and senior years with the subse-

quent critical evaluation of the student experience by seminar
—these and other devices will be used to enlarge and widen
the conception of the social task of education. No mere "social uplift" reformist movement for slum areas will suffice.
This inclusive educational objective looks toward the remaking of the social structure, both as a means toward better
educational opportunities, and as the actual process of at-
taining real education.

There will, of course, be teaching of family case work; but
the study of the family will not concentrate solely on the
problems of the working-class home as is often the case.
There will be study of marriage and the home; but not solely
of married life of the middle classes. There will be analysis
of delinquency and crime rates, and of the socio-economic
factors which affect antisocial behavior; but neither individual
rehabilitation nor social reform will occupy the educational
stage exclusively. There will be study of the problems of
political and civic articulation of a group now largely disfran-
chised, and practice in winning political rights. There will be
study of the economic power of consumers, in terms of intelligent buying. There will be an increasing understanding of
the religious and ecclesiastical life of an impoverished geographic section, and a consequent lifting of the level of religious expression among both races; but there will be no
arrogant assumption that the educated person's religion is
superior to the less sophisticated and sometimes more genuine insight of the less educated.

Lastly, there will be an intelligent effort to make sure that,
in this readjustment of curricular emphasis and teaching
methods, the real values of the older college curriculum are
not lost or surrendered. One of the primary objectives of collegiate work has always been that of transmitting the cultural
heritage from generation to generation. Wise teaching will
insure that this function is fulfilled, perhaps even more effectively, in the functional college. It is with this and other
questions of teaching that the next chapter deals.

XIII

TEACHING

What I am surest of is, that what I tried to teach was never so important as how I taught it.

—HENRY SEIDEL CANBY

IN THE traditional college, teaching was primarily, though not solely, an effort to convey information from teacher to student. It was called "passing on the social heritage." The teacher was assumed to know what the student ought to know; and education consisted of the effort to get the student to master the materials presented by the teacher.

Nevertheless, the testimony of discerning teachers who labored under this system bears heavily on the point stated by Dr. Canby at the head of this chapter. The *how* of the teaching was much more important than the subject-matter *what*. It is proposed that, in the functional college, use be made of this valuable insight of liberal arts teachers. Method is much more important than content because method actually determines the significance of content, and to an important degree, method *is* content. Beginning with a conception of our educational aims, we fashion our teaching method to fit these aims, and select curricular content appropriate to aim and methods.

THE INCLUSIVE AIMS OF TEACHING

Following several converging lines of study, mainly sociological, educational, and psychological, the argument of these chapters has led to agreement upon a threefold hierarchy of educational aims which can now be recapitulated:

1. *Attitudes* of life, and the habitual practices which embody these attitudes, are the fundamentally important matters of concern in the educative process. For the segregated college, those attitudes and habits are judged to be most desirable which are calculated to have a modifying effect upon caste and to promote optimum living for all persons both in the modified society of the future, and during the interim of modification.

2. *Skills and techniques* to implement these habits and attitudes should be acquired by the student as an integral part of his education. These tools fall primarily into two categories: (*a*) social techniques, calculated to minister to the needs of a submerged group struggling for emergence in American culture; and (*b*) personal techniques of survival and integration looking toward genuine enjoyment of living in spite of the differential working of caste.

3. The fullest and richest informational background available should be acquired by the student in his endeavor to implement purposeful living in accordance with the foregoing aims. The *subject-matter content* of college education is an important tertiary consideration.

WHAT IS THE CURRICULUM?

Everything that happens in the life of the student during his college years is "curricular." Whatever he experiences, and the manner of experiencing it, are what he "learns." Sometimes this learning is negative—he rejects the experience. Sometimes it is perverted—he learns not the intended lesson, but something else (as learning to "get by" on examinations). Sometimes the learning is positive—he accepts the new insight, or information, or skill, and builds it into his working attitudes as a part of himself, acting upon it. But whatever he experiences at college is part of the curriculum. That is why there is no separate chapter on curriculum in this study. Everything we have been discussing is "curricular" in that it describes the learning process, and thus defines what is to be learned.

We do not take this inclusive view of the curriculum on a dogmatic basis. Our choice is functionally determined. If we wish to carry forward our educational objectives, in the transformation of caste and the attainment of the good life during the transformation, lesser conceptions of the curriculum prove inadequate for our teaching purposes. To list them is to reject them:

1. The notion that college education consists in the mental

mastery of a prescribed list of books—whether they are the "one hundred best books of all time," or a less ambitious agglomeration of assorted textbooks. What neater device could the college find for perpetuating the "Do what de man say" psychology? The answers of life are all to be found in the books—go to them, read, note, and inwardly digest. Regurgitate for examination. Here is your diploma. You have done well what your superiors asked. Go in peace!

2. The notion that curricula can be fixed by analyzing child activity, or by canvassing adult life. Both of these ideas, which hold the mirror up to life and then lead the child through his paces to "fit him for life," exhibit a repugnant dichotomy. So to fashion education is either (a) to assume that there is now operating in America, for the Negro, a substantial degree of equality of opportunity and equality in expression through an unimpeded democratic process; or (b) to affirm that the present strictures and inequities are to be permanently retained. The so-called "sociological approach" fixes the caste system more firmly upon American society when it leads education to conform to established patterns.

3. A special form of the foregoing is the building of vocational training curricula on a job-analysis basis. The caste-determined vocational opportunities of the Negro college graduate cannot be accepted as the last word in ultimate possibilities. Here is "education for social control" with a vengeance.[1]

4. A statistical survey, giving an additive picture of standard practices in colleges. This method dooms us to the level of mediocrity. It is possible that the pioneering practice of a single obscure institution will be more significant for educational planning at a given point than the whole weight of the academic superstructure of the nation. Unless we leave open

[1] For discussion of this point see Horace Mann Bond, "The Curriculum and the Negro Child," *Journal of Negro Education*, IV, 159-68. Bond criticizes Weatherford for seeming to rivet rural peonage permanently upon the Negro child by teaching him to meet his "daily needs" through accommodation to rural life, e.g., in appreciation of "the beauty in the growing crops and the fallow field." See also Ch. IX above.

this door of possibility, we ignore the creative potentialities of deviants. This method also dooms us to what has been. A survey of what is cannot tell us new things.

5. Individual curricula based on analyses of needs and deficiencies of individual students. This halfway house in the journey to good curriculum construction is an especially enticing resting place. But to know the deficiencies of an individual, we must have not merely a means of measuring him in terms of his own achievement quotient, but also some larger frame of reference which helps us to describe "needs," "deficiencies," and "strong points." Deficiencies are relative. Christian virtues are Nietzschean vices. The "deficiencies" of a Negro student, as judged by a paternalistic white person, may well be the strong points of that same individual as judged by the standards of the functional Negro college.

The functional curriculum, which is life as experienced by the student, must have a broader base than any of these five. It must be built around the idea that education gets its meaning and sense of direction from its purposive effort to build better life for all; and this places first emphasis upon attitude.[2] Only in the light of such an inclusive societal framework can we have an adequate notion of the needs of the individual. Our social reference gives meaning and validity to judgments in individual cases. Intended social functioning becomes the larger framework for educational construction.

Not for a moment do we lose sight of the individual student. He is the focus of our attention. And because we wish fully to understand him, and fully to implement his highest capabilities, we must study him as he is—a part of the social whole which molds him and which he helps to mold; and as he may become—a constructive social force, finding his own enduring life satisfactions in bringing larger life to all men of all complexions.

[2] "Society's stake in the attitudes which a child acquires is even greater than in the skills and concepts he gains. . . . the practical effect of the shift of emphasis from knowledge and skill to attitude—from the intellectual to the affective aspect of mental life—is more significant than many a conflict of principle." H. S. Tuttle, *Social Basis of Education*, p. 5.

It is precisely at this point that the older idea of the curriculum as a group of formal disciplines missed the mark on one of the most important aspects of the learning process, namely, its conception of the manner in which intelligence is developed. Starting with the idea that the mind was a faculty of the individual somewhat analagous to his body, the classical educators worked on the theory that practice and drill developed the mind in much the same way as gymnastic drill and exercise developed the muscles of the body. Almost any subject matter could be effectively used for the purposes of mental gymnastics, provided it was difficult enough to make the student stretch and work. And because of the prevalence of this notion of the development of intelligence, and the practice of that theory in the colleges, education has been facetiously defined as "what remains after one forgets all he learned in college." This is an important, and thoroughly vicious, half-truth.

The other half of the truth is that the content of the intellectual activity is just as much a part of the end-result as the structure of the activity. Even in the gymnasium this is recognized—men do not expect to learn to box by swimming. Both activities may serve to strengthen body muscles and build stamina and endurance; but the specific skills of one sport are not those of another. How much more this is true in intellectual affairs is apparent when we consider the actual patterns of learnings which emerge from the two types of college education, the traditional and the functional. In the main, it is largely true that the content, the subject matter, of the classical education has little relevance to post-collegiate life; and the only way to give it that relevance is to achieve the relationship in the stuff of curriculum building. The individual who lives in a social group which does not habitually practice the processes of social redirection through group thinking and activity simply does not learn these processes. They are not a part of his personality, his equipment; but the individual who lives and works and studies and learns as a member of a collegiate group which includes him in the vital processes of social planning and building, by that very fact of participation in such a process, weaves these materials into the fabric of his intelligence.[3]

Our discussion of curriculum therefore began with the decision that the pattern of educational organization is the fundamentally determinative matter for functional education. The things which set the stage and actually determine the conditions of performance through which the student learns, that is, administrative policies and practices, cannot be considered as mere technical matters of efficiency, in a category by themselves. They are properly matters of curriculum building. Administrative procedures are curricular materials. Within the democratic framework of college operation, people live. They learn. The relationships of individual to individual in rebuilding the social structure are the vital matters in this learning. The college which wishes to make caste irrelevant will be itself a college without caste. Administrative procedures, staff selection, and the complex town-and-gown patterns are all matters of curriculum building. These are the warp of the educational fabric into which the individual weaves his thread of purpose. The fashioning of that warp actually determines the patterns of possibilities for the weavers, without dictating the choice of pattern.

PERSONNEL

The Staff problem is not merely one of getting the best equipped personnel. There is a functional relationship between the whole pattern of staff relationships and the basic

[3] Appendix B applies this same line of reasoning to the matter of comparative mental testing of races. It is clear that the child in whose home, school, and social life fine distinctions of meaning are customarily made, will have a much better opportunity to develop his own abilities in drawing fine distinctions of meaning than another child whose daily life is not thus environed. The intelligence quotient is not a measure of "native" intellectual abilities as much as it is a measure of the level of achievement of a given individual in terms of the selected standards as compared with his chronological age. And the level of achievement, which actually defines the I. Q., is, to an important degree, a function of the individual's environment. Intelligence is built up by the agglomeration of experiences. The mental fabric is woven with the ideas, distinctions, and intellectual habits the child finds in use about him; and with these he attacks new problems to find new solutions.

educational aim of the college. Two considerations make the selection of staff in the functional college a matter of prime importance. Every person has a voice in the deliberative councils; and every person on the campus contributes, positively or negatively, to the total pattern of campus life in which education is carried on. Added to these two considerations is a third, which has to do not so much with the selection of individual staff members as with the resultant pattern of staff composition. Since it is one of the objects of the functional college to transform the caste system, the staff must be so made up as to contribute to this objective.

Thus, for example, it is serious enough in the traditional college to have a teacher or administrator whose race attitudes are paternalistic; but to have such a person on the campus of the functional college would, to an important degree, nullify the efforts of the institution. Again, the segregated college which does not challenge the dominance of caste need not concern itself with the implications of its racial policy in the selection of workers whether an uniracial or interracial staff is to be used; but the functional college cannot overlook a matter which is vital to its success.

In general, then, the staff of the segregated college will be as strong, as effective, as well prepared through training and experience, as it is possible for the college to command. Staff persons will be selected, as individuals, primarily because the college feels that they have something of value to contribute to the larger purposes of socially functional education. They will be organized as a group so that the whole pattern of staff relationships and complexion will be designed to express in the academic microcosm the pattern of social relationships which the college hopes to see in the national macrocosm. The college which is working to transform caste will not recognize any caste distinctions in its staff arrangements, on or off campus. The college which wishes to liberate its students from bondage to what is, in order that they may aid in obtaining fullness of life not only for themselves but for others as well, will bring them into a collegiate society in which they find no recognition of the artificial barriers of caste. The college which wishes to promote fullness of life for all people will make sure that nothing in its own arrangements of staff relationships reflects surrounding social strictures or inhibits the growth of creative development in staff members as they participate in the society of the wider campus. In the main, this means an exceedingly painstaking process in the selection and training of personnel, and in the provision of adequate resources for their work. In addition, one special phase of the problem of staff selection calls for further comment, namely, the place—if any—of white teachers and administrators on the segregated campus.

COLLEGE WITHOUT CASTE

Many thoughtful Negroes have asked whether the time has not come for all whites to step out and leave the Negro colleges entirely in the hands of Negroes. In an earlier chapter it was pointed out that the question is not a simple, two-sided argument. But the issue is squarely joined in representative opinions like those of Woodson and Robinson. The case against the use of white teachers or administrators on segregated campuses is well argued by Woodson whose attitude can be summarized in these words: ". . . the unfortunate successors of the Northern missionary teachers of Negroes have thoroughly demonstrated that they have no useful function in the life of the Negro."[4]

The case for retaining, at least in the private schools, a certain number of white persons is stated with equal clarity and effectiveness by Robinson:

So far as the question of teachers from the North is concerned at present, the issue scarcely exists. For some time now there has been a definite movement toward placing the direction of Negro private education in the hands of Negroes. The movement has advanced so far that there is real danger that the interracial character of Negro private schools will be entirely lost. Many thoughtful Negroes have deplored this danger and have expressed their belief in the beneficial contributions to Negro education of this interracial factor and their hope that a

[4] Carter G. Woodson, *The Miseducation of the Negro*, p. 26.

considerable number of really emancipated white teachers will always
be identified with the Negro educational enterprise. With the same
reasoning they feel that the introduction of the interracial factor into
the staffs of the public schools of the North would help white and
Negro children in those schools to realize something of the true meaning
of American democracy.[5]

Both of these writers may be counted among those who
strongly wish the segregated college to serve the larger social
purposes under discussion in this book. Yet they disagree
heartily as to whether whites should play any continuing part
in Negro education.

And in the meantime, many of the white teachers and administrators have left the segregated campuses. More are
leaving yearly. Among those who remain, much searching of
heart goes on, and something of this kind goes through their
minds at times when, somewhat wistfully, they wonder
whether they are serving the best interests of all by staying
on: At every point, the Caucasian caste attempts to cut the
Negro off, to hem him in, to restrict and to isolate the submerged group. If we were to resign and leave the campuses,
then segregation would be complete. Nowhere else in all the
Southland would there be communities of white and black
folk living together in a normal, friendly, human way, sharing
their gossip and their hopes, playing bridge and prosecuting
research, engaging in exciting educational adventure and
matching skill on court and diamond. Nowhere would there be
persons of both races living and working side by side like
normal human beings, quietly transcending, deliberately ig-
noring, the artificial barriers of caste. It may be that the men
and women who graduate and go out from the gates of a
college which has refused to let the pressures of caste eliminate the interracial fellowship of its campus will have learned
a little more effectively to transcend and to transform the
world which confronts them. It is the sort of possibility, as

[5] W. A. Robinson, "What Peculiar Organization and Direction Should Characterize the Education of Negroes?" *Journal of Negro Education*, V (July,
1936), 398.

matters now appear at least to this writer, on which one feels justified in betting his life.

TEACHING TECHNIQUES

1. *Guidance.*—Within the larger social pattern of college life as defined by administrative policies, staff selection, and the wider campus, three types of teaching procedure are important. Guidance, instruction, and companionship are the three principal means of formal teaching. In the functional college, these three procedures may, in the main, closely resemble excellent procedures now followed in many colleges. We assume that the professional and technical abilities of trained experts in these fields will be used by the functional college; and we intend in these pages to discuss only the points relevant to our problem—not necessarily the points at which these procedures in the functional college differ from other colleges, but the points at which procedures are determined for us by our functional concept. If, at times, we appear to be rehearsing what is merely accepted best procedure, then we answer that in these instances many colleges are already functional, and we need to be more fully consicous of that fact.

If guidance could begin well down in the elementary school, it would be more effective. The almost total lack of comprehensive and thorough guidance programs in the public and private elementary and secondary schools from which Negro students come, means that until more funds are available for guidance programs for the pre-collegiate student, the college will have to begin the process. But guidance should begin not later than the moment of application for admission. This may imply negative as well as positive guidance. Institutional desires for tuition fees, or for larger enrollment as a means of getting increased appropriations, cannot be permitted to overrule the sane judgment that a particular student ought not to matriculate at *this* college. Using best available diagnostic devices, the college must help the student, in advance of matriculation, to discover himself as far as possible at his present stage of growth, and to select his college wisely. Such a guidance program not merely assumes integrity on the part of the several colleges; it also assumes a coöperative differentiation of function between institutions so that the student who does select a given college for his purposes will not find that his Alma Mater is the old woman who lived in the shoe, her efforts and energies spread over so many unrelated lines of endeavor that none of them is well handled. If it be objected that this notion of academic integrity and co-operative differentiation to prevent wasteful duplication of effort and to provide fullest and richest possibilities for all applicants is a pipe-dream, the answer is that unless we can get our segregated colleges to take these preliminary steps in setting their own houses in order, we cannot expect them to make a significant attack upon caste or upon the larger complex of social materials which surround them. Instead of struggling against each other, competing for students and for academic prestige, the colleges for Negroes have a bigger battle to fight. A genuine united front of segregated colleges is necessary. Then we can actually see guidance (not recruiting) begin with admissions.

Only one in every 500 of the Negro population is now in college, as compared with one in every 100 of the white population. Over this slender bridge of college-trained men and women march the hopes of educated Negro America. This is no time for intercollegiate sparring and shadow boxing. Only united efforts of all the segregated colleges can release a constructive force for enriching Negro life and making caste irrelevant.

Then what becomes of the idea of "selective admissions for training leaders?" In Chapter XI we pointed out that there are several types of leadership, that all are necessary in the democratic process, and that they usually emerge in persons of quite different abilities and temperaments. On the basis of information now available, colleges cannot hope to select in advance the particular persons who will or will not exercise these leadership functions. The assumption that only the person who has a particular academic and cultural finishing can qualify for leadership in a democracy simply does not square with the facts. Also, the college which thinks it is "training leaders" is dangerously close to a series of false notions: that only college-trained persons can be leaders, that all college-trained persons become leaders, and that especially students from this college are leaders.

A saner and wiser attitude on the problem of leadership training is found in the following steps which segregated colleges, collectively and individually, may take: (*a*) adequate differentiation of function between institutions, to eliminate overlapping and to insure adequate spread of academic offerings; (*b*) careful pre-admissions guidance to make sure that each student matriculates at the institution best calculated to serve his needs; (*c*) comprehensive attempts by each college to provide fullest opportunity, guidance, and encouragement to its enrollees in the development of the habits of critical intelligence, independence of thought and judgment in the light of the common good, and stability of temperament and character to enable the individual to contribute to dynamic and creative community activity in whatever capacity he may work. If these three efforts cannot immediately be carried through completely, the functional college still faces its own obligation of adhering to the program as far as circumstances permit.

It is assumed that the educational and vocational guidance which are carried on through the years of college residence are as adequate as professional training and group insight can make them. They aim at educational and vocational self-discovery by the student. Closely correlated with this in-college guidance process is the diagnostic and remedial work carried on by competent psychologists and counselors, to correct the ravages of the caste system on the individual personality. Finally, educational guidance, to be effective, must have expression in diversity and flexibility of curricular patterns;

but this adaptation to individual needs must always be kept within the larger framework of desired societal movement.[6]

The guidance program culminates in a placement service which enables the educational and vocational progress of the student to find issue in post-collegiate activity. This placement service concerns itself not only with teaching, graduate study, and closely allied academic fields; but it is as inclusive as the interests and abilities of its student clientele, and aims at opening avenues now closed by caste.[7]

2. *Instruction.*—In general, the college which is interested in escaping from conformity to caste patterns will aim at versatility and variety in its instructional techniques. Recognizing the inclusive nature of the curriculum and the implications of the wider-campus, the teachers will also be encouraged to depart from the time-honored classroom methods of lecture and recitation. Occasional lectures have their place, in supplying information or leading into insights which the students need at that particular stage of their experience, and which they could not gain for themselves without considerable waste of energy and time. But to limit the teaching process to the lecture system is to make it largely impossible for the college to become normative. Indoctrination is indoctrination, and the net result is the same whether it be radical or reactionary or liberal dogma. Acquiescence, acceptance by the student, conformity to the lecturer, are the things learned from the lecture. "What does he want?" the student asks; and his examination effort reflects his study of the wants of the professor. Assuming a static society, we teach the answers; but teaching another set of answers in the same authoritarian fashion will not create a dynamic society. It may bring revolt or social upheaval, but it will not bring

[6] See Ambrose Caliver, *A Personnel Study of Negro College Students.* "Instead of prescribing an education that will fit the whole race for a given station in life, personnel work is an agency that will enable every individual to prepare himself adequately and intelligently for any station suited to his individual capacities and interests, which fits into the needs of society of which he is a part." (P. 4.) "Needs of society" will, of course, be interpreted to include a normative effect on caste.

[7] See George W. Crawford, *Talladega Manual of Vocational Guidance.*

social reconstruction. Creative powers are not developed by indoctrination—they grow in practice.

So, too, with recitation. There possibly is a place—at most a greatly diminished place—for quizzing and drilling in college teaching. Some lines of study, such as mastery of language and mathematics, may call for repetitive practice which properly comes at times of felt need. These are questions for the teaching experts in their own fields to answer. Certain it is, however, that the recitation by means of which the professor goes around the class quizzing the students to see whether they have covered the assignment for the day, has no place whatever in a college which is attempting to cultivate initiative and self-direction in its students. If the curriculum is not valuable enough in itself to excite student interest, and if other supplementary techniques of student-teacher conference and sharing cannot be worked out to supplant the disciplinary threat of quizzing and recitation, then the college must admit its bankruptcy. The galaxy of "new" methods now being used in scores of colleges affords suggestive lines of departure which each teacher and institution may assess and test in experience. A list of the more common teaching techniques in an ascending scale of their appropriateness for the functional college might read: recitations, lectures, tutorials, conferences, group discussions, individual and group projects. In the real college, there will be fewer set schedules for bringing together masses of students to take notes on professorial lecturing, and more use of guided student initiative in the prosecution of projects and activities of social significance and educative value.

3. *Companionship.*—The whole of the student's life is educative. The whole of the teacher's life is part of that student education. "What you are speaks so loudly that I cannot hear what you say," wrote Emerson.

Most, if not all, of the segregated colleges are still small enough for the teacher and student to know each other with some intimacy. For the most part, the resident college for Negroes already enjoys the opportunities for student-faculty sharing of life which Harvard and Yale are spending several million dollars to attain in new small-unit housing schemes. No standard pattern ought to stamp itself upon all the colleges for Negroes; but whatever that pattern of housing and personnel organization may be, there will assuredly be deliberate provision for the whole of the teacher's life to be shared with the whole of the student's life. The college will safeguard its staff from nervous strain and overwork by providing frequent rest periods and opportunities for staff escape from the immediate pressures of student demands; but while the teacher is on the job, he knows that the whole pattern of his life is having its impact on the student. Willy-nilly, this is so; the functional college recognizes the fact and uses it for educative purposes.

This is the point at which guidance and instruction and personal remedial and stimulative work converge in a personalized give-and-take between older and younger learners. If the professor is freed from an endless grind of lecturing, and the student is freed from an equally silly series of note-takings, both will have more time and energy to devote to the high and serious business of getting acquainted and together exploring the fields of knowledge and scaling the heights of appreciation. Then real teaching begins.

Not every instructor will have a penchant for this personal camaraderie; but enough of this type ought to be on the campus so that the whole academic lump is leavened with a yeasty intellectual ferment, and the education of personal contact gives its fillip to the less informal academic procedures of classroom, laboratory, and library.

TEACHING AND TESTING: THE PROBLEM OF MEASUREMENT

Education is constantly in danger of being subordinated to certification. The college demands that the secondary school prepare students for collegiate work, and certify that they are so prepared. The graduate and professional schools in their turn demand that the college certify to the requisite abilities and preparation of their own graduates who apply for admission to the graduate school. Parents demand to know how their children are getting on. Teachers and administrators insist on some means of evaluating the work of their students before graduating them. Under the combined pressures of all these groups, it is difficult for the college to retain or regain its major educational goals. Certification dominates education. The student, in this certificational system, thinks of his own progress not in terms of education but of certification. He learns to compete for marks or for honors. He estimates the goal in terms of the degree.

Such a danger is not easily avoided. Certification will be necessary as long as American education retains its present institutional forms, but it ought to be possible to use measurement and certification as aids to education rather than as tyrants over it. The college which permits its education to be subordinate to its own tests and measurements and to its own degree-granting processes, cannot expect to be an effective factor in modifying either individual life or the larger social system. For here in the academic structure is the same tyranny of system over life, of fixed and immutable arbitrary standards which inhibit and obstruct adventurous and creative departure from established ways. Within the college itself we discover at work the identical psychological patterns which, in the larger social scene, we recognize as typical tools of the caste system.

If certification is to be an aid to, rather than a dictator of educational programs and policies, the testing and measuring process must be designed to serve both educational and certificational purposes. The cure for certificational dominance is not less but more measurement, and of a different kind, used for different purposes. A sane testing program would include these objectives:

1. To gauge educational progress of each student in terms of his own capacities and his own history, to determine a dynamic effort-quotient for him. The testing program for such a dynamic effort-quotient of each student is a means of measuring his own growth as related to his capacities and in-

terests. The growth is to be estimated in terms of his progress on the scale of socially desirable habits and attitudes as they are appropriately implemented with skills and techniques and well grounded in informational and factual materials. As the student builds his own synthesis of values and makes a beginning at a philosophy of living, he makes progress toward graduation. Degrees are granted largely on the basis of this dynamic effort-quotient as indicated by substantial (in view of his abilities) progress in socially desirable directions.[8] If the functional college is not to be accused of insincerity in making socially desirable attitudes and habits its primary aim, it should be ready to give the approval of its degree only to students who make appreciable progress in developing and implementing such life attitudes to a significant degree beyond their achievement at matriculation. It should withhold its degree from students who do not make such progress, regardless of courses and credits and marks accumulated in the registrar's office. These latter are a second-best medium of exchange to be used for certification, and in a modified and perfected form they have their usefulness in the second phase of the testing program.

2. To provide information and diagnostic data revealing the student's achievement along the lines of his special interests, in terms of the norms for entrance on post-collegiate activity in his chosen field, thus providing an objective basis for the double process of guidance and of certification. With

[8] President Lowell of Harvard in 1920: "The failure to maintain rigorous standards may well be connected with the American system of measurement by credits instead of by attainment. Courses, whether in school, in college, or in any kind of education, instead of being treated as an end, should be regarded as a means; and a test in them should be not a final award but a mere measure of progress. At present the credit for a course is treated like a deposit in a savings bank, without a suspicion that the deposit is not of gold that can be drawn upon at its face value, but a perishable article. To change the metaphor, we treat it like wheat poured into a grain elevator, whereas it is often more like fruit in a cold storage plant without the means of refrigeration. Indeed, it is sometimes more like the contents of an incinerator." A. Lawrence Lowell, *At War with Academic Traditions*, pp. 139-40. This testing of achievement is, of course, still within the framework of the subject-matter educational goals, not, as advocated in these pages, a measure of the student's achievement in terms of socially desirable life patterns.

American graduate schools set up as they are, it will be recognized that some undergraduates will fulfill the requirements of the functional college and receive its degree without
necessarily qualifying or wishing to qualify for a particular
type of graduate work. And it is not inconceivable that a
student may qualify for admission to the graduate school of
his choice without at the same time qualifying for the approval of his Alma Mater. Until the graduate schools radically alter their methods of admission (possibly becoming
functional themselves), the college will need to have a recognized process of certification and recommendation. Adequate
forms for cumulative information should lead to meeting the
needs at this point without great difficulty other than added
expense. We do not imply that the standards for the degree
of the functional college are higher or lower, less rigorous or
more rigorous, than the standards for certification to the
graduate school; but we do maintain that the two are different, and that distinctly different tests and measures should be
used for each of the two, without implying superiority or inferiority. One is primary for the college; the other is, at
present, essential for post-collegiate certification. Much the
same line of thinking applies in fields other than graduate
study. Qualification for teachers' certificates, or for entrance
upon particular vocational careers, becomes the basis for
measurement and certification of students interested in these
fields. At frequent strategic points through the course of collegiate residence, the student and his counselors will consult
about his progress in terms of the standards for admission
into his chosen field. As in the first testing program, so in
this second, guidance and testing are closely interwoven.

3. To enable the college to estimate itself in terms of its
own aims and objectives, to correct and improve its teaching
process with successive student generations. When a student
is marked "failure," who has failed—the student or the institution? Assuming a rational admissions process and a correlated diversification of curricula every student failure is an
important indication of possible collegiate inadequacy. The

functional college will study its failures as well as its successes, to improve its own procedures. The testing programs for the first two aims provide the raw data for this third objective of institutional research and self-examination.

Tests and measures adequate to this full program are not perfected; but considerable work is in progress at the present time, looking toward this end. It is a matter of time and money and hard work until we are able to make at least a significant beginning in this threefold testing and evaluating program. This process of differentiated evaluation is the means of escaping the tyranny of certification over education. Therein lies its peculiar importance for the functional college.

SPECIAL PROBLEMS OF TEACHING: THE RACIAL EMPHASIS

In the subject-matter realm, the question of dealing adequately with the special problems of Negro life and history is one which has engaged the attention of some of the ablest social scientists and educators. Here is an area of controversy over the specific content of education for Negroes which has caused no small amount of heated discussion in the last three-quarters of a century. Some men have argued that there is no such thing as "Negro" education—that the Negro is to be educated exactly like any other American citizen. Others have replied that in addition to all the regular courses of study, the Negro should be taught the lessons of race pride and self-respect by a study of the contribution of the race to the progress of the nation. Still a third group have wanted the Negro college and school to teach the young colored man about the African background as a basis for pride of ancestry; while a fourth group have insisted that biological inferiorities, which they alleged were present, dictated a special kind of education for "backward peoples"; and a fifth have contended that the special disadvantages suffered by the Negro in America have placed special burdens upon the Negro college—burdens which may be translated into opportunities.[9]

[9] Some of the more pertinent of recent writings dealing with this problem of the racial emphasis in Negro education are: Paul E. Baker, *Negro-White*

Now, to the extent that the earlier chapters of this book are correct interpretations of fact, the segregated institution has at hand a valid basis for choosing between these several conflicting conceptions of curricular materials. We may select those materials most suitable to the purposes of the functional college, at work to promote optimum living for all persons, and as a part of this effort, at work to modify caste.

Will there be a special kind of education in the functional college, a special curriculum? There will not be a special cur-

---

Adjustment; R. B. Binnion, "Solving the Negro Problem through Education"; Horace Mann Bond, "Human Nature and Its Study in Negro Colleges," "The Curriculum and the Negro Child," and *Education of the Negro in the American Social Order;* Andrew W. Brown, "The Reliability and Validity of the Seashore Tests of Musical Talent"; Forrest Brown, "Goodwill Tour in Virginia"; Bessie D. Bryant, "The Influence of Education upon the Negro's Standard of Living"; Ralph W. Bullock, *In Spite of Handicaps;* Ralph J. Bunche, "Education in Black and White" and "Critical Analysis of the Tactics and Programs of Minority Groups"; J. L. Clark, "Race-Relations Course in a State College"; Thomas L. Dabney, "The Importance of Negro History"; Robert P. Daniel, "One Consideration of Redirection of Emphasis of the Negro College"; Bertram W. Doyle, *Etiquette of Race Relations in the South;* W. E. B. DuBois, "America and the Negro Citizen" and "The Field and Function of the Negro College"; Edwin R. Embree, *Brown America;* H. Feldman, *Racial Factors in American Industry;* E. Franklin Frazer, *Negro Family in Chicago;* Lester B. Granger, "Race Relations and the School System"; George E. Haynes, "Negro Achievement as Shown by Harman Awards"; E. S. Jacobs, "Pioneering in Home Economics among Negroes of Tidewater, Virginia"; Charles S. Johnson, "On the Need of Realism in Negro Education" and *The Negro in American Civilization;* James Weldon Johnson, *Negro Americans, What Now?;* Harold Fletcher Lee, "Social Problems of the Negro in America"; A. LeR. Locke, *Decade of Negro Self-Expression;* Alaine Locke, "The New Negro"; Robert R. Moton, *What the Negro Thinks;* Franklin O. Nichols, "Preparation of Negro Youth for Marriage and Parenthood"; E. B. Reuter, *The American Race Problem;* W. A. Robinson, "What Peculiar Organization and Direction Should Characterize the Education of Negroes?"; B. Schriecke, *Alien Americans;* Gilbert T. Stephenson, "Education and Crime among Negroes"; Merz Tate, "Proposed Social Studies Programme for Bennett College for Women"; W. D. Weatherford and Charles S. Johnson, *Race Relations;* John P. Whittaker, "What is the Responsibility of the Liberal Arts College Toward Meeting the Occupational Opportunities for Students?"; R. S. Wilkinson, "Development of Home Economics in Negro Schools"; Doxey A. Wilkerson, "A Determination of the Peculiar Problems of Negroes in Contemporary American Society"; L. Virgil Williams, "The Need for the Development of Creative Abilities among Negro Students"; Carter G. Woodson, *The Miseducation of the Negro;* and *African Background Outlined, or Handbook for the Study of the Negro;* T. J. Woofter, Jr., *Negro Problems in Cities;* Donald Young, *American Minority Peoples.* For bibliographical information concerning these books and articles see the Bibliography.

riculum posited on alleged biological inferiorities. There will
be special curricular features designed to fortify the Negro
in his struggle against caste, and to help him enrich life—his
own life and that of others. It is not altogether unlikely that
the curricular departures of the functional college will suggest similar developments which may help other types of colleges to become functional in terms of their own special problems. To the extent that the segregated institution intelligently
meets its special as well as its general problems, it may give
guidance to American higher education in general.

Wilkerson[10] lists 130 problems which have been mentioned
by writers, either in books or in periodicals, in recent years,
each of which carries with it a special curricular suggestion
for the functional college. Each of these problems is one
which the Negro meets in American society, not because he
is biologically different from the dominant white group but
because the social situation especially thrusts these problems
upon him. These 130 problems Wilkerson classifies under
the following headings: (1) problems in the world of work;
(2) problems of civil liberty; (3) problems of health, housing, the family and the church; (4) problems of personal
and social integration, racial attitudes, stereotypes, and beliefs; (5) problems of education; and (6) problems of minority group strategy. Here is a preliminary suggestion of
the wealth of materials which awaits the seriously purposed
educators who set about to make available the instructional
equipment to meet the needs of the Negro under the American caste system.

The democratic processes of curriculum construction will
settle upon selected aspects of these problems, and of others
which occur to the teachers and learners. The selection of
specific materials and the decision as to the manner of using
these materials, are rightly left to the educative process itself.
No set of curricular materials ought to be superimposed from

[10] Doxey A. Wilkerson, "A Determination of the Peculiar Problems of Negroes
in Contemporary American Society," *Journal of Negro Education*, V (July,
1936), 324-50.

above. We are content with pointing to underlying considerations.

One of the clear necessities of a functional curriculum is
the study, in full perspective, of the plight and tactics of the
Negro as a submerged group in American culture. It is important that the study of race problems in America be kept
in its larger setting, viewed with relation to the plight and
techniques of submerged minority and majority groups in
other parts of the world. American race problems must be
studied "in their relativity, in their world aspect, without
which they are apt to increase resentment and not to serve to
liberate the mind and the individuality. The only way to
mental freedom is analysis. Only in this way can the pathological self-centeredness, resulting from the oppression psy-
chosis and the repression of self-determination, and the spell
of uniqueness be broken, and the obsession realized to be the
product of general laws."[11] This curricular development of the
strategy needed by a submerged minority group seeking emergence is seen in the entire spread of the functional college curriculum—from selection of staff and determination of administrative policies through to classroom methods and materials.
One focal point is a seminar for social science students and
professors, in which a careful canvass of the world scene
provides background and perspective for the American situation. The insights of this special group are available for the
whole college; and conversely, the lessons of total collegiate
experience are incorporated in the findings of this study
group. The student needs to know what social techniques and
skills are best adapted to the purposes of racial advancement
and the larger welfare of humanity. He needs to learn what
these are, and how and when to use them. He needs to know
the range and type of problems on which to work, and where
to find opportunities to begin and to continue that work in
his local community, in his state, in the nation, in the world.

Alongside this cultivation of social skills and techniques
lies a parallel task of discovering methods and resources for

[11] B. Schrieke, *Alien Americans,* p. 152.

personal integration and survival, for richness of living by transcendence of situations like the 130 problems which Wilkerson lists. Just what this personal integration is to be, is also a matter for the democratic educational process to discover rather than for the present writer to dictate. But the resources of high ethical and religious integration will be useful not only in avoiding the escapist flight into fantasy but also in enabling the individual to carry on against tremendous odds.[12] The individual needs to discover for himself the fuller opportunities that come from being on the "active fringes of culture."[13] In this constructive discovery lies his power to avoid the deleterious effects of segregation which might otherwise lay hold upon him—"disillusionment, frustration, loss of ambition, bitterness, anti-social impulses, deep sense of social inadequacy, warped personality."[14] Teaching in the segregated college will be aimed at the discovery and cultivation of the inner resources necessary for this amazing conflict of the individual with his social environment.

These two basic principles we lay down to guide the initial thinking of staff and students as they develop curricula in their functional colleges—the necessity for including in the curriculum the problems of minority group strategy as seen in world perspective; and the necessity for nurturing in the individual the inner resources for personal victory in the face of temporary defeat. What these mean in specific terms of activities and resource materials is a problem for the several colleges to solve jointly and individually. There are a number of valuable researches in this curriculum field which need to be done, and the experience of the next twenty years should shed much light upon problems of technique and procedure. The subsidiary questions of the study of Negro life and his-

[12] "It took a war to teach me that there was no real security anywhere except in the mind,—that if content and safety might be bedfellows, happiness and insecurity could be brothers in arms." H. S. Canby, *Alma Mater*, p. 155.

[13] "Historically, it is on these active fringes of culture that civilizations grow up." Charles S. Johnson, "The Development of the Personality of Students in Segregated Communities," *Quarterly Review of Higher Education among Negroes*, IV (April, 1936), 67-71.

[14] *Ibid.*

tory, the development of conscious race pride, and the like, are to be answered in terms of these two basic working conceptions with which the functional college approaches the questions of specific curriculum content.[15]

FUNCTIONAL TRANSMISSION OF THE CULTURAL HERITAGE

Perhaps the most vehement objection to the functional notion of collegiate education comes from the classicists who are concerned with the perennial problem of passing on the cultural heritage. The classical pattern of the college curriculum had as its organizing principle the conviction that the student should be introduced to the cumulative insights of the great men of all ages, that the individual should enter into his cultural birthright. The problem, then, was the seemingly simple one of discovering the best arrangement and sequence of studies through which the student might acquaint himself with the cultural heritage. In the course of time, greater and greater emphasis came to be placed upon the discovery of some means of accurately certifying that the student had covered the ground laid out for him by his teachers. The dual process of instruction and examination culminated in certification. Now, say the defenders of the subject-matter curriculum, if we do not lay out a systematic scheme for mastery of the broad fields of human learning, what assurance have we that the student will enter into his heritage? And what assurance have we that the chief end of education—passing on the cultural heritage—will be performed? The answer is first in a counterquestion, and then in an affirmation.

The counterquestion is this: What assurance have we that the classical method of curriculum construction and instruc-

[15] One hundred and fourteen interested persons contributed to the list of 353 "Problems in the Collegiate Education of Negroes," compiled by John W. Davis (West Virginia State College *Bulletin*, June, 1937). Practically every one of these 353 problems is curricular within the meaning of the term as we are using it—including all the experience of the collegiate youth. These are problems of the college as such, while Wilkerson's list (above) had to do primarily with the American scene to which the college addresses itself. There is no paucity of materials or of problems.

tion actually did pass on the cultural heritage? To be sure, the insights and cultural inventions of successive generations were preserved. They were mainly preserved in two forms: (1) in word-of-mouth, person-to-person transmission of folklore, tradition, etc., gradually developing into permanent records such as books, paintings, sculptures, and the like, which were preserved in libraries and museums, the collections being augmented by the slow accretions of the generations, and being available to the culturally curious; and (2) in the changing forms and operations of civilization, in which the modifications of the culture directly affected the daily experiences of the common man. Contemporary examples of this second form of transmission of the cultural heritage are: the operation of 28,221,291 automobiles and trucks in the United States in 1936,[16] and the use of radio receiving sets in 70 percent of American homes in 1935.[17] The whole technological structure of modern life is the tangible expression of the heritage of civilization. The schools are instrumental in giving the individual the tools of cultural understanding; but the surrounding culture educates in a thoroughgoing and effective fashion which only the most effective school even remotely approaches. What the child learns as he grows up in modern society—the habits of life and standards of value which operate day by day in his actual choices and desires—these are the things which functionally determine the manner and degree in which the cultural heritage is transmitted from generation to generation. It is as an integrated functioning part of the culture, not as a carefully preserved exhibit, that the cultural heritage is actually transmitted. It is not a proven fact that the classical curriculum did pass on the cultural heritage. It did perhaps help to preserve the heritage; but it did not make that heritage largely functional in the lives of men. Until definitive evidence is available, in the form of a

[16] "Automobile Facts and Figures," Automobile Manufacturers' Association (1937).

[17] *World Almanac,* 1936, p. 323, based on census estimates and reports of the Columbia and National Broadcasting Companies and the McGraw-Hill Publishing Company. The figures do not include 780,000 automobile radios.

comprehensive study of what college graduates actually do in their working and leisure time, what their standards of value are, what operational evidences can be found to support the contention that the classical curriculum gave the student the cultural heritage—until such evidence is in, we question the assertion that the standard subject-matter curriculum really performed the task claimed for it. Not solely or primarily, but only secondarily in the colleges, is the cultural heritage transmitted. Life itself teaches the individual.

The other side of the picture is our affirmation that, since actual experience educates, and since in experience the things which are genuinely learned are those things which are accepted as the basis for action, the effort to transmit the values of the cultural heritage must be closely associated with the student's conscious and constructive effort to realize his own genuinely felt desires. There is no final dichotomy between the transmission of the social heritage on the one hand and the growth of the individual on the other—provided the growth of the individual is seen in its social setting, and provided the transmission of the social heritage is seen in its operational nature. Education then is seen to be the effort to aid the individual in a continuous process of growth, at each stage of which he appropriates the values, insights, and tools of the culture which are appropriate and necessary to his growth, and at all stages of which a conscious effort is made to insure well-rounded rather than one-sided development.[18]

Viewed from this perspective, the pedantic academician who is less concerned with the actual operational social significance of learning and culture and more occupied with the cloistered preservation of the scholarship of the past and present, is parasitical. Perhaps it is socially permissible for a limited number of persons to occupy parasitical sanctuaries like those in which the lamp of learning and culture was kept alive through the Dark Ages—more so in an age like the

---

[18] See William H. Kilpatrick, "Education as Living for Better Living," *Educational Method*, XVII (January, 1938), 149-56.

present which appears to be cool in its appreciation of the liberal arts. Such a conception of an admitted immediate social irrelevancy of scholarly activity assumes that the world is to be abandoned to its fate. It is beyond redemption. All that can be done is to preserve cultural values inviolate so that if a better day dawns, the academician can safely come out of his retreat. But a nation, or a racial group, which is interested not in retrogression but in advance, can ill afford the doubtful luxury of permitting its more able and better trained members to retreat into academic irrelevancy. The preservation and transmission of the cultural heritage is organically linked with the advancement of the race.

Here again is a point at which the traditional educational procedure missed the mark by using an erroneous theory of learning. It often assumed that the cultural heritage was passed on merely by formal study about it. A truer insight insists that only those things are actually learned which are learned in and for use by the learner. The transmission of values demands that they be values for the persons to whom they are transmitted. If the cultural heritage is to be a vital and meaningful thing to the student, he must learn its vitality and meanings as he actually uses it in daily living.

RACIAL CONTRIBUTION TO CULTURAL ADVANCE

At this point we see a little more clearly wherein the Negro may contribute to American culture as he shares in it. The literature of this question is prolific, and much attention in curriculum planning is currently being directed toward it.[19]

[19] William S. Braithwaite, *Anthology of Magazine Verse and Yearbook of American Poetry*; Benjamin Brawley, *The Negro in Literature and Art in the United States* and *The Negro Genius*; Harry T. Burleigh, *Negro Spirituals* and *Old Songs Hymnal*; Countee Cullen, *Color, Copper Sun, Caroling Dusk*, and *The Black Christ*; W. E. B. DuBois, *Darkwater, The Gift of Black Folk, The Souls of Black Folk*, and *The Dark Princess*; Paul Lawrence Dunbar, *Complete Poems*; Elizabeth L. Green, *The Negro in Contemporary American Literature*; Langston Hughes, *Weary Blues* and *Fine Clothes to the Jew*; H. C. Lehman and Paul A. Witty, "The Negro Child's Interest in Writing Poetry"; James Weldon Johnson, *Autobiography of an Ex-colored Man, Book of American Negro Poetry, Book of American Negro Spirituals, God's Trombones, Along This Way*, and *St. Peter Relates an Incident*; Blair Niles, *Black*

Without presuming to dogmatize, we are here permitted to state certain inferences for functional education.

It is not yet proved, or disproved, that the Negro has special talents in particular lines. The stereotypes with which the caste system operates would lead us to believe that the Negro has certain artistic abilities and talents, especially in music and the plastic arts, not possessed to the same degree or in the same kind by Caucasians.[20] To some extent this notion is a reflex of the fact that it is in the arts, particularly the spirituals and jazz or swing music, that the Negro has attracted most favorable attention from the Caucasian. But it cannot be assumed that, merely because Caucasian ears have been pleased by the sorrow songs of slavery and by the hot rhythms of swing, the Negro has a peculiar talent for artistic creation along these lines. It might be argued with equal logic that the invention of gunpowder by the Chinese showed a peculiar talent for explosives, or that Gutenberg's press established the literary inventiveness of Germanic peoples. Whatever inferences are drawn must be established in the light of historical perspective, and must hold true when full consideration is given to all sociological and environing phenomena. There has been, for example, a general feeling among cultured persons that the German people had a peculiar musical genius. Although this notion has gone somewhat into eclipse in recent years, it was widely prevalent in the first quarter of the twentieth century. But if these same Germanic racial stocks are examined not at 1900 but at 600, what has become of the alleged musical ability? It takes a pre-Nazi Munich and Nuremberg with centuries of cultural growth and development, to produce the soil out of which genius

Haiti; Howard W. Odum, *Rainbow round My Shoulder, Wings on My Feet,* and *Negro Workaday Songs;* H. W. Odum and Guy B. Johnson, *The Negro and His Songs;* Dorothy Scarborough, *On the Trail of Negro Folk-Songs;* Edwin W. Smith, *Aggrey of Africa* and *The Golden Stool;* Hildegarde H. Swift, *Railroad to Freedom;* Thomas W. Talley, *Negro Folk-Rhymes, Wise and Otherwise;* Jean Toomer, *Cane;* Walter F. White, *The Fire in the Flint* and *Flight.* For bibliographical information concerning these books and articles see the Bibliography.

[20] See Appendix B.

flowers. And the flowering of genius is in large part (how large a part it is impossible to say, but certainly to a very significant degree) determined by the cultural chemistry of the social soil. No Vienna, no Beethoven. Mozart, composing at six and playing for royalty before ten, could logically be taken as an example of an alleged peculiar genius of the Germanic peoples for musical expression. But whatever explanation may be given to Mozart, that explanation cannot overlook the fact that he was born and nurtured in Salzburg, the Salzburg of the nineteenth—not the ninth—century.

So, too, with the Negro's musical expression in America. It began with the sorrow songs. It has reached its current zenith in swing music. The spirituals and the seculars were born of slavery. Stephen Foster, white, took many of the plantation melodies, cast them in wording appropriate to the pattern of master-slave relationships, and gave them to America, an America which avidly welcomed these plaintive songs of sorrow that did not challenge the caste pattern. The Fisk Jubilee Singers with their superlative rendering of the songs of aspiration and longing, of sorrow and yearning, sang their way into the consciousness of two continents, and set the pattern still used by many Negro colleges in winning Caucasian approval and contributions. The birth of jazz and the development of swing further testify to the manner in which Caucasian America welcomes the Negro as he contributes a cultural strain which is so frankly and openly "Negroid."

It is impossible to say whether the acceptance is based more on the intrinsic merit of the musical contribution or upon the fact that the marked difference between these musical forms and the established classical norms does not imply "musical equality." There is a degree to which the contribution of the Negro to American culture has been successful primarily because it either coincided with, or did not openly challenge, the dominant ideas of what was appropriate for a lower caste. On the other hand, the recognition accorded Negro artists on the basis of their work has an important bearing upon the self-respect of the group. There are those who feel, with some justification, that any activity which ministers to the self-respect of the Negro is distinctly valuable; but others will argue that self-respect which is bought at the price of conformity to caste is too dearly purchased —that self-respect ought to be a by-product of struggle against caste. These latter would sharply challenge the "rightness" of conformity to cultural and artistic stereotypes. They would not necessarily rule out the possibility of using highly stylized modes of expression which are predominantly "Negroid" in connotation, but they would object to the use of such modes if their use tended to perpetuate invidious caste implications. The task before the curriculum-makers, then, is one of finding out how to teach racial self-respect without the necessity of buying that self-respect at the price of caste-conformity; and at the same time to recover the values of a racial cultural heritage without conjuring up the sociological phenomena which are historically associated with the emergence of that heritage. How to enjoy the spirituals and seculars as folk songs, without implying that the singer is recalling with pleasure the days of slavery out of which they came; how to acknowledge the Negro's gift to America without admitting a special "Negroid" status; how to achieve the values of cultural richness and diversity through group differences without surrendering the values of freedom and enjoyment which can come only through integration; how to enable the Negro American to be both a Negro and an American—these are curricular problems before the functional college.

The particular pertinence of this racial-emphasis problem to the larger question of transmitting the social heritage lies in the fact that the answers to both questions must be discovered together. The Negro student must see that both his African and his Caucasian ancestry have shared in the making of the cultural heritage into which he as an individual is now introduced. He must appropriate the values of this inclusive human heritage, with a cultivated ability to discriminate between the transitory and the enduring, the trivial and the consequential, the ephemeral and the significant. And he must come to see that as a Negro he is also an American, and that the proper phrase is "Negro American" not "American Negro." A successful social orientation of the problem of transmission of cultures, both inherited and contemporary, would weigh all problems against the counterbalance of caste. The appropriation of the cultural heritage and the enrichment of contemporary culture will go hand in hand with the attempt to make caste irrelevant.

A high appreciation of the cultural heritage of the Negro, both the African and the American background, will not necessarily rule out an equally high appreciation of the non-Negro heritage. The amalgam of civilization certainly is not Caucasoid. It is human. The Negro needs to have no feeling either of inferiority, or of resentment, or of superiority, as he enters into the fullest participation and appreciation of all that is his as an American citizen—as a world citizen. The ferris wheel of civilization brings different national and racial groups to the zenith at successive periods of history. Let not him whose car is temporarily at the top forget that he ascended as others declined; and let not him who ascends think too long of the fact that others precede him.

The teaching materials of the functional college will be selected because they enrich and ennoble life. The experiences which are planned and executed, the selections made from the storehouse of history, the artistic and aesthetic materials utilized, the religious and ethical insights developed, the judgments made and the values accepted, the life attitudes formed and the habits built, will be calculated to enrich the life of the Negro student because they enable him to enrich the life of his fellow human beings, to enrich all and to impoverish none.

STRUCTURAL VARIETY

The how and the what of teaching will not conform to one standardized pattern in all the institutions of higher learning for Negroes. Within the general framework of the functional college, each institution pursues its own particular bent;

and to the degree that it successfully shares in the function
of reconstructing society, each institution will enjoy larger
freedom to work out its own destiny. There is a close parallel
between enlarged individual freedom and enhanced institutional liberty—both come as by-products of the struggle for
justice, equity, and decency in society.

The functional land-grant college will therefore be a better
land-grant college because it is discharging its social function.
The liberal arts college finds its larger release when it directly attacks the illiberal and inartistic caste structure. Teachers colleges and professional schools enlarge their own opportunities for training and placing effective workers when they
attack the fortress of their present difficulties in the racial
barriers. The private schools find their *raison d'être* in intelligent refusal to conform to the mores of caste. The state-
controlled institutions find that their own future and effectiveness are permanently enhanced not by short-sighted conformity
to legislators and politicians but by far-sighted and statesman-
like cultivation of state officials and administrators in growth
away from the tyranny of caste conformity.

The functional notion also heightens the meaning of other
structural patterns. The present four-year college may not be
the permanent pattern of higher education in America. The
junior college and the university may conceivably squeeze
from their respective ends, and largely eliminate the present
undergraduate college. But if the undergraduate college goes,
whatever takes its places in the educational structure will be
faced with the same weight of caste, and only as its whole
educational philosophy and practice are oriented to the need
of discharging its social function, will the new institution find
its most significant opportunities for service and growth.

Similarly, the future of the subject-matter patterns in the
liberal arts colleges appears to be a matter of some conjec-
ture at the moment. The so-called "General Education Movement" which is coming over the horizon will probably have
a marked influence upon the liberal colleges which survive
the nutcracker pressures of junior college and university.

Some colleges will have a four-year logical sequence of courses, combining required and elective work. Some will have an entirely individualized curricular pattern, following implicitly the needs of the unfolding experience of each student. Some will have a 2-2 sequence, using the first half of the college course to lay broad basic foundations and the second half to dig deeply into one field of concentration. Some will work on the principle of alternation between general and special, guiding the student from one to the other in a ladder process of action and interaction for growth. Some will evolve a 1-2-1 sequence, letting the first year be broadly exploratory and informative, aimed at acquaintance; the second and third years a period of concentration and specialization; and the last year one of integration and synthesis, again in broad terms. Still others will go onto a five-year basis leading directly to the Master's degree, and utilizing some combination or variant of the patterns just mentioned. It is to be hoped that educators will encourage variety and experimentation in educational structure and program as well as in technique and procedure—but it is also to be hoped that segregated colleges will increasingly see that their ability to realize *any* educational objective is inextricably bound up with their effectiveness in unloosing the binding cords of caste. The future of the colleges with their staffs and students, the future of the Negro American and the white American, that future of peace and plenty and creativity in living, wait upon the success of all high-minded efforts to make the way straight and to level the mountains of difficulty.

XIV

PROPHETIC EDUCATION

Whatever else one may have learned, if he comes into the World from his Schooling and Masters, quite unacquainted with the Nature, Rank and Condition, of Mankind, and the Duties of human Life . . . he is not educated; *he is not prepared for the World; he is not qualified for Society. . . . The Way therefore to judge whether Education be on a right Footing or not, is to compare it with the END; or to consider what it does in order to accomplish Youth for choosing and* behaving well in the various *Conditions, Relations, and Incidents of Life.* —GEORGE TURNBULL (1742)

TWO HUNDRED years ago, a chaplain to English royalty insisted that liberal education must be taken out of the cloister and made to serve the needs of society. His yardstick for measuring the value of education (quoted in part at the opening of this chapter)[1] was the degree to which the graduate was "qualified for Society," knowing well the "Nature, Rank, and Condition of Mankind," in order that he might "behave well in the various Conditions, Relations, and Incidents of Life." The purpose of the college was to train young men to fulfill satisfactorily the duties of their particular social stations. Here was education to serve a certain type of social need—the need for conformity in a society which was thought to be static.

An opposite point of view is demanded by the present American situation. Education is to serve the needs of society —yes. The student is to understand the nature, rank, and conditions of mankind—yes. But the needs of society are to be thought of not in terms of servile conformity but in terms of prophetic attack in behalf of enlargement of life for all people, black and white, and (instrumental to this end) release from the bonds of caste. The understanding of the stratification of men in classes and castes is to be expressed not in blind acceptance of the *status quo,* but in a critical analysis of it. Here is education to serve the needs of a dynamic society by helping to make it possible for social evolution to move toward enlarged opportunities for optimum living for all.

Turnbull would have had education come out of its monastic cloister to serve social need. So far, he was right. But

---

[1] From George Turnbull, *Observations on Liberal Education,* p. 175, quoted in Benjamin Franklin's *Proposals Relating to the Education of Youth in Pennsylvania,* p. 32.

Turnbull interpreted social need in terms of conformity to an eighteenth-century aristocracy; and in this, while he may have been more or less right for his day, to follow his lead in a twentieth-century democracy would be anachronistic. To the degree that the American college harks back to an eighteenth-century English tradition for its social orientation, it is outmoded. But the authentic eighteenth-century American tradition demands that education be socially potent. Education for democracy can be neither cloistered nor servile; it must be prophetic.

To be effectively prophetic, the college needs the best obtainable frame of reference for social orientation. This book is an attempt to work toward supplying that need for one group of colleges. The writer claims neither omniscience nor infallibility, nor does he expect his writing to revolutionize American education. He does dare to hope, however, that here and there a college may find in these pages some suggestions or insights which have meaning and value, some valid contributions to the social orientation of higher education.

THREE GENERAL INFERENCES FOR EDUCATION

1. The data herein reviewed appear to lead to the inference that there need be no fundamental differences between the colleges best suited to Negroes and the colleges best suited to whites. The stuff of human nature is generally the same regardless of race. Individual differences do not follow racial patterns; all Americans increasingly share a common social and cultural heritage; and while the post-collegiate opportunities and experiences of whites and Negroes may not now be identical in American society, in the main they are similar; and the functional college anticipates the time when there will be no racial disparities in opportunities to make a living, to enjoy life, and to contribute to the welfare and happiness of mankind. The college designed to serve best the needs of Negro youth will therefore be very much like a college which might be designed to serve best the needs of American youth in general (though not necessarily like many colleges now existing).

2. A contrary inference is also indicated by the data, an inference which qualifies the first. There are some points at which the segregated college will be different in emphasis or procedure from the nonsegregated—not, however, for biological or racial reasons. The Negro college will be somewhat different from the non-Negro college in certain respects because, American society being inequitable, the Negro needs to know more, to be better prepared and equipped, more finely sensitized in his social sympathies, and more completely developed in social intelligence and social maturity than his white brother, merely to win his way to normal happiness and constructive living in the face of the odds of caste, and simply to repay his social obligation in spite of the difficulties of American life. The Negro college needs to provide training for workers in a minority group working to improve its status and opportunities. This it does in addition to the tasks it shares in common with the nonsegregated colleges. The differences are matters of addition, not of subtraction.

3. In so far as its methods are sound, its insights useful, and its procedures satisfactory, the segregated college which seriously sets itself to the discharge of its social function may possibly, as a by-product, render a wider service to higher education in general. The problem of building self-controlled, socially-minded, ethically sensitive, vigorous men and women who are habituated in the processes of social intelligence is not peculiar to the Negro college. Again, the implementing of democracy in collegiate procedure is of concern not solely to the segregated institution. Therefore, the segregated college which builds sanely, soundly, and adventurously in the performance of its social function may find that its achievements shape the prototype of a Trojan horse by which American education can help to conquer the citadel of a professedly democratic, but essentially undemocratic and unethical society.

One final word. There are those who inquire whether the Negro college can safely take the risks involved in the discharge of its social function. At this early stage in its evolution, when it is scarcely half a century old in full collegiate stature, is the segregated college well enough established to run the hazard of eccentricity or of failure? Are there enough first-rate standard colleges open to Negroes, so that the group can afford to have some of its institutions leave the beaten track, without jeopardizing the higher educational opportunities of Negro youth? These are questions to be weighed carefully.

In reply, let another question be posed. Let it be asked whether the situation we face does not indicate that unless the Negro colleges are ready to abandon much that is in the mummery of the standardized college in order to become socially effective, they will actually work to miseducate, thwart, and misdirect Negro youth. The nonfunctional college is not merely irrelevant, it is miseducative and parasitical. In fact, the nonfunctional college for Negroes is traitorous. It acquiesces in the day-by-day defeat of the desires and aspirations of the Negro, and thereby miseducatively consents to the social stultification by which America is denied a contribution which might be made by one-tenth of its people.

We dare to hope that some colleges will wish to fulfill their social function, that they will wish to become prophetic rather than monastic or servile. Higher education will become effectively prophetic when not only its formal instruction, but equally its structure and procedures are redirected by the best available group thinking, with the aim of employing all the strength of critical intelligence, all the stamina of the human spirit, all the resources of ethical religion in the prophetic venture. Both by precept and by practice the college then foreshadows the society it foresees.

APPENDIX A
COTTON AND LYNCHINGS

In reality, lynchings come out of the state of mind of white people much more than out of the crimes committed by Negroes. —ARTHUR RAPER

THE purpose of this note is to examine the relationship between annual fluctuations in the per acre income of the cotton grower and annual fluctuations in the number of lynchings of Negroes by whites in cotton states.

There are three levels of phenomena which can be distinguished: (1) the excuses given for lynchings; (2) the actual occasions for lynchings; and (3) the underlying causes. The excuses usually have some relationship to the occasions, though not necessarily so; but usually neither excuses nor overt occasions are related directly to causes. It is necessary to drive back of excuses and occasions to underlying causes, to show the basic relationship of economic processes and race attitudes.

1. *The excuses given.*—It is popularly believed that lynchings commonly occur in retaliation for rape. The facts are that less than 20 per cent of all Negroes lynched have even been accused of rape. More than four-fifths of the excuses given have been other matters.[1] Moreover, in the cases where rape is alleged, there is strong presumptive evidence pointing to the conclusion that the "proneness to hysteria evidenced among white women where Negroes are concerned is undoubtedly a prominent factor in starting the mob after 'a Negro.'"[2] Again, Johnson has shown[3] that there is scant justification for the myth that Negroes

[1] "It may be assumed with full safety that in every case where there was the slightest intimation or suspicion of rape or attempted rape upon a white woman, newspaper accounts would mention the fact. For the purpose of giving the lynchers every benefit of the doubt let us include the 237 Negroes (9.4%) lynched for 'attacks upon women' with the 477 lynched for alleged rape. The greatest possible total is therefore 714 Negroes who can be charged with rape, alleged rape, attempted rape, suspicion of rape, or of offenses of any nature however slight, against a white woman, out of a total of 2522 lynched for all offenses (between 1889 and 1918). The maximum therefore would be 28.3 per cent, or less than one in three victims. If we confine ourselves to cases where Negroes were specifically charged with rape, the number of such accusations falls to slightly less than one in five." Walter White, *Rope and Faggot,* p. 253.

[2] *Ibid.,* p. 58: "In the great majority of cases where rape or attempted rape is alleged, the women can be divided into four classes: young girls ranging from the ages of twelve or thirteen to nineteen or twenty years of age, passing through the difficult period of adolescence; second (and this includes a considerable percentage of the alleged victims of attacks), women who range in age from the middle forties upwards; third, women who have been married for many years and usually to rather unattractive husbands; and fourth, spinsters."

[3] James Weldon Johnson, "The Lynching Shame," *Current History,* XIX (January, 1924), 596-601.

are irresponsible in sex attitudes and prone to rape white women; for the number of lynched Negroes accused of rape in a given period throughout the entire South is less than the actual number of citizens of New York City alone who were indicted for first-degree rape on evidence submitted to the New York Grand Jury.

White points out[4] that the Negro's alleged propensity for rape and sex crimes was unheard of in the United States prior to 1830 although Negroes were first brought into the country in 1619, and numbered 1,500,000 in 1820. During these two centuries of rapidly developing Negro population, charges of rape against Negroes were unknown, although there was ample opportunity for the commission of such crimes. The accusation of rape and sex crimes against the Negro appears suddenly with the sharply increased demand for cheap labor which came at a time when the invention of the cotton gin suddenly made the plantation system of growing cotton a highly lucrative enterprise—lucrative as long as labor costs could be kept at the slave level. And as the technique of mob violence came to be relied upon more and more as a means of intimidating and controlling the Negro population, justification of the lynchings was sought in a gargantuan build-up of the sex myth. Vehement condemnation of lynchings from Southern and Northern whites who disagreed with the practice brought more and more frequent charges of rape in defense of increasing mob brutality.

It is this line of evidence which leads to the question whether the reasons for the dominance of sex as a factor in lynchings centers principally in one objective—the economic ascendancy of whites over Negro labor. William Pickens has described the rape-lynching myth as "simply the shrewdest battle cry of the forces seeking the economic domination of the Negro. . . . The average man, even the most brainless, may be moved by it," and thus sex is used as "a red herring . . . whenever one discusses the economic, political or civic advancement of the Negro."[5]

But even if the full force of the alleged rape accusation were granted, it still remains true that about four-fifths of all the lynchings must be accounted for in some other manner. The list of excuses given for lynchings ranges from the preposterous through the absurd to the ridiculous. Perhaps an all-time high in obvious untruth is the case in Tuscaloosa, Alabama, where a helpless paralytic, confined to a wheel chair, was lynched "for rape." A Negro is lynched for refusing to give evidence; he is lynched for giving evidence. He is lynched for "running"; he is lynched for staying where he is and refusing to run. He is lynched for being related to a criminal; he is lynched for "conjuring." He is lynched for "introducing smallpox" and for "poisoning mules." The

[4] White, op. cit., pp. 88 f.
[5] Op. cit., p. 76.

following compilation of the excuses—not causes—alleged for lynchings over the last half century is made from the reports of the National Association for the Advancement of Colored People, and in every case this means simply a statement of the excuse which was reported in the press at the time the mob murder was committed:

Refusing to give evidence
Testifying in court
Poisoning mules
Eloping with a girl
Jilting a girl
Using abusive language
Bad reputation
Disorderly conduct
Throwing stones
Unpopularity
Enticing a servant away
Disputing a white man's word
Slapping a child
Disobeying ferry regulations
Running
Colonizing Negroes
Conjuring
Killing a horse
Violation of contract
Refusal to pay a note
Introducing smallpox
Testifying for one of his own race
Being troublesome
Quarrel over profit sharing (five lynched)
Expressing sympathy with the murder of a white man (five lynched)
Jumping labor contract
Not turning out of road for white boy in automobile
Expressing himself too freely regarding lynching of a Negro
Passing counterfeit money
Slapping a white woman
Fighting with a white man
Organizing sharecroppers' union
Too prosperous
Communistic activities
Killed in search of another
Writing insulting note
Talking disrespectfully to a white man
Planning to sue a white man in court
Threatening a white man
Testifying against a white man
Activity in politics
Being related to a murderer
In the neighborhood when a posse went by
Frightening children
Remaining in town where Negroes were not allowed
Defending a Negro
In 4th of July celebration
Mistaken identity
Relative of man lynched
Shot by posse in search of another
Insanity
For writing note to white woman
Boastful remarks
Talking of Chicago Riot
Trouble between white and colored cotton mill workers

For the year 1937, the excuses given for the eight lynchings were: rape, one; crime against nature and robbery, one; murder, four; wounding officer of the law, two. All these persons were in the custody of the law; three were taken from jails and five from officers outside the jails. Two were tortured with blow torches while chained to trees, and then one was shot. The others burned to death.[6]

2. *The occasions.*—The best analysis of the excuses, occasions, and

[6] Report of the Department of Records and Research of Tuskegee Institute, January 1, 1938.

causes of lynchings which has yet come from the press is *The Tragedy of Lynching,* written by a white Southerner,[7] and published under the auspices of the Southern Commission on the Study of Lynchings. It is a case study of the twenty-one lynchings in 1930, a painstaking, case-by-case analysis of the sociology of mob violence. The interested reader cannot do better than acquaint himself with the 480 pages of evidence.

The principal occasions for lynchings may be grouped under four general headings: Negro crime, white crime, economic duress, and other socio-economic disturbances.

The list of excuses makes it fairly clear that not all lynchings can be connected with Negro crime; yet, undoubtedly, many lynchings are perpetrated because it is believed that a Negro has committed some crime. But to a certain extent, Negro crime is chargeable to the white group, because of lack of proper penal and judicial procedures for Negroes, and lack of educational and cultural advantages generally. And as Dollard has pointed out,[8] a good deal of Negro crime is a reflex of the caste system. To lynch Negroes for crimes which are properly chargeable to the fact of caste is a bit of social irony worth nothing. And while it does not appear that there is a high correlation between the number of lynchings and fluctuations in the amount of Negro crime,[9] on the other hand, lynching, which is one form of white crime, does occur in the areas where the white crime rate is highest.[10]

But both Negro and white crime rates relate to numerous other sociological factors. "The highest crime rates among both Negroes and whites usually occur at the lowest economic levels.[11] The Southern Commission's study concludes: "Mobs and lynchings eventually can be eliminated if the irresponsive and irresponsible population elements can be raised into a more abundant economic and cultural life."[12] At the bottom of the whole sorry display of mob violence lies the stark fact of poverty—impoverished life, lack of education, lack of cultural opportunities, lack of money income to buy the basic necessities of life, lack of any adequate means of enjoying life. And the close relationship which appears between the annual fluctuations in economic conditions and the annual fluctuations in the number of lynchings is, as we shall see, a fairly sensitive index of a basic interaction of economic processes and race attitudes.

To be sure, other socio-economic circumstances, such as strikes or international war, have repercussions in the lynching curve. The num-

---

[7] Arthur F. Raper, of Agnes Scott College.
[8] John Dollard, *Caste and Class in a Southern Town,* Ch. XIII and XIV.
[9] Raper, *op. cit.,* pp. 33 ff and *passim.*
[10] *Ibid.,* esp. p. 33 n.
[11] *Ibid.,* p. 34.
[12] *Ibid.,* p. 38.

ber of lynchings rose sharply in 1917-19. As a matter of fact, anything which strongly affects the emotional overtone of life for the white population is likely to be the occasion for an increased number of lynchings. It is such facts as this which, with other evidence, lead to the conclusion that the real occasion for lynchings is the state of mind of white people.[13] The occasion may be anything which touches off the latent antagonism—powder explodes, whether touched off with flint and steel or with an electric spark. But beneath this occasion is the latent antagonism itself—the underlying cause.

3. *The causes of lynchings.*—Beneath the occasions for lynching, which it appears are to be found principally in the state of mind of the lynchers, are the causes of the lynching mind-set, imbedded deep in the social fabric. A significant illustration of the general fact that the basic causes of lynchings are these underlying social factors is the correlation of fluctuations in the purchasing power of cotton growers' per acre income and fluctuations in the number of lynchings of Negroes by whites in cotton states.

Race antagonisms, historically developed along lines of economic competition between racial groups distinguished by high visibility, are constantly present in the undercurrents of the social process. The caste system, constructed along racial lines, in terms of economic processes, thus appears as the actual cause of lynchings; and the annual variations indicate the degree of sensitivity of economic and racial factors within the caste framework. When times get bad, the resentment of the white group finds its expression, as we shall see, along well-grooved channels of social antagonism. Bad cotton years are nearly always accompanied by a rise in lynchings; better cotton years tend to be followed by a decline in lynchings.

The following considerations justify the use of the purchasing power of the cotton growers' per acre income as a rough index of fluctuations in economic conditions in the cotton states. The South is predominantly rural. Cotton is the principal cash crop, dominating everything else.[14] Annual fluctuations in cotton prices result in changes in farmers' incomes which subject rural populations to great vicissitudes. Not merely low incomes, but tragically irregular incomes, are the rule. "In a typical farm, considering the income of each year as successively 100, the average deviation of each year as compared to the previous one was 82% over a period of sixteen years."[15] In this economic sea of high billows and deep troughs, the mariner rides with a tiny boat and no reserve supplies. Nearly one-fourth of the income of the average tenant farmer

[13] See Arthur Raper, *The Mob Still Rides*, p. 23, quoted in part at the opening of this Appendix.
[14] R. B. Vance, *Human Geography of the South*, pp. 177, 185, 186, 200.
[15] *Ibid.*, p. 195.

TABLE 6

ANNUAL DEVIATIONS FROM NORMAL TREND IN THE PER ACRE INCOME OF THE COTTON PRODUCER IN THE HALF CENTURY ENDING 1932 (1917–18 OMITTED)[a]

YEAR	PER ACRE PRODUCTION OF COTTON (AVERAGE) IN LBS.	PRODUCERS' PRICE PER LB. AS OF AUGUST IN CENTS	PER ACRE INCOME OF PRODUCER (2) × (3) IN DOLLARS	APPROXIMATE TREND (FIVE-YEAR MOVING AVERAGE)	"TRUE" TREND (SMOOTH CURVE)	ANNUAL DEVIATIONS OF PER ACRE INCOME FROM THE "TRUE" TREND (4) − (6)	
						+	−
(1)	(2)	(3)	(4)	(5)	(6)	(7)	(8)
1885	169.9	8.39	14.24				
1886	164.3	8.06	13.24				
1887	175.1	8.55	14.97				
1888	169.5	8.50	14.06	14.33	14.46	...	.40
1889	176.9	8.55	15.12	14.84	15.22	...	.10
1890	195.5	8.59	16.79	15.07	15.29	1.50	
1891	198.7	7.24	14.38	14.88	14.88	...	.50
1892	168.7	8.34	14.06	14.52	14.46	...	.40
1893	175.3	7.00	12.37	13.51	13.37	...	1.00
1894	219.0	4.59	10.05	12.78	12.95	...	2.90
1895	172.2	7.62	13.12	12.23	12.52	.60	
1896	175.2	6.66	11.66	12.21	12.56	...	.70
1897	209.0	6.68	13.96	12.31	12.56	1.50	
1898	223.1	5.73	12.78	12.90	12.68	.10	
1899	185.0	6.98	12.98	13.04	12.93	.05	
1900	194.7	9.15	17.81	13.87	13.21	4.60	
1901	168.2	7.03	11.82	13.88	14.42	...	2.40
1902	184.7	7.60	14.03	14.89	15.03	...	1.00
1903	169.9	10.49	17.82	16.13	15.82	2.00	
1904	213.7	8.19	19.19	16.50	16.79	2.40	
1905	182.3	10.78	19.65	18.01	17.75	1.90	
1906	202.3	9.58	19.38	18.79	18.58	.80	
1907	172.9	10.36	17.81	18.90	19.21	...	1.40
1908	203.8	9.01	18.36	19.32	19.86	...	1.50
1909	156.5	13.60	21.28	20.30	20.08	1.10	
1910	176.2	13.95	24.57	20.55	21.07	3.50	
1911	215.0	9.60	20.64	21.60	21.34	...	.70
1912	201.4	11.49	23.14	22.73	21.84	1.30	
1913	192.3	12.50	24.03	21.66	21.43	2.50	
1914	216.4	7.36	15.92	22.69	21.62	...	5.70
1915	178.5	11.22	20.02	22.77	22.07	...	2.05
1916	165.6	17.34	28.72	26.82	25.82	2.90	
1917	167.4	24.12	45.40	31.51			
1918	164.1	28.93	47.47	48.07			
1919	165.9	35.41	58.75	42.01	41.75	17.00	
1920	186.7	15.92	29.72	40.73	38.72	...	9.00
1921	132.5	17.01	22.53	38.50	37.03	...	14.50
1922	148.8	22.03	34.03	36.81	35.93	...	1.90
1923	136.4	28.69	39.13	32.64	34.73	4.40	
1924	165.0	22.91	37.80	33.49	34.20	3.60	
1925	173.5	19.59	33.98	33.80	33.98	.00	
1926	192.8	12.47	24.04	33.52	32.94	...	8.90
1927	161.7	20.19	32.64	31.57	30.54	2.10	
1928	163.3	17.99	29.37	29.63	28.27	1.10	
1929	169.1	16.79	28.39	25.86	26.29	2.10	
1930	157.0	9.46	14.85	23.44	23.35	...	8.50
1931	211.5	5.66	11.97	19.17	19.67	...	7.70
1932	173.3	6.52	11.29				

[a] Basic data from the United States Department of Agriculture *Year Book*, 1935.

goes to support the credit superstructure which advances his eight
months of supplies and rations while he waits for the crop. Any cut
in his income is a serious matter. He feels it, and so do his neighbors.
A decline in the cotton growers' income per acre is an acute index of
his state of mind—that state of mind out of which comes the tendency
to lynch.

Table 6 gives the data for constructing the index of cotton growers'
income.[16] The data of columns 2 and 3 are found in the *Year
Book of Agriculture*, 1935 (United States Government Printing Office), pages 425-26. The approximate trend (5) is calculated by a computed five-year moving average centered to determine the trend point
for the fourth year of each successive group. This method of determining the statistical trend is selected because placing the trend point
opposite the third year of each group would have permitted the trend
index to reach two years into the future, whereas the psychological fact
calls for a trend which is primarily connected with the past. If the
logic of this last statement were pressed, it would call for centering
on the fifth year of the group; but this would act to vitiate the statistical result. Therefore the fourth year is used. The "true" trend, column
6, is estimated by plotting the data of columns 4 and 5, and running a
smooth curve guided by the points of the approximate trend. Measuring
the difference between the points determined by the figures of column
4 and the corresponding points on the smooth curve of the "true" trend
gives the data of columns 7 and 8. In no case does the use of the "true"
trend rather than the approximate trend give the deviation of this
index a position with reference to the lynchings index which is relatively
different from what it would have been if the approximate trend had
been used. The years 1917 and 1918 are omitted from the computations
because the World War interfered with the normal relationship between the fluctuations in cotton income and lynchings, causing both
factors to rise rapidly together, as is shown in Figure 8.

Table 6 may be read as follows: Column 6, the "true" trend, fairly
well represents the basic level on which the cotton grower is forced to
subsist over a period of years. Any betterment of his condition is indicated by a deviation above the trend, in column 7; while the figures
of column 8 point to the years in which he was forced to live below the
level of income indicated by the trend. Thus, in 1888, the per acre
income of the cotton grower was $.40 below the trend. In 1889 it had
gone up to only $.10 below the trend; in 1890 it rose to $1.50 above

---

[16] After all work on this index, and its correlation with the lynching index,
had been completed, *The Tragedy of Lynching* came into my hands, carrying
on p. 31 a brief analysis of the same facts, but without full supporting data.
I have thought it worth while to give a somewhat fuller account of the matter,
particularly because my results differ from Woofter's.

the trend, only to fall sharply to $.50 below the trend in 1891—and so on. The figures of columns 7 and 8 may be read as a rough index of the fluctuations of the per acre income of the cotton grower above and below the normal trend.

It is possible to make one further refinement of the data for the period beginning 1910. The United States Department of Agriculture [17] furnishes the index value of the American farmers' dollar in terms of his annual cost of living and production since 1910. Table 7 shows the results of translating the per acre income of the cotton grower into

TABLE 7

ANNUAL DEVIATIONS FROM NORMAL TREND IN THE PER ACRE INCOME OF THE COTTON PRODUCER, 1910–32, CORRECTED FOR COST OF LIVING AND PRODUCTION

YEAR	PER ACRE INCOME OF PRODUCER	INDEX OF PURCHAS- ING POWER[a]	PURCHAS- ING VALUE OF INCOME	FIVE-YEAR MOVING AVERAGE	SMOOTH CURVE	ANNUAL DEVIATION[b] (IN DOLLARS)	
						+	−
(1)	(2)	(3)	(4)	(5)	(6)	(7)	(8)
1910	$24.57	98	$25.55				
1911	20.64	101	20.54				
1912	23.14	100	23.14				
1913	24.03	101	23.91	$22.21	$21.91	2.00	
1914	15.92	100	15.92	20.59	21.42	...	5.50
1915	19.97	105	19.48	21.31	21.98	...	2.50
1916	28.50	124	24.08	23.47	23.48	.60	
1917	45.30	149	33.98	24.17	.....		
1918	47.40	176	29.39	26.71	.....		
1919	58.60	202	28.72	26.00	25.82	2.90	
1920	29.72	201	14.86	24.93	24.86	...	10.00
1921	22.53	152	16.68	23.03	23.18	...	6.50
1922	34.03	149	26.52	23.17	23.42	3.10	
1923	39.13	152	28.96	25.04	24.51	4.45	
1924	37.80	152	28.18	24.96	25.08	3.10	
1925	33.98	157	24.47	25.14	25.17	...	.70
1926	24.04	155	17.55	24.66	24.55	...	7.00
1927	32.64	153	24.16	23.16	23.26	.90	
1928	29.37	155	21.45	21.73	21.50	...	.05
1929	28.39	153	21.01	19.17	19.81	1.20	
1930	14.85	145	11.69	17.77	17.69	...	6.00
1931	11.97	124	10.54	15.11	15.04	...	4.50
1932	11.29	107	10.84				

[a] United States Department of Agriculture, as reported in the World Almanac, 1936, p. 365.

[b] War years omitted.

[17] *World Almanac* (1936), p. 365.

purchasing power in accordance with this index. It is unfortunate for the present study that comparable indices of the farmers' cost of living and production are not available for the period from 1890 to 1910 because, as we shall see, the statistical significance of the correlation of our two factors is markedly higher when the per acre income is corrected in terms of purchasing power.

In spite of the roughness of the data and the simplicity of the mathematical methods used, the result is a suggestive picture of the import of the annual fluctuations in terms of the position of the cotton grower above or below the long-term trend. The deviations from the long-term trend are therefore a useful rough index of the special state of mind of the cotton grower in any particular year, as to whether he feels pinched and resentful, or whether he feels a measure of enlargement of his narrowing world—a bit of psychological elbow room.

The index of overt race tension is constructed in a manner not dissimilar to the foregoing process. First of all, there appears to be no reason for believing that in normal times factors other than the economic situation fluctuate annually in accompaniment to annual fluctuations in the number of lynchings. The period of the World War was marked by a striking increase in the number of lynchings at the same time that cotton prices soared on a war-boom market (see Figure 8); but these abnormal years of race hysteria, in which, for example, Negroes were sometimes lynched for returning home in the uniform of the United States army, illustrate the fact that such extraneous factors do not normally fluctuate in accompaniment to the changed number of lynchings. White,[18] in his excellent book on lynchings studies a number of factors, mainly geographical in context and not connected with a time-sequence. He reports a correlation of lynchings and evangelical fundamentalism; but none of the factors he studies fluctuate annually to the accompaniment of annual variations in the number of lynchings. If these and other noneconomic factors influence lynchings, it is a long-term, more or less continuous pressure which is absorbed in the minimum continuing mass of lynchings below the trend line in our index.

On the other hand, certain factors give strong presumptive reason for looking for a significant correlation of the cotton income and lynching factors. First, lynchings are typically a rural phenomenon. Thus, in 1935, for example, not one Negro was lynched in a large city, or from a large city. Six lynchings occurred in counties in which were located towns of eight to fourteen thousand population; but in every instance the lynching took place in the smaller towns or in the open country. The largest urban community involved was Oxford, Mississippi, with a total population of 3,890. The other lynchings all took

[18] White, *op. cit.*

place in counties in which the largest town was 2,500 or less. In the seventy counties where occurred eighty-four lynchings in a five-year period, the only cities appearing were Vicksburg, Jackson, Birmingham, and St. Joseph.[19] This fact means that fluctuations in the income of cotton growers and fluctuations in lynchings in the cotton belt are in the same social context. Both are predominantly rural phenomena.

Secondly, the counties in which lynchings occur are relatively the poorer counties of their states, indicating that the whites as well as the Negroes in lynching counties live very close to the poverty line, probably below it. In 1935 the per capita value of products from farm and factory combined was below the respective state averages in four-fifths of the lynching counties, and in nearly four-fifths of them the per capita value of taxable property was below the state average. The per capita bank deposits and revenue receipts were below the state averages in nine-tenths of the counties in which lynchings occurred. The per capita retail trade was below the state averages in over four-fifths. Three-fourths of the counties had relatively fewer automobiles than their states, four-fifths had fewer electric subscribers, five-sixths had fewer income tax returns and fewer telephones.[20] Thus, a drop in returns to cotton growers thrusts thousands of farmers below the poverty line on which they have precariously hung; and this happens in the rural areas where the lynchings also occur. If there is a rough correspondence in fluctuations of per acre income of cotton growers and the number of lynchings of Negroes (as we shall see that there is), this correspondence may well be indicative of a significant relationship between economic conditions and race attitudes.

Reliable statistics on lynchings are available beginning with the year 1889.[21] Table 8 shows the manner of computing the index for annual deviations in the number of lynchings. The fact that the Federal Farm Board activities destroyed the validity of the market prices of cotton as an index of farmers' cash income for 1931 and succeeding years, terminates the study with the year 1930.

The interrelationship of the two indexes is shown graphically in Figure 8. A study of the two curves, which show the trends and the annual fluctuations, suggests the hypothesis that in the period before the World War, where there was a sharp decline in cotton prices in a given year, there was an immediate increase in lynchings (as in 1901);

[19] Arthur Raper, *The Mob Still Rides*, p. 15.

[20] *Ibid.*, p. 15.

[21] The National Association for the Advancement of Colored People has made the most exhaustive search for statistics on lynchings. Any bias this organization may show is a constant, having nothing to do with the relationship of the figures to cotton prices. The N.A.A.C.P. has merely listed all the lynchings reported in the press.

TABLE 8

ANNUAL DEVIATIONS FROM NORMAL TREND IN NUMBER OF LYNCHINGS OF NEGROES BY WHITES IN TEN SOUTHERN STATES, 1889–1932[a]

YEAR	NUMBER OF NEGROES LYNCHED IN TEN SOUTHERN STATES	APPROXIMATE TREND (FIVE-YEAR MOVING AVERAGE)	"TRUE" TREND (SMOOTH CURVE)	ANNUAL DEVIATION OF NUMBER OF LYNCHINGS FROM THE "TRUE" TREND (2) − (4)	
				+	−
(1)	(2)	(3)	(4)	(5)	(6)
1889	76				
1890	68				
1891	91				
1892	127	89.0	90.0	37.0	
1893	83	93.4	93.2	...	10.2
1894	98	96.2	95.0	3.0	
1895	82	90.4	91.0	...	9.0
1896	62	85.8	88.0	...	26.0
1897	104	85.6	85.0	19.0	
1898	82	80.8	82.0	...	.0
1899	74	77.6	79.0	...	5.0
1900	66	81.6	76.0	...	10.0
1901	83	72.2	74.0	9.0	
1902	56	70.0	70.8	...	14.8
1903	71	68.0	67.0	4.0	
1904	64	65.2	65.0	...	1.0
1905	52	59.2	62.0	...	10.0
1906	53	58.4	59.6	...	6.6
1907	52	59.4	58.2	...	6.2
1908	76	58.4	58.0	18.0	
1909	59	57.2	57.0	2.0	
1910	46	55.8	56.8	...	10.8
1911	46	56.0	54.0	...	8.0
1912	53	48.8	48.5	4.5	
1913	40	44.2	45.5	...	5.5
1914	36	43.4	43.0	...	7.0
1915	42	42.4	40.5	1.5	
1916	41	39.6	40.0	1.0	
1917	39	43.4	42.8	...	3.8
1918	59	49.2	...		
1919	65	48.0	...		
1920	36	50.0	51.0	...	15.0
1921	51	53.4	47.5	3.5	
1922	56	45.0	45.5	10.5	
1923	17	33.6	36.0	...	19.0
1924	8	28.6	28.5	...	20.5
1925	11	23.8	20.5	...	9.5
1926	17	13.8	15.5	1.5	
1927	16	12.2	12.0	4.0	
1928	9	11.6	12.0	...	3.0
1929	5	13.8	12.0	...	7.0
1930	22	11.8	11.0	11.0	
1931	7	9.6	9.2	...	2.2
1932	5				

[a] Basic data from the reports of the National Association for the Advancement of Colored People.

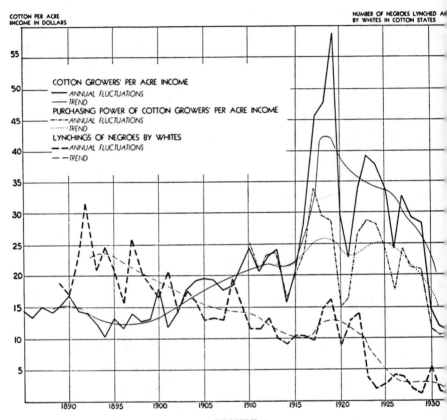

FIGURE 8

TREND IN PER ACRE INCOME OF COTTON GROWERS AND ANNUAL
FLUCTUATIONS FROM THE TREND; TREND IN NUMBER OF LYNCH-
INGS OF NEGROES AND ANNUAL FLUCTUATIONS FROM THE
TREND, 1888-1932; AND TREND IN PURCHASING POWER OF THE
COTTON GROWERS' PER ACRE INCOME WITH ANNUAL
FLUCTUATIONS, 1910-32

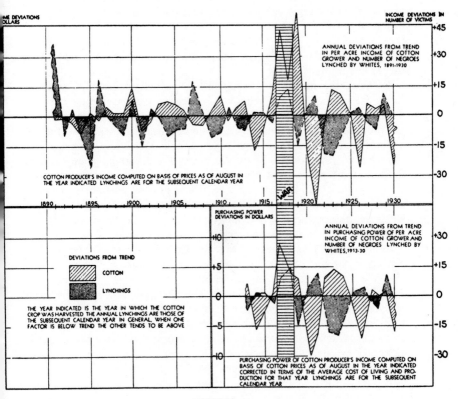

FIGURE 9

ANNUAL DEVIATIONS FROM TRENDS IN TWO FACTORS: PER ACRE
INCOME OF COTTON PRODUCERS AND NUMBER OF NEGROES
LYNCHED IN SOUTHERN STATES, 1891-1930

that where the decline was not as sharp, there was a one-year lag in the
decrease in lynchings (as in 1907); that where there was a moderate
decline which followed a single year of good prices which was preceded
by a number of lean years (as in 1891), the increase in lynchings lagged
one year; and that when a still further decline followed in 1894, the
reserves of the farmers being completely exhausted, the curve of lynchings returned sharply and at once. It would appear from a cursory
examination of the sections of the two curves for the pre-war period
that, except in 1893 and 1896, a drop in the cotton index was followed
by an increase in lynchings, principally within the twelve months of
the following year.

If, now, the indexes of variation are brought together in graphic
form, the meaning of the relationship becomes clearer. Figure 9 shows
the deviations from trend in the two factors: (a) per acre income of cotton producers and (b) number of Negroes lynched by whites in the ten
cotton states for the period 1890-1930 (World War years omitted). For
comparative purposes, the figure also shows the deviations from trend of
index (a) when corrected for purchasing power of the farmers' dollar
for the period beginning 1913. The cotton production figures are computed on the basis of the price as of August in each calendar year,
when the ginning begins. Lynchings are for the calendar year, January
to December. The lynchings of each calendar year are therefore paired
with the cotton income data of the preceding calendar year. The uniform
pairing of the indexes for this one-year lag in Figure 9 does not recognize the actual situation, however, for in three cases (as comparison
with Figure 8 makes clear) it has the effect of intruding sharp increases
of lynchings back upon comparatively prosperous cotton years rather
than of correlating these increases with the depression years which
were so marked as to have an immediate influence upon the lynching
curve, taking effect before the close of the calendar years. Thus, the sharp
increases in lynchings in the years 1894, 1901, and 1930 are directly
associated with drops in cotton income of these same calendar years;
but the uniform allowances of a one-year lag does not recognize these
exceptions. Statistical uniformity violates an important sociological fact.
Aside from these three years in which a sudden decline in cotton was
accompanied by an immediate rise in lynchings, Figure 9, in general,
appears to reveal a negative relationship between the cotton income of
a given year and the number of lynchings of the ensuing year. When
the purchasing power of the cotton growers' per acre income is above
its trend, the number of Negroes lynched by whites in cotton states
tends to be below its trend; and when cotton drops below trend, lynchings tend to rise.

The data of this study do not give startling statistical results. The
number of cases is too small—although we can hardly be expected to

produce more cases than exist! The index value of the farmers' dollar is not available earlier than 1910. The computation of a five-year moving average makes it necessary for us to drop the first three and the final years of even this short period, so that we have fully adequate data for only sixteen years. There is probably a closer correlation between the two factors than our inadequate index reveals, because the closer we get to adequate indexes, the more nearly significant does the coefficient of correlation become.

The coefficient of correlation according to the Spearman rank-difference method for the entire period from 1891 to 1930 (lynchings 1892 to 1931), omitting the two years of the war hysteria, is —.463. This relationship may not be taken as indicating a correlation sufficiently high for purposes of prediction. It is certain, however, that whatever relationship does exist between the two factors is due to the economic, not the racial factor. An increase in lynchings can hardly be said to affect the price of cotton in the preceding twelve months! Whatever causal relationship there may be supports the hypothesis that there is a genuine interrelationship between changes in economic conditions and the intensity of race attitudes. While this correlation is not high enough to suggest anything like an immutable causal connection, the study does tend to support the belief that there is a functional nexus between economic processes and overt race tension.

For the period in which we have adequate data, the results are more nearly conclusive. The Pearson product-moment method of computing the coefficient of correlation between cotton growers' per acre income and lynchings yields a result of —.61 for the period 1913-30 inclusive, war years omitted. When the coefficient of correlation is computed by the same method for the same period, using not the per acre income of the cotton producer, but the purchasing power of that income as corrected by the index value of the farmers' dollar, the result is —.6851, placing it definitely in the area of statistical significance.

Let it be remembered, however, that all that is given in this Appendix is a rough indication of the fact that, in general, when the economic situation grows more desperate (as indicated by a fall in the income of the cotton producer, and particularly, a fall in the purchasing power of that income), the deeply grooved habits of social antagonism find overt expression in an increased number of lynchings. Figure 9 shows that, when per acre income is corrected in terms of purchasing power of the farmers' dollar, the entire period from 1902 to 1928, inclusive (war years omitted), finds the cotton and lynchings indexes on opposite sides of the trend line, without exception. We are permitted to conclude that there is in this study of cotton and lynchings some solid, specific corroboration of the general thesis that economic conditions and race attitudes have been, and are, interrelated in the American South.

APPENDIX B

COMPARATIVE
RACIAL INTELLIGENCE

. . . there is no adequate proof of fundamental race differences in mentality, and . . . those differences which are found are in all probability due to culture and the social environment.   —OTTO KLINEBERG

WITHOUT entering into the devious and inconclusive arguments as to what constitutes a "race," it is assumed for the purposes of this note that a "Negro" is any person who is legally classified as a Negro in the Southern states. These are they who come to the segregated college. And the question before us is whether there is any scientifically valid or conclusive reason for holding that either Negroes or Caucasians (by this definition) are superior to the other group in intelligence.

It ought not to be necessary to discuss this question at all; but the persistence of a notion of the superiority of one of the two racial groups, and the frequency with which that notion is encountered in the American scene, demand that something more than summary dismissal be given the matter.

Perhaps the two most adequate statements of the present state of knowledge in this matter are the books by Garth and Klineberg.[1] It would have been possible merely to refer the reader to these (and other) sources; but to round out the materials for this present study, a little more than a passing reference seems demanded of the writer.

WHAT IS INTELLIGENCE?

Whether it is assumed that intelligence is a composite of a number of unitary abilities, or whether it is assumed that intelligence is itself a unitary phenomenon, in either case, it must be admitted that the actual functioning of mental processes at any given stage of an individual's development is not merely a matter of innate ability but also a matter of actual experience. Intelligence, the actual performance of intellectual processes, to an important degree is a function of the experience of the individual. And that experience is gained in terms of the society in which the individual lives. Intelligence, by which we mean the individual's "ability to learn and to utilize in new situations knowledge or skill acquired by learning" and "his selective adaptation through acquired knowledge,"[2] is actually built up through the day-to-day experiences of the individual. To be sure, psychological experimentation and study have established the fact that individuals (without reference to racial groupings) do vary greatly in their innate capacities, that is,

[1] T. R. Garth, *Race Psychology* and Otto Klineberg, *Race Differences.*
[2] Committee of the American Psychological Association, quoted by Garth, *op. cit.*, p. 70.

that the potentialities of development are significantly different as between individuals at birth. But this is not a racial matter; and, further, scientific study has also shown that the actual development of the individual toward the limits of his own potentialities is significantly affected by the social milieu in which he grows up. The actual intellectual performance of any individual at a given stage of his growth is obviously a direct product of that individual's experience. Potentialities are, to an important degree, fixed by heredity; but the actual pattern of intellectual processes which is intelligence in operation (the only intelligence we know at the present time), is, to an important degree, affected by the experiences of the maturing individual.

There are, then, two points at which differences between racial groups in intelligence may be looked for: one, the inherited biologically determined potentialities, and the other, the social milieu in terms of which the individuals in a racial group develop. It is the verdict of such scientific knowledge as we now possess that whatever differences may appear between white and Negro in America are to be understood in terms of the second of these factors, not the first. Garth puts it this way:

Differences so far found in the intelligence of races can be easily explained by the influence of nurture and of selection.[3]

The conclusion which must be drawn in the light of such scientific investigations as have been made is that there are no sure evidences of real racial differences in mental traits. While heredity operates according to laws, qualitatively considered, mental traits are distributed among all races, for all possess these human traits. Such a trait as intelligence, though really a racial possibility in all races, has been isolated and emphasized in some more than in others. But this is not saying that it could not be so emphasized in the unfortunate race.[4]

Much of the difference found in the results of studies of racial differences in mental traits is due to racial mobility, so that the one race has a temporary advantage over the other. . . . Removal of the barriers causing the eddies causes the emphasis to dissolve in the common racial stream.[5]

Klineberg's conclusion is quoted in part at the head of this Appendix. It agrees with Garth's statements in maintaining that, as far as any scientific information now available is concerned, there is no evidence to support the belief that biological inheritance gives one race a superiority over the other; and both men agree that the weight of the evidence suggests that such differences as now appear between racial groups

[3] Ibid., p. 84.
[4] Ibid., p. 211.
[5] Ibid., p. 221.

can be accounted for readily by the cumulative effect of differential opportunities and experiences. The converging lines of evidence may be summarized for our purposes somewhat as follows.

WHAT IS THE VERDICT OF COMPARATIVE MEASUREMENT?

It was long alleged that one or another racial or national stock was superior to others; but the allegation rested on assertion and protest rather than upon validated scientific evidence. More recently, anthropology entered the field, and following a period of disagreement and controversy, a clear opinion has emerged that, as far as anthropology is concerned, there is no basis for assuming that any racial group is innately superior to another in intellectual abilities. As far as anthropological and physiological data are concerned, the case for racial inequality is not proved;[6] and as Boas puts it, "The differences between races are so small that they lie *within the narrow range in the limits of which all forms may function equally well.*"[7] Believers in alleged racial differences in intellectual capacity find no support in the data of anthropology.

The conclusions of intelligence testing support the same point, but for slightly different reasons. Whereas anthropology tells us that all races share the relatively narrow range within which excellence of performance may be expected; psychological testing starts with the fact of known wide variations between individuals from moron to genius, and goes on to suggest that while actual aggregate differences between racial groups in intellectual performance are now indicated by much intelligence testing, these differences in performance do not point to innate or racial disparities. They probably are indexes of social and environmental differences which are subject to modification with changes in the culture.

This is to be expected both from the nature of intelligence testing and the nature of intelligence itself. Consider first the nature of intelligence testing. As Boas[8] and Pintner[9] summarize the conclusions, intelligence tests do not measure, and probably never will measure, innate intellectual capacities and abilities apart from the actual development of these abilities and capacities in terms of experience. Pintner says bluntly, "We shall never be able to make an intelligence test absolutely independent of environmental factors." In other words, when an attempt is made to compare one racial group with another, in terms of their performance on intelligence tests, there is legitimate reason to

---

[6] Klineberg, *op. cit.*, pp. I-III.
[7] Franz Boas, *Anthropology and Modern Life*, p. 41. Italics added.
[8] *Ibid.*, p. 56.
[9] Rudolph Pintner, *Intelligence Testing*, p. 97.

infer that the differences measured may actually be differences in the respective environments of the two groups.

This last point is of particular importance when we consider it along with the nature of the process by which intelligence is built. The actual fabric for thinking, the thing called intelligence, is not substantially some mysterious "given" factor or faculty; it is in large measure a developed pattern of action. The plying shuttle of native equipment carries the thread of individual experience through the warp furnished by the surrounding culture, and the resultant pattern of action which an individual uses as he approaches any situation (that is, as he thinks about it, studies it, uses his intelligence) is patently affected by the social process in which the individual has grown up. If the social warp for an individual has been one which afforded limited opportunities, his patterns of performance will be relatively simple; just as a more rich and varied milieu would tend to develop richness and variety and fineness of functioning. If, then, social usage made sharp and consistent distinctions between the societal patterns afforded to a large group of individuals, it is not impossible that the achievement of the group would reflect the distinction. Thus, with the known fact of astounding racial disparities under the American caste system, the marvel is that the patterns of intellectual activity for the two castes are not actually separated by a wide gulf. Psychological measurement to date has indicated a very large degree of overlapping, and a practical identity of range. The present difference in distribution, which is all that the most fanatical advocate of white superiority can possibly claim, may merely mirror the disparities of caste rather than an alleged immutable biological inheritance. Much larger differences between the two groups might have been expected merely because of the confining influence of caste and its accompanying practices.

Furthermore, the known influence of environment upon changes or variations in I.Q., while not conclusive in and of itself, furnishes another significant strand of corroborative evidence. Kilpatrick has summarized the data thus:

The psychological researches into the "problem of heredity and environment" show that with identical twins, admittedly equal at the start, environmental differences have brought about a difference in measured I.Q. as much as twenty-four points. Many studies of siblings, as well as the comparison of children found in "good" as compared with "poor" or "bad" homes corroborate these effects of environment on "general ability." The evidence seems conclusive that the kind of intelligence measured by the intelligence tests may and perhaps generally does improve when the environmental conditions are culturally improved.[10]

[10] William H. Kilpatrick, "Intelligence, Individual Differences, and Democracy," unpublished MSS.

These converging lines of evidence afford a key to alleged racial differences in intelligence, and a key to better educational procedures. Since disparities in the culture now are reflected in disparities in intellectual performance, the task of an educational system which is concerned with the ethical demands of the situation—and indeed, the task of American society if it is to give effect to its democratic profession—is to work to correct the social iniquities which cause the present intellectual inequities. When the cultural opportunities for all Negroes become substantially equivalent to the similar opportunities for all whites, it will then be appropriate to measure the comparative levels of achievement and draw inferences regarding the biologically inherited abilities of the two racial groups.

APPENDIX C

TALLADEGA COLLEGE COUNCIL: A PROGRESS REPORT

Democracy must be born anew every generation, and education is the midwife. —JOHN DEWEY

EVERY embodiment of a high ideal falls short of the goals it seeks to reach; and the individuals concerned with the creation and operation of the College Council at Talladega College are first to disavow any claims to perfection in their venture. The value of the effort is to be found in the fact that it gives concrete evidence to support the belief that something significant along this line can be done. The reader is urged to appraise this particular enterprise with rigor and with candor, but to appraise it in terms of its own historical setting. It is believed that the administrative departures outlined in this Appendix are a distinct step forward for this particular college.

One other word of qualification—even if this plan were perfect for Talladega, it would not necessarily fit elsewhere. Democracy in operation involves as a basic essential the possibility of variability in structure and in operation. Democracy courts the creative deviant, for therein lies the possibility of progress.

THE BACKGROUND

Talladega College is one of the colleges founded and nurtured by the American Missionary Association. While at least one member of the board of trustees of the college has always been elected from the citizenry of the town of Talladega, the growth of campus autonomy has been a slow, healthy process, marked by a gradual transference of the center of gravity of control from the parent body to the trustees of the college, and from them to the campus. The campus, in its turn, has included the trustees and the Association in its purview, in order not merely to maintain the values of historic connections, but also to insure the widest and most inclusive thinking on all matters of fundamental concern.

For many years, the authoritative body on the campus was the administrative committee, composed of the president, dean, treasurer and two elected faculty members. Subject to the board of trustees, this committee was charged with major and minor decisions on the campus, and with carrying out the decisions made by the Association and the trustees. The Association, whose executive secretaries commonly sat on the board of trustees as well, contributed its stimulating guidance through supervision of financial matters and visitation by the Association's field representatives. It was an administrative procedure with dual external control and committee local control which had more justification in the logic of operational evolution than in formal logic; but it worked, and worked well.

In 1933, the Association and the trustees jointly desired to take advantage of the transition period which usually accompanies a change of campus administration, to develop a larger degree of campus autonomy. Accordingly, they charged the president with increased responsibilities, giving him commensurate authority, and promising to stand by with critical friendliness as new campus procedures were worked out.

THE EXPLORATORY STAGES

No attempt was made to draw up a blueprint or to launch a scheme, in advance of a study of the needs and the possibilities of the local situation. But the exploratory study was launched with a controlling idea, namely, that democracy in administrative procedures demands that the freedom of action and decision be passed right on down the line from narrowest to broadest—president to faculty to students to society. If the flow of authority and responsibility is dammed up at any point along the line, it backs up and swamps the whole enterprise. A second idea, not clearly formulated at the beginning, but which emerged with peculiar forcefulness in the course of the study, was that whatever was to be done must be genuine—there must be no pulling of puppet strings, no going through the motions of democracy without the essential spirit of the thing as well.

After several faculty discussions and some student discussions two commissions were appointed. One, composed exclusively of faculty members, was asked to study the relationship of the faculty to the administration and the trustees. The second, which included an equal number of students and instructors, was asked to study all areas of student life and to bring in recommendations. After five months of study the two commissions reported, giving not merely general summaries of the areas they had been asked to explore, but also making specific recommendations for action. None of the specific recommendations for action were carried out at once. Instead, the whole body of data was taken under advisement by the president, the administrative committee, and the faculty. It soon appeared that the crux of the whole matter lay in the question of how to implement the democratic idea, so that all persons on the campus might have some share in making significant decisions.

As a means of studying the commissions' reports, mass meetings were tried. They proved unwieldy, but of some value. An essay contest was announced, open to all students, asking for essays on one of two subjects: "If I Were President of Talladega" or "A Proposal for Student Participation in the Government of Talladega College." The essays proved to be of little value, since they were, for the most part, merely patterned after student government projects which students had known in some high schools; and the Talladega students had already made it amply clear that they agreed with the administration in preferring to have nothing at all rather than a puppet show in which the administration and faculty made the decisions and the students governed themselves accordingly. There was a genuine desire for some means of getting the administration, the faculty, and the students to share in the governing process on an equal footing.

As the study proceeded, some progress was registered in the rejection of four possibilities:

1. Student self-government in which a definite area of college life is delimited, and within that area the students are placed in nominal control, always subject to the rules and supervision of the faculty and administration.

2. Faculty government of the college, in which the whole faculty, corporately, or delegated persons in the faculty as a committee or governing body, become the seat of control for the college.

3. Administrative control, in which the President or the Administrative Committee which is dominated by *ex officiis* administrative officers, direct the life of the college.

4. Student government not merely of themselves but of the college, which would result from any alleged democratic process which admitted students on a par with other members of the college family, and then arrived at decisions by majority vote.

As one or another of these possibilities was rejected, that rejection served to correct a corresponding misapprehension of the meaning of democracy. At one time or another, each of these ideas was advanced by some partisan, not always a person who would benefit directly from the adoption of the proposal. Throughout the discussion, the fear that "the other group" might outvote, or outtalk "the rest of us" lay behind a panicky insistence that "my group" must have at least a final veto over any proposal. This led to two more insights:

5. Majority votes, which are sometimes instruments for discovering popular wishes, are frequently devices for overriding minorities.

6. The process of democratically discovering the best mode of action in a given situation must therefore include the critical thinking of all persons and groups concerned in the matter; and if possible, no decision should be accepted when a significant minority opposes it in the name of the general welfare.

LAUNCHING THE COUNCIL

As the second year of study and discussion drew toward its close, a proposal from the campus was brought before the board of trustees, whose members had continually been apprised of the progress of campus discussions and were intelligently sympathetic with the attempt to meet the problem. As approved by the Trustees in legislative action which chartered the College Council (not "Student Council"), the policy-forming body on the campus is made up as follows: Six administrative officers (president, dean, comptroller, superintendent of buildings and grounds, men's counselor, women's counselor) who serve *ex officiis*; six faculty members, elected by the teaching faculty; and six students, one man and one woman elected by student vote from each of the three upper classes. These eighteen persons meet whenever called, and they are called whenever any Council member is informed by any campus resident that there is a felt need. They may meet four successive evenings, and not meet again for six weeks.

If the Council were to decide questions by voting, it is clear that the students are badly outweighed; or that either of the other two groups is badly outweighed if the students and one of the remaining groups should make common cause. But from the start, it was felt that instead of pushing things through by voting, the Council would think and discuss matters until a clear consensus of opinion emerged, not unlike the feeling of a "concern" in a Quaker meeting. In practice and in theory, that meant that one member—any member—of the Council could veto a proposal. One student, or one instructor, or one administrator, as long as he has conscientious scruples or logically defensible reasons for rejecting a proposal, can refuse to approve it. In the two and one-half years of operation of the College Council, no vote has ever been taken. Discussion clears the issues and reveals the trend of opinion. As the group mind begins to emerge, an attempt is made to formulate the thinking in a form acceptable to all. As long as there are objections, the matter is not settled; but when objections have been met, the secretary records agreement on the issue. Consensus is a satisfactory answer to the fears of groups which might be outvoted; it is a good way to meet the deficiencies of the majority-voting process.

A further safeguard lies in the fact that the meetings of the Council are open. There is never an "executive session." All discussions are carried on and all decisions made in full view and hearing of all who wish to come. The agenda of each meeting are posted in advance on six bulletin boards on different parts of the campus; and all interested persons are free to attend the meetings. Moreover, there is full opportunity and encouragement for persons from the floor to join in the discussion and to make their contributions at any point in a discussion. The attendance of students, faculty, and staff as participants in the meeting from the floor, has varied from a low of half a dozen to a high of about 90 percent of the campus population. The consensus of the eighteen Council members around the table must be arrived at in the light of the whole discussion, and in the presence of interested parties.

THE COUNCIL IN OPERATION

As actually functioning in these two and one-half years of its life, the Council has never met a stalemate. Not infrequently an evening of discussion will fail to uncover a consensus; but the educational process goes on in the dormitories and homes and the adjourned meetings which hold forth at a street corner or over the coca-cola bottles at the College Inn, and when the discussion is resumed the next evening, new insights are available. A particularly knotty problem once engaged the Council for four successive evenings. Simpler questions have been settled in as little as five minutes.

The range of subjects discussed covers the entire gamut of academic life and the wider campus—everything from athletic policies and fraternity life to use of the library, the systems of marking and promotion, and relationships of college and town. Nothing of general interest is ruled out. If a matter is of limited interest, it is usually referred to some smaller group for decision, unless the decision will affect a general policy or the program of a larger group, and the larger interest is thus involved. On occasion, a matter is taken to a student-faculty-staff mass meeting, where it may be presented through a panel discussion or a series of speakers. At other times, a general policy may be enunciated by the Council and the matter referred to the appropriate committee with power to act. Or the Council may arrive at a decision and refer the execution of the policy to an administrative officer. Or again, the Council may uncover a consensus of opinion regarding fraternities and sororities, and refer its thinking to the organizations concerned with a recommendation for their consideration.

A distinction is drawn between the making of policies and the administering of the same. The College Council is not an administrative body; it is a deliberative body. It formulates policies. All policies formulated on the campus are formulated by the College Council or under its surveillance. The machinery for carrying out the policies is made as simple as possible. The regular administrative officers—president, dean, comptroller, registrar, men's and women's counselors, superintendent of buildings and grounds, et al.—carry through their routine tasks in accordance with the objectives indicated by the Council. The manner of carrying out the objectives is sometimes suggested by the Council, but usually left to the administrative officer. The same freedom of choice of tools and procedures is given to the several committees. For the most part, if a committee's operation touches directly upon student life, students are members of the committee in at least as large numbers as faculty or staff persons. Every attempt is made to insure that the administrative machinery will be as inclusive and as considerate of all persons in its functioning as the Council is in its deliberations.

By this distinction between the determination of policies and their execution, the college also saves much valuable time and energy. For example, the Council is not asked to decide administrative matters that fall within the province of the social committee; but the social committee may wish to ask the Council to settle matters of policy for it from time to time. The Athletic Council makes up its schedules and carries through its season's program of intercollegiate and intramural sports, relieving the College Council entirely of all administrative detail and responsibility; but the policies determined upon by the College Council in the presence of and with the concurrence of the Athletic Council, are the guide for all administrative decisions of the Athletic Council.

Thus, at the college, the College Council makes the decisions in the clear light of full campus opinion and thinking and in the presence of interested parties. The policies are then executed by the administrative officers and committees specifically charged with responsibility for seeing that the particular policy is carried into action.

The relation to the trustees is an interesting one. As long as the legal responsibility for the welfare of the institution rests with the trustees, it is clearly unwise for them to abrogate their prerogatives of control. Accordingly, wherever there is now in operation a specific action by the trustees affecting a matter of policy, the Council may discuss and subsequently make recommendations to the trustees, action being taken only in the light of the trustees' resultant decision. This sometimes means delaying decisions on important matters for as much as six months. It is conceivable that some urgent crisis might make quicker action imperative; but in such an emergency, the college is just as well off with its Council as without it, for in either case, the same consultation with an off-campus group is necessary. Every effort is made to include the trustees in the process of campus thinking. The full minutes of Council meetings, which are posted on the campus after each meeting, are also mailed to the trustees so that they are at all times aware of discussions and decisions. Actions of the board of trustees with reference to the College Council have included four varieties: (1) specific action upon a specific request from the College Council; (2) enunciation of a policy with the request that the Council implement it; (3) delegation to the Council of full authority to determine and execute policies in a given matter; (4) joint conference with the Council in a concerted effort to discover a joint consensus.

The president has not abrogated his right to make decisions and to guide the college; but he has refused to bear the burden exclusively or limit the opportunity for such deciding and guiding. He has shared both opportunity and responsibility. He has insisted that he cannot morally act to guide or direct the college except as a participant in an inclusive democratic process. He is one member of the Council, and one member of the board of trustees. The idea is only four years old on Talladega's campus, and in its particular embodiment, at the time of this writing it has had only two and one-half years of life and growth. But it is a relatively effective tool of democratic administrative procedure. Few will doubt that it is superior to the machinery it replaced. Increasingly it appears to justify itself as an administrative device in line with the educational objectives outlined in Chapter XI.

BIBLIOGRAPHY

BIBLIOGRAPHY

SECTION I lists alphabetically all references to works quoted or cited in this book. Section II gives a brief bibliography of principal works in nine areas. In a very few instances, certain works are cited twice in this Bibliography, but usually a book or article is cited under the heading to which it principally belongs.

SECTION I. WORKS QUOTED OR CITED IN THIS BOOK

Allen, James S., The Negro Question in the United States (New York: International Publishers, 1936). 224 pp.

Arlitt, Ada Hart, "On Need of Caution in Establishing Race Norms," *Journal of Applied Psychology,* V (1921), 179-83.

Bagley, W. C., "The Army Tests and the Pro-Nordic Propaganda," *Educational Review,* LXVII (April, 1924), 179-87.

Baker, Frank E., "Has Education Failed?" *Social Frontier,* III (April, 1937), 199-201.

Baker, Paul E., Negro-white Adjustment (New York: Association Press, 1934). 266 pp.

Beard, Augustus Field, Crusade of Brotherhood (Boston: Pilgrim Press, 1909).

Beckham, Albert Sidney, "A Study of Race Attitudes in Negro Children of Adolescent Age," *Journal of Abnormal and Social Psychology,* XXIX (April-June, 1934), 18-29.

Bennett, Charles A., History of Manual and Industrial Education up to 1870 (Peoria: Manual Arts Press, 1926).

Bernard, L. L., "Attitudes and the Redirection of Behaviour," in Social Attitudes, ed. by K. Young (New York: Henry Holt & Co., 1931).

Boas, Franz, Anthropology and Modern Life (New York: W. W. Norton & Co., 1928). 246 pp.

Bode, Boyd H., Democracy as a Way of Life (New York: The Macmillan Co., 1937). "Kappa Delta Pi Lecture Series."

Bond, Horace Mann, The Education of the Negro in the American Social Order (New York: Prentice Hall, 1934). 501 pp.

—— "The Curriculum and the Negro Child," *Journal of Negro Education,* IV (April, 1935), 159-68.

—— "The Influence of Personalities on the Public Education of Negroes in Alabama," *Journal of Negro Education,* VI (April, 1937).

—— "The Liberal Arts College for Negroes: A Social Force," an address at the University of Louisville Municipal College Centennial Celebration, April 30, 1937.

Bonser, Frederick G., Fundamental Values in Industrial Education (New York: Teachers College, Columbia University, 1914). "Technical Education Bulletin," No. 10.

Bowen, Trevor, Divine White Right (New York: Harper & Brothers, 1934). 310 pp.

Brooks, William E., Lee of Virginia (Indianapolis: Bobbs-Merrill Co., 1932).

Bryant, Ora B., Jr., "News Items about Negroes in White Urban and Rural Newspapers," Journal of Negro Education, IV (April, 1935), 169-78.

Burks, R. S., "Relative Influence of Nature and Nurture upon Mental Development: A Comparative Study of Foster-Parents-Foster-Child Resemblance and True-Parents-True-Child Resemblance," Twenty-seventh Yearbook of the National Society for the Study of Education (Bloomington, Illinois: Public School Publishing Co., 1928), pp. 103-218.

Cade, John B., "The College: Obligations and Relations to the Community," Quarterly Review of Higher Education among Negroes, IV (April, 1936), 91-96.

Caliver, Ambrose, A Personnel Study of Negro College Students (New York: Teachers College, Columbia University, 1931).

Canby, Henry S., Alma Mater (New York: Farrar and Rinehart, 1936). 259 pp.

Capen, S. P., "Obligation of the University to American Democracy," School and Society, XLI (June 22, 1935), 817-22.

Cater, James T. (ed.), The College and the Social Process (Talladega, Alabama: Talladega College Press, 1934).

Chicago Commission on Race Relations, Negro in Chicago: A Study of Race Relations and a Race Riot (Chicago: University of Chicago Press, 1922). 672 pp.

Childs, John L., Education and the Philosophy of Experimentalism (New York: Century Co., 1931). 225 pp.

Coffman, Lotus D., "Province of Higher Education," Elementary School Journal, XXXVII (February, 1937), 411-14.

Cools, Victor G., "Why Negro Education Has Failed," Educational Review, LXVIII (December, 1924), 254-59.

—— "Negro Education and Low Living Standards," Educational Review, LXXII (September, 1926), 102-7.

Crawford, George W., Talladega Manual of Vocational Guidance (Talladega, Alabama: Talladega College Press, 1936). 146 pp.

Curti, Merle, "Social Ideals of American Educators," Report of the Commission on the Social Studies, American Historical Association (New York: Charles Scribner's Sons, 1935), Part X. 613 pp.

Daniel, W. A., The Education of Negro Ministers (New York: Doran & Co., 1925).

Dashield, J. F., "Racial Differences as Measured by the Downey Will-Temperament Test," Journal of Applied Psychology, VII (1923), 30-53.

Davis, John W., "Problems in the Collegiate Education of Negroes," West Virginia State College Bulletin, June, 1937.

Davis, Michael M., "Problems of Health Service for Negroes," Journal of Negro Education, VI (July, 1937), 436-44.

Davis, Thomas E., "Some Racial Attitudes of Negro College and Grade School Students," Journal of Negro Education, VI (April, 1937), 157-65.

Dession, G. H., "Making a Radical," Saturday Review of Literature, XV (April 3, 1937), 11.

Dewey, John, Human Nature and Conduct (New York: Henry Holt & Co., 1922).

—— Experience and Nature (Chicago: Open Court Publishing Co., 1925).

—— Individualism, Old and New (New York, 1930).

Dewey, John, "Education and Social Change," *Social Frontier,* III (May, 1937), 235-39.
—— My Pedagogic Creed (Chicago: Flanagan).
Dollard, John, Caste and Class in a Southern Town (New Haven: Yale University Press, 1937). 502 pp.
Douglass, H. Paul, Christian Reconstruction in the South (Boston: Pilgrim Press, 1909).
Doyle, Bertram W., "The Etiquette of Race Relations—Past, Present, and Future," *Journal of Negro Education,* V (April, 1936), 191-208.
Dublin, Louis E., "The Health of the Negro," *Annals* of the American Academy of Political and Social Science, CXL (November, 1928), 77-85.
DuBois, W. E. B., Souls of Black Folk (Chicago: McClurg & Co., 1907).
—— "The Segregated Negro World," *World Tomorrow,* VI (May, 1923), 136-38.
—— "The Field and Function of the Negro Colleges," *Fisk News,* VI (June, 1933), 1 ff.
—— Black Reconstruction (New York: Harcourt Brace & Co., 1935). 746 pp.
—— "Does the Negro Need Separate Schools?" *Journal of Negro Education,* IV (July, 1935), 328-36.
Ellwood, Charles A., Psychology of Human Society (New York: D. Appleton & Co., 1925).
Embree, Edwin R., Brown America: The Story of a New Race (New York: Viking Press, 1931). 311 pp.
Faris, Ellsworth, "Natural History of Race Prejudice," in Ebony and Topaz, ed. by Charles S. Johnson (New York: Opportunity, 1927), pp. 89-94.
—— "The Concept of Social Attitudes," in Social Attitudes, ed. by K. Young (New York: Henry Holt & Co., 1931). pp. 3-16.
Feldman, Herman, Racial Factors in American Industry (New York: Harper & Brothers, 1931). 318 pp.
Frank, L. K., "General Education Today," *Social Frontier,* III (April, 1937), 209-10.
Franklin, Benjamin, Proposals Relating to the Education of Youth in Pennsylvania (Philadelphia: 1749).
Fraser, Mowat G., College of the Future (New York: Columbia University Press, 1937).
Frazier, E. Franklin, "The Negro Community: A Cultural Phenomenon," *Social Forces,* VII (March, 1929), 415-20.
Freemon, Frank N., *et al.,* "The Influence of Environment on the Intelligence, School Achievement, and Conduct of Foster Children," *Twenty-seventh Yearbook* of the National Society for the Study of Education (Bloomington, Illinois: Public School Publishing Co., 1928).
Gaines, Francis P., The Southern Plantation: A Study in the Development and Accuracy of a Tradition (New York: Columbia University Press, 1925).
Garth, Thomas Russell, Race Psychology: A Study of Racial Mental Differences (New York: McGraw-Hill Book Co., 1931). 260 pp.
Goodsell, Willystine, The Education of Women (New York: The Macmillan Company, 1923). 378 pp.
Gover, Mary, "Trend of Mortality among Southern Negroes since 1920," *Journal of Negro Education,* VI (July, 1937), 272-80.
Graham, William L., "The Relation of Paine College to Its Community," *Quarterly Review of Higher Education among Negroes,* IV (July, 1936), 129-33.
Hawk, E. Q., Economic History of the South (New York: Prentice-Hall, 1934). 557 pp.

Haynes, George E., "The Church and Negro Progress," *Annals* of the American Academy of Political and Social Science, CXL (November, 1928), 264-71.

Herndon, Angelo, Let Me Live (New York: International Publishers, 1937).

Hoffman, F. L., "Race Traits and Tendencies of the American Negro," *Journal of the American Economic Association,* XI (1896), 1-329.

Holmes, Dwight O. W., The Evolution of the Negro College (New York: Teachers College, Columbia University, 1934). 221 pp. "Teachers College Contributions to Education," No. 609.

Horowitz, Eugene L., Development of Attitude toward the Negro (New York: 1936). "Archives of Psychology," No. 194. 47 pp.

Hundley, D. R., Social Relations in Our Southern States (New York: H. B. Price, 1860).

Hurlock, Elizabeth B., "The Will-Temperament of White and Negro Children," *Pedagogical Seminary and Journal of Genetic Psychology,* XXXVIII (December, 1930), 91-100.

Hutchins, R. M., The Higher Learning in America (New Haven: Yale University Press, 1936).

Jernegan, Marcus W., "Slavery and the Beginnings of Industrialism in the American Colonies," *American Historical Review,* XXV (January, 1920), 220-40.

Johnson, Charles S., "The Development of Personality of Students in Segregated Communities," *Quarterly Review of Higher Education among Negroes,* V (April, 1936), 67-71.

—— (ed.), Ebony and Topaz (New York: Opportunity, 1926).

——, E. R. Embree, and W. W. Alexander, The Collapse of Cotton Tenancy (Chapel Hill: University of North Carolina Press, 1935). 81 pp.

Johnson, James Weldon, "The Lynching Shame," *Current History,* XIX (January, 1924), 596-601.

Jones, Thomas Jesse, Negro Education, a Study of the Private and Higher Schools for Colored People in the United States, Bureau of Education *Bulletin,* Nos. 38 and 39. (Washington: United States Government Printing Office, 1916). 2 vols. 724 pp.

Jordan, David Starr, War's Aftermath.

Journal of Negro Education, "Survey of Negro Higher Education," II (July, 1933), 225-425.

—— "Survey of Health and Health Education of the Negro," Vol. VI (July, 1937).

Kallen, Horace M., College Prolongs Infancy, "John Day Pamphlets," No. 16. (New York: John Day Co., 1932). 28 pp.

Katz, Daniel, and F. H. Allport, Students' Attitudes (Syracuse: Craftsman's Press, 1931).

—— and Kenneth Brady, "Racial Prejudice and Racial Stereotypes," *Journal of Abnormal and Social Psychology,* XXX (July-September, 1935), 175-93.

Keith, Arthur, Place of Prejudice in Modern Civilization (New York: John Day Co., 1931). 55 pp.

Kelsey, Francis W. (ed.), Latin and Greek in American Education (New York: The Macmillan Co., 1911).

Kilpatrick, William H., "Education in the Social Process and the Lessons for the College," in The College and the Social Process, ed. by J. T. Cater (Talladega, Alabama: Talladega College Press, 1934).

—— "The Underlying Philosophy of Coöperative Activities for Community Improvement," Introduction to Youth Serves the Community, by Paul R. Hanna (New York: Appleton-Century Co., 1936).

Kilpatrick, William H., (ed.), Teacher and Society; First Yearbook, John Dewey Society (New York: Appleton-Century Co., 1937).

—— "Education as Living for Better Living," *Educational Method,* XVII (January, 1938), 149-56.

—— "Intelligence, Individual Differences, and Democracy." Unpublished MS. 10 pp.

Kinder, J. S., The Internal Administration of the Liberal Arts College (New York: Teachers College, Columbia University, 1934).

Klineberg, Otto, An Experimental Study of Speed and Other Factors in "Racial" Differences (New York: 1928). "Archives of Psychology," No. 93. 111 pp.

—— Race Differences (New York: Harper & Brothers, 1935). 367 pp.

—— Negro Intelligence and Selective Migration (New York: Columbia University Press, 1935). 66 pp.

Krout, M. H., "Race and Culture: A Study in Mobility, Segregation, and Selection," *American Journal of Sociology,* XXXVII (1931-32), 175-89.

"Ku Klux Conspiracy, The," Report of the Joint Select Committee [of Congress] on the Condition of Affairs in the Late Insurrectionary States (Washington: United States Government Printing Office, 1872). 13 vols.

Lasker, Bruno, Race Attitudes in Children (New York: Henry Holt & Co., 1929).

Lewin, Kurt, "Psycho-sociological Problems of a Minority Group," *Character and Personality,* III (March, 1935), 175-87.

Locke, Alain, "The Dilemma of Segregation," *Journal of Negro Education,* IV (July, 1935), 406-11.

Long, Howard Hale, "Some Psychogenic Hazards of Segregated Education of Negroes," *Journal of Negro Education,* IV (July, 1935), 336-50.

Love, John L., The Disfranchisement of the Negro (Washington: American Negro Academy, 1899). "Occasional Papers," No. 6. (In Bryson Library of Teachers College, Columbia University, New York.)

Löwe, Adolf, The Price of Liberty: A German on Contemporary Britain (London: Hogarth Press, 1937). "Day to Day Pamphlets," No. 36.

Lowell, A. Lawrence, At War with Academic Traditions in America (Cambridge: Harvard University Press, 1934). 358 pp.

McAlpin, Alice S., "Changes in the I. Q. of Negro Children," *Journal of Negro Education,* I (April, 1932), 44-48.

McConn, Max, College or Kindergarten? (New York: New Republic, 1929).

Martin, Everett Dean, Meaning of a Liberal Education (New York: W. W. Norton & Co., 1926). 319 pp.

Mead, Margaret, Sex and Temperament in Three Primitive Societies (New York: Morrow, 1935). 335 pp.

Miller, Kelly, "The Causes of Segregation," *Current History,* XXV (March, 1927), 827-33.

—— "The Reorganization of the Higher Education of the Negro in Light of Changing Conditions," *Journal of Negro Education,* V (July, 1936), 484-94.

Missouri, State of, "Negro Industrial Commission Report," *Monthly Labor Review* of the United States Department of Labor, XX (May, 1925), 988-89.

National Association for the Advancement of Colored People, Thirty Years of Lynching in the United States: 1889-1918 (New York: National Association for the Advancement of Colored People, 1919). 105 pp. Out of print.

—— Annual Supplements to Thirty Years of Lynching in the United States: 1889-1918 (New York: National Association for the Advancement of Colored People, 1919-35).

North, Sue, "Damyankees in Negro Schools," *American Mercury,* XXXV (June, 1935), 198-204.

Odum, Howard W., Social and Mental Traits of the Negro (New York: Columbia University Press, 1910). 302 pp.

―――― An American Epoch (New York: Henry Holt & Co., 1930). 379 pp.

―――― Southern Regions of the United States (Chapel Hill: University of North Carolina Press, 1936). 664 pp.

Oldham, J. H., Christianity and the Race Problem (London: Student Christian Movement, 1924).

Otto, Max C., "Philosopher of a New Age," Social Frontier, III (May and June, 1937), 230-32, 264-66.

Parham, Bettie E., "How the Conservative Negro Intellectual of the South Feels about Racial Segregation," Social Forces, XIV (December, 1935), 268-72.

Park, Robert E., "The Bases of Race Prejudice," Annals of the American Academy of Political and Social Science, CXL (November, 1928), 11-20.

―――― "Human Nature, Attitudes, and the Mores," in Social Attitudes, ed. by K. Young (New York: Henry Holt & Co., 1931).

Peterson, Joseph, "A Comparison of the Abilities of White and Colored Children," Comparative Psychological Monographs, Vol. I, Series 5 (July, 1923).

Phillips, Ulrich B., Life and Labor in the Old South (Boston: Little, Brown and Co., 1927).

Piaget, Jean, The Moral Judgment of the Child (London: Paul, Trench, Trubner & Co., 1932). 418 pp.

Pintner, Rudolph, Intelligence Testing (New York: Henry Holt & Co., 1931). 555 pp.

Progressive Education Association, Growth and Development: The Basis for Educational Programs (New York: Progressive Education Association, 1936). 292 pp.

Raper, Arthur, The Tragedy of Lynching (Chapel Hill: University of North Carolina Press, 1933).

―――― The Mob Still Rides: A Review of the Lynching Record 1931-35 (Atlanta: Southern Commission on Interracial Coöperation, 1936). 24 pp.

Reuter, Edward B., The American Race Problem (New York: Thomas Y. Crowell Co., 1927). 448 pp.

―――― "The Changing Status of the Mulatto," in Ebony and Topaz, ed. by Charles S. Johnson (New York: Opportunity, 1927).

Rice, S. A., "Stereotypes: A Source of Error in Judging Character," Journal of Personality Research, V (1926-27), 267-76.

Robinson, W. A., "What Peculiar Organization and Direction Should Characterize the Education of Negroes?" Journal of Negro Education, V (July, 1936), 393-400.

Rosenwald Fund, The Julius, School Money in Black and White (Chicago: The Julius Rosenwald Fund, 1934).

Schrieke, B., Alien Americans: A Study of Race Relations (New York: Viking Press, 1936). 219 pp.

Seligman, Herbert J., "The Negro Protest against Ghetto Conditions," Current History, XXV (March, 1927), 831 ff.

Sherif, M., The Psychology of Social Norms (New York: Harper & Brothers, 1936). 203 pp.

Smith, Thomas Vernor, The Democratic Way of Life (Chicago: University of Chicago Press, 1926). 211 pp.

―――― "Ideals in the life of Practice," in Growth and Development: The Basis for Educational Programs (New York: Progressive Education Association, 1936), pp. 119-22.

Spero, Sterling D., and Abram L. Harris, The Black Worker (New York: Columbia University Press, 1931). 509 pp.

Strong, A. C., "Three Hundred and Fifty White and Colored Children Measured by the Binet-Simon Measuring Scale of Intelligence," Pedagogical Seminary and Journal of Genetic Psychology, XX (December, 1913), 485-515.

Sumner, Francis C., "Environmental Factors Which Prohibit Creative Scholarship among Negroes," School and Society, XXII (September 5, 1925), 294-296.

—— "A Philosophy of Negro Education," Educational Review, LXXI (January, 1926), 42-45.

—— "Morale and the Negro College," Educational Review, LXXIII (March, 1927), 168-72.

Taylor, A. A., The Negro in Reconstruction Virginia (1926).

Thompson, C. H., "Education of the Negro in the United States," School and Society, XLII (November 9, 1935), 625-33.

Todd, Arthur J., Theories of Social Progress (New York: The Macmillan Co., 1926). 579 pp.

Toynbee, Arnold J., A Study of History (Oxford: Oxford University Press, 1934). 3 vols.

Tunis, John R., Was College Worth While? (New York: Harcourt Brace & Co., 1936).

Tuttle, H. S., Social Basis of Education (New York: Thomas Y. Crowell Co., 1934). Crowell's "Social Science Series."

—— Campus and Social Ideals (New York: the author, College of the City of New York, 1936). 88 pp. Limited ed.

United States Office of Education (Thomas Jesse Jones), Negro Education, Bulletin (1916), No. 30 (Washington: United States Office of Education, 1916).

—— Arthur J. Klein (ed.), Survey of Negro Colleges and Universities (1924), Bureau of Education Bulletin (1928), No. 7 (Washington: United States Government Printing Office, 1929). 964 pp.

Vance, R. B., Human Geography of the South (Chapel Hill: University of North Carolina Press, 1932).

Warner, W. L., "American Caste and Class," American Journal of Sociology, XLII (September, 1936), 234-37.

Washington, Booker T., "Observations on Negro Colleges," Worlds Work, XXI (April, 1911), 14230-38.

—— Up from Slavery (New York: Doubleday, Doran & Co., 1928 [1900]).

Weatherford, Willis D., and Charles S. Johnson, Race Relations (New York: D. C. Heath & Co., 1934).

West, A. F. (ed.), The Value of the Classics (Princeton: Princeton University Press, 1917).

White, Walter F., Rope and Faggot: A Biography of Judge Lynch (New York: Alfred A. Knopf, 1929). 272 pp.

Wiggins, Forest Oran, "Comment on an Article by Wilkerson on American Caste and the Social Studies Curriculum," Quarterly Review of Higher Education among Negroes, V (April, 1937), 77-78.

Wilbur, Ray Lyman, "Health Status and Health Education of Negroes in the United States," Journal of Negro Education, VI (July, 1937), 575-80.

Wilkerson, Doxey A., "A Determination of the Peculiar Problems of Negroes in Contemporary American Society," Journal of Negro Education, V (July, 1936), 324-50.

Wilkerson, Doxey A., "American Caste and the Social Studies Curriculum," *Quarterly Review of Higher Education among Negroes*, V (April, 1937), 67-74.

Williams, C. C., "Social Adjustment of Education," inaugural address at Lehigh University, *School and Society*, XLII (October 19, 1935), 521-26.

Williams, Paul R., "I Am a Negro," *American Magazine* (July, 1937), pp. 59 ff.

Woodson, Carter G., The Miseducation of the Negro (Washington: Associated Publishers, 1932). 207 pp.

Young, Kimball (ed.), Social Attitudes; a Symposium (New York: Henry Holt & Co., 1933). 383 pp.

SECTION II. SELECTED REFERENCES

Bibliographies

Caliver, Ambrose, Bibliography on Education of the Negro, Comprising Publications from January, 1928, to December, 1930, United States Office of Education *Bulletin* (1931), No. 17 (Washington: United States Government Printing Office, 1931). 32 pp.

—— and Ethel G. Greene, Education of Negroes: A Five-year Bibliography 1931-1935, United States Office of Education *Bulletin* (1937), No. 8 (Washington: United States Government Printing Office, 1937). 63 pp.

Cook, P. A. W., "A Guide to the Literature on Negro Education," *Teachers College Record*, XXXIV (May, 1933), 671-77.

Eaton, A., and S. M. Harrison, A Bibliography of Social Surveys. cf. "Negro Education" (New York: Russell-Sage Foundation, 1930). 467 pp.

Gray, Ruth A., Bibliography of Research Studies in Education 1935-1936, United States Office of Education *Bulletin*, (1937), No. 6 (Washington: United States Government Printing Office). 338 pp.

New York Public Library, The Negro: A Selected Bibliography (New York Public Library, 1930). 14 pp.

Russell Sage Foundation Library, Bulletin No. 111. cf. "The Negro" (New York: February, 1932). 4 pp.

Work, Monroe N. (compiler), A Bibliography of the Negro in Africa and America (New York: H. W. Wilson Co., 1929).

General Sources of Information

Crisis, The, ed. by Roy H. Wilkins (New York: National Association for the Advancement of Colored People).

Journal of Negro Education, The, ed. by Charles H. Thompson (Washington: Howard University).

Journal of Negro History, The, ed. by Carter G. Woodson (Washington: The Association for the Study of Negro Life and Culture, Inc.).

National Association for the Advancement of Colored People, Annual Reports, 1910-1937 (New York: National Association for the Advancement of Colored People, 1910-1937).

Negro Year Book: An Annual Encyclopedia of the Negro (Tuskegee Institute: Negro Year Book Publishing Co.).

Opportunity, Journal of Negro Life, ed. by Elmer Anderson Carter (New York: National Urban League).

Quarterly Review of Higher Education among Negroes, The, ed. by J. E. McKinney (Charlotte, North Carolina: Johnson C. Smith University).

Who's Who in Colored America: A Biographical Dictionary of Notable Living Persons of African Descent in America (New York: Who's Who in Colored America Corporation).

Education and the Social Process

Bear, R. M., Social Functions of Education (New York: The Macmillan Co., 1937).

Beard, Charles A., The Nature of the Social Sciences, Report of the Commission on the Social Studies of the American Historical Association Part VII (New York: Charles Scribner's Sons, 1934). 236 pp.

Bond, Horace Mann, Social and Economic Influence on the Public Education of Negroes in Alabama 1865-1930 (Doctor's dissertation, University of Chicago, 1936). 546 pp. MS.

———— "Horace Mann in New Orleans," *School and Society*, XLV (May 1, 1937), 607-11.

Bousfield, Maudelle B., "Redirection of the Education of Negroes in Terms of Social Needs," *Journal of Negro Education*, V (July, 1936), 412-19.

Boyer, Philip A., The Adjustment of a School to Individual and Community Needs (Philadelphia: University of Pennsylvania, 1920). 141 pp.

Brown, William Henry, The Education and Economic Development of the Negro in Virginia (Charlottesville, Virginia: Surber-Arundale Co., 1923) "Phelps-Stokes Fellowship Paper," No. 6. 150 pp.

Caldwell, I. S., A School That Teaches a Community, *Survey*, LIX (March 15, 1928), 764-65.

Commission on the Social Studies of the American Historical Association, "Conclusions and Recommendations," Report of the Commission on the Social Studies of the American Historical Association (New York: Charles Scribner's Sons, 1934). 168 pp.

Counts, George S., "The Social Foundations of Education," Report of the Commission on the Social Studies of the American Historical Association, Part IX (New York: Charles Scribner's Sons, 1934).

Coyle, Grace L. (ed.), Studies in Group Behaviour (New York: Association Press, 1937). 258 pp.

Curry, A. Bruce, "Religious Resources for Social Reconstruction," in The College and the Social Process, ed. by J. T. Cater (Talladega, Alabama: Talladega College Press, 1934).

Daniel, V. E., "What Are the Opportunities for Functional Citizenship in Colleges for Negro Youth?" *Quarterly Review of Higher Education among Negroes*, IV (January, 1936), 10-14.

Dewey, John, "The School as a Social Center," National Education Association *Proceedings* (1902), pp. 373-83.

———— Democracy and Education (New York: The Macmillan Co., [1916] 1935). 434 pp.

———— "The Higher Learning in America," *Social Frontier*, III (March, 1937), 167-69.

DuBois, W. E. B., "America and the Negro Citizen," in The College and the Social Process, ed. by J. T. Cater (Talladega, Alabama: Talladega College Press, 1934).

Duffus, R. L., Democracy Enters College (New York: Charles Scribner's Sons, 1936).

Finley, John H., "Creative Education for Creative Living," in The College and the Social Process, ed. by J. T. Cater (Talladega, Alabama: Talladega College Press, 1934).

Finney, Ross L., Sociological Philosophy of Education (New York: Macmillan Co., 1928).

Frank, Lawrence K., "The Task of General Education," *Social Frontier*, III (March, 1937), 171-73.

Fraser, Lionel B., "The Dilemma of Our Colleges and Universities," *Opportunity*, XV (June, 1937), 167-71.

Heaton, K. L., and G. R. Koopman, College Curriculum Based on Functional Needs of Students (Chicago: University of Chicago Press, 1936).

Hekhius, L., "College Curriculum and Modern Life," *School and Society*, XLV (February 13, 1937), 232-34.

Henningburg, Alphonse, "What Shall We Challenge in the Existing Social Order?" *Journal of Negro Education*, V (July, 1936), 383-92.

Johnson, Charles S., "On the Need of Realism in Negro Education," *Journal of Negro Education*, V (July, 1936), 375-82.

Jones, Thomas Jesse, Essentials of Civilization: A Study in Social Values (New York: Henry Holt & Co., 1929). 267 pp.

Kilpatrick, William H., "Public Education as a Force for Social Improvement," *School and Society*, XLI (April 20, 1935), 521-27.

―――― (ed.), The Educational Frontier (New York: Century Co., 1933).

McCulloch, Margaret, "The Function of the Negro Cultural College," *Journal of Negro Education*, VI (October, 1937), 617-62.

Midkiff, Frank E., "Negro Education and Race Relations in Southern United States," *Journal of Negro Education*, III (October, 1934), 586-92.

Newlon, Jesse H., "Educational Administration as Social Policy," Report of the Commission on the Social Studies of the American Historical Association, Part VIII (New York: Charles Scribner's Sons, 1934). 301 pp.

Oklahoma University, Higher Education and Society (Oklahoma City: Oklahoma University, 1936).

Palmer, A. M., The Liberal Arts College Movement (New York: Little & Ives, 1930). 187 pp.

Rice, J. A., "Fundamentalism and the Higher Learning," *Harpers*, CLXXIV (May, 1937), 587-96.

Rice, Richard, College and the Future (New York: Charles Scribner's Sons, 1915). 374 pp.

Richards, Edward A., "Consuming Education," *Harpers*, CLXXIV (May, 1937), 597-604.

Roosevelt, Eleanor A., "The Negro and Social Change," *Opportunity*, XIV (January, 1936), 22-23.

Snedden, David, Sociological Determination of Objectives in Education (New York: J. B. Lippincott & Co., 1921).

Taba, Hilda, The Dynamics of Education: A Methodology of Progressive Educational Thought (New York: Harcourt Brace & Co., 1932).

Zinsser, H., "What Is a Liberal Education?" *School and Society*, XLV (June 12, 1937), 801-7.

Comparative Racial Abilities

Anonymous Southerner, "Some Suggestions Relative to a Study of the Mental Attitude of the Negro," *Pedagogical Seminary and Journal of Genetic Psychology*, XXIII (June, 1916), 199-203.

Ausherman, Paul F., "The Establishing of Kwalwasser-Dykema Music Test Norms for the Negro Race," *Journal of Indiana State Teachers College*, VII (July, 1936), 132.

Baker, Mary C., "A Study of Certain Items of Achievement and Physical Capacity of College Women." (Master's thesis, New York University, 1932.) 53 pp. MS (on file in United States Office of Education Library).

Beckham, Albert Sidney, "A Study of the Intelligence of Colored Adolescents of Different Social-economic Status in Typical Metropolitan Areas," *Journal of Social Psychology*, IV (February, 1933), 70-91.

Blackwood, B., A Study of Mental Testing in Relation to Anthropology (1927). "Mental Measurements Monograph," No. 4.

Bousfield, Maudelle B., "The Intelligence and School Achievement of Negro Children," *Journal of Negro Education*, I (October, 1932), 388-95.

Brigham, C. C., A Study of American Intelligence (Princeton: Princeton University Press, 1923).

Bruce, Philip, The Plantation Negro as a Freeman: Observations on His Character, Condition, and Prospects in Virginia (New York: G. Putnam & Sons, 1889). 262 pp.

Burkhard, Russell, "Blockhead vs. Nordic: Racial I. Q's," *Education*, XLVI (April, 1926), 494-501.

Burks, B. S., "Relative Influence of Nature and Nurture upon Mental Development: A Comparative Study of Foster-Parents-Foster-Child Resemblance and True-Parents-True-Child Resemblance," *Twenty-seventh Yearbook* of the National Society for the Study of Education (Bloomington, Illinois: Public School Publishing Company, 1928), pp. 219-316.

Canady, H. G., "Intelligence of Negro College Students and Parental Occupation," *American Journal of Sociology*, XLII (November, 1936), 388-89.

Conference on Individual Differences in the Character and Rate of Psychological Development, Report of the; Iowa City, December 28, 1930 (Washington: National Research Council, 1931). 72 pp. MS.

Cooper, Peter, An Investigation of Racial Differences of College Students in Respect to Personality Traits (Talladega, Alabama: Talladega College, 1928).

Davenport, C. B., and M. Steggerda, Race Crossing in Jamaica (Washington: Carnegie Institute, 1929). Publication No. 395 of the Department of Genetics of the Carnegie Institute. 516 pp.

Davis, Robert A., "Some Relations between Amount of School Training and Intelligence among Negroes," *Journal of Educational Psychology*, XIX (February, 1928), 127-30.

Davis, Roland Clark, Ability in Social and Racial Classes (New York: Century Co., 1932). 114 pp.

Derrick, S. M., "A Comparative Study of the Intelligence of Seventy-five White and Fifty-five Colored College Students by the Stanford Revision of the Binet-Simon Scale," *Journal of Applied Psychology*, IV (1920), 316-29.

Ferguson, George Oscar, The Psychology of the Negro: An Experimental Study (New York: Science Press, 1916). "Columbia University Contributions to Philosophy and Psychology," No. 36. 138 pp. Also in "Archives of Psychology" (1916), No. 36.

Fukuda, T., "A Survey of the Intelligence and Environment of School Children," *American Journal of Psychology*, XXXVI (1925), 124-39.

Garth, Thomas Russell, "White, Indian, and Negro Work Curves," *Journal of Applied Psychology*, V (1921), 14-25.

———— A Review of Racial Psychology, *Psychological Bulletin*, XXII (1925), 343-64.

————, Bert E. Lovelady and Hale W. Smith, "The Intelligence and Achievement of Southern Negro Children," *School and Society*, XXXII (September 27, 1930), 431-35.

———— and C. A. Whatley, "The Intelligence of Southern Negro Children," *School and Society*, XXII (October 17, 1925), 501-4.

Goodenough, Florence L, "Racial Differences in the Intelligence of School Children," *Journal of Experimental Psychology*, IX (1926), 388-97.

Goodenough, Florence L., and G. Shapiro, "Performance of Pre-School Children of Different Social Groups on the Kuhlman-Binet Tests," *Journal of Educational Research*, XVIII (1928), 356-62.

Graham, James L., "A Quantitative Comparison of Rational Responses of Negro and White College Students," *Journal of Social Psychology*, I (February, 1930), 97-120.

——— "A Quantitative Comparison of Certain Mental Traits of Negro and White College Students," *Journal of Social Psychology*, I (May, 1930), 267-285.

Hankins, Frank H., The Racial Basis of Civilization: A Critique of the Nordic Doctrine (New York: Alfred A. Knopf, 1926). 384 pp.

Herskovits, Melville L., "On the Relation between Negro-white Mixture and Standing in Intelligence Tests," *Pedagogical Seminary and Journal of Genetic Psychology*, XXXIII (March, 1926), 30-42.

——— Some Effects of Social Selection on the American Negro (1926). "Publications of the American Sociological Society," No. 32.

——— The American Negro: A Study in Racial Crossings (New York: Alfred A. Knopf, 1928). 92 pp.

——— The Anthropometry of the American Negro (New York: Columbia University Press, 1930). 283 pp.

Hertz, Friedrich, Race and Civilization, translated by A. S. Levetus and W. Entz (New York: Macmillan Co., 1928). 328 pp.

Hewitt, A., "A Comparative Study of White and Colored Pupils in a Southern System," *Elementary School Journal*, XXXI (October, 1930), 111-19.

Hicks, J. Allan, Heredity, Maturation and Learning; Factors Affecting Individual Differences in the Development of Young Children, *Report* of the Conference on Individual Differences in the Character and Rate of Psychological Development (1930), pp. 15-18.

Jenkins, Martin D., "Socio-psychological Study of Negro Children of Superior Intelligence," *Journal of Negro Education*, V (April, 1936), 175-90.

Jenkins, Trixie, Intelligence and Language Ability of White and Colored Children. (Master's thesis, George Peabody College for Teachers, 1932.)

Jones, Eugene K., "Negroes North and South: A Contrast," *Missionary Review*, XLV (June, 1922), 479-82.

Journal of Negro Education, "Seventeen Writers Survey Race Psychology," Vol. III (July, 1934).

Jung, C. G., "Negroid and Indian Behaviour," *Forum*, LXXXIII (April, 1930) 193-99; XCV (March, 1936), 176-82.

Klineberg, Otto, "The Question of Negro Intelligence," *Opportunity*, IX (December, 1931), 366-68.

——— "A Study of Psychological Differences between 'Racial' and National Groups in Europe," *Archives of Psychology*, Vol. XX, No. 132 (1931-32).

Koch, Helen, and Reita Simmons, A Study of the Test Performances of American, Mexican, and Negro Children. "Princeton Psychological Monographs," Vol. XXXV, No. 5 (1920).

Lacy, L. D., "Relative Intelligence of White and Colored Children," *Elementary School Journal*, XXVI (March, 1926), 542-46.

Lambeth, Martha, and L. H. Lanier, "Race Differences in Speed of Reaction," *Pedagogical Seminary and Journal of Genetic Psychology*, XLII (June, 1933), 255-97.

Long, Howard Hale, "Test Results of Third Grade Negro Children Selected on the Basis of Socio-economic Status, II," *Journal of Negro Education*, IV (October, 1935), 523-52.

McFadden, John H., and J. F. Dashield, "Racial Differences as Measured by the Downey Will-temperament Test," *Journal of Applied Psychology*, VII (1923), 30-53.

McGraw, Myrtle B., A Comparative Study of a Group of Southern White and Negro Infants (New York: Teachers College, Columbia University, 1930).

Mayo, M. J., The Mental Capacity of the American Negro (New York, 1913). "Archives of Psychology," No. 28. 73 pp.

Murdock, Katherine, "A Study of Race Differences in New York City," *School and Society*, XI (1920), 147-50.

Muzzey, Dorothy, A Comparison of the Group Progress of White and Colored Children in Learning a Rhythmic Pattern. (Master's thesis, University of Iowa, 1932.)

Nutting, C. C., "Mentality of 'Inferior' Races of Man," *School and Society*, XXIV (July 24, 1926), 89-96.

Patrick, James R., A Study of Ideals, Intelligence, and Achievements of Negroes and Whites, *Bulletin* of the University of Georgia, Athens, Georgia, Vol. XXVII, No. 1 (December, 1926). 48 pp.

Perring, Louise F., "A Study of the Comparative Retardation of Negro and White Pupils in a Philadelphia Public School," *Psychological Clinic*, IX (May, 1915), 87-93.

Peterson, Joseph, "Comparison of White and Negro Children in the Rational Learning Test," in *Twenty-seventh Yearbook* of the National Society for the Study of Education (Bloomington, Illinois Public School Publishing Co., 1928).

—— "Methods of Investigating Comparative Abilities in Races," *Annals* of the American Academy of Political and Social Science, CXL (November, 1928), 178-85.

—— "Some Effects of Environment Factors and of Unreliability in Measurements on Rate and Variability of Psychological Development," in Conference on Individual Differences in the Character and Rate of Psychological Development, 1930 (Washington: National Research Council, 1930) pp. 35-40. 72 pp. MS.

—— and Lyle H. Lanier, Studies in Comparative Abilities of Whites and Negroes (Baltimore: Williams & Wilkins, 1929). "Mental Measurements Monographs," No. 5.

Phillips, Byron A., "The Binet Tests Applied to Colored Children," *Psychological Clinic*, VIII (December, 1914), 190-96.

Pintner, Rudolph, "Factors Affecting Performance," in Conference on Individual Psychological Differences (Washington: National Research Council, 1930).

Pressey, L. W., "The Influence of (a) Inadequate Schooling and (b) Poor Environment upon Results with Tests of Intelligence," *Journal of Applied Psychology*, IV (1920), 91-96.

Price, Joseph St. Clair, "The Intelligence of Negro College Freshmen," *School and Society*, XXX (November 30, 1929), 749-54.

Pyle, W. H., "The Mind of the Negro Child," *School and Society*, I (March 6, 1915), 357-60.

—— "Mentality of the Negro Compared with Whites," *Psychological Bulletin*, XII (1915), 22-71.

—— "The Learning Capacity of Negro Children," *Psychological Bulletin*, XIII (1916), 82-83.

Rogers, Agnes L., Dorothy Durling and K. McBride, "Effect on the I. Q. of Change from a Poor to a Good Environment," in *Twenty-seventh Yearbook* of the National Society for the Study of Education (Bloomington, Illinois: Public School Publishing Company, 1928), Part I, pp. 323-31.

Schwegler, R. A., and Edith Winn, "A Comparative Study of the Intelligence of White and Colored Children," *Journal of Educational Research,* II (December, 1920), 838-48.

Schwesinger, Gladys C., Heredity and Environment: Studies in the Genesis of Psychological Characteristics (New York: Macmillan Co., 1933). "Studies in Social Eugenics," No. 1. 489 pp.

Stoddard, George D., "The Social and Educational Conditions Surrounding the Appearance and Development of Individual Differences of a Psychological Sort," in Report of Conference on Individual Differences in the Character and Rate of Psychological Development, Iowa City, December, 1930 (Washington: National Research Council, 1930), pp. 20-33.

Streep, Rosaland, "A Comparison of White and Negro Children in Rhythm and Consonance," *Journal of Applied Psychology,* XV (February, 1931), 53-71.

Sumner, Francis C., "Mental Health Statistics of Negro College Freshmen," *School and Society,* XXXIII (April 25, 1931), 874-76.

——— and F. H. Sumner, "The Mental Health of White and Negro College Students," *Journal of Abnormal and Social Psychology,* XXVI (April-June, 1931), 28-36.

Sunne, Dagne, "Intelligence of Negroes," *Journal of Applied Psychology,* I (1917), 71-83.

——— "A Comparison of White and Colored School Children in Verbal and Non-verbal Tests," *School and Society,* XIX (1924), 469-72.

Thomas, W. I., "Race Psychology," *American Journal of Sociology,* XVII (May, 1912), 725-75.

Thompson, Charles H., "The Educational Achievements of Negro Children," *Annals* of the American Academy of Political and Social Science, CXL (November, 1928), 193-208.

Thorndike, E. L., "Intelligence Scores of Colored Pupils in High Schools," *School and Society,* XVIII (November 10, 1923), 569-70.

Towns, Grace, The Emotional Attitudes of Negro Girls in High School and College. (Master's thesis, Ohio State University, 1929). 76 pp. MS.

Varney, W. Drew, A Comparative Study of Intelligence of Negroes and Whites. (Master's thesis, University of Rochester, 1929). 160 pp. MS.

Viteles, Morris S., "The Mental Status of the Negro," *Annals* of the American Academy of Political and Social Science, CXL (November, 1928), 166-67.

Weintrob, J. and R., "The Influence of Environment on Mental Ability as Shown by Binet-Simon Tests," *Journal of Educational Psychology,* III (1912), 577-583.

Whitney, Frederick Lamson, "Intelligence Levels and School Achievement of the White and Colored Races in the United States," *Pedagogical Seminary and Journal of Genetic Psychology,* XXX (March, 1923), 69-86.

Whipple, Guy M., "Nature and Nurture," *Twenty-seventh Yearbook* of the National Society for the Study of Education (Bloomington, Illinois: Public School Publishing Co., 1928) Part I, Chap. XIII; Part II, pp. 282-96.

Witty, Paul A., and A. L. Decker, "A Comparative Study of the Educational Attainment of Negro and White Children," *Journal of Educational Psychology,* XVIII (October, 1927), 497-500.

Woodworth, R. S., Comparative Psychology of Races, *Psychological Bulletin,* XIII (1916), 388-96.

Yates, Charlotte, The Influence of New York City Environment upon the Intelligence Test Scores of Twelve-year-old Negro Girls. (Master's thesis, Columbia University, 1932).

Young, Donald (ed.), "The American Negro," *Annals* of the American Academy of Political and Social Science, Vol. CXL (November, 1928).

—— American Minority Peoples (New York: Harper & Brothers, 1932). 593 pp.

The American Caste System

Bond, Horace Mann, "Extent and Character of Separate Schools in the United States," *Journal of Negro Education,* IV (July, 1935), 321-27.

Bowers, Claude G., The Tragic Era (Cambridge: Houghton-Mifflin Co., 1929).

Burgess, Ernest W., "Residential Segregation in American Cities," *Annals* of the American Academy of Political and Social Science, CXL (November, 1928), 105-15.

Catterill, Robert S., The Old South (Glendale: Clark Publishing Co., 1937). 354 pp.

Christian Century, "Divisions Confronting the Methodists," LIII (January 1, 22, 29, 1936), 6-7, 147, 195.

Davids, Robert Brewster, A Comparative Study of White and Negro Education in Maryland. (Doctor's dissertation, Johns Hopkins University, 1936.)

Davis, Jackson, "British Africa and the South," *Virginia Quarterly Review,* XIII (November 3, 1937), 362-75.

Doyle, Bertram W., The Etiquette of Race Relations in the South (Chicago: University of Chicago Press, 1937). 247 pp.

DuBois, W. E. B., "Economic Future of the Negro" (New York: Macmillan Co., 1906). "American Economic Association Publications," Series 3, Vol. VII, No. 1.

—— "Passing of Jim Crow," *Independent,* XCI (July 14, 1917), 53-54.

—— and A. G. Dill, The Common School and the American Negro (Atlanta: Atlanta University Press, 1911). "Atlanta University Publications," No. 16. 140 pp.

Dunning, William A., Reconstruction: Political and Economic, 1865-1877 (New York: Harper & Brothers, 1907). 378 pp.

DuValle, S. H., The Legal Status of Negro Education. (Master's thesis, Indiana University, 1919.)

Edwards, Newton, "A Critique: The Courts and the Negro Separate School," *Journal of Negro Education,* IV (July, 1935), 442-55.

Faris, Ellsworth, "Racial Attitudes and Sentiments," *Southwestern Political and Social Science Quarterly* (March, 1929), pp. 479-90.

Foreman, Clark, "Race and Class in the New Society," in The College and the Social Process, ed. by J. T. Cater (Talladega, Alabama: Talladega College Press, 1934).

Frazier, E. Franklin, "The Status of the Negro in the American Social Order," *Journal of Negro Education,* IV (July, 1935), 293-308.

Gilligan, Francis J., The Morality of the Color Line (Washington: Catholic University of America, 1928). 222 pp.

Hankins, Frank, The Racial Basis of Civilization (New York: Alfred A. Knopf, 1926). 384 pp.

Harris, Abram L., "Negro Labor's Quarrel with White Workingmen," *Current History,* XXIV (September, 1926), 903-8.

—— "Prospects of Black Bourgeoisie," in Ebony and Topaz, ed. by Charles S. Johnson (New York: Opportunity, 1927), pp. 131-34.

Hart, Albert Bushnell, "The Realities of Negro Suffrage," American Political Science Association *Proceedings*, II (1905), 149-65.

Haygood, Atticus, Our Brothers in Black (New York: Phillips & Hunt, 1881). 252 pp.

Hill, J. A., "Composition of the American Population by Race and Country of Origin," *Annals* of the American Academy of Political and Social Science, CLXXXIII (November, 1936), 177-80.

Hobbs, Samuel H., Jr., North Carolina, Economic and Social (Chapel Hill: University of North Carolina Press, 1930). 403 pp.

Horton, R. W., "Not Too Much for a Negro," *Nation*, CXLI (December 11, 1935), 674-76.

Hubbard, M. W., and R. P. Alexander, "Type of Potentially Favorable Court Cases Relative to the Separate School," *Journal of Negro Education*, IV (July, 1935), 375-405.

Irby, Nolen M., A Program of Equalization of Educational Opportunities in the State of Arkansas (Nashville: George Peabody College for Teachers, 1931).

Johnson, Charles S., Shadow of the Plantation (Chicago: University of Chicago Press, 1934).

——— "Conflict of Caste and Class in an American Industry," *American Journal of Sociology*, XLII (July and September, 1936), 55-65, 252-55.

Johnson, Franklin, Development of State Legislation concerning the Free Negro (New York: Arbor Press, 1918). 207 pp.

Johnson, James Weldon, and H. J. Seligman, "Legal Aspects of the Negro Problem," *Annals* of the American Academy of Political and Social Science, CXL (November, 1928), 90-97.

Jordan, G. R., "Dare the South Answer?" *Christian Century*, LIII (May 6, 1936), 664-65.

Katz, Daniel, "Attitude Measurement as a Method in Social Psychology," *Social Forces*, XV (May, 1937), 479-82.

Kelsey, Carl, "Evolution of Negro Labor," *Annals* of the American Academy of Political and Social Science, No. 21 (1903), pp. 55-76.

Kennedy, R. C., "Alabama Dilemma," *Christian Century*, LII (July 10, 1935), 917-18.

Lasker, Bruno, "Some Obstacles of Race Coöperation," *Opportunity*, III (April, 1925), 101-4.

Lewinson, Paul, Race, Class, and Party (Oxford: Oxford University Press, 1932). 302 pp.

McNeil, H. L., "In Sheer Self-preservation the Negro Clergyman is Forced to Repudiate the Christian Church," *Christian Century*, LII (June 12, 1935), 796-97.

Moffat, R. Burnham, "The Disfranchisement of the Negro, from a Lawyer's Point of View," *Journal of Social Science*, XLII (1904), 31-62.

Nation, "Rising Tide of Prejudice," CXXII (March 10, 1926), 247.

Park, Robert E., "The Conflict and Fusion of Cultures with Special Reference to the Negro," *Journal of Negro History*, IV (March, 1919), 115-19.

——— "Concept of Social Distance as Applied to the Study of Racial Attitudes and Racial Relations," *Journal of Applied Sociology*, VIII (July, 1924), 339-344.

——— "Experience and Race Relations," *Journal of Applied Psychology*, VIII (September, 1924), 18-24.

Peterson, Gladys T., "Present Status of the Negro Separate School as Defined by Court Decisions," *Journal of Negro Education*, IV (July, 1935), 351-74.

Queen, S. A., and D. M. Mann, Social Pathology (New York: Thomas Y. Crowell & Co., 1925). "Crowell's Social Science Series," 690 pp.

Reckless, Walter C., and Harold L. Bringen, "Racial Attitudes and Information about the Negro," Journal of Negro Education, II (April, 1933), 128-38.

Sampson, J. M., "Race Consciousness and Race Relations," Opportunity, I (May, 1923), 15-17.

Schuyler, George S., "Travelling Jim Crow," American Mercury, XX (August, 1930), 423-32.

Sellin, T., "Race Prejudice in the Administration of Justice," American Journal of Sociology, IV (1935), 212-17.

Skaage, William H., The Southern Oligarchy (New York: Deven Adair Co., 1924). 472 pp.

Smith, William Roy, Negro Suffrage in the South, Studies in Southern History and Politics (New York: Columbia University Press, 1914), pp. 231-56.

Stephenson, Gilbert F., Race Distinctions in American Law (New York: D. Appleton & Co., 1920). 388 pp.

Stone, Alfred Holt, "The Economic Future of the Negro; the Factor of White Competition," VII (1906), 243-94. "Publications of the American Economic Association," Series 3.

Street, James H., Look Away: A Dixie Notebook (New York: Viking Press, 1936). 250 pp.

Symposium, Shall the Negro be Educated or Suppressed? (Hampton: Hampton Institute, 1889). 24 pp.

West, G. A., "Race Attitudes among Teachers in the Southwest," Journal of Abnormal and Social Psychology, XXXI (October-December, 1937), 331-37.

Woofter, Thomas J., Jr., Races and Ethnic Groups in American Life (New York: McGraw-Hill, 1933). "Recent Social Trends Monographs." 247 pp.

The Plight and Progress of the Negro under the Caste System

American Academy of Political and Social Science, The Negro's Progress in Fifty Years (Philadelphia: American Academy of Political and Social Science, 1913).

Brawley, Benjamin G., A Social History of the American Negro (New York: Macmillan Co., 1921).

―――― A Short History of the American Negro, 2d revised ed. (New York: Macmillan Co., 1927).

Brown, Ina C., The Story of the American Negro (New York: Friendship Press, 1936).

Bruner, C. V., Religious Instruction of the Slaves in the Antebellum South (Nashville: George Peabody College for Teachers, 1933).

Chadbourn, James Harmon, Lynching and the Law (Chapel Hill: University of North Carolina Press). 221 pp.

Dabney, Thomas L., "Organized Labor's Attitude toward Negro Workers," Southern Workman, LVII (August, 1928), 323-30.

DuBois, W. E. B., The Negro (New York: Henry Holt & Company, 1915).

Edwards, Paul K., The Southern Urban Negro as a Consumer (New York: Prentice-Hall, 1932).

Farnham, Dwight T., "Negroes, a Source of Industrial Labor," Industrial Management, LVI (August, 1918), 123-29.

Fowler, B. B., "Miracle in Gary; Negro Gropes toward Economic Equality," Forum, XCVI (September, 1936), 134-37.

Frazier, E. Franklin, "Psychological Factors in Negro Health," Social Forces, III (1925), 488.

Frazier, E. Franklin, "The Negro in the American Social Order," *Journal of Negro Education,* IV (July, 1935), 293-307.

Fuller, Thomas O., Pictorial History of the American Negro (Memphis: Pictorial History, Inc.). 375 pp.

Greene, Lorenzo J., and Carter G. Woodson, The Negro Wage Earner (Washington: Association for the Study of Negro Life and History, 1930). 381 pp.

Grover, Mary, and Edgar Sydenstricker, Mortality among Negroes in the United States, *Public Health Bulletin,* 174 (1928). 63 pp.

Hall, Charles E., and Charles W. White, Negroes in the United States 1920-1932 (Washington: United States Government Printing Office, 1935). 845 pp.

Harmon, J. H., Jr., A. G. Lindsay, and Carter G. Woodson, The Negro as a Business Man (Washington: Association for the Study of Negro Life and History, 1929). 111 pp.

Hart, Hastings H., "Peonage and the Public," *Survey,* XLVI (April 9, 1921). 43-44.

Haynes, George E., "Race Riots in Relation to Democracy," *Survey,* XLII (August 9, 1919), 697-99.

Hill, T. Arnold, "Present Status of Negro Labor," *Opportunity,* VII (May, 1929), 143-45.

―――― "The Liberal Arts College Graduate—His Occupational Outlook," in The College and the Social Process, ed. by J. T. Cater, (Talladega, Alabama: Talladega College Press, 1934).

Johnson, Charles S., "Changing Economic Status of the Negro," *Annals* of the American Academy of Political and Social Science, CXL (November, 1928), 128-37.

―――― The Negro in American Civilization (New York: Henry Holt & Co., 1930). "American Social Science Series." 538 pp.

―――― The Economic Status of the Negro (Nashville: Fisk University Press, 1933). 53 pp.

Johnson, Gerald W., The Wasted Land (Chapel Hill: University of North Carolina Press, 1937). 110 pp.

Kennedy, Louise V., The Negro Peasant Turns Cityward (New York: Columbia University Press, 1930). 270 pp.

King, Willis J., The Negro in American Life (New York: Methodist Book Concern, 1926). 154 pp.

Kingsley, Harold M., "The Negro Goes to Church," *Opportunity,* VII (March, 1929), 90-91.

Malcus, Ellison J., "The Negro Church in Rural Virginia," *Southern Workman,* LX (February, April, May, July, 1931), 67-73; 176-179; 201-10; 307-14.

Mays, Benjamin Elijah, and Joseph William Nicholson, The Negro's Church (New York: Institute of Social and Religious Research, 1933). 321 pp.

Mitchell, Broadus, Economic Effects of Slavery (Baltimore: Johns Hopkins University Press, 1924).

Morton, Richard L., The Negro in Virginia Politics 1865-1902 (Charlottesville Virginia: University of Virginia Press, 1919). "Phelps-Stokes Fellowship Papers," No. 4, 199 pp.

Mossell, Sadie T., "The Standard of Living among One Hundred Negro Migrant Families in Philadelphia," *Annals* of the American Academy of Political and Social Science, XCVIII (November, 1921), 173-218.

Nearing, Scott, Black America (New York: Vanguard Press, 1929). 275 pp.

Pickens, William, The New Negro, His Political, Civil and Mental Status and Related Essays (New York: Neale Publishing Co., 1916).

Reid, Ira DeA., Negro Membership in American Labor Unions (New York: National Urban League, 1930). 175 pp.

Roman, C. V., American Civilization and the Negro (Philadelphia: F. A. Davis Co., 1916).

Scarborough, William S., "The Negro Farmer in the South," *Current History,* XXI (January, 1925), 565-69.

Seligman, Herbert J., "Twenty Years of Negro Progress," *Current History,* XXIX (January, 1929), 614-21.

Sewall, J. L., "Industrial Revolution and the Negro," *Scribner's Magazine,* LXIX (March, 1921), 334-42.

Shores, Louis, "Public Library Service to Negroes," *Library Journal,* LV (February 15, 1930), 150-54.

Thompson, Charles H., "The Socio-economic Status of Negro College Students," *Journal of Negro Education,* II (January, 1933), 26-37.

—— "Court Action the Only Reasonable Alternative to Remedy Immediate Abuses of the Negro Separate School," *Journal of Negro Education,* IV (July, 1935), 419-34.

Weatherford, Willis D., The Negro from Africa to America (New York: Doran & Co., 1924). 487 pp.

Wesley, Charles H., Negro Labor in the United States (New York: Vanguard Press, 1927).

Williams, W. T. B., "Court Action by Negroes to Improve Their Schools a Doubtful Remedy," *Journal of Negro Education,* IV (July, 1935), 435-41.

Woodson, Carter G., A Century of Negro Migration (Washington: Association for the Study of Negro Life and History, 1918). 221 pp.

—— History of the Negro Church (Washington: Associated Publishers, 1921).

—— The Rural Negro (Washington: Association for the Study of Negro Life and History, 1930).

—— The Negro in Our History (Washington: Associated Publishers, 1932).

Woofter, Thomas J., Jr., Black Yeomanry: Life on St. Helena Island (New York: Henry Holt & Co., 1930).

—— A Study of the Economic Status of the Negro (Chicago: The Julius Rosenwald Fund. 1930), Part I, 58 pp; Part II, 56 pp.

Yarbrough, W. H., Economic Aspects of Slavery in Relation to Southern and Southwestern Migration (Nashville: George Peabody College for Teachers, 1932). 105 pp.

The Education of Negroes under American Caste

Blose, David T., Statistics of Education of the Negro Race, 1925-1926, United States Office of Education *Bulletin* (1928), No. 19 (Washington: United States Government Printing Office, 1928). 42 pp.

—— "Statistics of Negro Education in the Public Schools of Eighteen Southern States, 1933-34," *School Life,* XXI (November, 1935), 59.

Blount, George W., "Critics and Our Schools," *Bulletin* of National Association of Teachers in Colored Schools, XII (December, 1931), 23-24.

Caliver, Ambrose, "Some Tendencies in Higher Education and Their Application to the Negro College," *Opportunity,* VI (January, 1928), 6.

—— Background Study of Negro College Students, United States Office of Education *Bulletin* (1933), No. 8 (Washington: United States Government Printing Office, 1933).

—— "Liberalizing the Liberal College for Negroes," in The College and the Social Process, ed. by J. T. Cater (Talladega, Alabama: Talladega College Press, 1934).

Caliver, Ambrose (ed.), Fundamentals in the Education of Negroes (1934), United States Office of Education *Bulletin* (1935), No. 6 (Washington: United States Government Printing Office, 1935), 90 pp.

—— Availability of Education to Negroes in Rural Communities, United States Office of Education *Bulletin* (1935), No. 12 (Washington: United States Government Printing Office, 1935). 86 pp.

Clement, Rufus C., "Redirection and Reorganization of the College for Negroes," *Journal of Negro Education,* V (July, 1936), 474-78.

Davis, Jackson, "Recent Developments in Negro Schools and Colleges," *Bulletin* of the National Association of Teachers in Colored Schools, VIII (April-May, 1928), 5-10, 12.

Dillard, James H., "The Negro Goes to College," *World's Work,* LV (January, 1928), 337-40.

—— Selected Writings (Charlottesville, Virginia: John F. Slater Fund, 1932).

Favrot, Leo M., A Study of County Training Schools for Negroes in the South (Charlottesville, Virginia: John F. Slater Fund, 1923) ("John F. Slater Fund Occasional Papers"), No. 23. 85 pp.

—— "Some Facts about Negro Schools and Their Distribution and Development in Fourteen Southern States," *High School Quarterly,* XVII (April, 1929), 139-54.

—— "Provisions for Preparation and Training of Negro Teachers," *Bulletin* of the National Association of Teachers in Colored Schools, XI (January, 1931), 15-25.

—— "Schools for Negro Children: Past Practices and Present Hopes," *Nation's Schools* (October, 1932), 59-65.

Greene, Harry W., "The Ph.D. and the Negro," *Opportunity,* VI (September, 1928), 267-69.

Greenleaf, Walter J., "Negro Land-Grant Colleges," in his Land-Grant Colleges and Universities, Year Ended June 30, 1929; United States Office of Education *Bulletin* (1930), No. 28 (Washington: United States Government Printing Office, 1930).

Holmes, D. O. W., Present Status of College Education among Negroes, *Bulletin* of the National Association of Teachers in Colored Schools, XI (January, 1931), 75. (Washington: National Association of Teachers in Colored Schools).

Iles, R. E., "Standardizing the Negro College," *Peabody Journal of Education,* VI (September, 1928). 96-101.

Jackson, Reid Ethelbert, A Critical Analysis of the Curricula for Educating Secondary School Teachers in Negro Colleges of Alabama. (Doctor's dissertation, Ohio State University, 1937.) 326 pp. MS.

Johnson, Charles D., Relation of the Negro Problem to Education in the South. (Doctor's dissertation, University of Iowa, 1921.)

Johnson, Charles S., "The Education of the Negro Child," *American Sociological Review,* I (April, 1936), 264-72.

Jones, Lance G. E., Negro Schools in the Southern States (Oxford: Clarendon Press, 1928). 160 pp.

Jones, Thomas Jesse, "Recent Progress in Negro Education," United States Bureau of Education *Bulletin* (1919), No. 27 (Washington: United States Government Printing Office, 1919).

King, Willis J., "The Place of Religion in the Liberal Arts College," in The

College and the Social Process, ed. by J. T. Cater (Talladega, Alabama: Talladega College Press, 1934).

Knott, Harold E., Higher Education and the American Negro. (Doctor's dissertation, University of South Africa, 1927.)

Lane, David H., "Report of the National Advisory Committee on Education and the Problems of Negro Education," *Journal of Negro Education,* I (April, 1932). 5-15.

Leavell, U. W., Philanthropy in Negro Education (Nashville: George Peabody College for Teachers, 1930). "George Peabody College Contributions," No. 100. 168 pp.

McAllister, Jane Ellen, The Training of Negro Teachers in Louisiana. (Doctor's dissertation, Teachers College, Columbia University, 1929.) 95 pp. MS.

McCuistion, Fred, The South's Negro Teaching Force (Nashville: The Julius Rosenwald Fund, 1931).

———— Higher Education among Negroes (Nashville: Southern Association of Colleges and Secondary Schools, 1933).

Moton, Robert Russa, "Progress of Negro Education in the South," in National Education Association, Address and Proceedings (1929), pp. 107-11.

Newbold, N. C., "More Money for and More Emphasis upon Negro Education;—Not Reorganization and Redirection," *Journal of Negro Education,* V (July, 1936), 502-8.

———— "Unfinished Tasks and New Opportunities in Education in North Carolina," *North Carolina Teachers Record,* II (October, 1931), 66-76.

Noble, Stuart G., Forty Years of Public Schools in Mississippi, with Special Reference to the Education of the Negro (New York: Teachers College, Columbia University, 1918). 141 pp.

Payne, George E., "Negroes in the Public Elementary Schools of the North," *Annals* of the American Academy of Political and Social Science, CXL (November, 1928), 224-33.

Pechstein, L. A., "The Problem of Negro Education in Northern and Border Cities," *Elementary School Journal,* XXX (November, 1929), 192-207.

School and Society, "Admission of Negroes to State Universities and Colleges," XLII (August 31, 1935), 284.

Stowell, Jay S., Methodist Adventures in Negro Education (New York: Methodist Book Concern, 1927).

Ware, Edward T., "Higher Education of Negroes in the United States," *Annals* of the American Academy of Political and Social Science, XLIX (September, 1915), 209-18.

Washington, Booker T., "University Education for Negroes," *Indiana,* LXVIII (March 24, 1910). 613-18.

Whiting, Helen Adele, Booker T. Washington's Contribution to Education (Charlotte, North Carolina: Mimeograph Press, Klutz Mail Advertising Service, 1929). 160 pp.

Williams, W. T. B., Report on Negro Universities and Colleges (1922). "John F. Slater Fund Occasional Papers," No. 21.

Work, Monroe, "Two Generations since Emancipation," *Missionary Review of the World,* LIX (June, 1936). 289-90.

Wright, W. L., "The Small College in American Education," *The Crisis,* XLIV (March, 1937), 70.

The Question of a Racial Emphasis in Negro Education

Allen, Wilson S., Industrial Education for Negroes in Secondary Schools in Florida (Doctor's dissertation, Ohio State University, 1936). 186 pp. MS.

Anthology of American Negro Literature, An, ed. by R. V. Calverton (New York: The Modern Library, 1929).

Binnion, R. B., "Solving the Negro Problem through Education," *Current History*, XXX (May, 1929), 231-36.

Bond, Horace Mann, "Human Nature and Its Study in Negro Colleges," *Opportunity*, VI (February, 1928), 38-39.

Brawley, Benjamin, The Negro in Literature and Art in the United States (3d ed., New York: Duffield & Co., 1929).

—— The Negro Genius (New York: Dodd, Mead & Co., 1937). 366 pp.

Bunche, Ralph J., "Critical Analysis of the Tactics and Programs of Minority Groups," *Journal of Negro Education*, IV (July, 1935), 308-20.

—— "Education in Black and White," *Journal of Negro Education*, V (July, 1936), 351-58.

Burleigh, Harry T., Negro Spirituals (New York: Ricordi, 1917-24).

—— Old Songs Hymnal (New York: Century Co., 1929).

Chen, H. S., "Fallacies on Negro Education," *Educational Review*, LXXII (December, 1926), 278-79.

Clark, J. L., "Race-Relations Course in a State College," *Southern Workman*, LIX (February, 1930), 55-57.

Dabney, Thomas L., "The Importance of Negro History," *Southern Workman*, LVIII (December, 1929), 558-62.

Daniel, Robert P., "One Consideration of Redirection of Emphasis of the Negro College," *Journal of Negro Education*, V (July, 1936), 479-83.

Davis, John, "Unrest in the Negro Colleges," *New Student*, VIII (January, 1929), 13-14.

DuBois, W. E. B., The Souls of Black Folk (Chicago: McLurg & Co., 1904).

—— Darkwater (New York: Harcourt Brace and Co., 1920).

—— The Gift of Black Folk (Boston: Sturtford Co., 1924). 249 pp.

—— The Dark Princess (New York: Harcourt Brace & Co., 1928).

—— "Education and Work," *Howard University Bulletin*, IX (January, 1931), 5-22.

Frazier, E. Franklin, "Racial Self-Expression," in Ebony and Topaz, ed. by Charles S. Johnson (New York: Opportunity, 1927), pp. 119-21.

Granger, Lester B., "Race Relations and the School System," *Opportunity*, III (November, 1925), 327-30.

Green, Elizabeth L., The Negro in Contemporary American Literature (Chapel Hill: University of North Carolina Press, 1928).

Holmes, D. O. W., "Does Negro Education Need Reorganization and Redirection?—A Statement of the Problem," *Journal of Negro Education*, V (July, 1936), 314-23.

Hughes, Langston, Weary Blues (New York: Alfred A. Knopf, 1926).

—— Fine Clothes to the Jew (New York: Alfred A. Knopf, 1927).

Jacobs, E. S., "Pioneering in Home Economics among the Negroes of Tidewater, Virginia," *Journal of Home Economics*, XXI (February, 1929), 85-91.

Johnson, Charles S., "American Negro Art," *Opportunity*, IV (August, 1926), 238.

—— "On the Need of Realism in Negro Education," *Journal of Negro Education*, V (July, 1936), 375-82.

Johnson, James Weldon, (ed.), The Book of American Negro Poetry (New York: Harcourt Brace & Co., 1922).

—— The Autobiography of an Ex-colored Man (New York: Alfred A. Knopf, 1927).

Johnson, James Weldon (ed.), The Book of American Negro Spirituals; Musical Arrangements by J. Rosamond Johnson, Additional Numbers by Lawrence Brown (New York: Viking Press, 1925).

—— God's Trombones; Seven Negro Sermons in Verse (New York: Viking Press, 1927).

—— Along This Way (New York: Viking Press, 1933).

—— Negro Americans: What Now? (New York: Viking Press, 1934). 103 pp.

Lehman, Harvey C. and Paul A. Witty, "The Negro Child's Interest in Writing Poetry," Education, XLIX (February, 1929), 346-54.

Locke, Alain L. (ed.), The New Negro (New York: Albert & Charles Boni, 1925). 452 pp.

—— (compiler), Decade of Negro Self-Expression (Charlottesville, Virginia: John F. Slater Fund, 1928).

—— The Negro and His Music (Washington: Associates in Negro Folk Education, 1937). 141 pp.

—— Negro Art—Past and Present (Washington: Associates in Negro Folk Education, 1937). 122 pp.

Miller, Kelly, "The Function of the Negro College," Dial, XXXII (April 16, 1902), 267-70.

Nichols, Franklin O., "Preparation of Negro Youth for Marriage and Parenthood," Southern Workman, LIX (June, 1930), 253-56.

Odum, Howard W., Negro Workaday Songs (Chapel Hill: University of North Carolina Press, 1926).

—— Rainbow Round My Shoulder; the Blue Trail of Black Ulysses (Indianapolis: Bobbs-Merrill Co., 1928).

—— Wings on My Feet; Black Ulysses at the Wars (Indianapolis: Bobbs-Merrill Co., 1929).

—— and Guy B. Johnson, The Negro and His Songs; a Study of the Typical Negro Songs in the South (Chapel Hill: University of North Carolina Press, 1925).

Patterson, Fred D., "Avenues of Redirection in Vocational Education," Journal of Negro Education, V (July, 1936), 495-501.

Perret, A., "Highly Stylized, Not Primitive," Country Life, LXVIII (July, 1935), 42-43.

Scarborough, Dorothy, On the Trail of Negro Folk-Songs (Cambridge: Harvard University Press, 1925).

Schuyler, George, "The Negro Art Hokum," Nation (June 16, 1926).

Spaeth, Sigmund, "Dixie, Harlem, and Tin Pan Alley: Who Writes Negro Music, and How?" Scribner's, XCIX (January, 1936), 23-26.

Stephenson, Gilbert T., "Education and Crime among Negroes," South Atlantic Quarterly, XVI (January, 1917), 14-20.

Talley, Thomas W., Negro Folk-Rhymes, Wise and Otherwise (New York: Macmillan Co., 1922).

Thomasson, Maurice E., A Study of Special Kinds of Education for Rural Negroes (Charlotte, North Carolina: 1916). 104 pp.

Toomer, Jean, Cane (New York: Boni and Liveright, 1923).

Whittaker, John P., "What Is the Responsibility of the Liberal Arts College toward Meeting the Occupational Opportunities for Students?" Quarterly Review of Higher Education among Negroes, IV (January, 1936), 21-23.

Wilkerson, D. A., "A Determination of the Peculiar Problems of Negroes in Contemporary American Society," Journal of Negro Education, V (July, 1936), 324-50.

Wilkinson, R. S., "Development of Home Economics in Negro Schools," *Journal of Home Economics*, XX (June, 1928), 394-98.

Williams, L. Virgil, "The Need for the Development of Creative Abilities among Negro Students," *Journal of Negro Education*, IV (October, 1935), 500-4.

Woodson, Carter G., The African Background Outlined: or Handbook for the Study of the Negro (Washington: Associated Publishers, 1934).

Woofter, Thomas J., Jr., Negro Problems in Cities (New York: Doubleday Doran & Co., 1928). 284 pp.

Young, Donald, American Minority Peoples (New York: Harper & Brothers, 1932).

Larger Problems of American Caste

Adams, Romanzo, Interracial Marriage in Hawaii (New York: Macmillan Co., 1937).

Bolton, Euri Belle, "Measuring Specific Attitudes toward the Social Rights of the Negro," *Journal of Abnormal Psychology*, XXXI (January, 1937), 384-97.

Brownlee, F. L., "Experience in Work with Negroes," *Missionary Review*, LIX (June, 1936), 311-12.

Busch, John, "Race Attitudes of Children," *Religious Education*, XXI (January, 1926), 277-81.

Cox, Ernest Sevier, White America (Richmond, Virginia: White America Society, 1923).

—— Let My People Go (Richmond, Virginia: White America Society, 1925). 34 pp.

—— The South's Part in Mongrelizing the Nation (Richmond, Virginia: White America Society, 1926). 111 pp.

Curle, J. H., "Our Testing Time: Will the White Race Win Through?" (New York: George H. Doran, 1926). 301 pp.

Drachslerm, Julius, Democracy and Assimilation (New York: Macmillan Co., 1920). 275 pp.

DuBois, W. E. B., "Marxism and the Negro Problem," *The Crisis*, March, 1933.

—— and Lothrop Stoddard, Debate: Shall the Negro Be Encouraged to Seek Cultural Equality? (Chicago: Chicago Forum Council, 1929); *Forum*, LXXVIII (1927), 511-19.

Embree, Edwin R., Island India Goes to School (Chicago: University of Chicago Press, 1934). 122 pp.

Foster, A. L., "A Coöperative Adventure in the Field of Race Relations," *Opportunity*, VII (March, 1929), 98-99.

Grant, Madison, The Conquest of a Continent, or the Expansion of Races in America (New York: Charles Scribner's Sons, 1934). 393 pp.

Hammond, L. H., Southern Women and Racial Adjustment. (1920.) "John F. Slater Fund Occasional Papers," No. 19.

Harris, Abram, "The Negro and Economic Radicalism," *Modern Quarterly*, II (February, 1925), 198-208.

Haygood, Atticus, A Reply to Senator Eustis' Late Paper on Race Antagonism (New York: New York *Independent*, December 8, 1888). Reprinted as pamphlet, 1889, by Open Letter Club, Nashville, Tennessee.

Haynes, George E., Trend of the Races (New York: Missionary Education Movement, 1922). 205 pp.

Keith, Arthur, "The Differentiation of Mankind into Racial Types," Smithsonian Report (Washington: The Smithsonian Institute, 1919).

Kilpatrick, William H., "Resort to Courts by Negroes to Improve Their Schools a Conditional Alternative," *Journal of Negro Education,* IV (July, 1935), 412-18.

Lasker, Bruno, Jewish Experiences in America: Suggestions for the Study of Jewish Relations with Non-Jews (New York: Jewish Welfare Board, 1930). 309 pp.

Moton, Robert R., What the Negro Thinks (Garden City: Doubleday Publishing Co., 1929). 267 pp.

Muntz, Earl E., Race Contact (New York: Century Co., 1927). 407 pp.

News Week, "Virginia Wants United States to Send Negroes Back Home," VII (March 14, 1936), 13.

Odum, Howard W., Man's Quest for Social Guidance (New York: Henry Holt & Co., 1927). 643 pp.

Olivier, "Key to the Colour Question," *Contemporary Review,* CXLVIII (December, 1935), 665-73.

Patton, C. H., God's World (R. R. Smith, 1931).

Peabody Conference on Dual Education in the South, "Education and Racial Adjustment" (Atlanta: The Conference Executive Committee, 703 Standard Bldg., 1932).

Radin, Paul, "History of Ethnological Theories," *American Anthropologist,* XXXI (January-March, 1929).

—— The Racial Myth (New York: McGraw-Hill Book Co., 1934).

Reuter, Edward B., The Mulatto in the United States (Boston: Gorham Press, 1918).

—— Race Mixture: Studies in Intermarriage and Miscegenation (New York: McGraw-Hill Book Co., 1931). 224 pp.

—— (ed.), Race and Culture Contacts, American Sociological Society (New York: McGraw-Hill Book Co., 1934). 253 pp.

Sayers, James Denson, Can the White Race Survive? (Washington: Independent Publishing Co., 1929). 225 pp.

Shannon, B. D., The Racial Integrity of the American Negro (Nashville: Lamar, 1925). 64 pp.

—— The Negro in Washington: Study in Race Amalgamation (New York: 1930). 332 pp.

Speer, Robert E., Race and Race Relations (New York: Fleming H. Revell Co., 1929). 434 pp.

Stolberg, B., "Black Chauvinism," *Nation,* CXL (May 15, 1935), 570-71.

Stoddard, Lothrop, "The Impasse at the Color-line," *Forum,* LXXVIII (1927), 510-19.

—— Rising Tide of Color against White World-Supremacy (New York: Blue-Ribbon Books, 1931).

Stone, Alfred H., Studies in the American Race Problem (New York: Doubleday, Page & Co., 1908). 555 pp.

Strickland, W. W., Pagans and Christians (London: Westermann, 1931).

Tannenbaum, Frank, Darker Phases of the South (New York: Putnam, 1924). 203 pp.

Woofter, Thomas J., Jr., Basis of Racial Adjustment (New York: Ginn & Co., 1925). 258 pp.

INDEX

INDEX

Ability, differences in, 277; *see also* Intelligence

Achievement, measure of level of, 346*n*, 357, 403

Acting, an established social pattern, 107

Administration, *see* Colleges; Colleges, functional; Talladega College Council

Admission to college, 350; selective, for training leaders, 351

Adulthood, denied to student, 218-22; obligation of college to develop, 293; growth into, through democratic method, 303

Agrarian movement, radical aspirations defeated, 45; temporary flurry, 86

Agriculture, Negro shunted into, 43; competition between Negro and white man, 83*n*

Alabama, free Negroes and slaves in, 76; professional Negroes, 99

Alabama, Department of Education, quoted, 187

Amateur performances, college-community, 329

American Missionary Association, founded, xiii; educational work, 208-10; Talladega College founded and nurtured by, 209, 409

American Negro, phrase, 371

Amistad mutineers, xiii

Ancestry, African and Caucasian, 370

Antagonisms, racial, not unlike other group antagonisms, 24; social devices which function to perpetuate, 55; ready to respond to an incident, 61; *see also* Prejudice

Antipathy, racial, *see* Prejudice

Antisocial attitudes, cause of, 252

"Any white man is better than every Negro," 96

Apprentice system, pressure to eliminate Negro from opportunities of, 32, 42; helped to consolidate white artisan's position, 83*n*

Aristocracy, racial attitudes between Negro and, 35; in Reconstruction period, 40; fear rising tide of black political power, 45; at top of social strata, 73; *see also* Slave owners

Arlitt, A. H., 166

Army, Confederate, disaffection of lower-class whites in, 39

Army, Union, mountaineers swell ranks of, 37; slaves join, 39

Army Alpha tests, study of, 176

Artisans, white, competing with slave owners, 31 ff.; replace colored, 42; *see also* Whites, lower class

Artistic programs, college-community, 328

Arts, problem of self-expression, 143; extent of Negro talent, 368; recognition accorded Negro artists, 369

Askew, Sarah, 327*n*

Athletics and sports, 330-33; objections to commercial, 331; rationalizing of policy, 332

Atlanta, slaves prohibited from competing in labor market, 32

Atlanta Compromise, 86, 200, 204

Attitudes, nature of racial, 17-50; modifications of social, under recurring situations, 19; pressure of adult attitudes upon those of children, 21; rooted in experience, 21*n*; historical relationship between economic processes and race attitudes, 27-47, 82*n*; during Reconstruction period, 40; new potpourri of, 42; index of sensitivity of relationship between economic processes and racial, 47-50; tenacity, 54; shape social patterns, 55; accompanying social stratification, 78; characteristic interclass, in ante-bellum days, 78 ff.; tabulation of interclass, 78 ff., 84 f., 89 f.; pattern of social, in Reconstruction days, 84; interclass, of the 1930s, 89; caste-class complex of psychological, 92; defense rationalizations, 93; conflicting welter of, nurtured by caste-class

Attitudes—(*Continued*)
system, 105; developed as escape
mechanism, 106; which characterize
each of two castes, 113; of conflict,
153; objectivity of, about one's own
life and efforts, 157; in relation to
social redirection, 161-67; of higher
education toward social process, 239;
cause of antisocial, 252; how aim at
social? 252-54; selection of social, for
cultivation, 254-59; conflicts resulting
from alteration of a collective attitude, 306; importance of, in the educative process, 341, 344; relationship
of economic processes to racial, as
shown by lynchings, 383, 386, 387,
392, 397; *see also* Prejudice, race
Authority, problem of, in democratic
procedure, 279-81; of expert and
masses, 281-83
Autocratic administrative procedure,
263-65
Automobiles and trucks in U. S., 365
Autonomy and freedom played against
isolation and insularity, 139

Bagley, William C., 177
Bailey, Thomas P., quoted, 70, 192 f.
Beard, Augustus Field, quoted, 210
Benevolence cultivates dependence, 91
Benne, Kenneth, xv
Berea College, 151*n*, 244, 318
Birth, caste determined by, 72
Bizzell, W. B., quoted, 240*n*
Black Codes, 86
Black economy, meaning of, 145
Black Reconstruction (Du Bois), 246
Board, governing, legal responsibility
of, 289; coöperation in democratic
method, 290; white Southerners on,
318; relation of College Council to,
414
Boarding schools under Northern aus-
pices, 314
Boas, Franz, quoted, 403
Bode, Boyd H., 272*n*
Bond, Horace Mann, xv, 343*n*; on
social function of segregated col-
lege, 250
Bonser, Frederick G., quoted, 231
Book collections made available by col-
lege, 327

Brigham, *A Study of American Intelli-
gence,* 176
British master-servant pattern, x
Brunner, Edmund de S., xv
Bryant, Ora B., Jr., quoted, 60
Bryce, James, quoted, 20
Bunyan, John, quoted, 2
Burks, R. S., 166

Canby, Henry S., 341; quoted, 239*n*,
340, 363*n*; analysis of the New England college, 317
Capitalization of "Negro," 59
Carney, Mabel, xv
Carp, Bernard, xv
Carpetbaggers, 80
Case work, family, teaching of, 337
Caste system, class and caste in American society, 71-102; determined by
birth, may not change, 72; socio-
economic classes within each, 73;
ante-bellum stratification within Negro caste, 75; leaves lasting impression, 77; change in basic configuration, 80; dominance of white, threatened, 80; united white, demands
social superiority over all Negros,
86; Booker T. Washington's Atlanta
Exposition speech, 86, 200; perpetuated by paternalism, 91; literature
rationalizes alleged racial differences, 93; Negro's progress interpreted as improvement in condition,
not in status, 94; pragmatic axioms
of, 94 ff.; importance of etiquette in
preserving, 95; defines "his" place
for Negro, 97; baffling to whites, 97,
118; maldistribution of professional
services a function of, 98 ff.; pathological results of, 105-14; personality
maladjustments nourished by, 109;
Negroes passing into white caste,
112; third caste created to enforce
racial integrity laws, 112; transformation of, probably inevitable,
118; profits of, 119-23; perpetuated
by financial pressure urging segregation, 120; equalization would lower
level for whites, 120; costs of, 123-31;
cultural costs of, 127; dilemmas of
the Negro caste, 135-58; relation to
dilemmas of white caste, 135; segregation, 135-50; psychogenic hazards,

315; tabulation of colleges according to control, 316; estranged off-campus groups, 317; temptations to maintain aloofness, 319; percentage of Negroes in college, 351; testing its own aims and procedures, 358; racial emphasis in teaching, 359-64; three inferences as to differences between segregated and nonsegregated, 378-80; whether segregated can take risks involved in discharge of its social function, 379

Colleges and schools, *see also* Education; Talladega College; Teaching

"Colored" people, majority of human beings are, 9

Commercial sports, 330 ff.

Communication and understanding, lack of common bases of, viii

Communists, efforts to bring black and white workers together, 324

Community, segregated as ground for personal life, 148

Community-college relationships, 311-37; wide variety but four constant elements in the relationship, 315; the wider campus, 319; educational principles to be observed, 319; types of procedure appropriate to the program, 327; student participation, 334; program not mere social uplift, 336

Companionship of teacher and student, 354

Compensation patterns, 110

Competition, economic, *see* Economic processes

Compulsion an aspect of segregation, 137

Confederate Army, *see* Army

Conflicts, social, support attitudes of antipathy, 24; race not itself the cause of, 24; physical differences cause, 25; economic, determine racial, 25; for accommodation on a higher level, 153

Conformity the aim of academic education, 270

Connelly, Marc, 143

Consensus, reliance upon, a method of democracy, 276; as authority, 280; inclusive, v. majority vote, 290; avoidance of stalemate in face of

crisis, 291; a curb to ruthlessness of dominant groups, 297; of functional college with its culture, 298, 300; inclusiveness of, 298-301; of groups within the college, 299; method used by Talladega Council, 412

Contagion, a corollary of poor housing, 124

Contentiousness, problem of, 295-98

Controversial materials, treatment of, 5-8

Contumacy, problem of, 295-98

Cools, Victor G., 184; quoted, 201

Coöperation between white and colored workers in coal mines and cotton belt, 44

Corrective institutions, costs, 123

Cotton cultivation, coöperation between whites and Negroes, 44; variations in lynchings follow deviations in income from, 48, 383, 387-97; effect upon individual, 64; cost of, 122; system has made mental slaves of an entire region, 122; will it leave the Southeast? 122n

Cotton gin, effect of invention of, 37, 384

Cotton markets depressed to level of slave economy, 121

Cottrell, Donald P., xiv

County-wide library services, 327n

Craftsmen, Negroes trained as, 31; fight against slaves as, 32

Craft unionism, rise of, 83n

Crawford, Samuel W., 45n

Creative element, 19

Creativity, cultural, 142 ff.

Crimes, committed by whites against Negroes, caused by fear-hate complex, 61; correlation between lynchings and fluctuations in, 386

Cultural programs of college made available to community, 328

Cultural segregation, 136, 142

Cultural status, race the symbol of, 26, 54

Culture, self-expression and creativity v. eccentricity and sterility, 142 ff.; Negroid themes and modes of expression, 143; importance to Negro, 203; transmission of heritage, 264, 364-67; tangible expressions of the

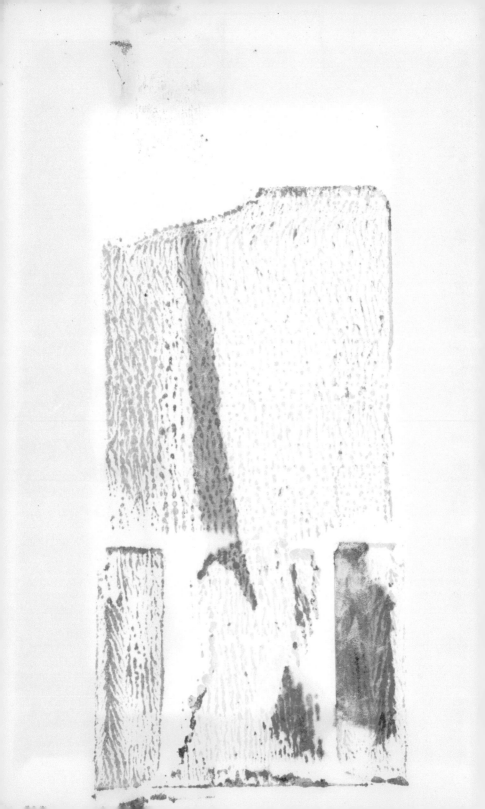